D1029119

OCCULT KNOWLEDGE, SCIENCE, AND GENDER ON THE SHAKESPEAREAN STAGE

Belief in spirits, demons, and the occult was commonplace in the early modern period, as was the view that these forces could be used to manipulate nature and produce new knowledge. In this ground-breaking study, Mary Floyd-Wilson explores these beliefs in relation to women and scientific knowledge, arguing that the early modern English understood their emotions and behavior to be influenced by hidden sympathies and antipathies in the natural world. Focusing on *Twelfth Night, Arden of Faversham, A Warning for Fair Women, All's Well That Ends Well, The Changeling,* and *The Duchess of Malfi,* she demonstrates how these plays stage questions about whether women have privileged access to nature's secrets and whether their bodies possess hidden occult qualities. Discussing the relationship between scientific discourse and the occult, she goes on to argue that, as experiential evidence gained scientific ground, women's presumed intimacy with nature's secrets was either diminished or demonized.

MARY FLOYD-WILSON is Associate Professor of English and Comparative Literature at the University of North Carolina at Chapel Hill. A recipient of a National Humanities Center Fellowship, she is the author of *English Ethnicity and Race in Early Modern Drama* (2003) and the co-editor of *Reading the Early Modern Passions: A Cultural History of Emotions* (with Gail Kern Paster and Katherine Rowe, 2004) and *Embodiment and Environment in Early Modern England* (with Garrett A. Sullivan, Jr., 2007). She has published articles in *Shakespeare Quarterly, English Literary Renaissance, Early Modern Literary Studies,* and *Shakespeare Studies,* and has co-edited a special issue of *Renaissance Drama.*

Frontispiece Title page woodcut, *De humani corporis fabrica librorum epitome* (Basel, 1543), Wellcome Library, London

OCCULT KNOWLEDGE, SCIENCE, AND GENDER ON THE SHAKESPEAREAN STAGE

MARY FLOYD-WILSON

CAMBRIDGE
UNIVERSITY PRESS

CAMBRIDGE
UNIVERSITY PRESS

University Printing House, Cambridge CB2 8BS, United Kingdom

Published in the United States of America by Cambridge University Press, New York

Cambridge University Press is part of the University of Cambridge.

It furthers the University's mission by disseminating knowledge in the pursuit of
education, learning and research at the highest international levels of excellence.

www.cambridge.org
Information on this title: www.cambridge.org/9781107036321

First published 2013

Printed in the United Kingdom by Clays, St Ives plc

A catalogue record for this publication is available from the British Library

Library of Congress Cataloguing in Publication data
Floyd-Wilson, Mary.
Occult knowledge, science, and gender on the Shakespearean stage / Mary Floyd-Wilson.
pages cm
Includes bibliographical references and index.
ISBN 978-1-107-03632-1
1. Shakespeare, William, 1564–1616 – Criticism and interpretation. 2. Occultism in
literature. 3. Literature and spiritualism. 4. Women in literature. I. Title.
PR2965.F56 2013
822.3′3–dc23
2012050275

ISBN 978-1-107-03632-1 Hardback

Additional resources for this publication at www.cambridge.org/9781107036321

To Madeline, my darling daughter and my sympathetic twin

Contents

Illustrations

Acknowledgments

Initial thoughts about this project began, appropriately enough, in a domestic space, where I wondered how my AS son faltered over interpreting affect but responded so profoundly and viscerally to the circulating emotions around him. My first stab at an argument received magnanimous and magical feedback from Mary E. Fissell. Her exceptional insights on early modern culture inform many of the central themes of this book. I also thank my fellow participants in Mary's colloquium "Vernacular Health and Healing," held at the Folger Institute, especially Bella Mirabella and Rebecca Totaro. For their kind and encouraging support of this project in its preliminary stages, Steven Mullaney, Mary Thomas Crane, and Phebe Jensen have my sincere gratitude. The audiences at Utah State University, Northwestern University, the University of Michigan, the Renaissance Gothic Conference in Cologne, the University of Melbourne, and the University of Warwick all posed crucial questions that sent me in exciting and productive directions. The conversations in Lorraine Daston's faculty seminar "Observation" held at the Folger Institute also helped shape my thinking about early modern science in instrumental ways.

This project would never have reached completion without the support of two important institutions and communities: the University of North Carolina at Chapel Hill and the National Humanities Center in Research Triangle Park. In addition to a fellowship provided by the Institute of Arts and Humanities, which gave me time to frame some early research questions, the University of North Carolina honored me with a W. N. Reynolds Leave as well as a departmental Research and Study Leave at vital stages in the writing process.

My year as the John G. Medlin Fellow at the National Humanities Center was a transformative experience. I am happily indebted to my fellow fellows, especially Elizabeth "Cassie" Mansfield, Colin Bird, Jessica Brantley, John M. Doris, Sarah Farmer, Holly Brewer, and Andrew

Escobedo. Particularly warm appreciation goes to Trevor Burnard and Florence Dore. The library staff, Eliza Robertson, Josiah Drewry, and Jean Houston, performed wonders every day. Indeed, I am enormously grateful to the entire NHC community, including (but not limited to) Geoffrey Harpham, Kent Mullikin, Pat Schreiber, James Getkin, Sarah Payne, Don Solomon, Lois Whittington, and Marie Brubaker.

Gail Kern Paster, Garrett Sullivan, and David Baker each read the manuscript in its entirety, and their brilliant and incisive commentary improved the project in more ways than I can measure. I am grateful to a large number of people for their questions, encouragement, assistance, advice, and insights, including Lara Bovilsky, Edmund Campos, Darryl Chalk, Tony Dawson, Lauren Garrett, Brett Hirsch, Laurie Johnson, Rebecca Laroche, Elaine Leong, Jeffrey Masten, Carla Mazzio, Vin Nardizzi, Tommy Nixon, Hillary Nunn, Jennifer Park, Kaara Peterson, Tanya Pollard, Kristen Poole, Beth Quitslund, Emma Smith, Pamela H. Smith, Michael Schoenfeldt, Laurie Shannon, Katie Shrieves, Alan Stewart, Valerie Traub, Katie Walker, Wendy Wall, Jordan Wingate, Paul Yachnin, and Julian Yates. Thanks to Kathryn Burns, Jane Danielewicz, Joy Kasson, and Megan Matchinske for their constructive reading of the initial project proposal. I am grateful to Bill Andrews, Claudia Funke, and Beverly Taylor for the professional opportunities they have made possible. Reid Barbour (who secured necessary library resources for me), David Baker, Gregg Flaxman, Darryl Gless, Shayne Legassie, Megan Matchinske, Jane Thrailkill, and Jessica Wolfe inspire me time and again as supportive colleagues and exemplary teacher-scholars. I am rich in funny, smart, generous friends: Ennis Baker, Dennis Baker, Florence Dore, Katie McKee, Deborah Morgan (KY), Will Rigby, Ann Walker, and Mary Wheeling have lifted my spirits, made me laugh, and helped me parent, making them indispensable to this book's completion.

A portion of Chapter 2 was previously published. See "Tragic Action at a Distance: *Arden of Faversham*," in Emma Smith and Garrett A. Sullivan, Jr. (eds.), *The Cambridge Companion to Renaissance Tragedy* (Cambridge, 2010), 188–99. I owe thanks to the Wellcome Library and to Wilson Library's Rare Book Collection at the University of North Carolina for supplying the book's images.

To Eyore: I miss our long lunches. Here's hoping you'll move again, close enough to fetch me tea on a regular basis. My dear PM: our alliance has brought me heaps of comfort, joy, and familial care. And your bereavement counseling is inimitable. I owe more than can be repaid to Mary Alice, who loves unconditionally, and I am blessed to have Jim, David, and Diana as my kin. My sympathies, secret and manifest, draw me like a magnet to my extraordinary children, Claude and Maddie. And to my partner, Lanis: simply recall what I once announced at a dinner party about my fortunate state. And then magnify the sentiment. Donna Fargo has nothing on me.

Introduction: secret sympathies

Occult Knowledge, Science, and Gender on the Shakespearean Stage situates early modern texts within a Renaissance cosmology of occult forces.[1] While scholars have attended to the relationship between the environment and embodiment in Renaissance literature, we have paid little attention to the animate qualities of that environment.[2] It is the task of this book to demonstrate that a comprehensive understanding of the animate early modern natural world must encompass what lies beyond nature: the preternatural realm. Spirits, demons, and unseen active effluvia comprised the invisible technology of nature's marvels. Hidden in nature, people believed, were antipathies and sympathies that compelled both bonds and animosities among an unpredictable mix of plants, minerals, animals, and humans. As I shall suggest throughout this study, our critical tendency to misconstrue the discourse of sympathies and antipathies as merely metaphorical has obscured how a pervasive belief in hidden operations shaped early modern perceptions of nature, gender, passion, motivation, knowledge, and theatrical experiences.

Drawing on the drama of the period, as well as books of secrets, receipt books, and medical treatises, *Occult Knowledge* argues that the early modern English, both elite and common, conducted their lives with the conviction that their emotions, behavior, and practices were affected by, and dependent on, secret sympathies and antipathies that coursed through the natural world. For early moderns, sympathies and antipathies provided an organizing structure for a whole range of actions and beliefs.[3] Historian Stuart Clark affirms that of all the "occult agents, perhaps the most discussed were the sympathies and antipathies that drew natural things together in 'friendship' and drove them apart in 'enmity' ('the way things differ and agree with each other')."[4] While the role of sympathies and occult forces has been examined in relation to the history of science and magic, as well as literature, little attention has been paid to their relevance for what we might call day-to-day living.[5] *Occult Knowledge* distinguishes itself from earlier discussions in its argument that occult agents were not the purview only of esoteric practitioners of magic.

Sympathies and antipathies not only produced involuntary emotional relationships but were also crucial levers by which ordinary people, as well as natural philosophers, supposed they could manipulate nature, heal or harm the body, and produce new knowledge. Indeed, it was the invisibility of nature's secrets – or occult qualities – that led to natural philosophy's privileging of experimentation, helping to displace a reliance on the inherited theories of ancient authority. In a direct challenge to Michel Foucault's characterization of Renaissance cosmology as a system of visual resemblances that condemned "sixteenth-century knowledge ... to never knowing anything but the same thing," *Occult Knowledge* asserts that this cosmology was not a visual or knowable system, but a veiled one that provoked scientific thought.[6] In Foucault's view, early modern nature was a configuration of analogies and similitudes revealed by its visible marks. But the materials I examine in *Occult Knowledge* contradict Foucault's episteme. Early moderns insist again and again that Nature hides her secrets. Moreover, as some historians of science now argue, it was the obscure unpredictability of occult forces that fostered the development of Renaissance natural philosophy. In their focus on occult operations, proto-scientific experts and practitioners sought to determine what constituted natural phenomena and how to distinguish natural events from supernatural causes and demonological manipulation.

Enchantment and superstition

Modern skeptical readers tend to question the degree to which people in the period subscribed to such "magical thinking."[7] But evidence suggests that belief in spirits, demons, and occult qualities was commonplace. Even when historians identify the secularizing effects of the Reformation, few still promote a pre-Enlightenment disenchantment thesis. Many historians maintain, instead, that supernatural mentalities, in the aftermath of the Reformation, were shaped on the one hand by demonological thinking and on the other by the culture's widespread subscription to providence.[8] From a reformist perspective, supernatural mysteries were the work of God. Demons were effective only because they knew how to influence nature's hidden forces. To censure the practice of natural magic, early modern detractors argued that such knowledge necessarily derived from demonological sources. Thus, while the world remained enchanted, an individual's access to its magic may have been increasingly proscribed.

A central assertion in arguments that emphasize disenchantment and secularization is that early modern writers judged belief in magical practices and spiritual entities to be superstition. But modern scholars often misunderstand exactly what superstition means to early modern writers. Literary critics, in particular, have observed that a superstitious engagement with fairies and magic was often associated with foolish women, old wives, or the ignorant.[9] What these critics neglect to recognize is that early modern superstition does not translate to mean simply naïve credulity (or a lack of modern rational skepticism). More often than not, superstition implied the risky assumption that one could engage with spirits or magic *and* avoid interacting with the devil.[10] Erasmus, notably, expressed hostility against "old wives" and fairy tales, exclaiming that

> A boy [may] learn a pretty story from the ancient poets, or a memorable tale from history, just as readily as the stupid and vulgar ballad, or the old wives' fairy rubbish such as most children are steeped in nowadays by nurses and serving women.[11]

But Erasmus also warned his readers of the implicit idolatry of such beliefs, for the danger of superstitious practices lies in their potential for devilish harm. He states:

> all curyous artes and craftes, of divynyng and sothesayeng, of juglyng, of doing cures by charmes or witchcraft in whiche althoughe there be none expresse conspiration [may engage] with dyvelles or wycked spirites yet nevertheless is ther some secrete dealyng with them. . .[12]

The reality of wicked spirits or devils is not in question. What Erasmus aims to combat is the ignorant notion that one can indulge in curious arts and escape the devil's entrapment. And yet, despite faith in an intervening God and intrusive devils, people also persisted in believing that they could direct or be affected by mysterious sympathies and antipathies in nature, in a preternatural realm removed from God's aid or the devil's interference. Reformist charges could not erase the "popular desire for some kind of instrumental application of sacred power to deal with the exigencies of daily life."[13]

Occult qualities and science

Occult Knowledge aims to complicate the disenchantment narrative in part by exploring the relationship between occult phenomena and scientific knowledge. Recent work in the history of science suggests that the early modern exploration of occult qualities proved central to the development of the experimental method. This perspective on the history of science implicitly challenges the historical break described by Foucault, who characterized modernity as a shift away from the sixteenth-century episteme of resemblances to a system of representation. After the Renaissance, Foucault argues, a world of resemblances gave way to one of "identities and differences."[14] But Foucault's account of the sixteenth-century world of sympathies is distorted in ways that prove crucial to the argument of this book. First, he maintains that the nature of sympathies is visually knowable. Relying heavily on Paracelsus' theory of signatures, Foucault contends that the hidden attractions or kinships between things (whether animal, mineral, or vegetable) could always be discerned by an external mark:

> Now there is a possibility that we might make our way through all this marvelous teeming abundance of resemblances without even suspecting that it has long been prepared by the order of the world, for our greater benefit. In order that we may know that aconite will cure our eye disease, or that ground walnut mixed with spirits of wine will ease a headache, there must of course be some mark that will make us aware of these things: otherwise, the secret would remain indefinitely dormant. Would we ever know that there is a relation of twinship or rivalry between a man and his planet, if there were no sign upon his body or among the wrinkles on his face that he is an emulator of Mars or akin to Saturn? These buried similitudes must be indicated on the surface of things; there must be visible marks for the invisible analogies.[15]

As we shall see in our discussion of medical receipts, the hidden logic of antipathies and sympathies determines what ingredients (such as aconite or walnut) make a cure efficacious. And while it is true that some similitudes had made themselves known by visual resemblances (such as the oft-mentioned likeness of the walnut's appearance to the brain), most sympathies and antipathies remained occult. Paracelsus argued that God embedded signatures in all things for the physician to identify, but he also conceded that use or experience ultimately confirmed the true value and hidden qualities of a substance.[16]

Second, in direct contrast to Foucault's claim that the Renaissance system of sympathies and resemblances meant that "sixteenth-century knowledge condemned itself to never knowing anything but the same thing," the hidden and illegible nature of these occult qualities actually provided a foundation for knowledge-making based on new experimental methods that emphasized the observation of effects over theoretical causation.[17] As we have noted, it has long been understood that sympathies and antipathies were the foundation for natural magic in the period, but scholars have also established that natural magic functioned as an early modern form of natural science. Indeed, Lynn Thorndike, Charles Schmitt, Brian Vickers, and many others, have debated the degree to which occult mentalities played a role in the development of scientific thinking.[18] Historians of science no longer subscribe to a single narrative of a scientific revolution, with its attendant forces of secularization and disenchantment. And, as John Henry has argued, an investigative focus on occult phenomena played a fundamental role in the development of scientific knowledge:

> The occult qualities or principles of matter . . . could only be evinced, it was claimed, by experimental procedures. Thus the professed belief in occult qualities came to be amalgamated with or embedded into other arguments in defense of the experimental method.[19]

Moreover, the concept of occult qualities compelled natural philosophers to determine the boundaries between and among preternatural, natural, supernatural, and demonic phenomena. While it was understood that demons knew most thoroughly the "properties and powers of all the elements, metals, stones, herbs [and] plants," many natural philosophers kept their focus on the secret workings of nature by sidelining demonic forces in their inquiries.[20] As Lorraine Daston has established, those philosophers examining the strange effects of sympathies and antipathies demonstrated an "unflinching commitment" to natural explanations.[21] In rejecting the common recourse to occult qualities in explanations of disease transmission, Giralamo Fracastoro, for example, developed his theory of contagion through an understanding of sympathies, antipathies, and invisible *species spirituales*.[22] To explain the perceived phenomena of sympathies and antipathies, natural philosophers of various stripes consistently appealed to material but invisible emission of effluvia.[23] Indeed, for many early modern proto-scientists, apparent instances of action-at-distance were elucidated by appeals to hidden emanations, whether characterized as spirits, corpuscles, or atoms.[24] In *Physiologia Epicuro-Gassendo-Charltoniana*, a text of mechanical philosophy that systematically interrogates the most notorious instances of sympathy and antipathy, Walter Charleton explains these forces as corporeal but imperceptible, even granting the reality of women's capacity to fascinate others due to the malignant spirits that emanate from their eyes and brains.[25]

"Boundary work," in its original use, refers to the demarcations in science studies between fields of knowledge, where experts and practitioners aim to determine what counts as legitimate science. Within early modern natural philosophy, boundary work sought to distinguish supernatural miracles from preternatural wonders and to provide natural explanations for the apparent powers of non-human matter and agents.[26] These natural explanations, however, were not necessarily motivated by an emergent scientific rationality, as a modern might suppose. Instead, the experimenter often sought to secure a boundary between demonic and non-demonic activities. As Sir Francis Bacon observes, experimentation could invoke malign spirits.[27] To probe nature's secrets safely means to keep the devil at bay. Attributing power to the sympathetic and antipathetic forces of the imagination "was the standard means of denying the actions of demons and witches."[28]

It is, notably, the pervasiveness with which writers appeal to sympathies and antipathies that drove Sir Francis Bacon to insist upon developing more expansive and incisive methods of inquiry. Notoriously, Bacon rails against "students of natural magic" in *Novum Organum* (1620), criticizing them for their tendency to "explain everything by Sympathies and Antipathies."[29] But Bacon also has a complicated investment in these same forces.[30] In fact, he wrote an introduction to a proposed *History of the Sympathy and Antipathy of Things* where he acknowledges the absolute centrality of such forces as the "spurs of motions and the keys of works" in nature. What he laments, however, is that men rely indolently on the "recital of specific properties, and secret and heaven-sent virtues" at the expense of "searching out the real causes."[31] As Katharine Park puts it, Bacon saw sympathies and antipathies as signs that more profound explanations existed at an even deeper level.[32] Bacon's *Sylva Sylvarum* proves devoted to examining and explaining a whole range of sympathetic and antipathetic phenomena, from emotional bonds, to fascination, to cruentation (bleeding corpses), to the effects of precious stones. As Lorraine Daston and Park observe in their work on wonders, the Aristotelian tradition of science sought to establish the regularities of nature, but a Baconian approach urged attention to where nature seemed to go awry.[33] In Guido Gilgioni's words, Bacon's *Sylva Sylvarum* indicates that it "is only by knowing and subduing the appetites of matter that man can master the intractable forces of nature, restoring humankind's original control of its appetites."[34] For Bacon, the wonders generated by antipathies and sympathies provide ready framed opportunities for conducting trials and experiments that will vex Nature until she reveals her secrets.[35]

Sympathies and humors

This study intervenes in the current scholarship on the history of emotion to explore how a pervasive belief in sympathies and antipathies shaped early modern interpretations of affective experiences. As Gail Kern Paster and Michael Schoenfeldt have demonstrated, the theory of humors was fundamental to sixteenth- and seventeenth-century explanations of human emotions and behavior. Critical appeals to humoralism have opened up new understandings of pre-modern psychological processes and shed light on questions of identity, agency, gender, race, and sexuality.[36] While this contemporary critical work has been enormously productive, *Occult Knowledge* advances the thesis that early modern writers established that some emotions could not be explained in humoral terms.[37] Unlike the humors, which "reflected universal characteristics of the four elements present in all terrestrial bodies," occult properties were idiosyncratic, peculiar, and often at odds with the observable, elemental world.[38] As the seventeenth-century writer Will Greenwood observes in *[Apographe storges], or, A description of the passion of love* (1657), where there is a "sympathy in Nature," there may be "an antipathy in Complexion," and where there is "a sympathy in Complexion," there may be "antipathy in Nature."[39] In other words, one's humoral complexion cannot function as an indicator of hidden sympathies and antipathies.

As manifest qualities, humors served as the basis for understanding passions, disposition, and temperament; however, people also attributed certain behaviors to the hidden sympathetic and antipathetic potencies coursing through the natural world. Sympathies and antipathies were thought to inhabit all animals, minerals, plants, and people. Their occult energies attract and repel other fauna, flora, and minerals, uniting and dividing an endless array of strange couples. As the sixteenth-century writer William Fenner observes, nature's hidden sympathies produced inexplicable bonds:

> The Philosophers call them *occultae qualitates, hidden qualities*, no reason can be given of them. No man can give a reason why the load-stone should be so deeply affected with iron, as to draw it unto it. It hath a sympathy with it; the wilde Bull hath a sympathy with a figgetree; nothing can tame him but it; the Elm hath a sympathy with the Vine: the Vine hath a sympathy with the Olive.[40]

We can find a similar occult logic in Desiderius Erasmus' colloquy on friendship, which establishes how sympathies found in nature determine the enigmatically close connection one may feel with another person.[41] Unable to explain certain peculiar attachments, Erasmus, along with many writers in the period, recites a list of perplexing attractions and repulsions, or sympathies and antipathies, long observed in the world:

> A Serpent is an Enemy to Mankind and Lizards: He loves Milk, hates the Smell of Garlick. A Crocodile is a mortal Enemy to Mankind. A Dolphin is a greater Lover of them. Every Kind of Animal by mere Instinct fears its

Enemy. A Horse mortally hates a Bear. An Elephant loves a Man wonderfully, but hates a Dragon, a Mouse, and a Swallow. A Dog is a very friendly
Creature to Man, and a Wolf as great an Enemy, so that the very Sight of him
strikes a Man dumb. A Spider is a great Enemy to a Serpent and a Toad. A
Toad is cured immediately by eating of Plantane.[42]

Hidden similitudes, such that would draw an elephant to man, could not be
discerned by mere appearance; knowledge of this sympathy was gained expe-
rientially or anecdotally. As Fenner notes, "No man can give a reason why"
these attractions and repulsions occur in nature, for they are recognized only by
their strange effects. Levinus Lemnius, in *The secret miracles of nature*, argues
the same point when he explains that "sympathy and mutual agreement,
whereby the one is by similitude wonderfully affected with the other, & thence
comes the attraction" is the result of "secret and hidden properties . . . [where]
we see the effects of things, but we know not the causes."[43]

On the emotional influence of secret sympathies, readers may be most
familiar with Marsilio Ficino's theory of the occult nature of love:

> Because the whole power of magic consists in love. The work of magic is the
> attraction of one thing by another because of a certain affinity of nature . . .
> just as in us the brain, lungs, heart, liver, and the rest of the parts . . .
> sympathize with any one of them when it suffers, so . . . all the bodies of
> the world . . . From this common relationship is born a common love; from
> love a common attraction. And this is the true magic . . . Thus also the
> lodestone draws iron, amber draws chaff.[44]

In all likelihood, it was Ficino's fifteenth-century translation of the
Hermetica that incited subsequent scholarly fascination with the potential-
ities of natural magic and helped bring about the expanding medical interest
in occult qualities.[45] Indeed, mostly removed from the critical debate about
the passions is a substantial body of scholarship on the intellectual history of
magical sympathies. Drawing on a range of ancient Greek writers such as
Empedocles, Posidonius, and Plotinus, Renaissance treatises on natural
magic describe a natural world of hidden forces of attractions and repulsions. Interest in Neoplatonic Hermeticism was shared by Giovanni Pico
della Mirandola, Agrippa von Heinrich Cornelius von Nettesheim,
Giambattista della Porta, and Paracelsus. In Pico's words, the magician's
role was to reveal "the wonders lying hidden in the recesses of the world, in
the bosom of nature, and in the storehouses and secrets of God."[46] It is
"universal sympathy that makes all magic possible."[47] We could argue that
the detachment of "sympathy" – as a modern affective term – from its roots
in magic and medicine is part of a larger history of dematerialization and

metaphorization that early modern scholars have delineated in their work on embodiment.[48]

Referring to "sympathy" in its modern sense underscores the fact that sixteenth-century understandings of sympathy had surprisingly little to do with moral philosophy. Some literary scholars have suggested a historical split developed in the seventeenth century between a pre-Cartesian, residually magic conception of sympathy and an emergent, consciously developed moral position.[49] But even as late as the eighteenth century, sympathy could still imply a mysterious, involuntary, and even contagious emotional experience.[50] In his writing on religious enthusiasm, for example, the Earl of Shaftesbury expresses concern that mobs spread panic by sympathetic contact and mere looks. Before the eighteenth century, sympathy was not just a somatic feeling but a somatic feeling that breached the boundaries of individual bodies.[51] Our current notion of sympathy as an ethical, emotional response is the residual afterlife of the embodied sympathy that engaged the pre-moderns. Indeed, early modern conceptions of contagious or infectious sympathies may have inhibited the development of the later moral sentiment, since sympathetic empathy presumes individuated boundaries between the subject and object.

For the most part, however, scholars have neglected to trace how universal sympathy may have played a significant role in vernacular and popular understandings of emotion in the early modern period. In *A treatise of the passions* (1640), Edward Reynolds indicates that the affections can be understood through two lenses; most passions are shaped by one's nature and place, but there are also emotions that seem to exceed the humoral paradigm. On occasion, people will experience an attraction that derives from "secret vertues and occult qualities":

> Love then consists in a kind of expansion or egresse of the heat and spirits to the object loved, or to that whereby it is drawne and attracted whatsoever therefore hath such an attractive power, is in that respect the object and general cause of Love. Now, as in Nature, so in the Affections likewise, we may observe from their objects a double attraction: The first is that naturall or impressed sympathie of things, whereby one doth inwardly incline an union with the other, by reason of some secret vertues and occult qualities disposing either subject to that mutuall friendship, as betweene Iron and the Loadstone: The other, is that common and most discernable attraction which every thing receives from those natures, or places whereon they [are] ordained ... [by] Providence.[52]

In a similar vein, Reynolds notes, nature produces instances of "strange *Hatred* ... amongst men; one mans disposition so much disagreeing from

anothers, that though there never passed any injuries or occasions of difference betweene them, yet they cannot but have minds averse from one
another." These extraordinary antipathies derive from the same occult
qualities that purportedly cause serpents and lions to fear fire, or that
compel an elephant to reject his meat "if a Mouse have touched it."[53]

We can find a dramatic example of an occult antipathy in Shakespeare's
The Merchant of Venice, when Shylock is asked by the Venetian court to
explain his desire to take revenge on Antonio. He suggests to the court that
they attribute his hatred to his "humour," but his explanation indicates that
he is infected by a peculiar and more irrational animosity than what choler
can produce:

> Some men there are love not a gaping pig,
> Some that are mad if they behold a cat,
> And others when the bagpipe sings i' th' nose
> Cannot contain their urine; for affection,
> Mistress of passion, sways it to the mood
> Of what it likes or loathes. Now, for your answer:
> As there is no firm reason to be rendered
> Why he cannot abide a gaping pig,
> Why he a harmless necessary cat,
> Why he a woollen bagpipe, but of force
> Must yield to such inevitable shame
> As to offend himself being offended,
> So can I give no reason, nor I will not,
> More than a lodged hate and a certain loathing
> I bear Antonio, that I follow thus
> A losing suit against him.[54]

Shylock's odd examples of men who cannot hold their urine when they hear
a bagpipe, or who grow mad in the presence of a cat, would have recalled for
some early modern audience members the strange and oft-repeated
catalogs of occult qualities. Giambattista della Porta, for example, remarks
on the mysterious nature of antipathies in a similar vein: "Some cannot
away to look upon a Cat, a Mouse, and such like, but presently they
swoon."[55] These peculiar aversions were understood as inexplicable and
illogical – occult, rather than humoral, in their causation. As Gail Kern
Paster rightly observes, Shylock "constructs his obduracy as a natural
antipathy of the sort common in humans and animals both," but Shylock
also alienates the term "humor" from its familiar significance as a quality
that can be shaped, purged, and modulated by the non-naturals.[56] The
inability to abide "a harmless necessary cat" is symptomatic of an internal
occult property that cannot be altered or understood. Shylock argues that

his hatred for Antonio is of the "strange" kind that Reynolds describes in certain men, mysteriously preexistent to "any injuries or occasions of difference betweene them."

Both Fenner and Reynolds cite the most prominent example of the "natural or impressed sympathie of things" in the lodestone and iron. The powerful draw of the magnet proves to be the epitome of nature's hidden sympathies. Writers in the period suggest that the lodestone's pull on iron is more than just an analogy for emotional attraction: the magnetic pull felt by lovers is the same force that the lodestone displays. In *A Midsummer Night's Dream*, for example, Helena laments that her attraction to Demetrius has the power of magic well before the fairies get involved. Demetrius is the adamant, a stone sometimes confused with the lodestone, which draws Helena like steel:

> You draw me, you hard-hearted adamant,
> But yet you draw not iron; for my heart
> Is true as steel. Leave you your power to draw,
> And I shall have no power to follow you.[57]

The secret sympathies that pull iron to the lodestone operate in the same preternatural sphere as the forces that draw particular people together.

Occult knowledges

As I have already asserted, accepted knowledge of how to manipulate nature's occult qualities was held by people from all walks of life, from the erudition of natural magicians to the experiential know-how of housewives.[58] Popular, inexpensive, and frequently reprinted, Albertus Magnus' *The Book of Secrets* maintains that "every particular or general nature, hath natural amity and enmity to some other ... And in [Man] be the virtues of all things, and all secret arts worketh in man's body itself."[59] As Allison Kavey argues, readers of *The Book of Secrets* would recognize that "[s]ympathy and antipathy between objects determines the composition of the natural world, and they act as levers by which readers could mold it according to their needs and desires."[60] William L. Eamon has demonstrated that many published secrets of nature were derived "directly from unlettered people: from craftsmen, empirics, monks, and peasants." One notable (though most likely fictitious) collector of secrets, Alessio Piemontese, claimed to have "acquired a great many good secrets, not only from men of great knowledge and great Lords, but also from poor women, artisans, peasants, and all sorts of people."[61]

When we turn to the practice of medicine, as Mary E. Fissell has shown, sympathetic reasoning played a crucial role in the diagnosis and treatment of diseases for "physician, surgeon and patient alike." According to seventeenth-century physician Nicholas Culpeper, "Sympathy and antipathy are the two Hinges upon which the whole Model of Physick turns."[62] While a history of popular medicine is beyond the scope of this book, scholars indicate that the medical knowledge of irregular practitioners and learned physicians generated the "same kinds of treatments, herbal remedies and manipulations."[63] Famously, Paracelsus maintained that the physician must "consult old women, gypsies, magicians, wayfarers, and all manner of peasant folk and random people, and learn from them; for these have more knowledge about such things than all the high colleges."[64] One story describes the famous surgeon Ambroise Paré obtaining a successful home remedy for healing burns from an "'old country woman' in an apothecary's shop."[65] While many medical writers condemned the ignorance of wise-women and herb women, others held that they were the best sources for understanding medicinal plants.[66] Medical writers could claim to know more about an herb's varieties and manifest qualities, but neither the learned nor the uneducated could explain the hidden virtues that made a plant effective. As Andrew Wear notes, "[m]edical knowledge in literate households seems to have been transmitted by word of mouth, by manuscript collections of remedies, by books, and sometimes by all three."[67] Attention to female irregular practitioners and receipt books suggests that women could accumulate experiential knowledge through their daily practices as caregivers in their homes and in their communities.[68] As Pamela Smith and Deborah Harkness have shown, much of what we now identify as science had roots in the practices and experiments of ordinary citizens, who conducted systematic observations of the natural world at the same time that Bacon developed his recommendations for changing knowledge production.[69] Such knowledge remained experiential (or in the case of Paracelsian signatures, mystical), and consequently both arcane and egalitarian.[70]

The widespread and even mundane status of occult knowledge is demonstrated by the strange recipes found in books of secrets and receipt books.[71] Indeed, some of the cures recorded in manuscript household receipt books indicate a routine faith in sympathetic forces. To stop bleeding, for example, readers are instructed to have "the party hold in their hand, or any where about their body a little of the herb *bursa pastoris* ... it will suffice though one wear it but in their pocket, or to their hatband."[72] Since no direct contact with the wound is needed, the cure points to an assumed

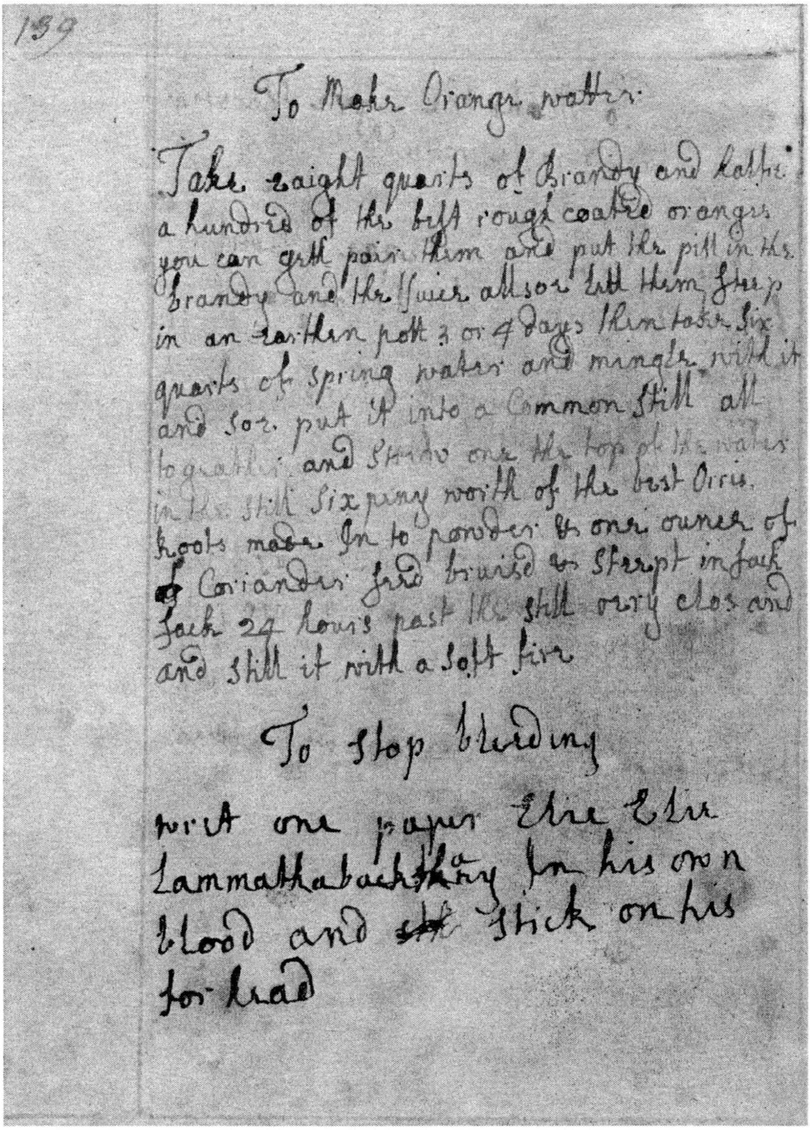
139

To Make Orange watter:

Take eaight quarts of Brandy and halfe
a hundred of the best rough coated oranges
you can gett pair them and put the pill in the
brandy and the Juice allso lett them steep
in an earthen pott 3 or 4 days then take six
quarts of spring water and mingle with it
and soe put it into a Common Still all
togeather and strow one the top of the water
in the still sixpeny worth of the best Orris
Roots made In to powder & one ounce of
of Coriander seed bruised & steept in sack
sack 24 hours past the still very clos and
and still it with a soft fire

To stop bleeding

writ one paper Elie Elie
Lammathabachthany In his own
blood and ~~sti~~ stick on his
forhead

Figure 1 Receipt for stopping bleeding. English medical notebook, seventeenth century, Wellcome Library, London

occult antipathy between blood and the herb. Another remedy to stanch
bleeding has the caregiver write a garbled "Eli, eli, lama sabachthani" in
blood on a piece of paper and place it on the patient's forehead.[73] In a recipe
for the "falling evill," the directions call for taking a man's shoe when you
see him fall. The caregiver must then "pisse in [the shoe] and wash well this
shoe and put the pisse in his mouth and hee shalbe whole."[74] In this case,
the odd therapy implies that contact with the shoe transforms the urine into
an antidote for falling. Until the late seventeenth century, a belief in hidden
causes and occult forces was held by most people, no matter their status,
educational background, or understanding of the cosmos.[75]

Gender and women's secrets

As I will demonstrate, the emergent importance of experiential knowledge
and the revaluation of occult qualities in this period heightened the culture's
interest in women's secrets. For early moderns, the "secrets" of women not
only functioned as an epistemological concept (women's knowledge of
occult operations), but also referred to "hidden and secret [occulta et secreta]
things about the nature and condition of women."[76] As Katharine Park has
argued, the experiential knowledge of nature's secrets (versus knowledge
based on theoretical structures) had long been associated with women.[77] As
the household members usually responsible for care-giving and bodywork,
women gained expertise in the presumed occult properties of plants, minerals, and animals when making medicines and food.[78] And yet many of the
male-authored household guides published in the seventeenth century
increasingly delimited the woman's role in the administration of household
physic, suggesting that their therapeutic knowledge had been appropriated
or redefined.[79] We should consider the printed texts' attenuation of wom-
en's domestic work in light of Deborah E. Harkness's assessment of female
practitioners in London: "women were at the very heart of London's
medical world. They were not marginal, they were not laughable, and
they were not expendable. Perhaps that is why so many male practitioners
found them so very threatening."[80]

As Park has also suggested, it was in the early modern period that
"women increasingly became the objects of knowledge rather than knowers
themselves."[81] This transition was complicated, however, by assumptions
about the occult qualities and powers thought to inhere in the female body.
According to Monica H. Green, in the fourteenth and fifteenth centuries,
the medical discourse on specifically female diseases began to adopt the term
"secrets" to refer to its subject matter. Labeling gynecological subjects

"secrets" captured their cultural associations with shame and privacy, but also located occult knowledge and forces within the bodies of women. At a time when a "secrets" literature was developing in other areas of medicine, science, and alchemy, manuscripts focused on the "secrets of women" also emerged and declared their goal to "make manifest those things which are hidden and secret [*occulta et secreta*] of the nature and conditions of women."[82] Green notes that the "heading *secrets of women* was meant to imply that the same kinds of occult (if unprovable) truths were being conveyed in these texts as could be found in other books of 'secrets,' such as those attributed to . . . philosophers and physicians."[83] The drive to make women's secrets manifest continued to shape medical and literary discourses well into the sixteenth and seventeenth centuries. As both occult objects and instruments of occult knowledge, women hold a crucial but often obscured position in the history of science that *Occult Knowledge* helps to trace.[84]

As a chapter in Pliny's *Natural History* indicates, "The remedies that women's bodies doe minister," the occult qualities of female flesh were sometimes understood to have curative potentials.[85] Pliny recites the commonplace that menstrual blood should be used in mad dog bites, due to a "powerful and predominant sympathie" between the blood and rabid canines.[86] Menstrual blood is also cited as integral component in anti-enchantment charms. It was held that women with "their monthly courses" could heal the sick with their hands.[87] Joannes Jonstonus mentions menstrual blood as an effective remedy for tumors, and more specifically, the menstrual blood of virgins as valuable in curing rosaea.[88] Countless writers debate the supposed effects of ingesting menstrual blood – it had the capacity to procure love, lust, madness, or impotence.[89] The poisonous nature of menstrual blood – a notion also traced back to Pliny – remained the early modern explanation for women's supposed capacity to bewitch or fascinate.[90] When the "terms" ceased or became corrupted, the venomous vapors were emitted through the eyes. Other recipes in the receipt books rely on the secret virtues of breast milk. One, in particular, indicates that it aids prognostication: "take the milke of a woman and drop it in [a man's] urine that is sicke and if it floats above he shall live and if it sinks he shall dye of that evil."[91]

Indeed, some writers took the extreme position that a woman's body predisposed her to witchcraft. The authors of *Malleus Maleficarum* (1489) had argued that all witchcraft derives from carnal lust, and the "mouth of the womb" is "never satisfied."[92] In the seventeenth century, Johann Jacob Wecker asserts that "you shall find more Women that are Witches than you shall find Men, by reason of their Complexion . . . every Moneth they are filled with more superfluities ... and they send forth venemous fumes to those that stand by them, and fill the body therewith."[93] Even those writers who dismissed the power of witches, such as Johann Weyer and Reginald Scot, believed that old women were able to infect others with their corrupted eye-beams. According to Agrippa, Giambattista della Porta, and Albertus Magnus, bold and assertive women, in particular, could transmit their unruly passions to others either at-a-distance or through the shared handling of objects. Reciting this notion, the secrets author Thomas Johnson writes that if one wears the "apparell of strumpet," one will become infected with a "certaine impudencie and shamles boldness" in the same way that a lodestone transfers, by contact, its magnetic effects to iron.[94] Such accounts of the preternatural female body are patently misogynistic. Less obvious, however, is how these fears and anxieties about women and their bodies have informed the history of science, the construction of knowledge, and the representation of emotion in the period.

Several prominent historians have delineated women's roles in the production of science by examining the gendered rhetoric of scientific writing, especially its feminization of Nature and her secrets. Indeed, the gendered implications of Francis Bacon's proposal that natural philosophers vex Nature to reveal her secrets have been hotly debated by historians of science. Famously, Carolyn Merchant observed that Bacon's search for natural knowledge was presented in language that metaphorically establishes a coercive physical relationship between a male inquisitor and a female nature.[95] Engaged with the question of scientific analogies, Katharine Park has shown that representations of Nature as a female allegorical figure tended to reflect the interests of natural philosophy. Whereas medieval and early Renaissance depictions of Nature show her clothed and veiled, hiding her secrets from prying eyes, later portraits of Nature depict her naked and exposed (yet still difficult to know or penetrate).[96] While scholars may disagree on the implicit gendered violence of Bacon's metaphors, there is little doubt that early modern people assumed that women, like Nature, were repositories of secrets.

It is Park's thesis in *Secrets of Women* that the uterus was perceived as nature's ultimate secret, and it became the "privileged object of dissection in medical images and texts" in the early modern period. The female womb "acquired a special, symbolic weight as the organ that only dissection could truly reveal, and as a result, it came to stand for the body's hidden interior."[97] Ultimately, Vesalius' anatomy demonstrates (spectacularly in the woman displayed on the title page of *De humani corporis fabrica* [Basel, 1543]) that the "principal secret of women was that the uterus held no secrets at all."[98] In a similar vein, Mary Fissell has argued that reproduction became "disenchanted" in seventeenth-century English vernacular texts. Previously associated with the Virgin Mary and the wonders of birth, representations of the womb in Reformation England increasingly focused on its capacity to foster disease and monstrous births.[99] Laurinda Dixon and Kaara Peterson have both established that medical writers, playwrights, and artists prove obsessed with uterine afflictions in this period – such as the suffocation of the mother, greensickness, and uterine fury – and they repeatedly identify the female body as innately ailing and contaminated.[100] We could argue that the pervasive pathologizing of the womb provides further evidence that a one-sex model held little sway in the everyday lives of early modern people. The number and complexity of uterine diseases, in particular, indicate a profound differentiation between the sexes, especially in therapeutic terms.[101]

But at the base of many of these discussions of the medicalization of the womb is the secularization thesis. Fissell's appeal to disenchantment, for example, implies that medical work in the period necessarily moves towards modern rationalism. However, Fissell also concedes that "'disenchantment' is not quite the right word, because the terrible womb could be described in terms just as supernatural as the miraculous womb."[102] Indeed, historians have overlooked how early modern medical writers not only identified the female body as a source of sympathetic and antipathetic forces but also detected occult qualities within the womb itself. The womb attracted the attention of "science" and medicine, I argue, not only because it was hidden but also because its occult status had accumulated associations with preternatural characteristics. As Joannes Jonstonus observes in *The idea of practical physick*, the womb's "occult qualities ... [are] apparent from hence, because it hath a singular Sympathy and antipathy with divers things; desires mans seed, is delighted with sweet things."[103] Alexandro Massaria in *De Morbis foemineis, the woman's counsellour* characterizes his "Treatise of the Diseases of women" as "so occult, intricate, and difficult to perform, that there is nothing to be found in all the Cabinets of nature, or secrets of the medicinal Art more abstruse and difficult."[104] As we shall see, many early modern gynecological texts suggest that the womb functions in the same way as the lodestone, attracting and repelling various entities on the basis of its inherently sympathetic and antipathetic qualities.[105]

A central text in the history of uterine afflictions, and often cited for its supposed disenchantment of the womb, is Edward Jorden's *A briefe discourse of a disease called the suffocation of the mother* (1603). Because Jorden made the significant argument that a young girl's strange fits were not the effects of demonic possession but the symptoms of a natural disease called "suffocation of the mother," his treatise has been hailed as a turning point in the secularization of disease and the medicalization of female illness. The "suffocation of the mother" is understood in the period to be a rising womb, often related to the cessation of menses, and it is identified by many scholars as early modern hysteria.[106] In the history of medicine, Jorden has been classified as an early skeptic, whose proto-scientific analysis furthered medical progress and anticipated the advent of modern psychological disorders. As D. P. Walker put it, the publication of Jorden's treatise seems to attest to a climate "favourable to the development of modern science."[107] But modern readers have overlooked the ways in which Jorden is a man of his times. As a physician, Jorden identifies himself as having expertise in diagnosing whether a disease is natural, preternatural, or supernatural, and he indicates that he can cure those diseases that prove to be natural or preternatural.[108] He does not dismiss the possibility of demonic possession, although he does identify it as a rare occurrence. Moreover, Jorden asserts that the devil can induce the "suffocation of the mother," for he understands, as many in the period argue, that the devil easily generates natural diseases.[109] As Jorden explains, not only can witchcraft engender the illness, "the divell" may function as an "externall cause" of a disease by "stirring up or kindling the humors of our bodies, and then depart without supplying continuall supernaturall power unto it" (25v and 31r). Once an external cause is remote, even if it may have been demonic, the resulting affliction is categorized as natural.

Interpretations of Jorden's treatise as an early instance of the secularization of medicine not only have missed his appeal to demonology but have overlooked his uncanny characterization of the female body. Once Jorden eliminates the possibility that the suffocation of the mother can be attributed to the devil's abiding presence, it is the diseased womb that takes on marvelous, preternatural qualities.[110] As Jorden explains, it is not surprising that people have been "deceyved by the rarenesse and straungenesse of these matters" in their ascription of uterine fury to demonic possession, for "these matters . . . are hidden out of their Horizon amongst the deepest mysteries of [his] profession" (2r). In other words, the female body itself hides occult secrets, which can only be known to the professional physician. Much of the first section of his pamphlet demonstrates the womb's sympathy, or "communitie and consent," with the rest of the body (1v). Whenever the womb proves in "any way depraved, the offence is communicated from thence unto the rest of the body" (6r). Therefore the effects of uterine afflictions are varied and "strange" (2r). The parts of the body, Jorden argues, suffer by "consent" or sympathy in two ways. One is by contagion, where an infectious disease "creeping from one part to another doth alter the qualitie of the parts as it goeth." The other is by "*similitude* of substance," where the "part consenting [to the womb] receiveth nothing from the other, but yet is partaker of his griefe" (7v).¹¹¹ The womb's occult forces explain not only its capacity to disorder the entire body but also its peculiar (and oft-cited) response to scent therapy. Since the "matrix . . . is delighted with sweete savours" due to a "naturall," but mysterious, "propertie," physicians can move the womb up or down by applying evil or sweet "savours" to the nostrils or the vaginal opening (21v).¹¹²

Much of Jorden's treatise is devoted to the wondrous symptoms that uterine afflictions produce. He cites a gentlewoman who would feel a "uterine affect" whenever she saw a "particular man." Another woman would fall into a "fit of the mother," when she feared admonishment, or when she saw another woman suffering a fit (23r).¹¹³ Suffocation of the mother, as Kaara Peterson details, could produce false deaths and revivifications.¹¹⁴ Citing an extraordinary anecdote drawn from Ambroise Paré, Jorden suggests that it was a uterine affliction that led Vesalius, famed for his anatomical dissections, to cut open a living gentlewoman of Spain. The violence of her fit made her look like a corpse. But on the second "cut of the knife she cried out and stirred her limbes, shewing manifest signes of life" (11r). The implicit irony of the story is that Vesalius, in aiming to make visible the peculiar secrets of the female body, found himself startled out of his profession by the occult qualities of the womb. Jorden closes his pamphlet with the assertion that he has omitted those cures that belong to him as a physician, thus making secret his expertise and designating the information in the pamphlet as common and commonplace (25v). In other words, Jorden authorizes in physicians a specialized knowledge of the female body that outstrips the experiences of laypeople, unlicensed caregivers, or, more particularly, women themselves. Seventeenth-century medical writers' ensuing interest in uterine disorders suggests that the feminization of nature's secrets affected the development and course of early modern medicine.

Such speculation about women's preternatural qualities was not limited to treatises on medicine, secrets, witchcraft, or books of magic. We can find evidence of these same concepts in household receipt books. In one seventeenth-century manuscript, the householder has transcribed a version of the notorious weapon-salve, the controversial remedy that instructed the caregiver to anoint the weapon with its marvelous balm, rather than the wound itself. In published writings, the question of the remedy's efficacy takes a back seat to the central disputes about the cure. Did the therapy rely on a sympathetic relation established between the injury and the knife? Did material yet hidden emanations move (at a close distance) from the weapon to the wound? Or was it the work of the devil?[115] In this particular manuscript account, the writer cites some of the usual ingredients of the weapon-salve found in various sources, including the moss of a dead man's skull. However, this version also warns the reader to exclude women, and any materials that women may have touched, from the administration of the cure. It is necessary to bind the weapon with linen, but it cannot be linen that has been "used About A woman's body, nor he that companieth with a woman, must neither Anoint the weapon, nor Come neare the same." Nor can the wounded "keep the company of women" while he heals.[116] The warnings underscore the fear that a woman's body could emanate contagious occult emissions that would disrupt the sympathetic action of the therapy.

Sympathy in the theater

One of my goals in *Occult Knowledge* is to show that early modern drama and performance were situated in a culture in which people experienced and sought to manipulate nature's sympathies and antipathies in their everyday lives. A striking example of the everyday nature of occult knowledge can be found in Philip Henslowe's diary. The theatrical manager records, among his accounting schedules, several secrets and recipes that depend on sympathetic forces for their effects, including instructions on how "To make a fowle fall dead," "To know wher a thinge is yt Is stolen," and "against frensye or one that is bytt wth a dogg." This final cure requires, among other things, writing certain words on parchment in bat blood and tying the paper to one's left arm on a Tuesday morning.[117] The how-to structure of early modern receipts – whether magical, curative, or legerdemain – has a kinship with theatrical enterprises. Obviously, the English Renaissance theater produced visual and auditory effects on stage. But there is also some evidence to suggest that dramatists and spectators believed those effects could stir an audience member's emotions against her will, in the same way that antipathies or sympathies in one entity might draw or repel the affections of another.

According to David Marshall, eighteenth-century sympathy is unavoidably theatrical: it occurs when "audiences in the theater, or people in the world are faced with the spectacle of an accident, or suffering, or danger." Adam Smith, Marshall contends, treated sympathy as a theatrical phenomenon: "acts of sympathy are structured by theatrical dynamics that ... depend on people's ability to represent themselves as tableaux, spectacles, and texts before others."[118] While sympathizing after the Restoration entailed moral, emotional, and even physiological, engagement, the theatrical experience that Marshall describes assumes a fundamental separateness between individuated minds and bodies. Theatrical performances roused people's passions, but, more significantly, they provided opportunities for the audience to reflect self-consciously on their actual distance from the spectacle being staged. This distance, I contend, did not exist for theater-goers in Shakespeare's London, who were subject to less predictable and more contagious sympathies.

Certainly, early modern antitheatricalists believed that spectators should be concerned about the occult or secret effects of theater: theatrical performances take "possession by subtle invasion," the players' "impressions of the mind are secretly conveyed over to the gazers," and their "wanton speeches do pierce our secret thoughts."[119] It worries Stephen Gosson that the abuses of the theater "cannot be shown, because they pass the degrees of the instrument, reach of the plummet, sight of the mind, and for trial are never brought to the touchstone."[120] At the heart of what Tanya Pollard identifies as the "early modern theater's preoccupation with drugs and poisons" is a hidden world of antipathetic poisons and sympathetic cures.[121] Some defenders of the stage characterized its potentially therapeutic effects in humoral terms, imbuing theater with the power to purge melancholy, for example. Others suggest a theater of secret forces and contagious emotions.[122] Although he does not apply the thesis to theater, Sir Philip Sidney defends the virtues of pleasurable poetry by citing how its efficacious cure of philosophy works on the patient without his knowledge:

> even those hard-hearted evil men ... will be content to be delighted – which is all the good-fellow poet seemeth to promise – and so steal to see the form of goodness (which seen they cannot but love) ere themselves be aware, as if they took a medicine of cherries.[123]

For Montaigne, the emotional experience of a theater-goer demonstrates most persuasively that certain passions are mysteriously transmitted from one party to another:

> [t]he frenzy which sets its goads in him [the poetry critic] who knows how to discern it also strikes a third person who hears him and relate and recite it, just as a magnet not only attracts a needle but also pours into it the faculty of attracting others. It can more easily be seen in the theatre that the sacred inspiration of the Muses, having first seized the poet with anger, grief, or

> hatred and driven him outside himself whither they will, then affects the
> actor through the poet, and then, in succession, the entire audience – needle
> hanging from needle, each attracting the next one in the chain.[124]

But for Gosson, spectators who hope for therapeutic effects simply open
themselves up to the theater's dangerous and occult charms: "look for no
salve at plays or theaters . . . to leave physic, you flee to enchanting."[125] And
for Anthony Munday, the plays themselves so often present "counterfeit
witchcraft, charmed drinks, and amorous potions, thereby to draw affections of men, and to stir them up unto lust, to like even those women of
themselves they abhor," so that the performances may encourage the
"ignorant multitude to seek such unlawful means" of manipulating their
neighbor's affections.[126] In other words, watching plays may be the first step
towards engaging the services of a cunning woman.

When he defends the moral power of theater in *An apologie for actors*
(1612), Thomas Heywood asserts that theatrical performances have the
uncanny power to elicit confessions from audience members against their
will. Recalling Hamlet's plan to catch the conscience of the king with the
staging of *The Mousetrap*, Heywood recites several stories in which audience
members are compelled by a performance to confess publicly secret crimes
that they have hidden for years.

> At Lin in Norfolke, the then Earle of Sussex players acting the old History of
> Fryer Francis, & presenting a woman, who insatiately doting on a yong
> gentleman, had (the more securely to enioy his affection) mischieuously and
> seceretly, murdered her husband, whose ghost haunted her, and at diuers
> times in her most solitary and priuate contemplations, in most horrid and
> fearefull shapes, appeared, and stood before her. As this was acted, a townes-
> woman (till then of good estimation and report) finding her conscience (at
> this presentment) extremely troubled, suddenly skritched and cryd out Oh
> my husband, my husband! I see the ghost of my husband fiercely threatning
> and menacing me. At which shrill and v[n]expected out-cry, the people
> about her, moou'd to a strange amazement, inquired the reason of her
> clamour, when presently vn-urged, she told them, that seuen yeares ago,
> she, to be possest of such a Gentleman (meaning him) had poysoned her
> husband, whose fearefull image personated it selfe in the shape of that ghost:
> whereupon the murdresse was apprehended, before the Iustices further
> examined, & by her voluntary confession after condemned. That this is
> true, as well by the report of the Actors as the records of the Towne, there are
> many eye-witnesses of this accident yet liuing, vocally to confirme it.

In a second anecdote, a female audience member's strange reaction to a
staged murder somehow leads the local church-warden to find the buried
skull of the woman's husband, which she had driven a nail into twelve years

before.[127] It is possible to reconcile these revelations with the popular notion that "murder will out" – a providential narrative that promised God's protection against the wicked.[128] And yet, Heywood's stories suggest that theater plays the instrumental role in the revelation of these wicked crimes. Notably, Heywood's accounts feature female murderers who are moved by theatrical performances to reveal their secrets involuntarily. Heywood's stories, I argue, offset the fear that an evil or bold woman's occult knowledge and hidden powers will adversely affect those in her presence. Rather than feeling sympathy, as in pity, for the characters on stage, Heywood's female spectators are sympathetically affected by the performances – as a lodestone draws iron – to bring their hidden crimes to light.

The cultural fear of women's embodied occult qualities should also inform our discussion of the transvestite stage. While the eroticization of boys had its own contagious dangers, it was also understood (as several books of natural magic make plain) that the spirits and invisible emissions emanating from a young boy's body were deemed healthful rather than harmful.[129] While we can only speculate, perhaps the fear of women's darting glances and magnetic wombs made their bodies too unruly for public display. We might take as an example a scene in Thomas Heywood's *A Woman Killed With Kindness* (1603). The cuckolded husband, Frankford, panics when the maid brings his children into the presence of his wife Anne. His anxiety suggests that women who fail to adhere to society's injunctions to be chaste, silent, and obedient will prove literally contaminating to those around them:

> Away with them, lest, as her spotted body
> Hath stained their names with stripe of bastardy,
> So her adult'rous breath may blast their spirits
> With her infectious thoughts.[130]

Anne's influence, Frankford fears, is not simply a moral issue of poor behavior producing poor behavior. He believes that the occult transmission of Anne's breath and thoughts could contaminate the spirits of their children. While Anne's pitiable state, as she begs for forgiveness, may invite sympathy from a modern audience, Heywood's play indicates, instead, that the close proximity between the mother and her offspring will generate sympathies of another sort: if unprotected, the children will soon resemble their mother in spirit and body by way of contagion.

Even as late as 1682, printed texts advised that a child's illness, when you can "find no other outward or inward cause," should license one to suspect a "venomous vapour, or Witch-craft."[131] In his account of women's supposedly infectious nature, Johann Jacob Wecker asks "Are not Children handled more safely by Men, than by Women?"[132] At the end of Heywood's play, Anne Frankford has denied herself food and drink and purified her body of its fleshly appetites and venomous vapors. In this desiccated and passive state, she finally garners a more familiar kind of sympathy, or pity, from her husband.[133] Given that Heywood and his contemporaries repeatedly demonstrate that sympathy for a living, breathing woman could prove dangerous to a spectator, an early modern audience may have been reassured to know that their emotions were stirred by a boy actor representing a woman's disordered passions. Rather than pointing to a one-sex culture, the all-male stage may have functioned as protection from the implicit power of women's embodied occult qualities.

The chapters

Histories of science and medicine have neglected to examine imaginative texts as sources of early modern society's ambivalent perceptions of women's secrets. But at the same time that natural philosophy began to privilege trials and experiments as legitimate sources of knowledge production, early modern drama staged stories that assessed the epistemological authority of women's practices as healers, distillers, and experimenters. It is in early modern drama, I argue, that we find accounts of gender, epistemology, and science which the non-literary texts fail to provide: accounts that suggest that as experiential evidence gained ground among natural philosophers, women's presumed intimacy with nature's sympathies and antipathies was either demonized or diminished. *Occult Knowledge* argues that, in its representations of women's bodies and women's knowledge, early modern drama participates in natural philosophy's production of epistemological boundaries. By focusing on the theater's staging of occult phenomena in everyday life, this book uncovers an obscured but important chapter in the social history of science when the construction of legitimate scientific knowledge depended on taming women's bodies and arrogating their secrets.

In my readings of *Twelfth Night*, *Arden of Faversham*, *A Warning for Fair Women*, *All's Well That Ends Well*, *The Changeling*, and *The Duchess of Malfi*, I argue that these plays repeatedly stage the question of whether women have a privileged access to nature's secrets but also whether women's bodies possess and transmit hidden, occult properties.[134] By examining the representation of women on stage who are viewed as possessing occult knowledge or powers, *Occult Knowledge* reinterprets the question of boundary work in the period. As we already observed, assessments of occult phenomena in early modern natural philosophy sought to draw distinctions between natural knowledge, demonology, and supernatural miracles. In this vein, the occult knowledge traditionally held by women (or irregular healers or cunning folk) was constantly subject to a sorting process; it could be classified as illicit witchcraft, specious nonsense, or useful information, ripe for more official appropriation. *Occult Knowledge* tracks the ways dramatic representations of female knowledge take part in this boundary work: the women depicted, for example, in *The Duchess of Malfi*, *A Warning for Fair Women*, *Arden of Faversham*, and *All's Well That Ends Well* come very close to being classified as witches but their knowledge or power proves too ambiguous to circumscribe.[135]

In the first chapter, "Women's secrets and the status of evidence in *All's Well That Ends Well*," I contend that Helena's success in curing the King of France in Shakespeare's comedy depends not only on the merit of her father's receipts but also on her understanding of hidden sympathies and antipathies. The play explores the question of whether Helena has a privileged access to nature's secrets and asks whether her body possesses hidden, occult properties. Throughout *All's Well That Ends Well*, the secret animating virtues of a recipe's ingredients, or of a talisman, are conflated with the potential effects of Helena's own mysterious qualities – somatic and epistemological.

Chapter 2, "Sympathetic contagion in *Arden of Faversham* and *A Warning for Fair Women*," examines the representation of infectious, bold women in these anonymous domestic tragedies. Both plays stage occult phenomena – including cruentation, or the bleeding corpse – as instances of contagious sympathy, an early modern concept of infection that presupposes a latent likeness between the disease and the victim. In *Arden of Faversham*, Alice Arden secretly infects those around her: this influence is analogized in the cunning man's proposal that he paint a poisoned portrait of her that would contaminate the viewer's eye-beams. The *Arden* playwright implies that theater, as a source of contamination, poses the same threat as Alice. In contrast, *A Warning for Fair Women* cites the same stories of confession that Heywood recounts and represents theater's contagious sympathies as morally corrective rather than dangerous.

In Chapter 3, "'As secret as maidenhead': magnetic wombs and the nature of attraction in Shakespeare's *Twelfth Night*," I highlight how contemporary correlations made between the lodestone and the womb can help us understand the circulation of desire in Shakespeare's comedy. The magnetic influence of the womb in *Twelfth Night* not only directs the characters' emotions and behavior but also, as Sebastian acknowledges, produces the occult bond of twinship – a secret sympathy that inspires attraction in the same way that the lodestone distributes its magnetic virtue by contact.

Chapter 4, "Tragic antipathies in *The Changeling*," establishes that the book of secrets at the heart of Thomas Middleton and William Rowley's *The Changeling* conflates the secrets of nature with women's secrets. Moreover, its theatrically deployed recipe, which verifies virginity, posits a hidden antipathetical relation between the properties of a virgin and the occult virtues of the mixed concoction. The natural operations hinted at in the book of secrets – the cosmological undercurrents of antipathies and sympathies – also govern the characters' emotional responses. As a case in point, Beatrice-Joanna hates DeFlores (as Alsemero explains and we discover) because he is her predestined contrary – her idiosyncratic poison. For Middleton and Rowley, directing or manipulating nature's hidden qualities proves to be a gendered enterprise. When Beatrice concocts a homeopathic scheme to drive out a poison with poison, she draws on her own experiential familiarity with occult properties. Her failure, however, signals one effort among many in the play to circumscribe nature's secrets as an entirely masculine realm.

In Chapter 5, "'To think there's power in potions': experiment, sympathy, and the devil in *The Duchess of Malfi*," I argue that John Webster presents Ferdinand's imprisonment and torture of his sister in language that invokes the discourses of natural magic, proto-scientific experimentation, and demonology to stage questions about the moral and spiritual dangers of manipulating nature. Compelled by his fear of women's secrets, Ferdinand attempts to plague his sister with "art" (echoing Bacon's bid to vex Nature to reveal her secrets). While Ferdinand fantasizes about the revelatory power of experimentation and scientific inquiry, his actual inquisition of the Duchess disintegrates into *maleficium*. Webster suggests that Ferdinand's obsessive endeavor to reveal his sister's secrets leads him, tacitly, to engage the devil's services. As a demonic disease, then, Ferdinand's lycanthropy is fitting punishment for his violations of nature.

Looking forward

Enlightenment science did not eradicate the power of occult qualities (which had been incorporated into mechanical philosophy). As Lorraine Daston and Katharine Park observe, "the active principles of matter and gravitation so central to Newtonian natural philosophy were every bit as occult or even miraculous."[136] It was, instead, the human body and its imagination that underwent the most severe rehabilitation. While the material imagination in the sixteenth and seventeenth centuries could impart sympathetic and antipathetic effluvia that acted on surrounding external matter, the powers of the imagination in the eighteenth century became confined to individual minds. Increasingly, when common or vulgar folk in the later periods reported strange marvels, these encounters simply highlighted their naïve credulity and feverish hallucinations.[137]

Certainly, there were sixteenth-century writers who had insisted that the manipulation of sympathies and antipathies belonged solely to the sphere of the erudite magus, and that vulnerable folks (such as women, children, the ignorant, and the elderly) lacked the resources to resist the infectious or delusional effects of strange phenomena. But as long as human minds and bodies could emit material effluvia, even civilized and temperate men prove impressionable in the earlier periods. In a world of coursing sympathies and antipathies, and sometimes by virtue of their central role as nurturers and healers in the household, women of all classes were presented on the early modern stage as possessing the capacity to act on others at-a-distance.

CHAPTER I

Women's secrets and the status of evidence in All's Well That Ends Well

In Shakespeare's *All's Well That Ends Well*, Helena cures the King of France with a medical receipt – a handwritten remedy – bequeathed to her by her father, a renowned physician who recently passed away. The medically official (and paternal) origin of Helena's medical expertise seems to legitimize her therapeutic practice. However, her capacity to restore the king to health derives not only from her father's specific prescriptive instructions but also from a more general, and potentially embodied, knowledge of nature's hidden sympathies and antipathies.[1] The occult properties attributed to things (as in talismans, or the secret virtues of plants or minerals) are equated, at several junctures in the play, with the presumed occult properties of women's bodies. Bertram's persistent resistance to Helena, staged in the final scene as skepticism of her claim that she has achieved his assigned tasks, can be read as an ambivalence about the cultural associations made between occult knowledge and female secrets.

Critics have long struggled to determine what kind of knowledge Helena possesses. She has been identified as a cunning woman associated with fairy magic, a Paracelsian, a domestic medical practitioner, and a student of her father's medicine.[2] There is no critical consensus as to whether Helena's therapeutic knowledge is masculine or feminine, mainstream or unorthodox, science or magic. To some degree, all of these critics are correct. In contrast to the doctors who fail to cure the king, Helena claims the kind of experiential knowledge found in receipt books. Receipt knowledge could be characterized as domestic, traditional, and even folkloric, but the content of medical receipts varied little from a physician's pharmaceutical prescriptions. Receipts, particularly in their how-to structure, also overlapped with the instructions found in books of natural magic, and books of secrets (which could include directions for theatrical illusions), as well as early treatises of proto-scientific experimentation.[3] All of these procedures share an emphasis on the effects of an experiential process without a clear sense of causation. The very title of the play, *All's Well That Ends Well*, suggests to its audience that if the effects are good (if the patient, for example, is made well), then the consequences should take precedence over causation. Such an assertion necessarily provokes challenges or questions (underlining the comedy's status as a "problem play"), but it does so, perversely, by insisting that we need not investigate what produces an outcome, if the results are favorable.

Helena's perception of her own agency, as well as the structural trajectory of the play itself, is derived from the assumption, inherent in medical recipes, that certain steps will generate probable outcomes even if the cause remains unknown. As noted in the introduction, many early modern medical receipts based their presumed efficacy on the hidden power of sympathetic and antipathetic action. And it is Helena's understanding of secret sympathies in nature that encourages her to apply receipt knowledge to experiences beyond the curing of the king. In the first half of the play, Helena puts a literal medical receipt into practice when she heals the king of his fistula. In the second half of the play, Helena interprets the conditions of Bertram's spiteful farewell letter (that she can call him "husband" once she obtains his ring and bears his child) as another receipt – a set of "how-to" instructions which, when followed, will generate desirable results. The restoration of the king depends on an experiential knowledge of recipes that anticipates an emerging scientific culture.[4] But the hidden maneuvers of the bed-trick hint that Helena herself may embody occult properties, thus returning *All's Well That Ends Well* to a world of natural magic.

The secrets of receipt knowledge

A comfort with occult causation can be traced to traditional medicine and natural magic. As a practice, medicine deployed whatever methods and ingredients that promised results. University-trained physicians were "accustomed to elaborate specialized versions of occult – that is hidden, but nevertheless natural – causation within medical theory."[5] They drew on treatments that combined Paracelsian methods, Galenic remedies, and magic in their therapies.[6] A "utilitarian attitude," Ian Maclean notes, "[is] appropriate to the medical art."[7] The official *Pharmacopoeia*, issued by the College of Physicians in 1618, includes among its approved ingredients items recognizable for their inherent magical virtues:

horn of unicorn or rhinoceros, the bone from the heart of a stag, elephant
tusk, bezoar stone, mummy taken from the tomb, frog spawn, crayfish eyes,
penis of a bull, flesh of vipers, nest of swallows, [and] oil of foxes.[8]

As Richard Kieckhefer has established, it is possible to trace an "indifference"
to what causes a remedy to work back to the medical material of medieval
manuscripts where the "distinction between occult and manifest power . . .
[is] perhaps beside the point."[9] In the same way that housewives or cunning
folk may not know why a cure proves effective, physicians were not always
able to articulate what caused a remedy to work. They often employed
remedies that "may only be explicable through a non-manifest cause or
process, which can be acknowledged without being fully grasped."[10]

The interest in occult causation increased in the early modern period,
Nancy Siraisi notes, "to accommodate a changing disease environment,
[and] a new attention to particulars."[11] Since the practice of medicine
typically valued effects over and above theory, practitioners doggedly pur-
sued knowledge through experimentation, often with a focus on understanding the occult. The only way to ascertain how to take advantage of
hidden properties or virtues in a potential medicament was through trial,
testing, and observation. As such, occult diseases and cures hold an important place in the history of science. In John Henry and John M. Forrester's
words, "it is in fact abundantly clear that those thinkers who promoted the
experimental approach did so as a means of trying to deal with the occult
qualities which, they had come to believe, were too important to be
excluded from natural philosophy."[12]

The medical writer Jean Fernel provides the period's most systematic
discussion of occult diseases and cures in *On the Hidden Causes of Things*.
Unlike Paracelsus' contention that God provides signatures in natural
substances for the physician to discern the appropriate cure for an ailment,
Fernel insists that the occult properties in plants, minerals, and animals
remain hidden, inviting our admiration rather than understanding. Trial,
experiment, and observation, however, can teach the physician the secret
powers of nature's medicaments. Implanted in everything, Fernel maintains, are sympathies and antipathies that stay "concealed and remote,"
except when discovered by experience.[13] Since this knowledge could be
obtained through everyday experiences, it was available to lay folk as well as
medical doctors. Consequently, physicians and irregular practitioners often
applied the same curative methods and prescriptions.[14] As the primary
caregivers in their communities, women could be very well versed in the
qualities and uses of a variety of medicaments.[15]

As noted in the introduction, close examination of household receipt books reveals a spate of cures that rely on occult forces and the hidden sovereign virtues of particular animals, minerals, or plants.[16] In a number of instances receipts suggest sympathetic magic, as when the cure for a dog bite requires hair from the biting dog. At other times, the correspondence between illness and cure lies in a recognizable similitude (not unlike Paracelsian signatures): ingesting fox lungs, for example, will heal a bad cough. Astrology can also play a role, helping to determine when a cure is administered, or when the simples for a recipe are to be gathered.

In one notable receipt, the cure not only depends on a secret sympathy developed between an animal and the patient but also provides the caregiver with secret knowledge. The instructions promise help in identifying the "secret or hydden dysease of any man and to heale the same":

> Take a younge whelpe that yet sucketh, and let him
> lye night and daye with the man the space of three dayes
> during the which time the patient shall take milke
> In his mouth and spite in to the whelpe's mouth then
> Take the sayde whelpe and cleave him in pieces, and you
> Shall knowe the sicke parte of the man by that of the
> Dog which you shall see either infected or whole and sound
> for certainly the whelp draweth to him self the
> secret and hidden disease whereof he dieth and the
> man shall be healed and you must bury the Dogge.[17]

The first stage in the recipe puts the dog and the patient in the same bed for three days, hinting that this time and contact cultivates a sympathetic relationship between the two. While spitting into a dog's mouth was a commonly practiced gesture of friendship, the writer insists that the patient spit milk into the mouth of a nursing puppy. Even if the man does not use dog's milk (for the receipt fails to identify its source), the action still mimics the puppy's attachment to its mother. Spitting also implies a transmission of the disease to the dog (at a time when theories of contagion often depended upon the concept of action-at–a-distance). It also connotes a purging on the man's part. Finally, an anatomy of the whelp gives the caregiver access to secret information and ensures the eradication of the disease in the patient.[18] The final instruction, "you must bury the Dogge," suggests that the writer believes the disease has been fully transferred to the animal.

In a similar vein, a common recipe for treating plague sources required the occult transfer of the disease from a human patient to live chickens:

Take a cock chicken & pull all the feathers of his tayle very bare, then hold
the bared part of the pullet close upon the sore, & the chicken will gape &
labor for life, & will dye; then do so with another pullet till it dye, & so with
another: till you find the last chicken will not dye, cannot be killed by the
infection being altogether extracted, for when all the venom is drawn out the
last chicken will not be hurt by it, & the patient will mend speedily; one
Mr. Whatts hath tried this on a childe of his, & 8 chickens one after another
dyed & the ninth lived, & the sore being hard & hot, was made soft by the
first chicken as papp, the 2d drew it clean away.[19]

As Charles Estienne explains in *Maison rustique*, placing the fundament of
any living fowl on an infection proves therapeutic because poultry have "a
naturall contrarietie [antipathy] against poison."[20] Not only does the writer
suggest that the chickens will counter the plague's poison, but the recipe
also promises to generate a renewal of skin, and presumably strength. While
the receipt books omit any discussion of causation, they do mark some
valuable cures as "proven." In this case, Mr. Whatt's good success with his
own child functions as anecdotal evidence, perhaps encouraging a family
member to apply as many as eight live chickens to her own ailing patient.

As with the notorious weapon-salve, some isolated receipts pointedly
draw on the concept of action-at-a-distance in their therapeutic instructions. Consider for example the following remedy "To stanch bleeding, or
cure a green wound by sympathy":

Take a peece of reesed [rancid] bacon hold it between hot tongs so let it drop
into a pot, then wipe some of the blood (whether it be of the nose or wound)
on a cloth, then annoint that cloth over with reesed bacon and keep it about
you in a constant gentle warmth, for if it be kept too hot, it will cause much
pain in a sore and you neede doe nothing to the wound but lap it up clenly.
I heard nothing but this cured a horse when a stake was run into him a good
way and it was no long time in healing. Sympatheticall powder will doe the
same, which is Roman vitterall [vitriol] calcined, that is keep your viterall in a
constant warmth & there will be a whitish powder grow on the outside,
which must be strowed on the blood and kept in constant warmth just as the
Bacon is ordered going before, not kept to hot by no means, nor cold.[21]

This recipe stands out not only for its expressed identification of sympathy
as the occult force that heals the wound but also for its embedded and much
simplified recipe for making the famed sympathetical powder itself.[22]
Occasionally receipts rely on the use of an amulet or talisman, implicit in
the recommendation that a child wear a wolf's tooth around his neck to
prevent dental pain, or in a receipt that stipulates wearing a bag filled with
foxes' stones around one's neck to avoid "the mother & fainting."[23]

While overtly supernatural word charms prove rare, they do appear from time to time.[24] Buried in the manuscript collection of recipes held in Robert Boyle's family, for example, is the following remedy:

> "A Receipt by way of Charm for an Ague"
> Our Saviour Jesus Christ seeing the cross He had an Agony upon him, the Jews asked art thou afraid and he said I am not afraid nor have I an Ague. All those that fear the Name of Christ and wear the name of Christ about them shall have no Ague. Amen, Sweet Jesus, Sweet Jesus, Sweet Jesus, Amen, Sweet Jesus, Amen. This is to be served [clothed] in a black silk and put to the pitt of the stomach an hour before the fitt comes and not [illegible] by the party but worn till all to pieces.[25]

The recipe fails to delineate how the caregiver or patient knows when "an hour before the fit comes" will be; perhaps the cautious wore the charm on their bodies at all times.

To get a fuller sense of how the very structure of *All's Well That Ends Well* may be influenced by the logic of these preternatural receipts, it is important to note the common ground these texts share with other how-to discourses, including books of secrets but also natural magic, legerdemain, and trickery. *Hocus Pocus Junior*, for example, provides recipes or secrets on how to produce marvelous effects where the cause remains unknown or hidden to the spectator.[26] How-to instructions on producing theatrical artifice also appear in books of secrets. While the first part of Girolamo Ruscelli's *The Secretes of the Master Alexis of Piemont* is devoted to remedies, cosmetics, and dyes, the second part provides secrets to a range of optical illusions and deceptions among its medical cures and face washes.[27] One trick reveals how "To make all thinges seme Blacke and Greene in the night."

> TAke the blacke inck of a Fishe called a skuttle, called *Atramentum Sepiae*, & take also Verdegrice, and mingle bothe togither, and put them in a lampe with the wieke, and set it a fier in a chambre, where there is no other light but that, and al that is in the said chambre walles and all shal seeme partly Greene, and partly Blacke, whiche is a meruelous thing to see.[28]

An audience to Ruscelli's trick might have trouble determining whether the illusion is natural or not. In the same way that the cured king in *All's Well That Ends Well* provokes questions about the nature of unusual phenomena, a staged spectacle can produce a similar state of category confusion. As Philip Butterworth has established, books of secrets and books of natural magic were primary sources for generating magical spectacles on stage.[29] To glimpse how a cure, a charm, and a trick might all be classed together, we need only look to the mix of receipts collected by Philip Henslowe in his diary. Among a set of therapies aimed to cure the "falling evill," to clean a wound, to heal deafness and blindness, and to drive away an ague, Henslowe records instructions for making a fowl fall down dead and a charm that will reveal lost items in one's dreams. What unites these receipts, and all the various genres of "how-to" texts, is their goal of producing effects.[30]

Prescriptions of rare and proved effects

From the start of the play, we can trace how Helena's interpretation of her world and her own agency relies on the occult logic and assumptions contained in some receipt books. Initially, she feels frustrated by her class position, lamenting, in particular, her seeming inability to produce substantial effects in the world – the very skill that receipt books will supply. When Parolles teases her on the uselessness of preserved virginity, she responds with a speech that seems to imbue the physical site (or the "there") of her virginity with expansive powers: "A mother and a mistress and a friend, / A phoenix, captain, and an enemy / A guide, a goddess, and a sovereign" (1.1.154–56).[31] Then, feeling stymied by her current circumstances, Helena states it is a pity

> That wishing well had not a body in't
> Which might be felt, that we, the poorer born,
> Whose baser stars do shut us up in wishes,
> Might with effects of them follow our friends
> And show what we alone must think, which never
> Returns us thanks.   (168–73)

Helena's deepest desire is to translate her wishes (and her body's potential) into results, but from the outset she imagines that her low birth prevents her from making anything happen.

Helena's frustration stems from her perception that the social gap between herself and Bertram is insurmountable. Indeed, she naturalizes their separation with an astronomical analogy that locates them in separate cosmological spheres. As a baser star (170), she sees Bertram as "a bright particular star / . . . so above me. / In his bright radiance and collateral light / Must I be comforted, not in his sphere" (81–84). It is only when she shifts her perspective from the "fated sky" (200) to the sublunary world that Helena discovers she may have some agency, remembering that "Our remedies oft in ourselves do lie / Which we ascribe to heaven" (199–200).

Helena's claim suggests, simultaneously, that therapeutic knowledge is classless and non-gendered and that a hidden power of reparation lies physically within her. In the first sense, if the primary source of a remedy's power stems from its occult ingredients, a receipt that circulated among a variety of people could retain its usefulness no matter who mixed and administered the cure. While some recipes may gain a reputation as originally concocted by a named person (Dr. Stevens' Waters; My Lady Kent's Powder), the exchange of recipes requires that their worth be detachable from individuals. If the recipe is followed correctly, then its success lies in the preparation, mixture, and application of ingredients, not in the intrinsic qualities of the caregiver. And yet, Helena may also mean that the remedy lies, quite literally, within her, perhaps anticipating how her own body and its secrets will play a role in the cures she effects.

Having rejected the astronomical hierarchy that placed Bertram out of her reach, Helena rethinks her attachment to him. Rather than disallowing her love on the basis of vertical hierarchies, Helena conceives that her affections may be compelled by unseen connections in nature that defy appearances and class distinctions:

> What power is it which mounts my love so high,
> That makes me see and cannot feed mine eye?
> The mightiest space in fortune nature brings
> To join like likes and kiss like native things. (203–06)

Prompted by the sentiment that her overreaching love stems from an unknown "power," Helena concludes that her attraction to Bertram is guided by hidden correspondences. Nature, she maintains, has the capacity to traverse the "mightiest space" in its impetus to unite sympathetic entities: "to join like likes and kiss like native things." Outwardly it may appear that Bertram's physical distance literalizes an insuperable social gap that nature reflects celestially, but Helena reinterprets her prospects based on unseen sympathies. Such occult attractions produce action at a distance – nature ensures that hidden "like" will join with hidden "like," no matter the separating space. For many spectators, curing the king would appear to have no predictable connection to attaining a husband. But since Helena finds herself emboldened by nature's wondrous capacity to close great distances between the act and the effect, her plan to heal the king's fistula functions as one (seemingly unrelated) step in a grander receipt to cure her own lovesickness.

Defying the rationale that a person should attempt only what can be measured manifestly, or through the senses, Helena privileges what cannot be discerned as readily: "Impossible be strange attempts to those / That weigh their pains in sense and do suppose / What hath been cannot be" (207–09). Her faith in the success of her own strange experiment rests on a trust in hidden affinities. It is Helena's occult philosophy that allows her to imagine that practice and experience may reveal something more about the sublunary world, which exceeds available epistemological frameworks. God knows all things, Helena reminds the king, but humans can "square our guess by shows" (2.1.149). Helena implies here that assumptions about the operations of nature gain or lose credence by the evidence that experiments produce.

The king's illness points up the inadequacy of the dominant systems of medical knowledge: as Lafew observes, the king had been "relinquished of the artists, – / ... both of Galen and Paracelsus / Of all the learned and authentic Fellows" (2.3.9–11). Helena's triumph over the Galenists and Paracelsians in particular valorizes experiential knowledge over theoretical frameworks, while also privileging the effects of occult operations over the discovery of causes. Although often at odds with one another for authority, both Galenists and Paracelsians provided a theoretical basis for medical practice, which included theories of causation – in terms of the disease and the remedy.[32] Galenists held that most illnesses stemmed from disordered humors, and their cures aimed to restore humoral balance to the body. Paracelsians maintained that diseases had external causes, asserting that every individual disease had a corresponding individual cure. The king identifies these physicians as "learned doctors" and members of the "congregated College," much like England's College of Physicians (2.1.114–15), before suggesting that Helena, in contrast, may be an empiric (120). Although empirics were associated with quackery, Helena does not dispute the label, perhaps because the title literally denotes a kind of healer who relies on experience, observation, and experiment, to the "exclusion of philosophical theory."[33]

Resistant to the cures applied by both Paracelsians and Galenics, the king's fistula proves mysteriously beyond the theoretical ken of the "congregated College." Unlike the stories told in Boccaccio's *The Decameron* and in William Painter's *Palace of Pleasure*, which locate the fistula on the ruler's stomach or breast, *All's Well That Ends Well* neglects to report the site of the affliction.[34] Several critics have insisted (with attention to the bawdy jokes made in other parts of the play) that the king suffers from a *fistula in ano*.[35] But Shakespeare's omission of the site of the fistula also points up the hidden nature of the king's disease. As an ulcer or open sore of "morbid origin," the king's fistula could easily be a symptom of an undiagnosed, mysterious disease.[36] Some early modern health practitioners insisted that an occult disease required an occult cure.[37] But developing and employing occult cures for occult diseases was a strain of medical practice that did not fit neatly into either a Galenic or a Paracelsian approach.[38]

As a physician, Helena's father would have been trained predominantly in Galenic humoralism, but with some Paracelsian theory as well.[39] His receipts, however, constitute his experiential knowledge, since the "how-to" instructions of receipt books provide only shrouded glimpses into the theoretical foundations of a cure. As both manuscript and published receipt books make clear, remedies get transmitted from generation to generation because they have been proven (either anecdotally or by the transcriber) to work. When the Countess and Lafew discuss Gerard de Narbon's reputation, they emphasize his "skill" as a practitioner above all else. In her description of the receipts, Helena underscores their "rare and proved effects" (1.3.208). These effects, she explains, derived in part from her father's reading, but more directly from his "manifest experience" (209). And the particular remedy she believes will cure the king has been "approved" or proven (214). As she explains to the king, the value of this receipt derives from her father's "practice" and "experience" (2.1.104–05).[40]

Without denying that God may have worked through Helena and her receipt, the play suggests that the recipes themselves contain secrets. Helena hints that "something" resides in her remedy that far exceeds her "father's skill" (1.3.228–29).[41] It is possible, she states, that this "good receipt" is "sanctified / By th'luckiest stars in heaven" (230–32), but her father's final instructions urged her to employ the remedies with "heedfull'st reservation" for the very reason that they contained within their "faculties inclusive" powers that surpassed even their recognized worth (211–12).[42] It is possible that the recipes' ingredients – or rather the properties within those ingredients – promise effects that defy most theoretical understandings of causation. When Helena presents herself to the king, she indicates that her father also advised her to keep the cure secret: "He bade me store [it] up as a triple eye / Safer than mine own two" (2.1.106–07). While the meaning of "triple eye" remains opaque, it connotes the mind's eye or a mode of perception that senses what remains hidden.

The audience witnesses the receipt's "rare and proved effects" when the king emerges healthy and active. What remains occulted, however, is what the cure involved, why it worked, and how it was effected. By staging the therapy off-stage, Shakespeare underscores the occult nature of the remedy.[43] Anticipating the other important behind-the-scenes event of the play – the bed-trick – the king's cure also invokes associations between the secrets of women's bodies and the secrets of nature. As noted in the introduction, the "secrets" of women in pre-modern Europe signified an epistemological concept as well as the "hidden and secret [*occulta et secreta*] things about the nature and condition of women."[44] Early modern medical discourse established correspondences between between nature's secrets and women's bodies, epitomized in the idea that the womb itself contained occult qualities.[45] For Sujata Iyengar and others, the concealed administration of the remedy in *All's Well That Ends Well* implies that Helena heals the king through her sexuality.[46] Lafew jumps to a similar conclusion when he refers to himself as Cressid's uncle (2.1.96) and to "Doctor She" (77) as a "medicine" that can "[q]uicken a rock" (70–72). And yet, since the remedy remains hidden, the audience never knows how Helena restores the king to health. She may have applied an ointment, given him a cordial, or cured him with her body. All we can say definitively is that the nature of Helena's treatment, whether its secrets lie in her body or in the receipt, is known only by its effects.

For Lafew, the mystery of Helena's curative methods, combined with the king's wondrous recovery, constitutes a supernatural act. Once Helena cures the king, Lafew reads from a text that describes the event as "A showing of a heavenly effect in an earthly actor" (2.3.22–23). The announcement frames Helena's performance in providentially conservative terms.[47] Rather than attributing power to Helena or her medicaments, the public version insists that she has functioned as God's instrument. By identifying a "heavenly" influence, the written narrative neatly counters the possibility of witchcraft or demonic intervention – an interpretation hinted at in Helena's earlier vision of the "odious ballads" and "vilest torture" that could incur should she fail to cure the king (2.1.171–73).[48] Lafew insists that the king's revival shows the "[v]ery hand of heaven" (2.3.30):

> They say miracles are past, and we have our philosophical persons, to make modern and familiar things supernatural and causeless. Hence is it that we make trifles of terrors, ensconcing ourselves in seeming knowledge when we should submit ourselves to an unknown fear. (1–5)

By questioning whether "miracles are past," Lafew challenges the dominant argument made by Protestant clergymen that "providential interference were *miranda* not *miracula*, preternatural wonders brought about by divine manipulation of secondary causes and elemental forces."[49] Lafew's interpretation of events seems to hearken back to an older Catholic world and indicates a deep dissatisfaction with the naturalists' inclination to explain away mysteries and wonders. Opposed to Lafew's retrograde view are the philosophers who attribute all strange occurrences to natural causes. Lafew's public announcement neglects to entertain the notion that Helena has administered a preternatural cure that relies on occult operations of nature. But his critique of philosophical persons who substitute "seeming knowledge" for supernatural causation is also an acknowledgment of how categories of unusual phenomena were shifting in the period. As Stuart Clark observes, "supernatural explanations were challenged by preternatural, and preternatural by natural alternatives."[50]

The most intriguing aspect of Lafew's perspective is his pairing of "supernatural" with "causeless." Strictly speaking, a supernatural event cannot be causeless, for something supernatural has been instigated by the first cause, God himself. More than likely, a "causeless" thing refers to an occult phenomenon, where the cause remains hidden from human discernment. Lafew maintains that the explanation of causes provided by natural philosophers is "seeming knowledge," implying that philosophers appeal to unproven theories when the causation remains "unknown," or that they naturalize the phenomenon without providing an assured causal explanation of the strange effects. But Lafew's binary thinking only allows for two possibilities: the king might have been cured by the "seeming knowledge" of the Galenists or the Paracelsians (who failed in their endeavors), or the king has been cured by God, with Helena as His instrument. The possibility that Helena herself may possess secret knowledge or occult power does not occur to him.

When thou canst get the ring upon my finger

While the first half of the play introduces us to Helena's possession of receipt knowledge and the success it generates, the second half charts Helena's attempt to reframe Bertram's mocking tasks into a receipt that will turn him into her proper husband.[51] Although ordered by the king to marry Helena, Bertram refuses to accept his status as her husband. Seeking autonomy from both his mother and Helena (whom he may view as a sister), Bertram also fears spending, as Parolles puts it, his "manly marrow" in a "box unseen" (2.3.263–65). As a euphemism for female genitalia, the unseen box, with its secret powers, threatens to trap him at home; Bertram runs to the wars to escape a confinement he associates with the women in his life. He does not depart, however, without leaving Helena a message. Echoing the impossible challenge or task of a fairy tale, Bertram writes to her:

> When thou canst get the ring upon my finger, which never shall come off,
> and show me a child begotten of thy body that I am father to, then call me
> husband; but in such a "then" I write a "never." (3.2.55–58)

Recognizing the folk-tale cast of Bertram's pronouncement, critics have
treated his ultimatum as a riddle, linking it with more overt riddles in the
play such as Diana's introduction of Helena as "one that's dead is quick"
(5.3.300).[52] Typically, the rhetoric of a riddle calls for an ingenious answer that
resolves the puzzling or equivocal aspects of a question. Betram's note,
however, describes difficult tasks (he deems impossible), which will produce
particular results if accomplished. Certainly Helena does not interpret
Bertram's statement as riddle. She identifies it, instead, as her "passport"
(3.2.54), in the sense that it authorizes her to take action.[53] Since accomplish-
ing Bertram's tasks would necessitate proximity, Helena implies that the letter
proffers an ironic invitation to follow him into another country. Moreover, by
insisting that the letter functions as her "passport," Helena construes
Bertram's message not only as permission to act but also, more importantly,
as a kind of receipt – a recipe for remedying the alienated state of her marriage.
In his effort to be contrary, Bertram has, paradoxically, provided step-by-step
instructions on how Helena can produce the effects she seeks.[54]

Helena's insistence on privileging hidden sympathies comes to fruition in
the bed-trick. Although Bertram believes he sleeps with Diana, Helena
takes comfort in his inability to discern her presence. She marvels that men
"can such sweet use make of what they hate … so lust doth play / With
what it loathes, for that which is away" (4.4.22–25). Her logic suggests that,
if driven by a natural antipathy, Bertram would have been repulsed by her
presence without knowing why. Instead, the consummation of the marriage
supports her belief in their sympathetic bond. For the same reason that the
king's therapy had erotic connotations, the bed-trick functions largely as a
remedy. Bertram indicates as much when he implores Diana to give in to his
"sick desires, / Who then recovers" (4.2.36–37). By substituting herself for
Diana, Helena may intend that their sexual experience will remedy
Bertram. Of course, for Helena, sex promises not only a cure for greensickness (or lovesickness) but also the begetting of Bertram's child.

While the bed-trick underlines the correlation between secretive women
and women's secrets, it is the exchange of rings that raises the possibility that
Helena has introduced a new and occult ingredient to her undertaking.
Rather than merely acquiring Bertram's ring, as his letter instructed, Helena
makes a trade during the bed-trick, giving him a ring as well. As Diana tells
him before their meeting: "on your finger in the night I'll put / Another

ring, what in time proceeds, / May token to the future our past deeds" (4.2.62–64).[55] The acknowledged sources to the play make no mention of Helena owning a ring. They do, however, ascribe a special virtue to Bertram's ring, indicating that it may function as an amulet that provides protective or enchanting powers.[56] But whatever virtues Bertram's ring may have held in the sources have been enhanced and transferred to Helena's ring in *All's Well That Ends Well*.

In the play's final scene, Bertram brings out Helena's ring with the intention of using it as the "amorous token" (5.3.69) in his impending nuptials with Lafew's daughter Maudlin. Lafew immediately recognizes the ring as Helena's property, but when Bertram denies her ownership, the king requests to inspect it:

> mine eye,
> While I was speaking, oft was fastened to't
> This ring was mine, and when I gave it Helen,
> I bade her, if her fortunes ever stood
> Necessitied to help, that by this token
> I would relieve her. Had you that craft to reave her
> Of what should stead her most? (82–88)

The king's concerns about Bertram's craft and Helena's fate stem directly from the ring's purpose: he gave it to her as a protective device. Yet it remains unclear exactly how such protection would operate. Early modern audiences may have identified the king's token as an amulet or talisman that defends by means of its occult forces. Presumably imbued with preternatural properties by the king, the ring would provide help of a mysterious sort, even at a great distance. As a consequence, the king assumes that Bertram must have applied a kind of "craft" or trickery to wrest the ring from Helena's possession.

In his effort to demonstrate that he recognizes the ring as formerly his own, the king compares his knowledge of it with the alchemist's comprehension of nature's mysteries:

> Plutus himself,
> That knows the tinct and multiplying med'cine,
> Hath not in nature's mystery more science
> Than I have in this ring. (102–05)

In superficial terms, the king wishes to convey his deep familiarity with the token; however, his analogy also equates it with "nature's mystery." Plutus has acquired, through alchemical practices, knowledge of how to achieve certain effects, whether they be the transmutation of metals, or the concoction of life-giving elixirs. He penetrates nature's mysteries, not by adhering to theoretical notions of causation, but by experiment. The king, in turn, grasps the "science," or certain knowledge, of his ring by its mysterious feats.

Not surprisingly, given that rings function broadly as tokens of commitment and more specifically as proof of intimacy, most critics read them as symbols of sexuality. In the same way that the ring exchange in *The Merchant of Venice* plays off of bawdy allusions to female genitalia, the rings in *All's Well That Ends Well* have been read as references to vaginal and anal eroticism. The ring stands in, I will suggest, for the occult powers thought to reside in the female body while also pointing to a rich tradition of medicinal rings, thought to contain wondrous virtues, which circulated in England up through Queen Mary's reign.[57] Through a series of allusions, Shakespeare invokes a well-known English story about King Edward the Confessor, his magical ring, a beggar, and wandering pilgrims that links Helena's ring with these popular, quasi-magical, "cramp rings," which derived their original occult power from a royal blessing.[58] A telling clue to this story appears in the king's epilogue, when he states (for no apparent reason other than to garner applause) that "The King's a beggar now the play is done" (1).[59]

The epilogue alludes to a story concerning the end of King Edward the Confessor's life, which tells of an encounter he had with a beggar near a church dedicated to St. John the Evangelist.[60] As the king was leaving the church an old man begged of him alms in worship of St. John. The king had no money but gave the man his ring instead. Several years later, two pilgrims from England, traveling in the holy land, lost their way at night. They subsequently encountered an old man who provided them food and shelter. As they prepared to depart, he revealed himself to be St. John the Evangelist. He then produced King Edward's ring and requested that they return it to him with the message that he and King Edward would soon meet in heaven. The ring was buried with the king upon his death but later retrieved for its miraculous properties. After Edward was canonized and his shrine built in Westminster Abbey, the ring earned distinction for its power to cure the illnesses of many visiting pilgrims. Moreover, as Lynn Jones has observed, the ring not only became "the primary symbol of Edward's rule and sainthood," but also instituted the "Wedding Ring of England" as central to the coronation ceremonies of English royalty.[61]

This "pilgrim ring" instigated a trend of "medicinable" tokens, which were consecrated by the reigning king or queen, whose handling and blessing infused the metal with a virtue that healed an array of disorders.[62] Whether or not Helena makes it to the final destination of her pilgrimage, St. Jacques, or Santiago de Compostela, her intentions would have reminded early modern audiences that St. James was the brother of St. John the Evangelist.[63] Shakespeare's subtle references to the legend of King Edward's ring underscore implications that Helena's ring is more than a symbol. Helena has given Bertram not only a symbolic representation of female genitalia but an amulet or talisman as well.

The embedded provenance and status of the ring necessarily provoke questions about its religious implications as well. Associated with the condemned idolatry and magical thinking of the "old faith," Helena's ring could represent a nostalgia for certain lost Catholic practices. And yet to identify the ring's powers too strictly with Catholicism would miss the attachment people felt to procedures they believed to be efficacious, no matter their religious identity. The presence of a charm in the pages of Robert Boyle's family receipts, for example, attests to the difficulty of drawing such distinctions. As Keith Thomas notes, "Sir Christopher Hatton sent Queen Elizabeth a ring to protect her against the plague."[64] As we have seen, there are, among the handwritten recipes for waters, salves, and oils, recommendations that people rely on the power of an amulet to generate a cure at-a-distance. Once we accept as commonplace the early modern mentality that recorded such prescriptions as useful, we are compelled to reevaluate our interpretations of what a theatrical audience might expect or believe.

Notoriously, critics have been divided on the play's conclusion. Those who emphasize the fairy-tale structure deem Helena's return as triumphant.[65] Her success in achieving both parts of Bertram's receipt echoes her marvelous cure of the king. But many others feel discomfort with the play's final scene, objecting that we have no indication that Helena's feats will elicit Bertram's affections.[66] The relationship looks coerced, and our modern view disallows the possibility that a man's heart could be transformed merely by the circumstantial evidence of Helena's accomplishments. The play itself seems to invite divergent responses, for even before Helena emerges on stage, the final scene presents the audience with questions about what constitutes knowledge and proof. Echoing the receipt books, and their notations of "*Probatum est,*" the courtiers interpret both rings as evidence of past actions.[67] Knowing that he gave his ring to Helena, the king insists it functions now as a kind of proof. "If it should prove" that this ring belonged to Helena (5.3.116), the king argues, then we must conclude that Bertram committed villainy: the ring serves as "fore-past proofs" of Bertram's guilt (122). Not only does the king insist that his old ring points to Bertram's misconduct, the Countess contends that Bertram's old ring provides "a thousand proofs" that Diana is his wife (201). As a strange set-up to Helena's demonstration of proof, false evidence leads these spectators to erroneous assumptions.

Diana's convoluted story of why she has Bertram's ring is merely a lead-in to Helena's theatrical entrance, helping to stage her return as a marvel. Framed as a wondrous resurrection, Helena's appearance provokes in her immediate audience the same interpretations that attended her cure of the king. They may wonder if they are witnessing a supernatural, preternatural, or natural phenomenon. The king himself articulates this category confusion when he questions whether Helena is real or a demonic illusion produced by an exorcist, beguiling "the truer office" of his eyes (302). The king's concern that his eyes have been tricked underscores the artifice inherent in Helena's theatricality and perhaps helps to justify Bertram's reluctance to accept her with open arms. As Kent R. Lehnhof has observed, Helena's theatrical exhibition of curative knowledge may have invoked for some spectators the "early modern mountebank and the medicine show."[68] In her answer to the king, Helena's use of the word "shadow" implicitly acknowledges that the situation may look like staged deception, but her primary message (which laments her estrangement as a wife) is meant to stir Bertram's passions:

HELENA: No, my good lord;
  'Tis but the shadow of a wife you see,
  The name and not the thing.
BERTRAM: Both, both. O, pardon!
HELENA: O my good lord, when I was like this maid,
  I found you wondrous kind. There is your ring.
  And, look you, here's your letter. This it says:
  "When from my finger you can get this ring
  And are by me with child," et cetera. This is done.
  Will you be mine now you are doubly won?

(303–11)

As if still unsure of Helena's presence as a substantial body, Bertram addresses his answer to the king, "If she, my liege, can make me know this clearly, / I'll love her dearly, ever, ever dearly" (312–13). Critics have long lamented the lack of warmth in Bertram's response. Although we may interpret his answer as a stalling tactic – a desperate attempt to postpone his inevitable confinement to marriage – Bertram also implies that Helena's appearance and brief testimony fail to establish that she has met his incredible demands. Moreover, he raises the emotional stakes with this final challenge. Whereas the letter promised only that Helena would gain the right to call him "husband," he now claims that making him *know* how she fulfilled the terms of his letter will result in his passionate devotion. Bertram's hypothetical declaration not only prompts the question of whether more knowledge would produce love in him but also raises doubts as to whether Helena can provide him with further knowledge. She only has the effects of her experiences – that is, her apparent pregnancy and his ring.

Whether we sympathize with Bertram or not, his implicit skepticism is warranted. Helena offers very little definitive proof that she has followed the letter's prescriptions. Since the ring remains in Diana's possession, she cannot present it as evidence. Bertram's original letter demanded that she show him "a child begotten of thy body that I am father to" (3.2.56–57), which Helena erroneously recites in this scene as "are by me with child" (5.3.310).[69] We may assume that Helena looks pregnant, since she appears to function as the visual punch-line to Diana's riddle:

> Dead though she be she feels her young one kick.
> So there's my riddle; one that's dead is quick.
> And now behold the meaning. (5.3.299–301)

But as historian Cathy McClive has shown, the "uncertainty" of early modern pregnancy was "such that only when the 'fruit' indicated its live presence and could be declared 'quick' was the 'truth' of the belly revealed." Indeed, quickening itself raised questions about the "ownership of knowledge," which rarely gave the pregnant woman an "epistemological advantage" over medical experts.[70] Jonathan Gil Harris notes that the play's homophonic suggestions of swelling also raise the specter of a phantom pregnancy.[71] Moreover, Shakespeare's revisions to his sources intensify the uncertainties of Helena's claim. In Painter's *Palace of Pleasure*, the Helena character emerges at the end with two twin boys whose fair appearance assures her husband that he "know[s] the thynges she had spoken, to be true."[72] The only proof fathers ever had of paternity were in the effects – by seeing a resemblance in their children. And any lingering suspicion that Helena used her body to cure the king could cast doubt on Bertram's paternity. If pregnant, the seminal cause remains occult knowledge to all but herself.

When Bertram makes his final request to "know" what Helena has done "clearly," she promises that "If it appear not plain and prove untrue, / Deadly divorce" will divide them (314–15). But what makes Helena so confident that she can "prove" her claims? A clue may lie in Bertram's earlier statement to the king, regarding Helena's ring: "If you shall prove / This ring was ever hers, you shall as easy / Prove that I husbanded her bed in Florence "(125–27). While Helena's claim of pregnancy and Diana's possession of Bertram's ring may be unpersuasive to Bertram, learning the true provenance of the second ring represents a different kind of knowledge. Bertram's bid to "know" Helena's actions may connote a carnal experience (as Diana uses the term in this same scene). And the commonplace analogy between female genitalia and rings prepares audiences to hear the sexual connotations of *knowing*. Moreover, an audience who believes in the secret properties of Helena's ring – ornamental and embodied – may also believe the ring has affected a change in Bertram. From this perspective, Bertram's experiential knowledge of Helena's body (during the bed-trick and beyond the play's ending) would not only corroborate her story but also prove to be his cure. Indeed, the revelation of the ring's occult powers could be the final step towards remedying Bertram's emotional estrangement. Although audiences may be disappointed that Bertram fails to declare love for Helena, his conditional statement, "If she, my liege, can make me know this clearly / I'll love her dearly, ever ever dearly" (312–13), may function as a final – though enigmatic – receipt. To "know this clearly" may simply mean to know her in bed again, but intentionally this time.

Shakespeare's *All's Well That Ends Well* captures a transitional period in early modern England when an emergent scientific world-view had yet to be disentangled from its natural magical origins. While critics have suggested that Helena's "hands-on, experimental knowledge" represented by her receipts may anticipate the "Scientific Revolution," they have also assumed that magic is necessarily antagonistic to the modern philosophical pursuit of knowledge.[73] In a play that highlights the gap between older and younger generations, Helena's occult knowledge marks her as, simultaneously, retrograde and modern.[74] For many early modern proto-scientists, occult phenomena generated interest in the hidden activities of nature. It was in this period that the very "idea of hidden causes and marvelous cures" proved instrumental in generating questions about the limitations and possibilities of human knowledge.[75] The belief in occult qualities led natural philosophers to turn to the "empirically undeniable reality of their effects ... a major stimulus to the empirical investigation of nature."[76] Rather than establishing undisputed theories of causation, natural philosophers sought experiential knowledge. Consequently, their established truth claims privileged degrees of probability over and above certainty.[77] As Bertram's provisional response in the final scene indicates, the secret operations of Helena's deeds cannot be fully grasped. But as the play's title reminds us, the effort lies in shifting one's focus from questions of causation to an observation of effects. If we identify *All's Well That Ends Well* too readily with an uncomplicated notion of the "Scientific Revolution," we will bury more deeply their shared investment in the occult.

CHAPTER 2

Sympathetic contagion in Arden of Faversham and A Warning for Fair Women

While Helena's secret knowledge in *All's Well That Ends Well* helps ensure the comic restoration of the king's health, the women who influence the occult operations in the anonymous tragedies *Arden of Faversham* and *A Warning for Fair Women* prove to be malign forces in their households and communities. Critical interest in *Arden of Faversham* and *A Warning for Fair Women* has centered on their representation of domestic life and the impact these private matters had on public concerns. And while both tales of mariticide involve uncanny episodes, such as bleeding corpses and mysterious portents, scholars tend to neglect the relevance of these strange events. In this chapter, I will argue that these phenomena point to the influence and effects of sympathetic contagion, a concept in the period that explains not only the contraction of certain diseases but also the invisible penetration – from one body to another – of poisonous vapors, material spirits, and strong emotions.[1] But unlike modern understandings of infection, contagion in the early modern period was commonly marked as a sympathetic response, which meant that the victim possessed a predestined affinity with the invasive element. As Thomas Lodge writes, "contagion ... is no other thing but a like disposition by a certaine hidden consent communicated by touch unto another," including the contact of imperceptible effluvia.[2] In contemporary writings on contagion, the "bold" woman, whose strong emotions infected those around her, was repeatedly cited as an exemplum of occult transmission.[3] As with all preternatural episodes, the effects of sympathetic contagion produced fundamental questions about causation and agency: were such responses moral, natural, demonic, or providential? While the non-dramatic accounts of these real-life murders tended to privilege either demonic or providential causation, the dramatic versions prove more equivocal. This categorical evasiveness can be attributed, I contend, to the recognition that theatrical efficacy – theater's capacity to move or alter its spectators – also depends on sympathetic contagion.[4]

Literary critics have long acknowledged that the domestic tragedies *Arden of Faversham* and *A Warning for Fair Women* have similar provenances and investments: they stage true crime stories as reported in Holinshed and redacted in popular print, and they portray unnatural wives involved in their husbands' murders.[5] In particular, scholars have focused on why these domestic tales of murder would have merited inclusion in the national histories of England. Lena Cowen Orlin observes that Holinshed devotes nearly five two-column folio pages to Arden's demise, despite the historian's classification of the story as a "private matter" "impertinent" to history. By having such a prominent place in a public history, Orlin argues, Arden's story "generates its own authorizing undertow ... creating a space for successor histories that similarly engage contested domestic relationships."[6] Catherine Belsey has contended that the profound interest in the Arden murder is prompted by "Alice Arden's challenge to the institution of marriage" as a "site of a paradoxical struggle to create a private realm and to take control of it in the interests of the public good."[7]

But for John Stow and Holinshed's *Chronicles*, the primary interest of Arden's story is not the political importance of domestic affairs but the mysterious aftermath of his murder. By their accounts, an impression of Arden's body remained in the grassy field where he had lain for two years after his death. In Holinshed's words:

> This one thing semeth verie *strange and notable* touching maister Arden, that in the place where he was laid, being dead, all the proportion of his bodie might be seene two yeares after and more, so plaine as could be, for the grasse did not grow where his bodie had touched; but betweene his legs, his armes, and about the hollownesse of his necke, and round about his bodie, and where his legs, armes, head, or anie other part of his bodie had touched, no grasse growed at all of all that time. So that manie strangers came in that meane time, beside the townesmen, to see the print of his bodie there on the ground in that field.[8]

In the marginal glosses to the 1586 edition, a commentator observes: "A *wonder* touching the print of Ardens dead bodie two yeares after he was slaine."[9] In similar language, John Stow's history reports that this incident was one notable thing about Arden's story, for the corpse left a "marvelylows ... picture" in the ground for people to wonder at.[10] Indeed, Arden's corpse is classified in the *Chronicles*' index among thirty or so other "wonders," including a child speaking strange speeches and a fish shaped like a man.[11] Arden's story, in other words, entered the *Chronicles* for its taxonomic similarity to other strange and inexplicable "wonders." Richard Baker follows Holinshed's precedent in *A chronicle of the Kings of*

England (1643) when he presents the tale of the body's imprint alongside reports of a monstrous birth near Oxford and multiple sightings of giant dolphins.[12] The wonder of Arden's corpse, as we will see, provokes questions about natural and supernatural causation that linger for almost one hundred years.

Not only have critics overlooked the uncanny elements of these stories in the sources, but they have also neglected the preternatural elements of domestic drama.[13] One exception is historian Peter Lake, who notes the occurrence of "semi-supernatural happenings" in both *Arden of Faversham* and *A Warning for Fair Women*.[14] In Lake's reading, the plays are strictly framed by the "interventions of divine providence, on the one hand, and of the devil and the forces of sin and evil, on the other." These tales of lust, adultery, and murder, Lake maintains, exist in a world "stretched tight between God and the devil, with the room for human agency between the two reduced, at times, almost to nothing."[15] Lake's tendency to treat drama as unambiguous historical data limits his perspective: as I shall demonstrate, a significant defense of theater rested on its preternatural, yet non-demonic, capacity to act on its audience in particular ways. In staging these crimes the dramatists not only leave open the possibility of natural causation, but also acknowledge that ordinary citizens may possess either occult properties or experiential knowledge that allows them to direct, interpret, or merely trigger hidden sympathies.

In *Arden of Faversham*, Alice's effect on others is manifest and occult: not only does she prove able to persuade people to act, but she also contaminates those around her in secret ways, much as would the poisoned portrait that the cunning man, Clarke, offers to paint of her. While Clarke has the knowledge to harness and direct occult forces, Alice's contagion emanates from her very person. Ironically, the Faversham authorities find further evidence of Alice's guilt in her uncanny effect on her husband's corpse: Arden's lifeless body begins to bleed again in her presence. As we shall see, such instances of cruentation provoked controversy over causation *and* wielded evidentiary power in criminal cases. The same sympathetic forces that sustained Alice's hidden influence and Clarke's natural magic also facilitated the "spectatorial infection or pollution" associated with the theater.[16] But unlike modern understandings of disease, sympathetic contagion entails the victim's hidden (and perhaps involuntary) consent, thus suggesting that only certain spectators can be corrupted. We find similarly strange occurrences in *A Warning for Fair Women*. At the center of this play is a cunning woman, Nan Drurie, who draws on secret knowledge to entice another woman, Anne Sanders, to betray her husband. When one of the murder victims in this play, John Beane, bleeds anew in the presence of his murderer, the other characters debate whether this sympathetic response should be ascribed to providence or to more ambiguous preternatural forces. Characters cite, as comparable instances of occult operations, anecdotes in which theatrical performances elicited involuntary confessions of murder from women in the audience. *A Warning for Fair Women* closes with the staged confessions of its two main female protagonists, Mistress Sanders and Mistress Drurie. Countering the notion that contagious sympathy threatened only to corrupt the audience, *A Warning for Fair Women* celebrates theater's capacity to reveal and restrain the secrets of women.

Arden of Faversham

One of the mysteries of *Arden of Faversham* is John Arden's willingness to forgive his wife's infidelity, despite his knowledge of her repeated betrayals and his suspicion that she tried to poison him. Franklin, Arden's only confidant, concludes that his behavior is attributable to Alice's enchanting powers:

> He whom the devil drives must go perforce.
> Poor gentleman, how soon he is bewitched.
> And yet, because his wife is the instrument,
> His friends must not be lavish in their speech. (13.152–55)[17]

Modern readers may be inclined to dismiss Franklin's language as a metaphorical description of love; however, in a play that involves the practices of a cunning man, a bleeding corpse, and an inexplicable imprint in the grass, it makes sense to take its references to enchantment seriously. Indeed, Mosby and Alice characterize each other's love as enchantment. Alice swears that Mosby has conquered her by "witchcraft and mere sorcery" (1.200). Later, she exclaims to him, "I was betwitched," vaguely accusing Mosby of "all the causes that enchanted" her (8.78–79). Mosby answers back,

> I was bewitched – that is no theme of thine! –
> And thou unhallowed hast enchanted me.
> But I will break thy spells and exorcisms,
> And put another sight upon these eyes
> That showed my heart a raven for a dove. (93–97)[18]

Mosby finds himself vulnerable to Alice's wounding eyes, for it is Alice's "policy," he claims, "To forge distressful looks to wound a breast / Where lies a heart that dies" (55–57). Once accused of witchcraft, Alice insists most vehemently that if Mosby fails to look at her, she will kill herself (112). She is adamant that he listen and speak to her until they have reestablished their mutual bond. Even when Mosby determines in private that he will "cleanly rid [his] hands" of Alice (43), he cannot seem to separate from her.

Even those audience members who knew nothing of Neoplatonic theories of love would recognize that the eyes were "instrumentes of Inchauntment," as Thomas Lupton acknowledges in *A thousand notable things* (1579).[19] As Ioan P. Couliano explains, Marsilio Ficino followed Plato and Galen in his understanding that love's arrows were not "mere metaphor." Love occurs when the "pneumatic ray" penetrates through the "pupils into his spiritual organism and, on arrival at the heart . . . [it] can degenerate into a bloody infection."[20] Cheap print publications, which disseminated information widely to people of various degrees of literacy, made available naturalist explanations for the phenomenon, as described here in the popular *The problemes of Aristotle* (1595):

> in the beginning loue doth rise from one beame and glance of the eye: for he doth see and desire at the selfe same time. And as soone as he doth desire, the louer sendeth cótinuall beames of the eie towards that which he loueth. And those beames are like vnto arrowes, because the louer doth dart them into the bodie.[21]

In *The vanitie of the eye*, George Hakewill observes that vaporous emanations can prove both mutual and unconscious, so that "men and women, doe interchangeably hurt one an other in this kinde."[22]

But the beams and vapors emitted from an individual's eyes did not always transmit love, for the "evil eye" and fascination operated on the same principles: fine vapors are discharged from one person's eye to penetrate the victim's eyes.[23] Women in particular (especially those who have "double apples in theyr eyes") had the greatest power to "hurt with their looking."[24] While fascination and ocular infection were most often associated with witches, all women could prove dangerous. Indeed, when Ficino gives his account of love as an infection transmitted by the eyes, he reminds his readers of Aristotle's description of how menstruating women can stain a mirror with their gaze. The surface of the mirror made visible the imperceptible emanations that polluted the air and infected those in her presence. As Sergius Kodera points out, the "story of the bloody mirror was one of the most famous and frequently cited testimonies for occult phenomena such as infection, fascination, or [the] evil eye during the Middle Ages and the Early Modern period."[25] In *The mirror of alchimy* (1597), Roger Bacon identifies the basilisk's capacity to slay men with its lethal gaze as a precedent for the commonplace that a "menstrous woman [who] beholde[s] her selfe in a looking glasse ... will infect it, so that there will appeare a cloude of bloud."[26] Even the supposedly skeptical Reginald Scot in *The discoverie of witchcraft* concedes that vapors emitted by the eye can pierce "the inward parts, and there breed infection." Citing the cockatrice's deadly looks and the "grosse vapors" left on a "looking glasse" by menstruating women, Scot acknowledges that such spirits can be conveyed from one body to another.[27] It may not be a coincidence that Alice reminds spectators of the mythical basilisk when she laments that her passionate devotion to Mosby will destroy her in the same way that a basilisk strikes a traveler (1.214). For many writers, the basilisk functions as an apt analogy for how the "passions of the mind can work out of themselves upon another's body."[28] Henry Cornelius Agrippa, Giambattista della Porta, and Johann Jacob Wecker each mention the cockatrice and basilisk in their descriptions of how women emit poisonous vapors from their eyes and infect others with their passions.[29]

   These same writers also suggest that when a woman is unnaturally "bold" or proves to be a "strumpet," she possesses the power to "infect decent people with physical disease and immoral behavior."[30] While experts on vision were beginning to argue for a receptive theory of eyesight as opposed to an extramissive model, contagious sympathy remained viable through comparable theories that the body itself emitted vapors or infected inanimate objects.[31] As Thomas Johnson in *Cornucopiae, or diuers secrets* (1595) states:

> It is supposed that in like maner the smock or other apparrell of a strumpet beeing worne of others, giueth a certaine impudencie and shameles boldnes to those parties ... Euen so if a Woman behold her selfe ofte in the glasse wherein an whore hath accustomed to looke in, it maketh her not onely impudent bold but also the more prompt to further offending.[32]

Della Porta attributes similar effects to the "harlot":

> A Harlot is not only impudent in her self, but she also naturally infects therewith, all that she touches and carries about her; so that if a man do often behold himself in her glasse, or put on her garments, it will make him impudent and lecherous as she is.[33]

It is no accident that Albertus Magnus delineates features of the marvelous in *The Book of Secrets* by establishing that all things possess a particular disposition such "as boldness is in an harlot." Through the power of sympathy, such dispositions and emotions can be acquired, as when a "man put[s] on a common harlot's smock, or look[s] in the glass (or [has] it with him) in which she beholdeth herself, he goeth bold and unfearful."[34]

Identified as a "strumpet" five times in *Arden of Faversham*, Alice exhibits the power of the archetypical "bold" woman. She demonstrates a knack for bringing people into her murderous web. She privately negotiates Michael's involvement, she relies on Susan's loyalty, she speaks to Green in secret, persuading him to murder, and she has the hard-bitten Black Will and Shakebag hoping to please her.

Despite Alice's implication that it is Mosby who plays the role of basilisk, the playwright repeatedly identifies Alice as the origin of contagion. When she insists on seeing Mosby in the play's first scene, she alludes to a mythological story that mingles sympathetic magic, love spells, and poison: "Were he as mad as raving Hercules / I'll see him," recalling the effects of Nessus' poisoned shirt on the classical hero (1.116–17). In an effort to secure Hercules' love through magic, his wife Deianira sent him Nessus' blood-soaked shirt, but its potency proved to be deadly rather than binding.[35] Further underscoring Alice's infectious nature is Clarke's plan to poison Arden with a portrait of her. Rather than catching her reflection in a mirror, Clarke offers to "temper poison with his oil" (229) and paint a portrait of Alice that will operate according to the same occult logic as the evil eye. As Mosby explains, once the painting is displayed,

> whoso looks upon the work he draws
> Shall, with the beams that issue from his sight,
> Suck venom to his breast and slay himself.
> Sweet Alice, he shall draw thy counterfeit,
> That Arden may, by gazing on it, perish. (230–34)

Drawing on the extramissive theory of eyesight, wherein the active eye emits eye-beams or pneuma to unite with particles projected by the object, Clarke's poison scheme relies on a theory of action-at-a-distance that echoes explanations of fascination as a natural but occult force.[36]

Eugene Hill has argued that Clarke's method of poisoning spectators with a portrait alludes to "contemporary anti-theatrical discourse." Citing William Rankins and Steven Gosson, who both lament the destructive and poisonous influence of theatrical spectacles, Hill identifies such language as a trope of moral corruption rather than a reference to material contamination.[37] And yet, a distinction in this discourse between moral and physiological infection proves difficult to maintain. Indeed, Hill quotes Matthieu Coignet's complaint that tragedy "infecteth more the spirits, & wrappeth them in passions, then drunkenness it self would do" – a statement that emphasizes the physicality of theater's impact on its audience.[38] In his discussion of acting in the period Joseph Roach has noted the belief that early modern performance functioned much like infection, for the actors' animal "spirits" were understood to become "agitated by the passions of the imaginer, [to] generate a wave of physical force, rolling through the aether, powerful enough to influence the spirits of others at a distance."[39] Clarke's articulation of poisoned eye-beams not only alludes to the antitheatricalists' fear of physical contamination, but also directs us to interpret *Arden of Faversham*'s representation of enchantment and emotional contagion in literal rather than metaphorical terms.[40]

Alice immediately recognizes the indiscriminate danger such a picture could pose: as she notes, anyone who comes into the "chamber where it hangs, may die" (237). Her anxiety that Clarke's poison cannot be directed at their chosen victim echoes concerns articulated in the period not only about the theater but also about the environmental threat of pestilence. An analogy between infectious women and the plague emerges when Franklin and Arden encounter a strange mist that cloaks their surroundings. Since the plague, it was thought, often settled in fog and bad air, mists could spread contagion. As they cross the river in a boat, Franklin asks the Ferryman, "Friend, what's thy opinion of this mist?" Curiously, the Ferryman compares the heavy mist to a "curst wife":

> I think 'tis like to a curst wife in a little house, that never leaves her husband till she has driven him out at doors with a wet pair of eyes. Then looks he as if his house were afire, or some of his friends dead.
>
> ARDEN: Speaks thou this of thine own experience?
> FERRYMAN: Perhaps ay, perhaps no; for my wife is as other women are, that is to say, governed by the moon.
>
> (ii.10–17)

Franklin's initial question presumes that the Ferryman will have experiential knowledge greater than their own on the nature of fog and mist. The Ferryman's folksy response implies both experience (as Arden indicates) and a traditional knowledge that some may dismiss as superstition. He assesses the mist based on the supposition that bold women – wicked and shrewish women – have the power to usurp their husband's role. It is unclear from the passage as to whether the husband or the wife possesses a "wet pair of eyes," which could denote crocodile tears or more dangerous emanations. But in his reference to the belief that all women are governed by the moon, the Ferryman hints that such cursed behavior can be attributed to the woman's menstrual cycle, perhaps alluding to the notion that venomous spirits dart from the eyes of menstruating women.[41] The casual equation between an uncanny mist and the behavior of all wives underscores the correspondence between nature's secrets and women's secrets.

While the all-encompassing nature of a mist would seem to pose danger to all exposed, early modern plague treatises indicate that the infection of pestilence, or even poison, requires that the victim possess an inherent compatibility with the invasive corruption. As Stephen Bradwell explains in *Physick for the Sickness* (1636), "where the *Seminarie Tincture* hath no Analogie, there is none, or verie slight *Infection*."[42] Drawing on Paracelsus, many plague tract authors understand this "analogy" to be a secret "predestined sympathy" between the disease and the body.[43] Pierre Drouet in *A new counsell against the pestilence* (1578) explains that contagion depends upon "some naturall likenesse betweene the thing Agent, and the Pacient."[44] For Thomas Thayre, a body free of corruption cannot be infected "because there is not that matter for infectious ayre to work upon."[45] In the same strange way that some people fear the sight of cheese, or dread the presence of a cat, they may also have a hidden, sympathetic weakness that primes their body for certain infections.[46]

Given that some bodies are prone to corruption, this concept of sympathetic contagion carries a moral charge and suggests that Alice's victims, particularly Mosby and Arden, may deserve their fates. It is, however, through the representation of the cunning man, Clarke, that the playwright also suggests that knowledge of nature's secrets can provide ordinary people with the means to protect themselves from infection. Few critics have considered the importance of Clarke in *Arden of Faversham*, no doubt because his particular strategies for murder are not what ultimately kill Arden.[47] Yet his character reminds us that cunning men and women were fully ensconced in the community, providing assistance to folk in their daily lives. Emma Wilby observes that the "common people of early modern Britain possessed a wide repertoire of spells and rituals with which they could practice magical self-help, but in those instances where more sophisticated magical knowledge was needed," they consulted "cunning folk."[48] According to Alan Macfarlane's research, "nobody was likely to have lived more than ten miles from one."[49] Although cunning folk were often attacked by Reformist theologians as "agents of *maleficium*," most people respected the cunning man for the "arts and techniques" he offered in support of their "material and psychological welfare."[50] Notably campaigns against cunning folk led to very few prosecutions. Indeed, it appears that most people did not accept "blanketing witches and cunning-folk as 'all alike.'"[51] The same porous boundaries between "the natural and non-natural, divine and demonic, real and illusory" that enabled the conflation of witches and cunning folk among strict demonologists also made it difficult to distinguish some of the cunning man's labor from the

concoctions people mixed in their kitchens on an everyday basis.[52] Cunning
men and women were understood to deal in cures, as well as in the recovery
of stolen property, the discovery of thieves, counter-witchcraft, and fortune-
telling.[53] The portrayal of Clarke exemplifies how "cunning" knowledge
could be also construed as indistinguishable from the expertise of artisans,
distillers, empirics, surgeons, naturalists, or even housewives.

In the sources, Clarke is identified as a "painter" who has experience with
poisons. In the play, he is a painter by trade, but Mosby also calls him a
"cunning man" (1.227–28). His proposed schemes for murder indicate that
he understands various secrets of art, nature, and *pharmakon*. His familiarity
with poisons would most likely stem from his knowledge of mixing paints
and, to an equal degree, remedies. As a painter and a cunning man, Clarke
has knowledge – in range and kind – that resembles the contents of certain
books of secrets.[54] John Bate's *The mysteries of nature and art* (1634), for
example, illustrates a similar though even broader array of knowledge. In
addition to presenting technical instructions for building fireworks and
waterworks, Bate's manual provides recipes for mixing paints compounded
of roots and berries and tempered with oils, together with cures for various
illnesses.[55] Notably, some of Bate's cures demand special care, for their
misuse, he warns his readers, would constitute poison.[56] Other remedies
indicate that their success lies in occult operations. A dried black toad hung
around one's neck, for example, will stem a person's bleeding.[57] Bate's work
presents a mish-mash of information, combining experiments he has tried
himself, specialized knowledge he has borrowed from erudite sources, and
household recipes long available in cheap print. Clarke's position in
Faversham resembles the mingled status of the books of secrets – they are
both mundane and occult. Or rather, they suggest that the mundane and
the occult are not mutually exclusive categories.

The implicit association between Clarke's practices and more routine,
domestic activities is underlined when Clarke gives Alice a recipe and
ingredients for poisoning her husband's food. Despite Alice's infectious
nature, she proves unable to mix and administer poison successfully. In
Holinshed, this scheme fails because Alice botches the recipe. Although the
painter had given her explicit instructions to put the poison in the bowl
before pouring in the milk, "she forgetting, did cleane contrarie, putting in
the milke first; and afterward the poison."[58] Alice's misstep in the source
points not only to the painter's expertise but also to the experimental
component of mixing home-made concoctions. The plan goes wrong in
the play as well, for Arden recognizes with his first bite that "there's something in [his] broth / That is not wholesome" (1.365–66). This time,

however, Alice blames the failure on Clarke. She criticizes the texture of the poison, complaining that the powder was "too gross and populous" when she needed a "fine confection" to give the broth a "dainty taste" (424–25). Although Alice may simply be rationalizing her own mistake, her evaluation of the poison's quality indicates, at the very least, a presumption of knowledge on her part. The fact that Arden is able to counteract the poison with Franklin's ready "box of mithridate" further underscores a familiarity with toxins and their antidotes (382). Indeed, mithridate was commonly used as a "preservative" against catching the plague, theoretically providing a way for people to redirect or mitigate contagious infections.[59]

Although Alice blames Clarke for the failure of the poisonous broth, she also proves profoundly interested in how the cunning man works. When she learns from Mosby that Clarke claims the capacity, for example, to "compound by art / A crucifix impoisoned, / That whoso look upon it should wax blind, / And with the scent be stifled" (1.610–13), she is prompted to interrogate Clarke on his skill and technique. She is particularly interested in how he can direct harm toward others without putting himself in danger:

> Why, Clarke, is it possible
> That you should paint and draw it out yourself,
> The colours being baleful and impoisoned,
> And no ways prejudice yourself withal?   (621–24)

Alice's inquisitiveness serves no vital role in the plot except to reveal her curiosity about his secrets – secrets that prove most remarkable in their similarity to commonplace household customs. Clarke's techniques for self-protection are almost laughable in their banality:

> I fasten on my spectacles so close
> As nothing can any way offend my sight;
> Then, as I put a leaf within my nose,
> So put I rhubarb to avoid the smell,
> And softly as another work I paint.   (627–31)

With rhubarb up his nose and glasses on his face, Clarke is able to mix hazardous poisons without impairment to himself. As a fellow schemer with Alice and Mosby in the plotting of Arden's murder, Clarke's moral corruption should ensure his punishment at the play's end, but Clarke alone escapes retribution for his misdeeds. However ludicrous Clarke's rhubarb may seem, it stands in for a broader knowledge that enables him to dodge even the most far-reaching, and seemingly providential, arm of justice.

As we noted earlier, the public notoriety of Arden's murder had less to do with the politics of marriage and more to do with questions of causation: whether to categorize strange phenomena as either natural or supernatural. In the source materials, these questions focus on two events: the wondrous discovery of Arden's murder and the strange imprint of his corpse in the grassy field. Regarding the first event, the writers tend to subscribe to the providential maxim "murder will out," suggesting that God may have had a hand in ensuring that witnesses found incriminating evidence.[60] In the *Theatre of God's Judgments* (1597), for example, Thomas Beard exclaims that the discovery of Arden's murder was "wonderfull" and "exceeding rare" due to "some tokens of blood which appeared in his house."[61] Samuel Clarke in *A mirrour or looking-glasse both for saints and sinners* (1654) presents the story under the heading "The Admiràble Discoveries of sundry Murthers," noting that the crime was revealed "by some blood that appeared in the house."[62] More explicitly, the ballad of Mistress Arden's crime has Alice lament that: "God our secret dealings soone did spy, / And brought to light our shamefull villany."[63] In the dramatic version, however, Alice and Susan make an effort to wash away the blood, but it refuses to disappear:

SUSAN: The blood cleaveth to the ground and will not out.
ALICE: But with my nails I'll scrape away the blood.
    The more I strive, the more the blood appears!
SUSAN: What's the reason, Mistress, can you tell?
ALICE: Because I blush not at my husband's death.

(14.255–59)

Rather than providing proof to the authorities of Alice's guilt (confirmation they gain from an array of signs), the stubborn blood seems to respond to Alice's physical presence. In fact, the playwright develops this spectacle (and departs from other versions of the story) by staging a scene of cruentation in which Arden's dead body begins to bleed anew when Alice approaches.

A veritable test case for attempting to draw boundaries between natural and supernatural events, cruentation provoked a variety of explanations. For strict providentialists, heaven or God orchestrates cruentation scenes to ensure that "murder will out." Perhaps best known for its appearance in Shakespeare's *Richard III*, cruentation can be traced to ancient Germanic practices that coalesced into the "Ordeal of the Bier," a judicial procedure that required suspects in a murder to approach and sometimes touch the victim's body. If the corpse bled or moved, then the murderer was identi-fied.[64] In *Daemonologie* (1597), James I acknowledges cruentation as a reliable means to discover "secret murther, [for] if the dead carcase be at any time thereafter handled by the murtherer, it wil gush out of bloud, as if the blud wer crying to the heaven for revenge of the murtherer."[65]

As Malcolm Gaskill has established, early modern communities relied on the collective ritual of cruentation to help identify the guilty. And as the following anecdote indicates, the process was not necessarily framed as divine intervention:

> In 1572 a Cheshire coroner summoned murder suspects to Nantwich church "that they might stand by, and be present about the corps, that all the people according to the opinion of Aristotle & the common experiment, might behold & see whether the body would expel excrements and fall to bleed afreshe in the sight of them all."[66]

By recognizing that they were conducting a trial that drew on Aristotle and common experience, the coroner and, presumably, the people in attendance appear to view cruentation in a proto-scientific vein. Such a perspective suggests collective interests and beliefs about nature that may border on magic but resist a supernatural explanation. Indeed, to arrange such an "experiment" in hopes that God would intervene would be profane to some reformist thinkers, since humans cannot summon God's power.

Hilary M. Nunn goes so far as to suggest that stories of bleeding corpses were rarely "attributed . . . to divine intervention." Instead, she notes, they pointed to "motivations, whether physical or spiritual, within the supposedly lifeless corpse itself."[67] For natural philosophers (who vary on the details) the bleeding is "action-at-a-distance" produced by unseen yet material emissions circulating among the parties present, some identifying it as the effect of emanations from the murderer's eye.[68] Levinus Lemnius, for example, in *The secret miracles of nature*, suggests that the blood flows when the corpse's choler becomes heated:

> But I shall more easily grant this, that blood will run forth of the wound, though it be bound over with swathbands, if he that did the murder stand by. For so great is the force of secret Nature, and so powerful is Imagination, that if there be any life left, or the dead body be warm, the blood will boyl, and wax hot by choler kindled in the dead body.[69]

Writing in the mid seventeenth century, Walter Charleton assimilates cruentation to the emergent mechanical philosophies. He suggests the blood responds in part to the "Phansy of the Person assaulted by an Assassine, having formed an Idea of Hatred, Opposition, and Revenge, and the same being Characterized upon the Spirits, and by them diffused through the blood."[70]

The problemes of Aristotle (1595) treats cruentation as a provocative puzzle and prudently covers several theories of causation:[71]

> This proceedeth of a diuine cause, and not of a naturall, because his bloud dooth call for reuenge against the murtherer. But if there be any naturall cause of it, this is it. The committer of this wicked fact calling it to minde, is verie sorie for it and repenteth him of it, and is in anguish of mind, and in a great heat, through the strong imagination which he hath conceiued, and by that meanes all his spirits doe stirre and boyle and repaire vnto the instruments of the sight, and so goe out by the beames of the sight of the eies vnto the wounds which are made, the which if they bee fresh, doe presently fall a bleeding. Secondly, this is done by the helpe of the ayre which is breathed in, the which being drawne from the wound, causeth it to bleed.

In its legitimization of a range of interpretations, the text even poses the possibility that the blood may hold no evidentiary significance ("the ayre which is breathed in"). And while the writer ostensibly privileges the "divine cause," he proves most interested in a preternatural explanation, providing enough detail to constitute a theoretical conception of action-at-a-distance. What this theory allows is that strong human passions can heat the imagination to such a degree that "spirits" (those fine vapors that flow in the blood) emanate out of the body through the eye-beams to stir up the blood of the corpse.

In *Arden of Faversham*, the scene of cruentation helps to corroborate Alice's guilt, but more importantly, it stages the event as another example of sympathetic contagion. The mayor brings Alice before her husband's corpse, thus spurring her to speak:

> Arden, sweet husband, what shall I say?
> The more I sound his name the more he bleeds.
> The blood condemns me, and in gushing forth
> Speaks as it falls and asks me why I did it.   (16.3–6)

Without a narrator in *Arden of Faversham* to insist that God directs the bleeding of Arden's corpse, the audience may believe that as Alice speaks her husband's name her passions and eye-beams provide the heat that causes his blood to flow. Ironically, it is the same occult emissions that brought others into her murderous web that now guarantee her execution.

Arden of Faversham closes with an epilogue, spoken by Franklin, who informs the audience of a future event to be noted "above the rest":

> Arden lay murdered in that plot of ground
> Which he by force and violence held from Reede;
> And in the grass his body's print was seen
> Two years and more after the deed was done.   (Epilogue, 10–13)

While the playwright does not elaborate on why this wonder should be noted, it is the grass imprint of Arden's body that garners most of the controversy outside the dramatic account. While the playwright proves more interested in representing Alice's capacity to infect her community, the prose accounts struggle to determine whether the body's print is natural, preternatural, or supernatural.

The corpse's impression in the ground proves difficult to categorize, in part, because it does not fit within the expected (and providentialized narrative) of "murder will out." The outline cannot be construed as evidence of the crime, for it lingered for two years or more after the murderers had been caught and executed. Seventeenth-century chronicler Richard Baker acknowledges that the uninformed reader may mistakenly assume that the corpse left a mark on the ground "for the murther."[72] But, as historians must explain, the fate of John Arden's body points to his guilt rather than his misfortune. John Stow explicitly identifies Arden's wrongdoing: "This filde he had taken by extortion from Cooks widow, then Reede's wife, and given them nothing for it." Stow then explains that the fate of Arden's corpse can be attributed to the widow's curses:

> the sayd Reads wife dyd not only shed many a teare, but also cursyd the same Arden, to his face continually, and in every place where she was prayenge that a vengeaunce and plage myght light upon hym and that all the world might wondar over hym, and cowld nevar be otharwyse perswadyd tyll God had sufferyd hym to come to this end.[73]

Holinshed reports Arden's inhospitable behavior more equivocally, noting that "some have reported" that Arden had "most cruellie taken" this field from a Widow Cooke who "after married to one Richard Read." But once again, it is the woman's bitter curses that precipitated the marvelous imprint:

> Reads wife not onelie exclaimed against [Arden] in shedding manie a salt teere, but also curssed him most bitterlie even to his face, wishing manie a vengeance to light upon him, and that all the world might woonder on him.[74]

As Keith Thomas has observed, Protestant reformers condemned cursing as a "magical manipulation of the Almighty's powers which no human being should attempt."[75] Most people, however, still assumed curses retained their efficacy, especially when pronounced by the poor or oppressed. But curses also led easily to charges of witchcraft, in part because the Church was so reluctant to countenance the possibility that "God might avenge the poor by responding to their supplications."[76]

In subsequent redactions of the murder, writers prove anxious to attribute the efficacy of the widow's curse to God, insisting that the marvel should be understood within a providential framework. However complicated it may have been to reconcile a curse with providence, it was more dangerous to imply that an individual woman's imprecations could hold such power.[77] In Holinshed, an editor adds significant commentary in the margins: "God heareth the teares of the oppressed and taketh vengeance."[78] For Richard Baker, the imprint qualifies as a miracle:

> out of whose hands the said Master *Arden* had uncharitably bought the said close [enclosure], to her undoing. And thus the divine justice even in this world oftentimes works miracles upon offenders, for a mercifull warning to men, if they would be so wise to take it.[79]

The providentialism of these accounts returns with great force in an unusual account of the Arden story in John Webster's *The displaying of supposed witchcraft* (1677). While most retellings of the Arden crime fall into the genre of history, Webster's text is a skeptical, proto-scientific analysis of the supernatural, aimed at dismantling superstitions and citing, for example, how the mediations of air, or the natural power of the imagination, often generate what looks like diabolical intervention. Despite his skeptical agenda, however, Webster does not rule out the possibility of supernatural forces. Indeed, he turns to the story of Arden's murder to demonstrate "that there are effects that exceed the ordinary power of natural causes."[80]

Citing Holinshed's *Chronicles* as a reliable source of "unquestionable testimonies," Webster introduces the mystery of the body's imprint. Is the body's print a "wonder," generated by natural, yet occult, forces? Or is it a miraculous sign of God's righteous vengeance against an oppressor of the weak?

> As it is most certain that this is a true and punctual relation given us by *Hollingshead*, as being a publick thing done in the face of a Nation, the print of his body remaining so long after, and viewed and wondered at by so many; so that it hath not left the least starting hole for the most incredulous Atheist to get out at. So likewise it may dare the most deep-sighted Naturalist, or unbelieving Atheist, that would exalt and so far deifie Nature, as to deny and take away the existence of the God of Nature, to shew a reason of the long remaining of the print of his body, or the not growing of the grass in those places where his body had touched for two years and more after? Could it be the steams or Atoms that flowed from his body? then are why not such prints left by other murthered bodies? which we are sure by sight and experience not to be so. And therefore we can attribute it justly to no other cause but only to the power of God and divine vengeance, who is a righter of the oppressed, fatherless and Widdows, and hears their cries and regardeth their tears.[81]

Although Webster entertains the possibility that the impression could have been generated by "steams or Atoms" that may have "flowed from [Arden's] body," he questions why this natural phenomenon would occur only with this murdered body and not with all others. In other words, the strange occurrence cannot be entirely natural if it is also anomalous. While it is Webster's agenda throughout *The displaying of supposed witchcraft* to dismiss supernatural explanations, he cites his interpretation of the Arden case as evidence that he is not a blind "Naturalist" or an "unbelieving Atheist." For Webster, most spectacles prove to be, on close consideration, products of nature. And those examples that escape easy explanation are typically "preternatural": they appear wondrous, but they can be attributed to secret or occult operations of nature. But Arden's corpse, it turns out, is the exception that proves the rule. The debate Webster outlines concerns proto-scientific questions of causation, but the underlying problem is whether the widow possessed occult powers. If Webster subscribed to the explanation that the body emitted "steams" or "atoms" after death (a theory that corresponds with the preternatural theories of cruentation), he might also be compelled to construe the imprint as a naturally sympathetic response to the widow's curses.

In the play *Arden of Faversham*, not only does the cause and significance of the grassy impression remain open to interpretation, but the playwright also alters the sources to relegate the widow to the background. It is, instead, her second husband, Dick Reede, who confronts Arden about his exploitative practices. Reede appeals to God in Arden's presence,

> God, I beseech thee, show some miracle
> On thee or thine in plaguing thee for this.
> That plot of ground which thou detains from me –
> I speak it in agony of spirit –
> Be ruinous and fatal unto thee!
> Either there be butchered by thy dearest friends,
> Or else be brought for men to wonder at,
> Or thou and thine miscarry in that place,
> Or there run mad and end thy cursed days.   (13.30–38)

Arden calls Reede's words "curses" that are bound to fall on the "shooter's head" (40–41). In response, Reede swears to charge his "distressful wife" and children to pray God for "Vengeance on Arden ... / To show the world what wrong the carl hath done" (49–51). But we have no evidence that his wife and children have followed his instructions. And as Orlin points out, "the legitimacy of Dick Reede's claim is neither proved nor disproved."[82] It remains unclear why the *Arden* playwright chooses to put the curse in

Reede's mouth instead of his wife's. Some critics have argued that the text downplays Arden's culpability: perhaps it mitigates the severity of Arden's exploitation of his tenants to have a man, rather than a woman, accuse him of wrongdoing.[83] It should be noted that the *Arden* playwright blurs the question of culpability from the opening scene when Arden receives "letters patents from his majesty, / All the lands of the Abbey of Faversham" (1.4–5), making him the beneficiary of an estate confiscated in the Reformation. Some spectators would have assumed that these lands carried with them a divine curse, thus implicating Arden in his own downfall from the very start.[84] With the original provenance of the property in mind, Reede's curse, which calls on God to take "Vengeance on Arden," may be a fulfillment of God's initial plan rather than a summoning of divine intervention. In other words, the boundary disputes over land carried with them boundary disputes over demonic, divine, or natural phenomena. Whether or not the playwright diffuses Arden's guilt as a landlord, he certainly underscores Arden's culpability as a husband who "winke[s]" at his wife's behavior.[85] While the imprint ostensibly signifies his wrongdoing as an overseer, it also shames him as the easy victim of his wife's scheming. And according to the logic of sympathetic contagion, it was Arden's hidden consent that precipitated his own demise.

A Warning for Fair Women

A Warning for Fair Women has received attention for its vexed representation of a wife's legal and moral agency and its odd mingling of emblematic and illusionistic theater.[86] Often categorized with *Arden of Faversham* as a domestic tragedy that portrays a real crime, this anonymous play directly raises questions about genre, since its opening scene portrays the figures of Comedy, History, and Tragedy discussing their relative successes on the stage. Tragedy plays host and commentator throughout *A Warning for Fair Women* and identifies the play in its closing speech as a "true and home-borne Tragedie" in contrast to the expected fare of a revenge play (Epilogue, 2729).[87] Discussion of the play's generic and structural features, however, overlooks the tragedy's metatheatrical layering: within the play an instance of cruentation compels a murderer to confess, and this wonder is compared to cases in which the performance of a tragedy elicits confession from guilty women in an audience. It is these same cases that supply Thomas Heywood in *The Apology for Actors* (1612) with examples that demonstrate the morally corrective power of the theater. *A Warning for Fair Women* then concludes with Anne Sanders' scaffold confession, extracted not by theater or cruentation, but by another female character, Nan Drurie, who functions throughout the play as a kind of cunning woman. Mistress Drurie's occult knowledge, which proves both dangerous and difficult to categorize, is recuperated by her ready acknowledgment of guilt and her willingness to work with the authorities in their prosecution of Mistress Sanders. As in *Arden of Faversham*, occult forces and preternatural phenomena shape the action of *A Warning for Fair Women*, affecting the agency of the women as well as the men. But unlike *Arden*, *A Warning for Fair Women* imagines contagious sympathy affected by a theatrical performance not as corruption but as an antidote to the menace of women's secrets.

For many critics, the puzzle of *A Warning for Fair Women* is why Mistress Sanders would transform so rapidly from contented wife to adulteress. Frances Dolan has argued that Anne Sanders feels discontent with her subordinate status, thus making her vulnerable to Mistress Drurie's corrupting influence. For Peter Lake, Mistress Drurie's "devil-like" presence is what ensures Anne's fall.[88] But to label Nan Drurie "devil-like" provokes questions. Is she a demonic force? Does she possess secret knowledge or powers? Or is she simply a sinful woman who proves very persuasive? The play does not answer these questions but presents Mistress Drurie, instead, as a figure who challenges easy categorization. In Arthur Golding's *A Briefe Discourse*, one of the play's sources, we learn that Mistress Drurie had been accused not only of poisoning her husband but also of "witchcraft and sorcerie" well before she conspired to murder her neighbor, Master Sanders.[89] But our initial introduction to Mistress Drurie in the play establishes her as an important woman in her community, valued for her knowledge and skills as a surgeon, an unusual profession for a woman in this period.[90]

As a licensed surgeon, Mistress Drurie possesses authoritative medical knowledge. In practice, however, she acts as a cunning woman, a bawd, and a housewife. Soon after the play begins, Master Browne begs Mistress Drurie to apply physic to him for his "inward griefe" (193), which turns out to be his sudden desire for Mistress Sanders. In response, Mistress Drurie establishes that she and Mistress Sanders regularly formulate their own remedies and special waters:

> Why *Aqua coelestis*, or the water of balme,
> Or *Rosa solis*, or that of Doctour *Steevens*
> Will help a surfeit. Now I remember me,
> Mistris Sanders hath a soveraigne thing,
> To help a sodaine surfeit presently. (197–201)

Citing commonplace concoctions readily available in published receipt books, Mistress Drurie's therapeutic cures appear unexceptional. As house-wives, she and Mistress Sanders provide purges and remedies for their households, and they take part in a community exchange of recipes.[91] But when Browne, by way of innuendo, conveys his desire for love rather than physic, Mistress Drurie begins to reveal a skill and cunning that exceeds what a housewife, or even a surgeon, would provide. She presents herself as experienced in tending to "secret maladie[s]" (189), assuring Browne that her man Roger is trustworthy enough to hear of "love, or secrets due to that" (186). Roger, in turn, claims that "Few women can my mistris force with-stand" (310). Confident that Mistress Sanders "may be tempred easily like waxe, / Especially by one that is familiar with her" (448–49), Mistress Drurie looks to be a panderer. Indeed, Roger observes that Mistress Sanders will not be the "first by many, / That [Drurie has] wonne to stoope unto the lewre" (450–51). Well-versed in remedies and surgery, Mistress Drurie implies that she possesses other knowledge as well. If anything, her "evil" is associated with knowing too much.

Mistress Drurie's expertise in surgery appears to have little to do with her capacity to persuade Mistress Sanders to stray. Indeed, as she explains, it is her purported skill in palmistry, over and above her surgery practice, that provides her with a steady income:

> And where I cure one sicknesse or disease,
> I tell a hundred fortunes in a yeere.
> What makes my house so haunted as it is,
> With merchants wives, bachlers and yong maides,
> But for my matchlesse skil in palmestrie?   (688–92)

Certainly the eclectic nature of Mistress Drurie's business, combined with her reputation for persuading women to "stoope," makes us doubt the veracity of her fortune-telling. And yet, the fraudulence of Mistress Drurie's palmistry is only a minor technique in her craftiness. Astonishingly, Mistress Drurie persuades Mistress Sanders that her choice to betray her husband would constitute a submission to providence (720). In so doing, Mistress Drurie takes advantage of the difficulties people face in determin-ing how to distinguish supernatural signs from preternatural or natural phenomena.

When Nan Drurie and Anne Sanders initially discuss her anger toward her husband, Anne states that it is her "destinie" to feel vexed before midday. When Anne saw "yellow spots upon [her] fingers" that morning, she knew she would be "chaft ere noone" (667–70). In response, Mistress

Drurie offers to read her palm for "Faire signes of better fortune to ensue" (677). Reading Anne Sanders' fortune, Nan Drurie predicts her husband's death and the subsequent gain of a more "gallant" spouse – changes that she deems God's decree (697). Indeed, Mistress Drurie's most persuasive line of reasoning is the argument that Anne must accept the inevitability of her future, for to "repine / Against his providence" would be to sin (719–20). Although disinclined to "change or [to] new affection," Anne readily agrees she must submit to "that which God and destenie sets downe" (756–59). While Nan helps direct Anne's actions, she does so by offering her a vision of her "destenie." We may view Mistress Drurie's cunning as more trickery than actual magic, but she persuades Anne Sanders to sin by means of her skill in palmistry. What proves most "devil-like" in Nan Drurie's performance is her presentation of preternatural knowledge – her analysis of the crooked lines on Anne's palm – as God's plan. Anticipating Iago's poisoning of Othello, Nan feels confident that her prophecy will "hammer so within [Anne's] head" and then kindle "loves fire" in her breast (766–67).

How one determines the relationship between the play's realistic scenes and the emblematic interludes directly shapes an interpretation of Mistress Drurie's role. While the playwright appears to have diverged from Golding in presenting Mistress Drurie as a surgeon rather than a witch, the symbolic dumb shows identify her as a "damned witch" (858) and an "accursed fiend" (824). By hearkening back to an older theatrical tradition in the interludes, the playwright reminds audiences of the influential spirits – both evil and good – that animate the world around them. While the representational scenes indicate that Nan Drurie is a fount of knowledge, the interludes imply that her knowledge has dark origins. And once Browne murders Master Sanders, both Mistress Drurie and her boy Roger are associated with devils. It is never clear, however, whether Nan Drurie knowingly practices devilish arts; instead, the playwright implies, she abuses her knowledge in such a way that she has invited the devil into her life. Mistress Drurie epitomizes the dangers of women possessing experiential knowledge – whether it be licensed, secret, or even fraudulent. Like Alice Arden, Nan Drurie is not identified by her community as a witch; however, as the dumb shows indicate, her expertise and interventions may prove to be witchcraft just the same. It is the ambiguity of her status – her seeming respectability – that makes her so treacherous. In the end, once she confesses and succeeds in persuading Mistress Sanders to confess, her threat as a knower of secrets is contained. The force that engenders Mistress Sanders' disgrace – much more than her feelings of subordination or lust – is the influence of a woman who knows too much.

While Mistress Drurie may affect her knowledge of secrets, no one in the play would deny the reality of premonitions or occult sympathies. Well before Browne attacks him and Master Sanders, for example, the servant John Beane worries that an accidental stumble may "betoken some mischance" (1003). Soon thereafter, "olde John, and Joane his maide" (1010) share their presentiments concerning Beane's welfare. Joane, who has hopes of marrying Beane, dreams of seeing him lie "upon a green banke," where she pins "gilliflowers" on his ruff before his nose begins to bleed (1031–33). Beane, in turn, reports a dream in which he is almost gored by raging bulls (1037–38). On the day of the murder, Joane's own nose bleeds three drops, and she immediately thinks of John Beane (1440–41). One could argue that these premonitions help ensure that Old John and Joane will discover the injured man at the optimum time, but their fortuitous discovery depends, instead, on how quickly their beasts move towards the site. The animals lead them to Beane as if they are "bewitched," says Old John (1432). Joane's sympathetic bleeding, which seems to have occurred at the moment of Beane's assault, reveals a preternatural circuitry of emotional connections among the play's more common folk.

The extraordinarily slow demise of John Beane is the wondrous event that inspires the play's most pointed questions regarding supernatural intervention. Having been left for dead with ten or eleven deadly wounds, Beane manages to survive until he can give evidence against his murderer, Browne. He dies promptly thereafter. The playwright stresses the fantastic nature of Beane's survival by making him a living example of cruentation. Mute and weak, Beane is brought before the murderer in a chair. The face-to-face encounter prompts his wounds to "break out afresh in bleeding" (1991). In response, Browne sees Beane's wounds as "fifteene mouthes that doe accuse me, / In ev'ry wound there is a bloudy tongue, / Which will all speake, although he hold his peace" (1996–98). Both underlining and undermining the evidential weight of the blood, Beane croaks out his final words: "Yea, this is he that murdred me and Master Sanders" (2000–01). Several witnesses in the play conclude that Beane's fate must attest to God's intervention. Master Barnes proclaims that it was "The wondrous worke of God, that the poor creature, not speaking for two dayes, yet now should speake to accuse this man, and presently yeeld up his soule" (2011–14).[92] One of the Lords of Court states that "the power of heaven sustained him" (2065), and the second Lord agrees "'Twas Gods good wil it should be so" (2072).

However definitive Beane's case may appear, his miraculous survival prompts witnesses to recall other strange incidents that are less easily reconciled to God's "good wil." After reasserting that they have beheld the "wondrous worke of God," Barnes raises the question of causation yet again: "Sure the revealing of this murther's strange" (2019). Master James reassures him that "in the case of blood, / Gods justice hath bin stil miraculous." But James's faith does not inhibit other folks from reciting stories of equally strange discoveries of murder:

MAIOR: I haue heard it told, that digging vp a grave,
    Wherein a man had twenty yeeres bin buryed,
    By finding of a naile knockt in the scalpe,
    By due enquirie who was buried there,
    The murther yet at length did come to light.
BARNES: I haue heard it told, that once a traueller,
    Being in the hands of him that murdred him,
    Told him, the fearne that then grew in the place,
    If nothing else, yet that would sure reueale him:
    And seuen yeares after, being safe in London,
    There came a sprigge of fearne borne by the wind,
    Into the roome where as the murtherer was,
    At sight whereof he sodainely start vp,
    And then reveald the murder.
M JAMES: Ile tell you (sir) one more to quite your tale,
    A woman that had made away her husband,
    And sitting to behold a tragedy
    At Linne a towne in Norffolke,
    Acted by Players trauelling that way,
    Wherein a woman that had murtherd hers
    Was euer haunted with her husbands ghost:
    The passion written by a feeling pen,
    And acted by a good Tragedian,
    She was so mooued with the sight thereof,
    As she cryed out, the Play was made by her,
    And openly confesst her husbands murder.
BARNES: How euer theirs, Gods name be praisde for this.

(2020–50)

Barnes' concluding comment on these stories points to the murky boundaries of preternatural thinking. The phrase "How ever theirs" indicates that, even in a play where providence is a favored theme, there remains a realm of mysterious causation that has no recognizable relation to providence. Nor, for that matter, can these instances be clearly ascribed to the devil. For Barnes, the Beane incident should be attributed to God, but he makes no general claim for these other strange discoveries.

It is no accident that the final tale James recites posits an implicit parallel between cruentation and theatrical experiences. As we noted in our discussion of *Arden of Faversham*, some argued that cruentation occurred when the murderer's spirits, stirred up and released by his guilty passions, caused the victim's wounds to bleed afresh. The sight of flowing blood might then compel the murderer to confess his crime. In a similar way, as the character James suggests, the "good tragedian" so affectively plays the role of a haunted woman who has murdered her husband that the performance moves a guilty wife to confess to her own mariticide. It is this very anecdote that Thomas Heywood cites in *An apologie for actors* to demonstrate the ethical efficacy of dramatic performances: the performance of this and similar "exercises," he writes, "have beene the discoverers of many notorious murderers, long concealed from the eyes of the world." As a "domestike, and home-borne truth," the story of this woman's confession constitutes for Heywood the most persuasive example of English theater's moral purpose.[93] Moreover, Heywood's other primary example of theater's beneficial achievements is the Mayor's story of digging up a corpse with "naile knockt in the scalpe." In Heywood's account, actors perform a scene where they drive a nail into the temple of a sleeping man, whereupon a woman in the gallery shrieks and then begins to murmur, "O my husband, my husband." Not long after, the church warden discovers a skull buried in the churchyard "with a great nayle pierst quite through the braine-pan."[94] Upon this report, the woman confesses to killing her spouse by driving a nail through his head. In these confessions, the sympathetic contagion of dramatic performances provoked these women (who had successfully hidden their crimes for years) to reveal their secrets involuntarily. For Heywood, theater's capacity to move the passions of its audience may produce strange discoveries, but they are not discoveries that he necessarily attributes to providence. Instead, the actors' performance works mysteriously on the spectators, provoking some and soothing others. As Richard Norwood writes in his diary (1612):

> [I] went often to stage plays wherewith I was as it were bewitched in affection and never satiated, which was a great means to withdraw and take off my mind from any thing that was serious, true, or good, and to set it upon frivolous, false, and feigned things.[95]

Taking a more positive view, Heywood characterizes performances as "bewitching" in their power to "new mold the harts of the spectators and fashion them to the shape of any noble and notable attempt."[96]

Well before Heywood wrote his treatise, the playwright of *A Warning for Fair Women* had already promoted the value of presenting a plot of domestic and "home-borne" truths that focuses on local crime rather than more exotic stories of vengeance. And as a "warning" directed specifically at women in the audience, the play acknowledges the metatheatrical effect of generating revelations – especially the confessions of evasive and secretive women – through the staging of crimes and confessions. It is no accident that the last portion of the play concerns Mistress Sanders' refusal to confess to her involvement in the murder of her husband. Protected by Browne, who remains devoted to her, and by the Minister, who falls in love with her after her arrest, Mistress Sanders stubbornly maintains her innocence with the expectation that Mistress Drurie, Roger, and Browne will "take the murder upon" themselves. Although instructed in prison by a Doctor on repentance, it is only Mistress Drurie who persuades Mistress Sanders to confess her sins. Mistress Drurie has openly acknowledged her guilty involvement in the crime, and she urges Anne Sanders to avoid the impulse to "wilfully shut up our hearts" (2597). In response, Anne finds herself transformed:

> Your words amaze me, and although ile vow
> I neuer had intention to confesse
> My hainous sinne, that so I might escape
> The worlds reproach, yet God I giue him thanks
> Euen at this instant I am strangely changed,
> And wil no longer driue repentance off,
> Nor cloake my guiltinesse before the world.   (2602–08)

Like Heywood, the *Warning* playwright presents theater as having the power to discover secrets through the staging of confessions; the implicit hope may be that the good tragedian's performance of Anne's confession will stir and move other women to reveal the secrets shut up in their hearts. And by making Mistress Drurie an instrument of the state, the playwright recuperates the dangerous threat of her cunning and performative capacity to discern and manipulate the secrets of others.

In the pamphlet account of the Sanders murder, Golding argues that the presentation of the homicide's details and aftermath should produce repentance in its readers for their own misdeeds. Golding points out that because the criminals' "faults came into the open Theater," they "seemed the greater to our eyes," but the enormity of these crimes should not make "ours the lesse, because they ly hidden in the covert of oure hearte. God the searcher of all secrets seeth them, and if he list he can also discover them."[97] For the *Warning* playwright, however, God may or may not intervene in the revelation of the hidden. Like Heywood, he indicates that the stirring effects of theatrical performances can act as a catalyst for such discoveries. The climax of the play is Anne's presentation of herself as an open book: "were my breast transparent / That what is figured there, might be perceiv'd" (2653–54). Where *Arden of Faversham* explores the dangers of contagion posed not only by the theater but also by the passions of bold women, *A Warning for Fair Women* ends in a fantasy where the sympathetic contagion of theatrical performances controls and exposes women's secrets in morally corrective ways. Both plays represent strange and uncanny worlds where the boundary disputes over epistemology and preternature also invoke questions of female agency and the potential power of performance. While it is unquestionably true that these domestic crimes garnered historical attention for the political significance of private matters, it is also true that early modern writers returned to these stories repeatedly in an ongoing effort to determine the nature, and the gender, of nature's secrets.

CHAPTER 3

"As secret as maidenhead": magnetic wombs and the nature of attraction in Shakespeare's Twelfth Night

At first glance, Shakespeare's *Twelfth Night* represents a world that has little in common with the uncanny environments of *Arden of Faversham* and *A Warning for Fair Women*. In contrast to these domestic tragedies, *Twelfth Night*'s allusions to female occult knowledge can be glimpsed only on the borders of the main plot. Fabian, for example, facetiously refers to a local wise-woman who can purportedly read bewitchment in a person's urine. And we could argue that Maria's ability to manipulate Malvolio with a forged letter hints at skills in the occult application of word-spells, infection, poison, and medicine. The scheme will succeed, Maria argues, because her "physic will work with him" (2.3.152–53).[1] Indeed, the trick functions as a "dish o' poison" that she has "dressed him" in (2.5.102), for Malvolio's "very genius hath taken the infection of the device" (3.4.116–17). But Malvolio's vulnerability to Maria's trickery – rooted in his time-pleasing ambition – also marks him as an outsider to the comedy's central amatory structure, in which men and women are unknowingly but innately driven by nature's hidden sympathies and contagions.

As this chapter will demonstrate, *Twelfth Night* is filled with references to occult properties, sympathies, and antipathies, which not only serve as clues to early modern cultural practices and beliefs but also suggest the hidden organizing structure of the play's actions. We recognize *Twelfth Night*'s haphazard couplings, combined with its multiple instances of twinning and doubling, as standard characteristics of romance comedy. I contend, however, that this comic construction also renders legible the hidden operations of the early modern physical universe. The discourse on magnetism, in particular, which notes strange correlations between the lodestone and the womb, provides a lens for interpreting the play's representation of attraction. The same force that draws metals to stones can also activate extraordinary bonds between people. Shakespeare's *Twelfth Night* depicts human desire as swayed by occult, and potentially magnetic, influences.

Stephen Greenblatt notoriously ends his essay on Shakespeare's *Twelfth Night*, "Fiction and Friction," with an assertion about the transvestite theater: "The open secret of identity – that within differentiated individuals is a single structure, identifiably male – is presented literally in the all-male cast."[2] Since this essay's publication, scholars have questioned the ascendancy of the one-sex model, most notably establishing how humoral discourse insists on physiological distinctions between men and women.[3] But the use of a one-sex model in early modern writing cannot be separated from a central problem it aimed to address: how to unlock the hidden mysteries of the womb. Indeed, one of Greenblatt's central sources, French physician Jacques Duval, viewed the womb as a "fantastic treasure house to which he [had] acquired the key."[4] Whether it hid the enigmatic diseases of women, the mysteries of reproduction, or the truths of female desire, the early modern womb habitually swerved from "a single structure, identifiably male."[5] While the all-male cast makes it unlikely that female wombs wandered the early modern stage, *Twelfth Night* proves haunted by the power of the matrix.[6] This chapter will argue, against Greenblatt, that the not-so-open secret of the play is the pervasive and occult influence of the magnetic, sympathetic early modern womb.

The early modern physics of attraction

From antiquity to the early modern period, the most observable effect of nature's occult qualities was the attraction of iron to the lodestone. Erasmus' wonder at the phenomenon is not atypical: "What a mighty Power of either Sympathy or Antipathy is there between the Steel and the Loadstone, that a Matter heavy by Nature should run to, and cleave to a Stone, as tho' it kissed it; and without touching it, should fly backward?"[7] For Pliny, only the echo rivals the lodestone as nature's greatest wonder:

> [I]s there any thing more wonderfull, and wherein Nature hath more trauelled to shew her power, than in [the lodestone]? True it is, that to rockes and stones she had given voice (as I haue already shewed) whereby they are able to answer a man, nay, they are ready to gainsay and multiply words vpon him ... And yet behold, Nature hath bestowed vpon it, sence, yea & hands also, with the use thereof ... a marvellous matter that this mettall, which tameth and conquereth all things else, should run toward I wot not what, and the nearer that it approcheth, standeth still, as if it were arrested, and suffereth it selfe to bee held therwith, nay, it claspeth and clungeth to it, and will not away.[8]

The echo and the lodestone make evident the existence of nature's secrets, hidden away in seemingly senseless rocks and metals. One sounds out an absent presence, and the other grasps to hold its sympathetic twin.

Early modern writers made little distinction between the force that compelled magnetism and the mystery of human desire. Not only did people find themselves inexplicably, and sometimes involuntarily, drawn to others, but they also regarded these emotions as strangely infectious. As Henry Cornelius Agrippa explains in *Three Books of Occult Philosophy*, the lodestone's attractive property can influence "all things that are near" it.[9] Just as the lodestar transfers its virtue to the lodestone, the lodestone communicates its power of attraction to the iron it draws. To describe this sequence, Robert Norman in *The new attractive* (1592) compares magnetism to a musk that passes its scent to a pair of gloves, which then perfume a whole trunk of clothes.[10] Likewise, when human passions circulate as a contagion among close company, the transmission depends on the very same physical dynamic as when a lodestone infuses its power into a succession of iron rings.[11] In *A table of humane passions* (1621) Nicholas Coeffeteau suggests that the distributive virtue of the lodestone is indistinguishable from a reciprocal chain of human affections:

> They say the Adamant or Loadstone doth not only make an impression vpon iron which it drawes, but doth also impart his vertue by his touching; so as the iron which it hath toucht, drawes other iron vnto it, and makes as it were a continued chaine. In the same manner, a friend brings his friends to him he loues, and he reciprocally imparts vnto him his friends; whereof there is framed a common bond, which makes them ready to succor one another, as if they were members of one body.[12]

Coeffeteau implies that the lodestone is not merely a trope for the generative quality of friendship but a discernible effect in nature that helps us conceive the presence of invisible properties or virtues that constitute our mysterious affective attachments.

That the pull of a lodestone and the attraction of a lover were indistinguishable energies can be detected in the purported use of adamants and lodestones to redirect human passions. Stephen Batman calls the adamant "a Precious stone of reconciliation and of loue. For if a woman be away from hir husband, or trespasseth against him, by vertue of this stone Adamas, she is the sooner reconciled to haue grace of hir Husband."[13] In *The Book of Secrets*, Albertus Magnus claims that if a husband lays a lodestone "under the head of [his] wife, and if she be chaste, she will embrace her husband; if she be not chaste, she will fall anon forth of the bed."[14] The implicit logic in these recommended practices is that humans and stones are affected and moved by the same sympathetic and antipathetic forces in nature.

If the adamant and lodestone were thought to affect women's desires in particular, the assumption may derive from early modern medical writings, which repeatedly describe the womb as a kind of magnet. While nature's greatest secret is the lodestone, the other "ultimate natural secret," as Katharine Park has argued, is the uterus.[15] Rather than treating the womb as an animal, as many of their classical predecessors did, early modern physicians identified the womb with occult qualities.[16] In the sixteenth-century health guide *De morbis foemineis, the woman's counsellour*, Alexandro Massaria maintains that without a "magnetical attraction to the Act of copulation by a sympathy" between a man and a woman, then the "very Act it self would be abhorred."[17] In *The problemes of Aristotle* (1595), the writer illustrates the contention that "the womb and nature doe draw the seede, as the Lodestone doth yron" with an anecdote about a maid whose womb drew in "seede" that had been left behind in her bath water.[18] As Thomas Chamberlayne asserts, "The first use of the Womb is to attract the seed by a familiar sympathy, just as the load-stone draws iron."[19] Jane Sharp in *The midwives book* begins a chapter on the matrix by asserting that the womb has "an attractive faculty to draw in a magnetique quality, as the Load-stone draweth iron."[20] While the female womb may appear, in visual terms, to be male genitals inverted, its power of attraction was understood to distinguish it in functional terms.

Early modern writers derive their understanding of the womb's magnetic nature from Galenic explanations of procreation and digestion, internal physiological processes which, they believed, functioned in similar ways. As Galen argues in his treatise *On the Natural Faculties*, the forces of attraction, retention, and expulsion characterize the movement of the body's organs. And yet the "true essence of the cause" of these motions remains occult. The optimal way to comprehend how attraction, retention, and expulsion activate the natural faculties, Galen proposes, is to consider the mysterious power of the lodestone. The liver and the womb, in other words, attract and repel in the same way that a magnet does.[21]

With its foundation in Galen, the early modern equation between the womb and the lodestone should be understood not as mere analogy but as a strategy for representing their shared yet hidden physics. Moreover, the medical discourse maintains that the womb had a sympathetic influence on the operation of the heart, liver, and brain.[22] Consequently, women were thought to experience most physical diseases, as well as extreme emotional distress, predominantly in the womb. Whether troubled by a disease of retention (such as greensickness, a fit of the mother, or uterine fury), a difficult birth, or excessive passions, the recommended treatments focused on the womb's attractive, expulsive, or retentive virtues. Lazare Rivière observes, for example, that retention difficulties can be cured by placing a range of "Attractive things beneath" the matrix, such as the blood of a wild goat (which "hath mighty vertue to bring down stopped Courses"). The aim is "to rouse and awake the Expulsive faculty."[23] Similarly, scent therapy relied on the womb's hidden properties or virtues. Indeed, in addition to the application of smells and specific virtues, medical texts advised midwives and physicians to apply the lodestone, or the aetites stone, to draw a child out of the womb, or to prevent premature birth, depending on where the stone was placed. Placing such stones around the neck or on the navel would supposedly help avert a miscarriage, whereas the "magnetick virtue" of the stone held near the "privities" would help draw out a child in a stillbirth or difficult delivery.[24] In the seventeenth century, steel was routinely prescribed for most diseases of retention. As Nicolaas Fonteyn in *The womans doctor* (1652) states, "the use and virtue of Steele is to unlock obstructions" and its composition works to "bring down *Courses* [initiate menstruation]," and provoke urine.[25] While critics have noted that steel pills were often recommended for greensickness, the assumption has been that physicians anticipated the need for iron in cases of anemia. In actuality, these practices underscore a belief that the womb and the lodestone operated in similar ways.

The matter of twins

More surprising, perhaps, than the early modern correlation between the womb and the lodestone is that the period's most renowned scientific inquiry into magnetism, William Gilbert's *De Magnete* (1600), attributes the affinity between the lodestone and iron to their shared formation in the "womb" of the earth. Gilbert's treatise charts a series of experiments that led to his chief discovery: the compass needle moved because the earth itself was magnetic.[26] Unlike his predecessors and contemporaries, Gilbert does not identify magnetism as a sympathetic force but argues, instead, that the act of the lodestone and iron is mutual.[27] And while he dismisses as fable any explanation that attributes magnetism to occult qualities, he makes the radical argument that the lodestone actually possesses an animate soul.[28] And for Gilbert, "mother" earth is "the fount and source and producer of all these forces and properties."[29] Since the lodestone and iron were generated together in the earth's womb, they prove to be uterine siblings, or twins:

So far we have been telling of the nature and properties of loadstone, as also of the properties and nature of iron; it now remains that we point out their mutual affinities – their consanguinity, so to speak – and that we show the two substances to be very nearly allied. In the upper most part of the terrestrial globe ... these two bodies come into being and are generated in the same matrix, in one bed, like twins.[30]

In other words, the likeness between the womb and the lodestone runs both ways: the lodestone's properties provide an explanation for the strange powers of the womb, and the womb's powers provide an explanation for the wondrous nature of the lodestone.

Remarkably, it appears that accepted beliefs about the female's role in procreation may have affected how scholars received Gilbert's assertion. Neither William Barlow nor Mark Ridley, for example, attributes the lodestone's power to the earth's womb.[31] In fact, when Ridley makes mention of the lodestone's origins in *A short treatise of magneticall bodies and motions* (1613), he describes its environs only as the "bowels of the earth."[32] In the final chapter of his treatise, Ridley directly challenges Gilbert's assertion that the lodestone's "*Magneticall* substance" derives from the earth. The two substances are distinct, he argues, for the earth's "*Magneticall* substance [is] unknown to us," beyond human understanding, and a wonderful effect of God.[33] Ridley then reminds his readers that it was the "skillful Potter" who "made the earth and all Magnetical bodies at the creation, and gave life and vigor to all things."[34] By appealing to the potter analogy, Ridley gets at the heart of what makes Gilbert's arguments so anarchical. Not only does Ridley remind his readers of the primary authority of God, the skillful potter of all things, but he also invokes Aristotle's discussions of both causation and procreation. In the terms of Aristotle's *Physics*, the potter represents the efficient cause, and the clay signifies the material cause. And in *Generation of Animals*, the potter molds clay in the same way that men contribute soul and form to the procreation process, while women provide only matter.[35] Ridley's resistance to attributing the lodestone's soul and animation to the earth's matrix stems from his biased understanding of the womb's role in human reproduction.

Of course, the Hippocratic two-seed theory of reproduction competed with Aristotle's notions.[36] If women contributed seed to the process of procreation, then the more dominant seed, either male or female, would determine the child's hereditary traits. But even when writers adhered to a one-seed theory, they believed that women, both at conception and during pregnancy, could affect the physical appearance of the child. No matter the theory, birth-marks and monsters were often attributed to the womb's sympathy with the mother's over-active imagination and its capacity to imprint its images and characteristics onto the unborn fetus. An excess of female matter could help precipitate a monstrous birth. As Leah DeVun explains, writers who drew on Aristotelian authority maintained that:

> A hermaphrodite occurred when matter contributed by the mother (in the form of menstrual blood) exceeded the amount needed to produce one fetus, but was not enough for two. The extra matter could form either conjoined twins or a single fetus with extra appendages, including a second set of genitals.[37]

In fact, Gilbert's claim that the earth's womb generated the twinship between the lodestone and iron meshes with circulating theories on the breeding of twins. While medical discourse disputed the number of cells in a womb, many agreed that excess matter or seed could produce either multiple births, supernumerary parts, or conjoined babies, depending on how and whether the seed was divided. Except in cases of superfetation, Aristotle identifies twins as preternatural and attributes them to an excess of generative matter: twins, in other words, veered off "the common course of Nature."[38]

Albertus Magnus in *De animalibus* adapts Aristotle's notion to a two-seed theory of reproduction. He offers four explanations for the division of seed in the womb: the male seed may enter the womb in an interrupted manner, particularly in a womb that proves too long; the female seed may enter the womb in "successive parcels"; the male sperm is "taken in by the womb in successive turns"; and finally, the movement of the uterus during coitus will divide the mingled contribution from both male and female. In the last three accounts, it is the womb's movement, and the resulting division, which brings about twins.[39] While a general early modern audience may not have known these theories in detail, the popular and widely circulating *Problemes of Aristotle* insists that twins are "not so strong as other men" because "the seed and substance which should have been for one man, is divided into two."[40] A later text, *Aristotle's Masterpiece*, indicates that "Twins are conceived ... through the strange disposition of the womb."[41] As reports of conjoined twins make clear, early moderns also believed that a division of generative matter in the womb could even produce opposite sex twins.[42]

As uterine siblings, twins were understood to have a particularly strong sympathetic connection, much like the lodestone and iron.[43] "Hippocrates' twins," a phrase that appears frequently in early modern literature, functioned as shorthand for characterizing the most intimate forms of this bond.[44] As Augustine notes (in refuting an astrological explanation for the phenomenon), Hippocrates' twins lived their lives in such sympathetic rhythm that they fell ill at the same time.[45] In his discussion of hermaphrodites in *The Secrets of Women*, Pseudo-Albertus Magnus explains that in addition to the manifestation of monstrous bodies, it is also possible to discern "monstrous spirits," and he cites the behavior of twins as the best example:

> One of whom had the power in his right side that no matter where he was carried, he opened all bars and closings. And the other had the power in his left side of closing all locks that had been opened . . . The cause . . . does not derive from constellation alone, but from a special disposition of the matter to receive the impression.[46]

Giambattista della Porta cites the same anecdote to establish that "particular creatures have particular gifts" or "some hidden property" within them. For many early modern writers, twins epitomize the wondrous effects of nature's secret sympathies.[47]

Twelfth Night

Shakespeare's *Twelfth Night* (performed the same year as the publication of Gilbert's *De Magnete*) is indebted to the notion that attraction between people is indistinct from the magnetic force that draws iron to the lodestone. Secretly directing the movement of human desire are two hidden magnetic influences: the twins' sympathetic bond and the afflicted wombs of Viola and Olivia. As emotional doubles, Viola and Olivia are each grieving the loss of a brother. Since profound passion necessarily vexed the early modern womb, each woman's sorrow generates a uterine pathology. And such distressed wombs had the power to affect the passions of those around them. As for the twins, Shakespeare traces Sebastian and Viola's occult bond to their mother's womb, for their formation as uterine twins makes them two halves of a whole. Indeed, Antonio alludes to the notion that twins derive from divided matter when, struck with wonder, he asks Sebastian if he has "made division" of himself. Sebastian and Cesario look to be, he exclaims, "[a]n apple cleft in two" (5.1.215–16). As scholars have observed, Antonio's language invokes the discussion in Plato's *Symposium* when Aristophanes states that Zeus weakens humans by cutting them in half, like a "sorb-apple which is halved for pickling." In that story, the world is comprised of halves seeking other halves, and "when one of them finds his other half . . . the pair are lost in an amazement of love and friendship and intimacy." For Plato, the tale defines love as "the desire for and pursuit of the whole" and provides an origin story of the sexes.[48] But for Sebastian and Viola, or any pair of early modern twins, the story mythologizes an authentic and occult bond between them.[49] Once separated from each other by shipwreck, their yearning infuses those around them with sympathetic contagions, producing the chaotic and superficially illogical couplings that mark early modern romantic comedies.

When the characters in *Twelfth Night* articulate the experience of attraction, they consistently invoke preternatural powers. Orsino accounts for Olivia's appeal, for example, by citing the allure of a numinous gemstone: "'tis that miracle and queen of gems / That nature pranks [Olivia] in attracts my soul" (2.4.83–84). For some early modern writers, the "queen of gems" was the pantarbe, which the *OED* identifies as "a mythical precious stone with magical properties, esp. resistance to fire and the capacity to attract gold."[50] Ficino named the Pantarbe as the highest-ranking stone, most infused with celestial influence. Only the lodestone exceeds its power:

> But O that somewhere we might easily find a Solar or Lunar stone so overpowering in its order, as we have in the loadestone and iron in the order of the Northern Pole-Star! True, they do report the Appollonius of Tyana found among the Indians a Solar Stone, pantaura by name . . . it attracts other gems itself just as the lodestone does iron. . . . [but] the power of the Bear prevails in [the lodestone].[51]

Either Olivia is literally adorned with the queen of gems, or (more likely) Orsino means that nature has infused Olivia's presence and appearance with a power akin to the queen of gems. In a similar vein, Antonio interprets his desire as an occult influence, characterizing Sebastian's appeal as "a witchcraft [that] drew [him] hither" (5.1.70).[52] Olivia describes her attraction to Cesario as an instance of secret contagion, for his "perfections / With an invisible and subtle stealth / . . . creep in" at her eyes (1.5.266–68).

Of course, in all these cases, the characters feel unrequited attraction, which exaggerates the sense that nature compels desire in ways that remain abstruse to humans. In Orsino's case, Olivia refuses to admit his suits, sending word that she intends to mourn her brother in isolation for seven years. Curiously, Orsino interprets Olivia's resistance not only as evidence of her ability to love him but also as a pathology that his love can cure.

> O she that hath a heart of that fine frame
> To pay this debt of love but to a brother,
> How will she love, when the rich golden shaft

> Hath killed the flock of all affections else
> That live in her – when liver, brain, and heart,
> These sovereign thrones, are all supplied and filled
> Her sweet perfections with one self king!   (1.1.32–38)

With obvious phallic connotations, Orsino declares his wish to penetrate and anatomize her body. That Olivia feels such grief for her brother encouragingly demonstrates, for Orsino, her capacity for passion. But embedded in Orsino's fantasy to win Olivia's heart is his desire to tame the unruly nature of the matrix.[53] If he implies vaginal intercourse here, then the rich golden shaft would kill "the flock of all affections . . . / That live in" Olivia's womb. By characterizing Olivia's grieving "affections" as both numerous and the target of his extermination, Orsino implies that they are potentially detrimental to her, implicitly drawing on the medical association between uterine diseases and affections.[54] If ruled by the flock of affections that "live in her," Orsino may believe that Olivia suffers from the retention of menses, an affliction that led to greensickness.

While early modern texts often associated greensickness with a virgin's "emerging sexual appetites," it was also attributed to profound sadness, grief, and fear.[55] "[S]tubburne carefulnes, immoderate feare and great sorrowe doe stoppe the menstruis," writes Philip Barrough.[56] Marked by a lack of appetite and withdrawal from society, greensickness transformed, as Gail Kern Paster has observed, "the very blood that is the social and biological sign of the virgin's maturation" into the "site and origin of a disease of self-poisoning."[57] Orsino believes that once the shaft affects Olivia, then all her faculties – liver, brain, and heart – will surrender themselves to loving him. The health of the womb, as we noted earlier, sympathetically affected the functioning of the heart, liver, and brain. Orsino longs to fill Olivia's hidden recesses and organs so completely with love for him that he, rather than her absent brother, will rule her womb's sympathetic qualities. As many audience members would know, a commonly recommended cure for greensickness was copulation (or more vaguely, marriage).[58] In other words, Orsino may imagine that his narcissistic desire to eradicate Olivia's current affections will have a curative effect on her as well.

Buried in Orsino's language, however, is a story of magnetism that counters Gilbert's originary (and feminized) narrative of the lodestone's occult qualities. Orsino's "shaft," often glossed by editors as cupid's arrow, is also a term for the Pole Star. As Robert Record writes in the *The castle of knowledge* (1556), "the lesser Beare . . . is the chiefe marke whereby mariners gouerne their course in saylinge by nyghte, and namely by 2 starres

in it . . . many do call the Shafte."[59] Not only does "Orsino" refer to a noble
Italian family but it also means "little bear," suggesting the Pole Star or
lodestar that sailors used to guide their ships.[60] The compass needle, having
been rubbed by the lodestone, was thought to point to the Pole Star. Rather
than attributing its force to the earth's womb, earlier writers (including
Ficino) often claimed that the lodestone acquired its special virtue from the
"lesser Bear." It may be Orsino's nominal sympathy with the lodestar that
spurs Feste to mock him as a mariner without direction: "I would have men
of such constancy put to sea, that their business might be everything and
their intent everywhere, for that's it that always makes a good voyage of
nothing" (2.4.74–76). Certainly, the transformational effect of Orsino's
"rich golden shaft" on Olivia's "flock of . . . affections" remains the stuff
of his self-loving, and conspicuously masculine, fantasy.

It is in his conversations with Cesario that Orsino invokes physiological
differences between men and women to assert that male desire, even if
unreciprocated, is superior in strength and quality to female desire. Implicitly
he rejects the one-sex model, for he differentiates between the sexes on the basis
of how their natural faculties compel motion in the body. Male passions, he
insists, possess a constancy that females lack. Drawing on Galenic language,
Orsino tells Cesario that women lack retention – a term we have seen used to
describe both magnetic force and the body's natural faculties.

> There is no woman's sides
> Can bide the beating of so strong a passion
> As love doth give my heart; no woman's heart
> So big, to hold so much. They lack retention.
> Alas, their love may be called appetite,
> No motion of the liver, but the palate,
> That suffer surfeit, cloyment, and revolt;
> But mine is all as hungry as the sea,
> And can digest as much. (2.4.91–99)

As we noted earlier, Galen accounts for the natural faculties of organs – their
motions of attraction, retention, and expulsion – as occult forces that
function like the lodestone.[61] For Orsino, the experience of love is equivalent to the process of digestion.[62] Female passions act as an unruly, superficial appetite of the stomach, or womb, which misjudges what it can
accommodate, leading to gluttony and purging. Men, on the other hand,
feel desire as a motion or faculty of the liver. The attractive force of their
natural faculty proves as strong as the sea's hunger, alluding perhaps to the
pull of the tide. And unlike expulsive women, men are able to assimilate and
digest whatever they take in.

Certainly Orsino has humoral discourse on his side. As Gail Kern Paster has shown, women were commonly typified as "leaky" or unable to retain fluids. Whether that fluid was menstrual blood, breast milk, or Olivia's great "Ps," incontinence was understood to be a female condition.[63] Their physical condition, Orsino asserts, is evidence of their inability to sustain either an affective state or a bond.[64] But, in contradiction to these humoral commonplaces, the magnetic power of the matrix imbued it with a strong retentive faculty. Not only did the womb necessarily retain the male seed, but it also held infants during pregnancy for nine months.[65]

Cesario directly answers Orsino's allegation that females lack constancy. In describing a woman he identifies as his father's "daughter," Cesario portrays a physiological condition that refutes Orsino's theory of male and female passions. Plagued with a green and yellow melancholy, this "daughter" suffers, quite literally, from retention:

> In faith, [women] are as true of heart as we.
> My father had a daughter loved a man
> As it might be, perhaps, were I a woman,
> I should your lordship.
> ORSINO: And what's her history?
> VIOLA: A blank, my lord. She never told her love,
>   But let concealment, like a worm i' th' bud,
>   Feed on her damask cheek. She pined in thought,
>   And with a green and yellow melancholy
>   She sat like patience on a monument,
>   Smiling at grief. Was not this love indeed?
>
> (105–14)

As Anthony Fletcher has observed, early modern audiences would have been quick to recognize that "green and yellow melancholy" alludes to greensickness, the illness (as observed with Olivia) attributed to the womb's retention of menses.[66] Symptomatically, Cesario's sister "pines," or wastes away, while the "worm i' the bud" (a synonym for poison, which evokes the noxious effects of putrefying blood) "feed[s] on her damask cheek." Such indicators attest to the womb's retentive capacity and the strength of women's passions.

The example of Cesario's sister does not simply suggest that Orsino is wrong about the intensity and duration of female love but also reminds us of Viola's own extraordinarily retentive state. Grieving, lovesick, and withdrawn behind a disguise, Viola's circumstances and experiences amplify the womb's retentive qualities. As Cesario tells Olivia, "What I am and what I would are as secret as maidenhead" (1.5.189–90), alluding not only to the commonplace association between secrets and female genitalia but also to her shrouded identity and hidden grief. For Cesario's portrait of his "sister" depicts a woman, like Olivia, who keeps "fresh / And lasting in her sad remembrance" her "brother's dead love" (1.1.30–31). But unlike Olivia, Viola arrived in Illyria stripped of the social circumstances that would allow her to mourn the loss of her brother properly. Soon after she learns that Sebastian may have drowned, Viola longs to join Olivia in her bereavement. The captain's statement that Olivia has "abjured the sight / And company of men" in mourning her own brother's death elicits Viola's passionate wish: "O that I served that lady" (1.2.36–37). Thwarted by the Captain's insistence that Olivia will accept "no suit[s]" (41), Viola chooses instead to disguise herself. Grief, more than prospective danger, directs her decision.[67] Cesario describes his "sister" as suffering for love, but Viola's retention was originally triggered by her secret mourning for her brother. In Cesario's terms, his sister's gift for concealment counters the stereotypical charge that women cannot keep a secret. Identified with the allegorical Patience, the "sister" sits on a monument smiling at grief.[68] Not only was "patience" the principal advice given to mourners in the period – "have patience to bear it out" – but Cesario also equates Patience with a carved statue erected over a grave whose sole purpose is to commemorate the dead.[69]

As David Schalkwyk has argued, if Viola were to expose herself as a devoted female, she would risk losing the intimacy she has gained as Orsino's male servant.[70] But Viola's "concealment" sustains much more than her relationship with Orsino. It is the retentive state of Viola's womb that enables the manifestation of her Cesario persona.[71] Her disguise helps her personate the brother whose loss afflicts her. Not only does she imitate her brother, fashioning her appearance and actions in his image, but she also suffers the physical effects of suppressing her grief.[72] Indeed, many accounts of greensickness assert that its symptoms included the development of masculine traits: some sufferers supposedly grew beards.[73] If we doubt that Viola's retained grief complicates her desire for Orsino, the point is swiftly brought home when Cesario answers Orsino's question, "But died thy sister of her love, my boy?": "I am all the daughters of my father's house / And all the brothers too; and yet I know not" (2.4.118–20). On the question of Viola's prospective death, Cesario's answer encodes the loss of a sister and a brother. An early modern spectator may have wondered whether Viola puts her health at risk in refusing to declare her love to Orsino – a possibility that Orsino raises with his question. Sebastian's absence is not only the more obscure cause of his sister's suffering but also the hidden reason why Viola's fate remains in the balance.

By disguising herself as Cesario, Viola can withdraw from the world, hide her sorrow, and resurrect Sebastian with her impersonation. She incorporates her brother into herself, thus refusing to acknowledge fully the painful import of her loss.[74] When she hides her identity, Viola imagines her eventual reemergence as a birth – when she can be safely "delivered to the world." She swaps her name, Viola, which recalls the "Vial" or womb that Shakespeare urges the young man in Sonnet 6 to make "sweet" with his "treasure," for "Cesario."[75] Her new name underlines her retentive state, for a Caesarian birth was employed when the womb lacked the expulsive faculty to deliver an infant.[76] Although Viola initially imagines she will disguise herself as a eunuch, Cesario recognizes himself as both male and female – "As I am man" and "As I am woman" (2.2.34–36) – or a hermaphroditic monster. Cesario may not possess a second set of genitals, but in choosing to cross-dress rather than mourn, Viola generates an identity that reunites her, spiritually, with Sebastian. If one adopts Paul Dean's view that "Cesario is the [Platonic] Form of which Viola and Sebastian are the material embodiments," we might translate this to mean that Cesario embodies the twins before their division in the womb.[77] Cesario represents, perhaps more than a eunuch or a hermaphrodite, a spiritually conjoined twin.

It is not coincidental that at the moment of the twins' reunion Shakespeare reminds the audience that Sebastian and Viola are uterine siblings, whose formation in the womb established their occult bond:

VIOLA: Of Messaline. Sebastian was my father.
Such a Sebastian was my brother, too.
So went he suited to his watery tomb.
If spirits can assume both form and suit
You come to fright us.
SEBASTIAN: A spirit I am indeed,
But am in that dimension grossly clad
Which from the womb I did participate.

(5.1.225–31)

In his reading of this scene, Greenblatt observes that it is "through the magical power of the name of the father [that] we learn that the threat to the social order and the threat to the sexual order were equally illusory."[78] But if our response to the twins' reunion emphasizes the "name of the father," we overlook the competing authority of the mother's womb. In Sebastian's use, "spirit" refers first to his soul before it takes on flesh, but it also describes the work of generation. Whether a medical writer subscribed to a one-seed or two-seed theory of procreation, most stressed that a more active male seed or spirit infused its form on the mother's matter or menses.[79]

What attests to the influence of the womb is Sebastian's acknowledgment that he "participate[d]," or shared, in that gross dimension. While most editors gloss "participate" as a reference to common humanity – all men and women take on a fleshly garment – Sebastian also means that he shared the womb and the process of embodiment with his twin sister.[80] Not only was the womb the site where the spirit gains a body, but it was also where twins, or multiple births, were determined. Sebastian's statement alludes to the early modern belief that it was predominantly the womb that affected the division of seed in the conception of twins. By implying that he and his sister were physically produced by a division in their mother's womb, Sebastian suggests that they share a spirit – both figuratively and literally. His story of their origins underlines the sympathetic nature of twinship; because he and Viola shared a womb, they also share an occult bond that mimics the lodestone and iron.

By personifying her loss of Sebastian through Cesario, Viola has functioned as an emotional lodestone, attracting Orsino (her lodestar), Olivia (her dispositional twin), and even Antonio into her contagious orbit. Just as the magnet had a distributive effect on the iron rings it contacted, Viola's yearning infects those around her. It is Olivia, in fact, who describes her attraction to Cesario as "catch[ing] the plague," an illness that in Paracelsian terms would attach itself to an "organ to which it was related by a predestined sympathy."[81] As we noted earlier, Olivia feels Cesario's "perfections / With an invisible and subtle stealth / . . . creep in" at her eyes (1.5.265–68). While we may dismiss these lines as mere admiration of Cesario's physical traits, the scene suggests that Olivia is drawn to Cesario's hidden, sympathetic qualities.

Olivia catches the "plague" when Cesario inadvertently woos her with language that not only expresses his mourning but also identifies himself as an embodiment of occult sympathies. In the same way that Viola's grief for her brother gets expressed indirectly in Cesario's description of a sister who concealed her love, Cesario's portrait of himself as an echo outside Olivia's gate communicates both lovesickness and mourning:

> Make me a willow cabin at your gate
> And call upon my soul within the house,
> Write loyal cantons of contemnèd love
> And sing them loud even in the dead of night;
> Halloo your name to the reverberate hills,
> And make the babbling gossip of the air
> Cry out 'Olivia!' O, You should not rest
> Between the elements of air and earth,
> But you should pity me.   (1.5.237–45)

Many critics have noted that *Twelfth Night* alludes to an Elizabethan version of the Narcissus myth, in which Narcissus falls in love with his twin sister, who looks just like him. When his sister drowns, he pines away for his own image because it reminds him of her.[82] As Paul Dean observes, Cesario plays "Echo to everyone else's Narcissus."[83] But even beyond the Ovidian myth, Shakespeare presents Viola/Cesario as an embodiment of occult sympathies. For Viola's name not only alludes to a "vial," but also, more obviously, signifies a stringed instrument – a viol or a lute. After the lodestone and iron, the other most popular account of nature's secret sympathies was when a lute would, without contact, resonate with another plucked lute in its vicinity. As James Hart explains in *Klinike, or The diet of the diseased* (1633), "Now, as concerning the operating vertue by sympathy . . . the things sympathising are not far remote one from another: as in the unisone harmony and consent of two lutes or vialls may easily appeare."[84] Cesario's account of Olivia's name – an anagram of Viola, reverberating through the hills – certainly expresses Viola's confused emotions of desire and grief. At the very same time, Cesario has unwittingly narrated the consonant vibrations that Olivia experiences as she listens. As Olivia characterizes her reaction to Cesario, her attraction feels like "enchantment" (3.1.104). Her response has its basis in an intrinsic sympathy for Viola's secret loss and its emotive equivalence to her own.

It is Sebastian's attempt to define the nature of Olivia's attraction to Cesario that has become the most critically debated textual crux in *Twelfth Night*:

> So comes it, lady, you have been mistook.
> But nature to her bias drew in that.
> You would have been contracted to a maid,
> Nor are you therein, by my life, deceived.
> You are betrothed both to a maid and man.   (5.1.252–56)

Criticism has focused on the direction and consequences of nature's bias. Greenblatt maintains that nature's bias corrected Olivia's homoerotic attachment to Cesario by shifting it towards Sebastian.[85] The analogy, Greenblatt contends, refers to the weighted bowl in the game of balls, which swerves as it rolls along the pitch. In this reading, "drew in" means contracted, so that nature pulled Olivia towards the heterosexual coupling of marriage. Challenging Greenblatt, Laurie Shannon has established how classical and early modern writers, including Cicero, Erasmus, and Montaigne, subscribed to the commonplace notion that "like seeks like." With reference to Foucault's account of the resemblances and similitudes that structure pre-modern cosmology, Shannon suggests that

Sebastian's phrase "in that" refers to Olivia's attraction to Cesario. In a homo-normative culture, it is nature's bias to draw similar partners together.[86] Other critics have tempered the debate. For example, Mario DiGangi maintains that Sebastian's statement generates a radical indeterminacy in the direction of nature's bias.[87] It may be, DiGangi suggests, that nature does not determine a single route of attraction. By representing Viola's desire for Orsino alongside Antonio's longing for Sebastian, the play represents desire as having no correlation to gender.

But even when we allow that desire can run in multiple directions, Sebastian's understanding of nature's "bias" remains opaque. This opacity, in fact, points to yet another way to read Sebastian's line: nature's sympathies remain hidden. If we interpret "drew in" as "ensnare" or "delude," then the phrase gestures to the commonplace that Nature is veiled and that humans cannot penetrate her "secrets."[88] In his colloquy on friendship, Erasmus' speaker makes clear that nature's biases are often concealed. He expresses an admiration for Nature's inclination to mix "secret Amities and Enmities in all Things, for which there is no probable Reason to be given, unless for her own Entertainment."[89] Just as Nature delights in jokes, as Paula Findlen has shown, Nature find her own secrets amusing.[90] While Nature draws people into her mysteries, she also refuses to disclose occulted knowledge. In this scenario, Olivia has "been mistook" by Nature's predilection for concealment. In contrast, Sebastian insists, Olivia has not been "deceived" in her betrothal to him. This is not to deny that a secret sympathy drew Olivia to Cesario, for occult forces have directed all the crisscrossed attractions in the play. But the logic of these attractions is veiled. Nature's sympathies are shrouded in wombs, rocks, lodestones and only prove visible through rare and marvelous effects – as in the physical manifestation of identical twins. The generic structure of comedy makes the orchestration of such effects possible. It is *Twelfth Night*'s doubling, twinships, and marvelous resurrections that give us a glimpse of nature's occult principles of attraction.

Sebastian's presence, in the flesh, reasserts the twins' separated condition, establishing that the "occasion" is now "mellow" for Viola to "be delivered to the world" (1.2.38–39). But when the siblings recognize each other, Cesario adamantly denies Viola's presence and defers their embrace:

> If nothing lets to make us happy both
> But this my masculine usurped attire,
> Do not embrace me till each circumstance
> Of place, time, fortune, do cohere and jump
> That I am Viola ...   (5.1.242–46)

By refusing physical contact with Sebastian, Cesario resists the natural magnetic force that compels them together.[91] The lodestone impressed Pliny in its anthropomorphic ability to "draw and grasp," clasping or embracing iron as if it had hands. In della Porta's *Natural Magick*, "embrace" is the term used repeatedly to characterize the occult response of iron to the lodestone.[92] But to bring back Viola is to lose Cesario – the play's parthenogenetic, theatrical fantasy, produced not by a woman's womb but by the staging of a woman's womb and its retentive and occult qualities. Indeed, *Twelfth Night* depicts wombs as such powerful forces that the presence of actual wombs would disrupt the theatrical representation of their occult influences. As a cross-dressed woman, Cesario/Viola secrets away her maidenhead and her grief; but as a doubly cross-dressed male actor, the secret is there is no secret. In other words, the transvestite theater may be a reaction to nature's secret sympathies, rather than an expression of a gender that "is teleologically male and insists upon a verifiable sign that confirms nature's final cause."[93] Nature's best-kept secret – the womb – not only differentiated women from men but also formed the physiological shape and secret biases of everyone, both on and off the stage.

CHAPTER 4

Tragic antipathies in The Changeling

Near the middle of Thomas Middleton and William Rowley's *The Changeling*, the principal female protagonist, Beatrice Joanna, discovers a book of secrets in her fiancé Alsemero's closet. Critics have typically treated the recipes in the book (two are divulged by Beatrice's reading them aloud), together with the concoctions in Alsemero's "physician's closet" (4.1.20), as not only eccentric in nature but also unessential to the plot as a whole, except as a fantastic way for Beatrice to discern her maid Diaphanta's virgin status, or as a thematic connection to the tragedy's investment in secrets of all kinds.[1] I will argue in this chapter that this book of secrets is, in fact, central to understanding *The Changeling*'s hidden logic, a logic akin to the veiled physics of attraction we traced in *Twelfth Night*, which attributes people's strange behaviors and motives to the hidden sympathies and antipathies that course through the natural world. As we have observed, many of the receipts in books of secrets rely on the occult qualities in plants, minerals, animals, and humans to produce their promised effects. Much in the same way, Alsemero, Beatrice Joanna, and DeFlores are compelled to feel and act by sympathetic and antipathetic forces that remain obscured from their full comprehension and prove discernible only by their responses. This chapter will also elaborate on *The Changeling*'s acknowledged indebtedness to the trials of Lady Frances Howard, a complex historical narrative that underscores the cultural tendency to attribute occult power to women's bodies.[2] The trajectory of *The Changeling*'s plot and the outcome of the Howard trial both suggest that when women act as inquirers or experimenters in the secrets of nature, the results prove unnatural and dangerous to the social order.[3]

Just before her wedding night with Alsemero, Beatrice loses her virginity to DeFlores in coerced payment for his murder of her first fiancé, Alonzo. At the very moment when she articulates her anxiety that Alsemero will detect her deflowered status in their marriage bed, Beatrice discovers among his belongings various paraphernalia that he employs to discern the secrets of others. In his closet – "A right physician's closet" – are not only vials and potions but also a manuscript titled "*The Book of Experiment, Called Secrets in Nature*" (24–5). Recognizing that her husband must "practice physic for his own use," Beatrice flips through the book, landing on the pages where the corners have been dog-eared (29). The first receipt reads "How to know whether a woman be with child or no" (25):

I hope I am not yet. If he should try though!
Let me see: folio forty-five – here 'tis,
The leaf tucked down upon't, the place suspicious:
"If you would know whether a woman be with child or not, give her two spoonfuls
    of the white water in Glass C" –
Where's that Glass C? O, yonder I see't now –
"– and if she be with child, she sleeps full twelve hours after; if not, not"
. . .
Ha! That which is next, is ten times worse:
"How to know whether a woman be a maid, or not."
If that should be applied, what would become of me?
Belike he has a strong faith of my purity,
That never yet made proof; but this he calls
"A merry sleight, but true experiment" –
The author "Antonius Mizaldus":
"Give the party you suspect the quantity of a spoonful of the water in the Glass M,
    which upon her that is a maid makes three several effects: 'twill make her
    incontinently gape, then fall into a sudden sneezing, last into a violent laughing –
    else dull, heavy, lumpish."   (26–50)

While the secrets Beatrice reads focus on women's bodies, the genre of secrets books typically covered a wide range of topics, including cooking, medicine, fireworks, magic tricks, ink-making, and more. Simply put, books of secrets provided instructions on how to produce certain effects; however, the ultimate cause of those effects remained occulted. Historians offer a variety of perspectives on the genre's significance and primary audience. Paulo Rossi argues that secrets literature is built on an epistemological divide between the elite magician and the ignorant masses. William Eamon has suggested that books of secrets anticipated the scientific revolution in their emphasis on practicable experiments. Focusing on English publications, Allison Kavey emphasizes how the popularity and cheap availability of certain books of secrets gave common readers a "sense of themselves as practitioners, as authorities, and as active participants in, rather than victims of, the world around them."[4]

As we noted in our discussion of *All's Well That Ends Well*, the publication of secrets could serve a wide range of social purposes. Girolamo

Ruscelli's *The seconde part of the Secretes of Master Alexis of Piemont* (1560), for example, presents an array of preparations, including instructions for special waters – many for improving the skin – as well as prescriptions "To make one have a good memorie," "To make Oile of Roses," "To make that a woman shall eate nothing that is set upon the table," "To make a woman that is wont to haue daughters to beare Sonnes also," "To preserue a man from Poison," and "To be assured and safe from all Sorcerie and Enchantement."[5] Many of these recipes depend on occult qualities or virtues in plants, animals, and minerals that follow a hidden logic of contraries and amities. In a receipt, for example, which promises to deter barking dogs, the sympathetic magic is apparent: "Take a blacke Dogge and plucke out one of his eies and holde it in your lefte hande, and by reason of the sauour and smell thereof the Dogges will not barke at you."[6]

Alsemero's book, the play reveals, is a personal collection of recipes in which he has recorded secrets gathered from other sources, thus representing the complex circulation of knowledge that took place among active readers, practitioners, and expert authors.[7] His scripted annotation identifies the virginity test as "'A merry sleight, but true experiment' – / [from] The author 'Antonius Mizaldus.'" As several critics have noted, Antonius Mizaldus, or Antoine Mizauld, was a secrets author who published *De Arcanis Naturae* (1558) among other books, including *Memorabilium, utilium ac jucundorum Centuriae IX Arcanorum* (1566), which contains several virginity tests.[8] Repeatedly cited as the source for other books of secrets, including Thomas Lupton *A thousand notable things* (1579) and Johann Jacob Wecker's *Eighteen books of the secrets of art and nature* (1660), Mizauld's name may have been familiar to some of *The Changeling*'s audience.[9] Alsemero also indicates that he acquired Mizauld's receipt from a Chaldean, a claim that may allude to books of secrets' common acknowledgment of oral sources, including cunning folk and herb women (4.2.112). Beatrice's examination of the book and closet makes plain that Alsemero's idiosyncratic collection of secrets also follows a personal alphabetical coding system that correlates the recipe with the correct vials of ingredients.

While it is true that virginity and pregnancy tests appear in some books of secrets, Alsemero's (or Beatrice's) emphasis on recipes keyed to the secrets of the female body points to the cultural associations made between nature's secrets and women's secrets. Modern audiences may assume that the "secret" of Alsemero's book refers explicitly to the hidden nature of an early pregnancy, or to the veiled status of sexual experience, but, as we have seen, early modern spectators would readily associate secrecy with certain

operations in nature. As noted in the Introduction, secrets literature developed at the same time that male medical writers began to classify knowledge
of women's health and illness as "secrets of women." While female health
practitioners may have had greater access to women's bodies in thirteenth-
and fourteenth-century Europe, men began, in this same period, to appropriate gynecological knowledge in printed form.[10]

Not only does Alsemero's book seem to conflate the experiments of
general secrets books with the gynecological genre, it also suggests that
the virginity test relies on the activation of occult qualities both in the
female body and in the mixtures contained in the glass vials. As Alsemero
observes during Beatrice's (falsified) test, the "composition" (4.2.134) contains a "secret virtue" that is "ne'er missed … Upon a virgin" (138–39).
When Beatrice cleverly, and comically, tries the recipe out on her virginal
maidservant Diaphanta, the experiment produces an array of observable
and external symptoms just as the book promised: Diaphanta gapes,
sneezes, laughs, and then becomes melancholy. The hidden condition of
her virginity is made manifest by the occult qualities of the potion.

Readers in the audience may have come across similar virginity tests in a
range of published genres, including lapidaries, histories, and encyclope-
dias.[11] However, the key difference between these published virginity tests
and the one staged in *The Changeling* is that other trials typically produced
observable responses in the non-virgin, a phenomenon that corresponds to
the assumed incontinence of leaky, sexually experienced woman. Readers of
Albertus Magnus, for example, were promised results if they placed a
lodestone under the head of an unchaste wife: if she proves unchaste, she
will "fall anon forth of the bed."[12] The anonymous *The booke of pretty
conceits* (1612) presents the following tests for proving "if a maiden be cleer":

> Burn Mother-wort, and let her take the smoake at her nose, and if she be
> corrupt, she shall pisse, or else not. Otherwise take gray Nettles whilst that
> they be greene, and then let her pisse on them, and if she be no Maiden, they
> will wither forthwith, or else not.[13]

Johann Jacob Wecker's *Eighteen Books of the Secrets of Art and Nature* (1660)
provides similar chastity tests:

> The Jet stone, (which is very frequent with us, wherewith we make Beads
> withall to pray, and to number and summe up our Prayers,) some scrapings
> of it, or the stone beaten in a Mortar, and sifted, so being brought into very
> fine pouder, and then drank with wine or water; if the woman do make water
> presently and cannot hold it, that is a sign she hath lost her Maiden-head; If
> she were never defloured, she will hold her water, and her retentive faculty is

strengthned by it. White Amber is as good as the former (or Crystall,) which they call Electrum, if being poudred, it be drank with wine fasting, and so taken inwardly: for if she be polluted, this will make her make water.[14]

A majority of virginity tests in the period involve the ingestion of jet stone, or gagates. In the encyclopedia *Batman vppon Bartolome*, for example, the entry on the "gagite" stone emphasizes that the cause of its effectiveness remains occulted:

> if a maide drinke of the water thereof, she pisseth not: and if she be no maide & drinketh therof, shée pisseth anon, and also against her will, as *Dioscorides* saith: And so by this stone a maiden is anone proued, as diuerse Authors affirme . . . while the vertue that is hid within is vnknowen.[15]

Both Holinshed's *Chronicles* and John Maplet's *A greene forest* characterize the occult virtue of the gagates stone as effective not only in proving virginity but also in repelling serpents with its perfume.[16] Robert Chester, in *The anuals of great Brittaine* (1611), ascribes these powers to the stone in verse:

> Gagates smelling like to Frankensence,
> Being left whereas the poisonous Serpents breed,
> Driues them away,
>
> . . .
>
> This stone being put in a faire womans drinke, (105)
> Will testifie her pure Virginitie,
> A most rare thing that some men neuer thinke,
> Yet you shall giue your iugdement easily,
> For if she make her water presently,
> Then hath this Woman lost her honestie.[17]

Since jet or gagates makes the unchaste "leaky," modern audiences may assume the effect is somehow linked to the physical consequences of the woman's deflowering.[18] But, as Wecker explains, the process relies instead on secret elements in both the gagates and the virgin. Gagates, he notes, strengthens the virgin's retentive virtue. In other words, inherent in gagates is an occult quality that proves sympathetic to virginity and antipathetic to serpents and non-virgins. Minerals, plants, and animals will affect sullied and unsullied women in different ways, as indicated in Giovanni Benedetto Sinibaldi's *Rare verities: The cabinet of Venus unlocked, and her secrets laid open* (1658): "Some say that deflowered virgins cannot endure the smell of the Lilly, as being the Hieroglyphick of virginity. Others say that Bees will presently smell out unchaste persons; for they are great lovers of chastity."[19] In John Fletcher's *The Faithful Shepherdess*, it is a "virgins hand" that can rouse the "secret virtue[s]" in herbs.[20]

It is *The Changeling*'s deployment of a virginity test that has, for several critics, linked Beatrice Joanna's story to the scandals of Lady Frances Howard. Lady Howard divorced her first husband, the Earl of Essex, on the grounds that he was impotent. The court demanded that she prove her virginity to substantiate the claim. A select group of matrons and midwives were brought into the courthouse to examine her. As John Chamberlain reported,

> the Lady hath ben visited and searcht by some auncient Ladies and midwives expert in those matters, who both by inspection and otherwise find her upon theyre oath a pure virgin: which some Doctors thincke a straunge asseveration, and make yt more difficult then to be discerned.

Although contemporary writers questioned whether physical evidence of an intact hymen could be discerned, the midwives' examination of Frances Howard's body was initially admitted to court as proof of her virginity.[21] Since Howard wore a veil, rumors later circulated that she had provided a substitute for the test, just as Beatrice employs a bed-trick with her maid Diaphanta. When Beatrice indicates that she will put Diaphanta's "honesty / Upon an easy trial" (4.1.97–98), the maid fears she will search her "[l]ike the forewoman of a female jury" (100). Physical assessments of virginity were customarily deemed unreliable not only because examinations yielded ambiguous results but also because people had access to recipes that instructed women in the falsification of virginity. Such prescriptions, for example, provided special ointments that promised to mimic the hymen, or they called for strategically placed animal intestines filled with blood.[22] These forgeries presented searchers (and husbands) with apparently manifest signs of virginity. By staging and subverting a different sort of virginity test in *The Changeling*, Middleton and Rowley shift the focus away from the strictly physical evidence of blood and hymens to emphasize, instead, a set of reproducible symptoms that denote a hidden or occult quality inherent either in the virgin's body or in virginity itself.

While Diaphanta's line may be a direct allusion to Lady Howard's annulment case, the representation of a woman misusing occult knowledge resonates with Lady Howard's purported involvement in Sir Thomas Overbury's murder. After her separation from the Earl of Essex, Lady Howard was soon married to Robert Carr, the Earl of Somerset. When Overbury died, Lady Howard, the Earl of Somerset, and their alleged accomplices were accused of murder. Overbury had disliked Lady Howard and disapproved of the match. He had also garnered a great many state secrets from Somerset (according to Sir Francis Bacon), which he may have threatened to reveal. As reported in various accounts of the trial testimony, both Lady Howard and her confidante Anne Turner took an active role in obtaining and compounding much of the poison that purportedly killed Overbury. According to the deposition of the apothecary James Franklin, Anne Turner bought a water called *aqua fortis* from him; she tried it out on a cat who "languished" and cried for two days before dying. Franklin then maintained that Turner brought him for an interview with Countess Howard:

> [she] told him that *Aqua fortis* was too violent a Water, but what think you (quoth she) of *White Arsenick*? He told her, it was too violent. What say you (quoth she) to *Powder of Diamonds*? He answers, I know not the Nature of that. She said, then he was a Fool, and gave him Pieces of Gold, and bade him buy some of that Powder for her.[23]

In this scenario, the Countess is represented as more knowledgeable in the hidden nature of poisons than the apothecary.[24] The countess, it was noted, had sent to Overbury, on one occasion, an array of tarts and jellies. Other witnesses in the trial indicate that Lady Howard had a history of consulting with cunning women, and an anonymous letter introduced in the proceedings stated that she was good friends with a Mrs. Thornborough who was "knowne to practice chimistrie much, and to make extractions, oynments powders and waters in great varietie: for what purpose god knowse."[25] It was also understood that Lady Howard had consulted the well-known conjurer Simon Forman for help with inhibiting the desires of her first husband Essex and winning the affections of her second husband Carr.[26] According to a reported deposition of Mrs. Forman, Mrs. Turner returned to their house after Forman's death and demanded several items, including a picture of wax and another of a naked woman. Several "Enchantments . . . written in Parchment" were shown to the court, including one fastened to "a little piece of the Skin of a Man." Some of the enchantments mentioned devils' names, who were to torment the Earl of Somerset and Anne Turner's lover, Sir Arthur Manwaring, if their "Loves should not continue." Anne Turner also, reportedly, confessed to consulting a Dr. Savories, who "practiced many Sorceries upon the Earl of Essex's Person," blaming both magic and women for Essex's supposed impotence.[27]

As several medical historians have noted, aristocratic women such as Lady Howard and Beatrice routinely learned medical therapies, which they applied to their families as well as their community.[28] Beatrice establishes her easy familiarity with physic when she praises DeFlores on his appearance and offers him her own medicinal treatment (as she works towards coercing him into killing for her):

BEATRICE: What ha' you done
  To your face alate? You've met some good physician;
  You've pruned yourself, methinks: you were not wont
  To look so amorously.
DEFLORES: Not I.
  'Tis the same physnomy to a hair and pimple
  Which she called scurvy scarce an hour ago:
  How is this?
BEATRICE: Come hither – nearer, man.
DEFLORES: I'm up to the chin in heaven.
BEATRICE: Turn, let me see –
  Faugh! 'Tis but the heat of the liver, I perceiv't;
  I thought it had been worse.
DEFLORES: Her fingers touched me –
  She smells all amber!
BEATRICE: I'll make a water for you shall cleanse this
  Within a fortnight.
DEFLORES: With your own hands, lady?
BEATRICE: Yes, mine own, sir: in a work of cure
  I'll trust no other.

(2.2.73–86)

While it seems doubtful that Beatrice has noted any improvement in DeFlores' complexion, she focuses on the state of his skin as a way of offering him the benefit of her therapeutic knowledge – knowledge common to women of her station. In her observation that DeFlores suffers from "heat of the liver," Beatrice also demonstrates a capacity for diagnoses. As noted above, her proposed cure – a special water for the skin – falls into a popular category of recipes found in various receipt books and books of secrets. Such waters usually required distilling a range of ingredients, and it was not unusual for women to house distilling equipment in their kitchens, alongside the simples they gathered from a garden and the more exotic ingredients they purchased at an apothecary.[29] As Beatrice makes clear, she regularly makes her own cures. Smelling of ambergris would have been customary as well, either from an oil (distilled in the household), or from a plague water (applied for protective purposes), or from a pomander worn about the neck or waist.[30] Such therapeutic knowledge, whether held by a "right physician," the lady of the house, or the local wise-woman, did not necessarily vary in its content.[31]

Inadvertently or not, Middleton and Rowley's portrayal of Beatrice's discovery of the book of secrets raises questions about the role of gender in knowledge-making. Beatrice penetrates her husband's private closet, discovers experiments he uses to know female bodies, and then carries out her own scientific trial in an endeavor to subvert his findings. Later when DeFlores indicates that Beatrice should have hired an apothecary's daughter to sleep with Alsemero, he insinuates that such a bed-mate would have the means, through secret recipes and methods, to fake her virginity (5.1.22). DeFlores' joke reiterates the same vexed issue: the knowledge of female secrets falls ostensibly under male authority (the apothecary father), yet women have access to this knowledge and the capacity to manipulate it.[32] One could argue that Beatrice's deception – from the moment she penetrates Alsemero's closet to her performance of virginal symptoms – demonstrates women's inability to uphold the social code necessary in the conduct of scientific experiments.[33] As Stephen Shapin has shown, an experimenter's gentlemanly status shaped the perceived truthfulness and empirical reality of his findings.[34] It is possible to interpret Beatrice's subterfuge as evidence that knowledge-making in the sciences is a masculine activity. And yet, as the intersection between receipt books and books of secrets suggests, the knowledge Alsemero seeks can also be construed as belonging to a feminine, domestic domain. Not only does Alsemero aim to detect, in the simplest sense, a woman's secret, but he also acknowledges the cultural association between closets, women, and secrets when he identifies Diaphanta as Beatrice's "cabinet," or the keeper of her clandestine knowledge.[35]

But if Beatrice initially rivals Alsemero in both knowledge and skill, her application of this knowledge ensures her downfall. Alsemero's inquiries into the secrets of nature make him vulnerable to Beatrice's trickery, but Beatrice's experimentation leads to her destruction. Beatrice experiments not only with the occult ingredients in Alsemero's cabinet but also with the hidden antipathies and sympathies that compel human relations.

Middleton and Rowley repeatedly equate the attraction and repulsions among people with the ingestion of cures and poisons. Not unlike Alice in *Arden of Faversham*, Beatrice's attractiveness has an uncanny, almost enchanting, effect on the men around her, which seems exacerbated by her virginal status. DeFlores describes her virginity not only as a reward for his crimes but also as a "sweet" substance that he has "drunk up," as if it had curative powers (5.3.169–71).[36] Alsemero characterizes his desire for Beatrice as unwilled and initially ominous (1.1.2). After encountering her, he abruptly changes his plans to go to sea, despite the favorable winds and propitious astrological signs that he would normally heed. His companion Jasperino proves puzzled, questioning his motives, "What might be the cause?" (40). Enraptured by Beatrice, Alsemero acknowledges that his hesitation to leave may stem from "some hidden malady / Within" that he "understand[s] not" (24–25). The play's most fervently passionate relationship – Beatrice's hatred of DeFlores and his obsessive longing for her – is defined most explicitly in occult terms, as an innate antipathy known only by its effects. In conversation with Alsemero, Beatrice describes her revulsion for DeFlores as an inexplicable "infirmity":

> Nor can I other reason render you
> Than his or hers, of some particular thing
> They must abandon as a deadly poison,
> Which to a thousand other tastes were wholesome:
> Such to mine eyes is that same fellow there,
> The same that report speaks of the basilisk.   (105–10)

A recurrent example in the catalogs of occult virtues, the mythical basilisk epitomized the natural antipathy between humans and serpents. DeFlores (or the deflowerer), who is often compared to a serpent, is the antipathetical contrary to the virginal Beatrice. Significantly, Beatrice acknowledges here that her hatred has no basis in manifest causes or rational reasons. Indeed, DeFlores himself insists that Beatrice "knows no cause" for her animosity towards him and attributes it to her "peevish will" (102). And yet willfulness fails to explain her sense that DeFlores is her particular poison.

Alsemero, whom we later learn is well versed in nature's secrets, explains that her response to DeFlores indicates that he is her natural antipathy:

> This is a frequent frailty in our nature;
> There's scarce a man amongst a thousand sound,
> But hath his imperfection: one distastes
> The scent of roses, which to infinites
> Most pleasing is, and odoriferous;
> One oil, the enemy of poison;
> Another wine, the cheerer of the heart
> And lively refresher of the countenance.
> Indeed this fault – if so it be – is general:
> There's scarce a thing but is both loved and loathed.   (111–20)

According to this logic, every man and woman has an imperfection or frailty in his or her nature that pulls back from its occult contrary, embedded somewhere in the webbed correspondences of hidden attractions and repulsions.[37] The scent of roses, a manifest quality, pleases most people; however, a few individuals possess an inherent property that responds negatively to the rose's occult virtues. Some even prove unable to stomach the usually curative qualities of wine and oil. In her flirtatious reply to Alsemero's analysis, Beatrice asks "And what may be your poison, sir?" Alsemero's answer, "What might be your desire, perhaps – a cherry" (122–23), teasingly suggests that she could be attracted to the very thing that he finds repulsive. Outstripping even her love for Alsemero is Beatrice's hatred for DeFlores, for "[t]his ominous, ill-faced fellow more disturbs [her] / Than all [her] other passions" (2.1.53–54). Her agitation and trembling in his presence signify the physical danger he poses to her. As Alsemero notes, DeFlores is Beatrice's poison, a role she underscores when she calls him viper (3.3.165), serpent (5.3.67), and standing toad-pool (2.1.58).

Lists of amities and contraries, of the kind that Alsemero references, often appear in books of secrets and natural magic. In representative fashion, Giambattista della Porta in *Natural Magick* writes:

> Hemlock and Rue are at enmity; they strive each against other . . . Much Rue being eaten, becometh poison; but the juice of Hemlock expels it; so that one poison poisoneth another . . . A Dog and a Wolfe are at great enmity; and therefore a Wolves skin put upon any one that is bitten of a mad Dog, asswageth the swelling of the humour . . . A Swine eats up a Salamander, without danger, and is good against the poison thereof . . . A Dog is most friendly to a man; and if you lay him to any diseased part of your body, he takes away the disease to himself.[38]

In attributing Beatrice's loathing of DeFlores to an occult cause – he is her specific, preternatural poison – Middleton and Rowley undermine any familiar sense of individual agency or intentionality. Beatrice does not choose, however willful she may be, to feel aversion for DeFlores. Nor does she mask perverse desire with revulsion. Some critics cite Beatrice's inexplicable hatred of DeFlores as repressed attraction, thus interpreting her passion in Freudian terms as a longing rooted in her unconscious, and such readings help make sense of the force of Beatrice's aversion to DeFlores.[39] But if we adhere to the early modern rationale of antipathies, Beatrice's hatred is a sign that DeFlores' physical presence poses a genuine threat to her well-being.

As discussed in the Introduction, contemporary writing on the passions indicates that certain emotions can only be explained by appealing to a language of inexplicable aversions and attractions based in occult qualities. Nicolas Coeffeteau in *A table of humane passions* (1621) explains how some feelings of hatred between men spring from these mysterious contraries in nature:

> naturall *Hatred* takes her beginning from a certaine antipathy, and contrariety of nature which is found in creatures, the which as it were abhorre one another, and cannot frequent or conuerse together, although the subiect of this *Hatred* appeare not, and that shewes it selfe more in the effect then in the cause; whereof wee haue prodigious examples in nature, in plants, in beasts, and in men.[40]

Although nature has mapped out these antipathies and sympathies, humans can only discern them through an experience of their effects. Early modern writers did not attribute these particular responses to the complexities of social relations. They identified them, instead, as derived from the secret nature of all organic matter – a world of particulars set in a network organized by occult likenesses and opposites. Plants may grow together out of hidden mutual sympathies for the same occult reasons that people may love one another. Albius invokes this reasoning in *The Changeling's* subplot when he wonders about his compatibility with such a young wife. Despite his manifest difference in age from Isabella, Albius speculates that they may have hidden attractive qualities: "Yet why may not this concord and sympathize? / Old trees and young plants often grow together, / Well enough agreeing." Lollio responds with a bawdy joke, "Ay, sir, but the old trees raise themselves higher and broader than the young plants" (1.2.21–25) underscoring the more observable, and socially regulated, differences between man and wife that make Albius anxious.

Some writers not only suggest that people, animals, and plants can encounter their poisonous enemies in nature as contrary counterparts, but also contend that one's antipathetical enemy can infect at a distance.[41] As the mystical writer Robert Fludd writes,

> The Cock doth Antipathetically abhorre the Fox. All Snakes and Adders do fear and fly from the Ashen-tree ... Also one blear-eyed person is able to infect another afar off by the secret emission of his contagious beames. We see that Onions draw teares from a person *ad distans*, by the emission of its beames. Again, we observe, that as like being wholsome and sound, doth commonly, by a Sympatheticall affection embrace his like; So also like being corrupted, doth Antipathetically, and that *ad distans* poyson and infect his like.[42]

Attractions and repulsions, hatred and love, invigoration and poison – they all operate at a distance – through the emission of beams. Encountering one's contrary in nature, in other words, can prove dangerously infectious even without direct contact. Moreover, Fludd proposes, once sympathetic entities are corrupted, they will infect other similar substances, thus producing a contagious chain of events.

We should understand that early modern writers are not simply suggesting that emotional antipathies function like poisons. They are arguing that an antipathy is a poison and that poisons are antipathies. As David Gentilcore has observed, "belief in the occult or hidden nature of poisons persisted" through the seventeenth century, "despite the beginnings of more experimental notions towards the secret arcana of nature." Dread of bewitchment and of poison were understood to be one and the same fear.[43] Many modern scholars do not fully comprehend how early modern writers explained poison and antidotes, for they are often quick to mark a distinction between a Paracelsian or homeopathic notion of "like cures like" and the Galenic argument that humoral balance is achieved through contraries.[44] But, in fact, Galen sought to cure poisonous infections with contraries *and* homeopathy.[45] Usually, it was argued, poison did not affect the body with manifest qualities of heat and cold but impinged on the whole substance, producing an occult effect.

Antidotes to poisons operated on occult qualities as well.[46] In one tradition, epitomized in Galen's theriac, poison was extracted by poison, by way of similitude or sympathy. Hence, a key ingredient in theriac was viper flesh. As Ambroise Paré explains, theriac draws out poison as the lodestone draws iron:

> There be some who thinke it not fit to lay treacle [theriac] thereto, because, as they say, it drives the poyson in. But the authority of *Galen* convinceth that opinion, for he writeth that if treacle be applyed to this kind of wounds before that the venome shall arrive at the noble parts, it much conduceth. Also reason confutes it; for vipers flesh enters the composition of treacle which attracts the venome by the similitude of substance, as the Load-stone draweth iron, or Amber strawes.[47]

In a similar vein, Philip Barrough observes that

> *theriaca*, and such like medicines against poison doe not worke their operation by driuing the poison from them (as they being in a wonderfull errour doe affirme) but rather they worke by drawing the poyson to them (as Galene teacheth, in his booke *de theriaca ad pisonem*).[48]

Hence, the secret sympathies and antipathies that draw together and repel various animals, plants, and humans are the basis for nature's provision of antidotes. When poisoned, animals preternaturally know how to locate their own cures because they are drawn to the remedying plant, as Pliny observes:

> The Elephant if he chance to let the [Lizard] Chameleon go downe his throat amongst other herbes or leaues (which this Lizard alwaies is like vnto in colour) he goeth straightwaies to the wild Oliue, the only remedie he hath of this poyson. Beares, when they haue eaten Mandrage apples, licke vp Pismires to cure themselues withall. The Stag and Hind feeling themselues poysoned with some venomous weed among grasse where they pasture, goe by and by to the Artichoke, and therewith cure themselues.[49]

The complex question of whether a poison's antidote functions as a sympathetic or antipathetic process frames Hugh Plat's description of the bezoar or bezar stone in the 1653 edition of *The jewel house of art and nature,* a popular book of secrets. Noting that the bezar is "of excellent virtue against poison," Plat explains its supposed origins:

> The stone is taken out of a beast in India much like a Hart . . . The occasion of this stones growing, some write to be this: This beast going down to the den of Serpents, doth with his breath compel them to comeforth, and then eats them; then he goes and plungeth himself into water till he perceiveth the fury of the venome to be past, and all then they will not drink a drop; after this, they feed upon many healthy herbs known to them upon natural instinct, to be of virtue against poyson, and by the mixture of these herbs with the Serpents eaten before, these Bezar stones are very strangely engendered within them.[50]

The curative properties of the bezar stone develop from a layered process in which the venom and healthy herbs ingested by the beast counteract one another in the production of a secret virtue. Since the stone contains both poison and its contrary, it is difficult to say whether its antidotal properties stem from antipathetic or sympathetic action. But as Frances Herring observes, most argue that "by similitude of substance," poison is expulsed "by the attractiue virtue" of an applied poison.[51]

As the object of Alsemero's affections and DeFlores' obsession, Beatrice initially appears to possess a fascinating or magnetic quality that draws men to her, identified with her fetishized virginity and her marriageability. But like Lady Howard, Beatrice's power also lies in her knowledge of nature's secrets: knowledge that undergirds the mixing of waters, potions, and salves. Howard purportedly demonstrated her capacity to outstrip the local apothecary with her expertise in poisons, much in the same way that Beatrice usurps Alsemero's closet. And just as Howard presumably orchestrated Overbury's death for her own political and personal advantage, Beatrice develops a plot in which she arranges the murder of her fiancé Alonzo in order to devise a marriage to Alsemero. But it is her knowledge of occult qualities that frames her plan, for she intends to use one "poison" to drive out the other. When seeking a solution to her marriage problem, Beatrice's thoughts shift to DeFlores: "The ugliest creature / Creation framed for some use . . . / Why men of art make much of poison, / Keep one to expel another. Where was my art?" (2.2.43–47). Identifying herself with men of art who understand the sympathetic nature of poisons and antidotes, Beatrice implies that she has the skill and experience to execute a plan that relies on the same principles. While the distinction appears to be that she metaphorically deploys a person-as-a-poison to eradicate another person-as-a-poison, Middleton and Rowley repeatedly characterize DeFlores as a walking, human poison. While Beatrice threatens to be another Lady Howard – a woman whose uncanny body and occult knowledge could prove potentially dangerous to all the men around her – her decision to deploy DeFlores as a poison backfires, for he succeeds, instead, in poisoning her.

We can, of course, argue that Beatrice poisons herself morally as soon as she decides to use DeFlores as her instrument in murder. She seems naively to believe that by using DeFlores as her weapon in Alonzo's murder, she has preserved her innocence. More particularly, she imagines that the social disparity between herself and DeFlores shields her from the crimes she has commissioned: "Think but upon the distance that creation / Set 'twixt thy blood and mine, and keep thee there" (3.3.130–31). DeFlores argues, in response, that employing his services has altered her irrevocably. Indeed, he insists that she has become just like him – his "equal" and his twin:

> Look but into your conscience, read me there –
> 'Tis a true book, you'll find me there your equal.
> Push! Fly not to your birth, but settle you
> In what the act has made you, you're no more now;
> You must forget your parentage to me –
> You're the deed's creature: by that name
> You lost your first condition; and I challenge you,
> As peace and innocency has turned you out
> And made you one with me. (132–40)

As DeFlores tells it, Beatrice has reenacted the fall. In the same way that Eve alienated herself from her "first condition" by eating the apple, Beatrice's deed has divided her from "peace and innocency." In his final statement, just before the rape, DeFlores maintains that she will "love anon / What thou so fear'st and faint'st to venture on" (169–70).[52] Her antipathy, in other words, will become her likeness, or her sympathy. By Act 5, the transformation appears complete when Beatrice exclaims that she feels "forced to love [him] now" (5.1.48).

Beatrice conceives of her fall as the moment she must "engender with a viper" (3.3.165), suggesting that DeFlores poisons her when he takes her virginity. At the end of the play, Beatrice exclaims that her blood has been tainted, both literally and metaphorically. Bleeding from the fatal wound that DeFlores inflicted, she warns her father to keep away from her with the admonition that her blood will contaminate him:

> O come not near me, sir, I shall defile you:
> I am that of your blood was taken from you
> For your better health; look no more upon't,
> But cast it to the ground regardlessly,
> Let the common sewer take it from distinction.   (5.3.149–53)

Without question, she speaks to the moral corruption she has brought to their aristocratic lineage, as well as the heated blood of lustful passions, but she also intends to save Vermandero from a physical poisoning.

And yet, we can also argue that DeFlores begins to poison Beatrice at-a-distance even before she engages his services. Middleton and Rowley indicate that DeFlores radiates an occult poison, potentially infecting others in his company. This is most explicitly suggested in Tomazo's intimations of danger in DeFlores' presence. He identifies his sudden revulsion towards DeFlores as a "contrariety in nature" (5.2.13), a phrase often used to describe a hidden antipathy. Tomazo then characterizes him as

>   so foul
> One would scarce touch him with a sword he loved
> And made account of; so most deadly venomous,
> He would go near to poison any weapon
> That would draw blood on him – one must resolve
> Never to use that sword again in fight,
> In a way of honest manhood, that strikes him;
> Some river must devour it, 'twere not fit
> That any man should find it. What again?
> He walks a-purpose by, sure, to choke me up,
> To infect my blood.   (15–25)

Although modern audiences may hear these assertions as merely the fantastical thoughts of a grieving brother, Tomazo's logic has its precedents in early modern writings on antipathetical effects. Not only does Tomazo suggest that DeFlores is a preternatural embodiment of poison, but he also echoes Fludd's assertions that an antipathy or a poison can corrupt or infect a person without contact. Tomazo imagines that any sword used on DeFlores would absorb his venomous quality, changing it from a simple weapon to one with assuredly deadly effects. Honorable swordsmen would be compelled to drown such a blade to avoid undue advantage in a fight. He fears that DeFlores walks close to him with the "purpose" of choking him up and infecting his blood (24–25).

At her death, Beatrice identifies DeFlores as a meteor, a sublunary phenomenon associated with prophecy and contamination (5.3.154).[53] In this moment she realizes that her initial loathing of DeFlores was a premonition that he would be her demise. If DeFlores can willfully poison others at-a-distance, as Tomazo suspects, then it is possible that Beatrice became infected before she enlisted him as her deputy in murder. Certainly her characterization of DeFlores in the early parts of the play associates him with poison: as we noted earlier, she has called him a basilisk, a serpent, and a standing toad-pool. His presence to her is "ominous" and "disturbs" her more "than all [her] other passions." Merely seeing him brings her thoughts "of some harm towards" herself. "Danger" lingers in her mind, so that she can "scarce leave trembling of an hour after" he leaves her (2.1.90–91). DeFlores acknowledges that Beatrice cannot "abide the sight" of him, "as if danger, or ill luck hung in [his] looks" (35–36). As the reference to the basilisk indicates, *seeing* plays a crucial role in instances of poisoning at-a-distance. In the same way that a "the louer sendeth côtinuall beames of the eie towards that which he loueth," DeFlores yearns to be in Beatrice's line of vision.[54] Despite being repeatedly spurned, he is determined to follow her and vex her, forcing errands to "come into her sight" (31). Even when chastised for haunting her, he declares "I must see her still" (78).

As Beatrice's specific poison, DeFlores finds himself drawn to her sound, healthy, and uncontaminated body and spirit. Robert Fludd argues that nothing "operateth more Antipathetically, and contrary to nature . . . than the corruption of an empoysoned or infected spirit, doth with a wholesome spirit of his like Species" for the reason that the poisonous spirit seeks "help and succor in its distress from the sound spirits."[55] As noted above, DeFlores describes his satisfaction in taking Beatrice's honor as if it were a health-giving or "sweet" substance that he has "drunk up." While the occult qualities of her virginity provide him with relief, his spirit converts her into the very poison she sought to escape.[56]

Even if we blame DeFlores for plaguing Beatrice with his constant presence, we must also consider his theory that Beatrice may have a natural appetite for poison. He imagines successfully attaining her for the very reason that all women have aberrant or wayward appetites. Drawing on the commonplace equation between an appetite for food and sexual desire, he refers to some instances in which women willingly opt for "Slovenly dishes":

> Hunger and pleasure, they'll commend sometimes
> Slovenly dishes, and feed heartily on 'em –
> Nay, which is stranger, refuse daintier for 'em.
> Some women are odd feeders   (2.2.150–53)

DeFlores invokes early modern characterizations of women, suffering from various uterine disorders, driven to eat strange things. Books of wonders tell stories of pregnant women compelled to eat human flesh – sometimes their husband's, sometimes their neighbor's.[57] Others with child would

> haue eate nothing but earth, ashes and coales of the harth, plaster pulled out of the walles, salt-peter in sellers, Snailes, Frogges, Peares, Apples, and Plummes not halfe ripe, and when their desire hath not beene fully satisfied, their Children have suffred for it.[58]

Similar appetites affected virgins afflicted with greensickness, who often suffered from a form of pica, eating chalk or clay. Most writers explain these unnatural appetites with the argument that obstructed menstrual blood or other crude humors are essentially poisoning the body from within. Since "similar seek out similar," women hunger for equally venomous substances.[59] While some writers suggest that the women should be restricted from eating odd materials, Levinus Lemnius states that he does not "deny to them that desire such things ... I let them use their own desire so far as I am confident it will not hurt them, and I conjecture the disease may be batter'd by it ... So we drive forth one disease with another."[60] Lemnius' view implies that not unlike animals, who instinctively seek out natural antidotes to the poisons they have ingested, greensick women eat strange substances to counter their body's production of poison. In other words, Beatrice's virginal body may house secret, occult qualities known only by the observable effects of her behavior.

When Beatrice decides to use DeFlores as a poison to drive out another poison, she alludes to the healing practices, which she calls a masculine art. Her goal, of course, is not to heal anyone but to rid herself of both Alonzo and DeFlores. But if curing with poison is a masculine art, many early modern spectators would readily associate simple poisoning with women's secrets. Whether or not they were identified as witches, ordinary women, it was thought, could emit poison with their breath or their eyes (often due to disordered menstruation).[61] And as the household members who performed most of the bodywork, women were presumed to have an experiential knowledge of both poisons and cures.[62]

Beatrice achieves her goal, in that DeFlores kills Alonzo. What she cannot control, however, is DeFlores' uncanny influence on her. As Beatrice's natural contrary, DeFlores seems to exist in the world of *The Changeling* for the purpose of either contaminating her (and engendering her sins), or punishing her with "poison" for the sins she commits on her own. DeFlores' occult nature may indicate that he is an otherworldly creature, perhaps the mysterious "changeling" of the play's title.[63] As anthropologists observe, changelings served an important cultural function in early modern society. In the face of developmental disabilities, for example, some parents believed their natural child had been replaced by a fairy. In certain cases of infanticide, parents had labored to compel the return of their true child by starving or abusing the changeling child. A difficult infant could be seen as a scapegoat of sorts, and the object of deep antipathy, who brought danger and disorder into the home.[64]

Changelings were thought to result from an exchange between the visible, natural world and an unseen world, and explained otherwise inexplicable events in the natural world, such as a baby who failed to thrive. It is possible to view DeFlores as a changeling creature – not an infant, of course, but a mature source of disorder and transformation who infects Beatrice's household.[65] In poisoning Beatrice and alienating her from her father's blood, DeFlores transforms his former contrary into his twin – or into another changeling. But if, as DeFlores hints, Beatrice's aberrant, female appetite drove her to seek out poison, then the cause of her downfall stems not from a separate fairy world but from a secret sympathy or antipathy hidden in her body. Middleton and Rowley do not invite the audience to feel sympathy for Beatrice, for she is a fallen woman whose contagious blood threatens to infect others. *The Changeling* suggests, instead, that to feel sympathy in a world of hidden occult forces is a dangerous enterprise.

CHAPTER 5

"To think there's power in potions": experiment, sympathy, and the devil in The Duchess of Malfi

The range of interpretive questions evoked by John Webster's *The Duchess of Malfi* is vast. Some of the topics critics perennially debate include the heroic and moral status of the Duchess, the construction of privacy, the significance of remarriage, and the representation of female subjectivity.[1] Two questions, in particular, have produced varied responses: Why is Ferdinand so deeply disturbed by his sister's private life? And what engenders his lycanthropy?[2] Notably, Frank Whigham has argued that Ferdinand is driven by an incestuous inclination that compensates for a more desperate, aristocratic desire to "evade degrading associations with inferiors."[3] His lycanthropy brings him to "his logical end in total isolation . . . in an inward hair shirt, he is finally *sui generis*."[4] Lynn Enterline pinpoints the crisis not in a crumbling aristocracy but in Ferdinand's fragile masculinity; unable to tolerate his twin sister's difference or her likeness, his lycanthropy is an extreme form of melancholia that marks his self-alienation.[5] Both of these readings, however, understand Ferdinand and his afflictions in modern, secular terms, failing to acknowledge in the play what Albert Tricomi has identified as an exploration of "the function of the unseen world of spirit in human affairs."[6] Webster, I will argue, situates Ferdinand's drive to discover his sister's secrets within a discourse that not only affirms the potential interference of witches and demons but also invokes the natural philosophical goal of uncovering nature's secrets.

Historians have debated whether assumptions about women's experiential knowledge of the secrets of nature played a role in witchcraft accusations in the period. Some scholars have argued that witches emerge when a community expresses anxiety about the management of the household or motherhood.[7] Since women were the people who most visibly and routinely tended to bodies, they were easily caught in the cultural link between "magical healing and maleficent harming."[8] Although not explicitly about witches, *The Duchess of Malfi* presents a society in which women's everyday knowledge – of recipes, cures, or their own bodies – is regularly associated with witchcraft.[9] Moreover, it portrays men seized with the attendant fear that women's bodies could exercise an uncanny power over their own.[10]

At the time of Webster's play, the idea of controlled scientific experiments, which produced replicable and verifiable data, had not yet emerged in natural philosophy. Experiential knowledge or experience, however, was undergoing rapid changes in meaning and status during this time, establishing a foundation for the experimental science to come. While the earliest conceptions of experiment were associated with legitimizing specific recipes or remedies, experiential knowledge took a variety of forms. Experience could be accidental or gained through the methodical study of something. Moreover, it could be an understanding acquired through a trial or test aimed at proving or disproving a conjecture.[11] Although not equivalent to experimental science, these acts of manipulating nature (often the practices of housewives, artisans, distillers, or apothecaries) not only produced knowledge but also contributed to the development of scientific activities.[12] Despite a shared history, the definition of elite scientific experimentation in the late seventeenth century depended on its differentiation from everyday practices.

Well before the emergence of scientific experimentation, however, early seventeenth-century natural philosophy demonstrates its investment in delineating legitimate and illegitimate methods for producing natural knowledge. Webster's tragedy, I will argue, participates in this boundary work. Invoking the cultural commonplace that both women and nature hide their secrets, Webster frames women's bodies as central objects of inquiry.[13] Indeed, Ferdinand's efforts to discover his sister's secrets are staged as an inquisition that mingles the discourses and practices of proto-scientific experimentation, natural magic, and demonology, thus capturing the relative lack of epistemological demarcations in the period.[14] Since "scientists" examine and provoke the same occult forces that demons deploy, they could unknowingly engage malign spirits. Webster suggests that it is Ferdinand's attempts to plague his sister with "art," or *maleficium*, which results in his contracting lycanthropy. His disease proves an apt punishment for a man who foolishly believes he can manipulate nature without the devil's participation.[15]

In Act 3, scene 1, Bosola and Ferdinand debate the impetus of the Duchess's secret actions. Unable to rationalize why she would marry below her social rank, Bosola suggests that she has been compelled by sorcery. Ferdinand responds with what appears to be a skeptical view, dismissive of the possibility that herbs, potions, and charms can move the will. Any witchcraft at work here, he argues, lies in her rank blood. For Ferdinand, his sister's sinful and base desires are morally equivalent to sorcery:

BOSOLA: I do suspect, there hath been some sorcery
   Us'd on the Duchess.
FERDINAND: Sorcery! to what purpose?
BOSOLA: To make her dote on some desertless fellow,
   She shames to acknowledge.
FERDINAND: Can your faith give way
   To think there's power in potions, or in charms,
   To make us love whether we will or no?
BOSOLA: Most certainly.
FERDINAND: Away, these are mere gulleries, horrid things
   Invented by some cheating mountebanks,
   To abuse us. Do you think that herbs, or charms
   Can force the will? Some trials have been made
   In the foolish practice, but the ingredients
   Were lenative poisons, such as are of force
   To make the patient mad; and straight the witch
   Swears by equivocation, they are in love.
   The witchcraft lies in her rank blood.

$$(3.1.63–78)^{16}$$

This debate identifies the Duchess's emotions and behavior as secret, aberrant, and incompatible with ready categories of understanding. Moreover, Ferdinand and Bosola put occult qualities and their powers at the center of an epistemological investigation. Bosola articulates a belief in the possibility that certain people (men or women) have sufficient knowledge of the occult properties of herbs to prepare charms and potions that will move the affections of others. As we shall see, women in the play are most consistently associated with knowledge of the sympathies and antipathies in ingredients. Ferdinand's position alludes to the contemporary controversies over the limits and powers of witches; in his view, they have the capacity to poison but they are unable to produce recipes or charms that move the will. Ferdinand seems to articulate an empiricist methodology. He insists on the weakness of sorcery based on reports of a contrived trial, in which someone other than the witches tested the nature of these potions by observing their effects in an experimental vein. As Sir Francis Bacon argued, "superstitious narrations of sorceries [and] witchcrafts" should be included in the examination of natural causes, not only to determine the exact "offences" of those practicing but also "for the further disclosing of nature."[17] But Ferdinand's insistence that love potions cannot accomplish what the witches intend, and produce instead only frenzy in their victims, also echoes Johanus Weyer's argument in *De praestigiis daemonum*, who maintains that all supposedly magical love potions "stir up frenzy" rather than love.[18] Famously, Weyer discounted the power of witches – specifically female witches. He argued that women's naturally weak and melancholic condition made them innately vulnerable to the devil's illusions. For Weyer, female witches have no knowledge of nature's secrets, and any power they claim is exclusively the work of the devil.

In a play filled with demonological references, as Tricomi has demonstrated, it is striking that Ferdinand neglects to acknowledge the devil's expertise in nature's secrets.[19] Almost all early modern writers would concede that the demonological manipulation of potions, charms, and herbs could move a person's affections. Indeed the very danger posed by the trial that Ferdinand describes is the potential intrusion of demons. Bacon urges experimentalists to separate "from *Superstitious* and *Magical Arts* and *Observation*, any thing that is cleane and pure naturall." Evidence of witchcraft has to be weighed carefully, he warnes, for the very reason "that [their effects] may be by a *Tacite Operation* of *Malign Spirits*."[20] Witchcraft narratives could prove helpful thought-experiments, but it was never advisable to experiment with witchcraft itself.[21] For the reformist writer William Perkins, charms and potions were often efficacious but those who used them had been unknowingly ensnared by the devil:

> superstitious persons, men or women, as vse Charmes and Inchantment for the effecting of any thing vpon a superstitious and erroneous perswasion, that the Charmes haue vertue in them to doe such things, not knowing that it is the action of the deuill by those meanes; but thinking that God hath put vertue into them, as hee hath done into hearbs for Physicke.[22]

Superstition for Perkins, and many writers in the period, is not a foolish belief in witchcraft but the ignorant assumption that people have the capacity to effect or produce certain actions in nature that can only be ascribed to the devil.[23]

Both Bosola and Ferdinand could be accused of superstition for the simple reason that they neglect to acknowledge the devil's participation in acts that look like sorcery. But Ferdinand's omission of the devil, combined with his unconsidered equation between the effects of theater (gulleries achieved by cheating mountebanks) and the effects of witches' poisons, anticipates his own foolish dabbling in witchcraft practices. Not only does Ferdinand ignore the possibility of demonic intervention but he also neglects to grant what witches can accomplish with their potions and herbs. Even if they cannot direct a person's affections, their ingredients can induce madness, which undermines the victim's will. It is ironic that the very man who degenerates into a frenzy potentially caused by occult forces overlooks the significance of this power.

And yet Ferdinand's ascription of witchcraft to the Duchess's blood not only attributes her behavior to sexual corruption but also alludes to the pervasive notion that dangerous occult properties could reside in women's bodies, particularly in their menstrual blood, their eyes, and their breath. Even Weyer grants that the "fetid breath [of] old women can sometimes" inadvertently "infect those of tender years whom they handle."[24] Although Ferdinand does not attribute great knowledge to witches, he insists that any woman has the potential to degenerate into a witch. In an earlier scene, Ferdinand maintains that the mildest acts of immorality can instigate this transformation: "be not cunning," he warns his sister, "For they whose faces do belie their hearts, / Are witches, ere they arrive at twenty years, / Ay: and give the devil suck" (1.2.229–32).

Further complicating our view of Ferdinand's position on witchcraft are his veiled references to his own experience with the occult virtues of herbs. In the scene that precedes his conversation with Bosola, he describes his discovery of the Duchess's sexual activity as akin to digging up a mandrake root. Webster does not clarify whether Ferdinand intends his statement, "I have this night digg'd up a mandrake ... And I am grown mad with't," literally or metaphorically (2.5.1–3). But the dominant effect of the mandrake, according to most medical texts, is its soporific powers, which may explain why it is Ferdinand's strange desire to sleep that terminates his bitter ranting in this scene.[25] Moreover, the mandrake root was known as an herb employed by witches, for it was thought to achieve the very results that Ferdinand describes in the trials of lenitive poisons. As William Bullein writes in *Bulleins bulwarke of defence against all sicknesse* (1579):

> of Mandrack, whych in old tyme, it was called *Circaeum*, of Wytches, whych had vertue (sayd they) or craft to transforme, both man beast, and herbe out of kynde. Among all other, they wrought Wonders by this herbe, to prouoke, bewitch, or cast men into mad blynd fantasies, or [frenzies], called Loue, whych rather may be termed, noysome beastly Lust, and when it is wrought by herbes, foolishnesse.[26]

While it remains unclear whether the mandrake has contributed to Ferdinand's madness, the Cardinal's assessment of his brother's behavior indicates that Ferdinand's intemperate response to his sister's duplicity is unusual. For many critics, Ferdinand's tirade can only be explained by ascribing his passions to a hidden desire: either he longs for his sister's body, or he desires the pre-Oedipal connection he shared with her as a twin. But for early modern audiences, the occult causes of Ferdinand's madness would not be solely psychological. In addition to wondering if the mandrake has affected him, spectators would take seriously Ferdinand's fear that his sister's supposedly tainted blood could literally poison him. Ferdinand's impulse to purge the Duchess's "infected blood" (26) is epitomized in the wild impulse to "kill her now" in himself and in the Cardinal (64–65). The deferred revelation of their twinship may also imply that Ferdinand's lunacy is a symptom of a disrupted sympathetic bond. And when the Cardinal compares the wild "tempest" of his brother's rage to "men convey'd by witches through the air / On violent whirlwinds" (51–52), the analogy affirms belief in the ever-present influence of witches and demons. Acknowledging that Ferdinand's behavior may be prompted by preternatural forces does not disallow incest as a hidden cause, but it shifts the origins of such desires away from modern psychological categories.

Since the torture and murder of the Duchess attest to Ferdinand's violent domination, we may be inclined to overlook his profound fear of his sister. Her willfulness does not just ruin his reputation or bring him in contact with "degrading . . . inferiors," but it also proves threatening, he believes, to his own well-being.[27] When he surprises the Duchess in her closet, his behavior betrays confusion – he wants to torture her and her husband, but he also dreads the "violent effects" of confrontation (3.2.95). Though initially bent on discovery, Ferdinand refuses to see Antonio, wishing instead that he could change eyes with the deadly basilisk (87–88). This wish is soon followed by his vow never to look on his sister again (137). While he may intend this pledge as a moral judgment, his dazzled eyes at her death indicate that merely looking at the Duchess feels hazardous to him.[28] When she pleads to live freely on the basis of her youth and beauty, his retort suggests that her powers are hidden and dangerous: "So you have some virgins / That are witches" (140–41).

When they discuss whether herbs or charms can move the will, neither Bosola nor Ferdinand identify the practice of sorcery or witchcraft explicitly with women; however, as Wendy Wall has observed, the play does regularly allude to women's expertise in the mixing of waters, antidotes, and cures. When wooing Antonio, the Duchess refers to the curative properties of gold. Once Antonio circulates the rumor that Bosola has poisoned his wife, he avoids bringing in a physician by alluding to the Duchess's well-known skill in concocting her own antidotes. Cariola's analogy that she will guard the Duchess's secrets in the same way one keeps poison from children gestures to the shared space of apothecaries and housewives.[29] While Wall acknowledges that domestic receipt knowledge is uncanny, she does not attend to the way Webster blurs the boundaries between domesticity and witchcraft.[30] But in a scene that many critics treat as digressive, Bosola attacks the household's resident "Old Lady" (who may be the Duchess's midwife) for storing suspicious and unnatural ingredients in her closet:

OLD LADY: It seems you are well acquainted with my closet?
BOSOLA: One would suspect it for a shop of witchcraft, to find in it the fat of
    serpents; spawn of snakes, Jews' spittle, and their young children's ordure,
    and all these for the face. I would sooner eat a dead pigeon, taken from the
    soles of the feet of one sick of the plague, than kiss one of you fasting.

                                                                  (2.1.36–43)

While Bosola intends to shock and expresses disgust with his list of materials that the Old Lady supposedly mixes into her cosmetic washes and unguents, audience members would know that the actual substances people used in recipes (found in kitchens, closets, and apothecary shops) were not entirely distinct from this list.[31] The application of animal dung was commonplace, as well as derivatives of lizards and serpents. One's apothecary might offer human fat or human skulls, or such odd (from a modern view) ingredients as the bark of mandrake or a stag's pizzle.[32] In referring to the curative measure of placing flayed pigeons on a patient's feet, Bosola obliquely reminds us that many of these medicinal and therapeutic practices depended on hidden sympathies and antipathies.[33] But Bosola's diatribe demonstrates how easily women's domestic knowledge could be conflated with illicit or dangerous practices.[34] It is the shared foundational knowledge of nature's hidden sympathies and antipathies (more than the strangeness of any particular ingredient) that makes this conflation possible.

Despite his condemnation of the Old Lady's supposed practices, Bosola does not dismiss her as a viable source of knowledge on women's secrets. Suspicious that the Duchess is pregnant, Bosola aims to produce symptomatic and observable effects of her condition through a physical experiment, calling it a "pretty" trick, reminiscent of the language found in books of secrets:

> I observe our Duchess
> Is sick a-days, she pukes, her stomach seethes,
> The fins of her eyelids look most teeming blue,
> She wanes i'th' cheek, and waxes fat i'th' flank;
> And, contrary to our Italian fashion,
> Wears a loose-bodied gown: there's somewhat in't.
> I have a trick, may chance discover it,
> A pretty one; I have bought some apricocks,
> The first our spring yields.   (66–74)

He subjects the Duchess to a trial founded on notions of aberrant female appetites.[35] Baiting her first with apricots, he then attempts to turn her stomach with his claim that they grew in dung. But even with the eye-witness notes he has gathered, Bosola remains uncertain that his hypothesis is correct. To confirm his conclusion, Bosola consults with the Old Lady, asking her to verify that the Duchess's "techiness and most vulturous eating" of apricots are "apparent signs" of breeding (2.2.1–3). He may attack the Old Lady for being a kind of witch, but he is willing to draw on her receipt knowledge, as well as her familiarity with women's bodies, to ascertain the Duchess's secrets.

Not only does Bosola indicate belief in the efficacy of receipt knowledge – specifically female receipt knowledge – but his ensuing mockery of the Old Lady also inadvertently suggests that male-dominated fields of knowledge are unable to access the secrets of women. When the Old Lady attempts to rebuff Bosola, he launches into an anecdote of glass-making that castigates women for their ignorance and excessive appetites:

BOSOLA: There was a young waiting-woman, had a monstrous desire to see the glass-house –
OLD LADY: Nay, pray let me go:
BOSOLA: And it was only to know what strange instrument it was, should swell up a glass to the fashion of a woman's belly.
OLD LADY: I will hear no more of the glass-house, you are still abusing women!

(5–12)

The Old Lady is, in part, correct that Bosola aims to abuse women. The waiting-woman he describes is driven by a monstrous desire to see the male instrument that would make a woman pregnant, suggesting not only that she has little understanding of breeding but also that her sexual desires are unnatural and prodigious.[36] But beyond the insult, Bosola has shifted the topic away from a domestic, effeminate sphere to a more masculine and proto-scientific realm of secret knowledge – glass-making. Glass-making in England was recognized as a craft with its own technological secrets.[37] To blow glass was to experiment, or to intervene in nature, and well before the Royal Society staged experiments glass-blowers staged their techniques for the public. Across the garden from the Blackfriars Theatre, which had presented *The Duchess of Malfi*, stood a working glass-house where spectators may have stopped after a performance.[38]

While the alchemical lab remained behind closed doors, and the scientific lab had yet to materialize, glass-houses were public places of

A—Blow-pipe. B—Little window. C—Marble. D—Forceps. E—Moulds by means of which the shapes are produced.

Figure 2 *Opera di Giorgio Agricola de l'arte de metalli* (Basel, 1563), Rare Book Collection, Wilson Library, University of North Carolina at Chapel Hill

experiment, commercial activity, production, magic, and performance.[39] But for Bosola, the glass-house story functions as a fantasy in which a proto-scientific practice would make women's secrets transparent. If the Duchess's belly were made of glass, then Bosola would not be forced to consult receipt books or old ladies. Indeed, Bosola reveals his effeminized position in the anecdote itself, for his desire to know who fathered the Duchess's child casts him as the foolish waiting-woman.

Throughout the play, this kind of rhetorical move (in which Webster's male characters cite advancements in technology or new knowledge) typically devolves into a joke about the failure to uncover the secrets either of women or of nature. The Cardinal, for example, alludes to glass-making and the telescope when he critiques women's inconstancy:

> A man might strive to make glass malleable,
> Ere he should make them [women] fixed.
> . . .
> We had need go borrow that fantastic glass
> Invented by Galileo the Florentine,
> To view another spacious world i'th' moon,
> And to look to find a constant woman there. (2.4.14–19)

Echoing Bosola's complaint that we still lack the proper spectacles to read what is written in the stars, the Cardinal diminishes the usefulness of Galileo's glass to protest that nothing can ensure the constancy of a woman. The mad Ferdinand invokes the dissections performed in the "Barber-Chirurgeons' Hall" when he threatens to "flay off" the physician's skin to "cover one of the anatomies" the physician "hath set i'th' cold" (5.2.75–77). As Katharine Park has argued, the early modern anatomist marked the ultimate translation of authority, in which the secret knowledge of therapies and cures long known to women gave way to male authority over the female body and its supposed secrets. The anatomized woman on the title page of Vesalius' *De Humani corporis fabrica* (who had claimed pregnancy, much like Cariola does, to avoid torture or death) reveals nature's ultimate secret – the uterus – to everyone's gaze.[40] Consequently, for Vesalius, the "principal secret of women was that the uterus held no secrets at all."[41] But for Webster, the anatomists reveal little more than the violence of their methods.

Ferdinand's confessed interest in the experiments conducted to test the efficacy of witchcraft should frame our interpretation of the odd trials he has the Duchess undergo when he imprisons her. If we consider Ferdinand's contrived tortures as fledgling experiments, then Bosola functions as the technician in his ventures.[42] Constrained in part by a gentlemanly bias toward contemplation over action, Ferdinand fits Steven Shapin's description of the proto-scientist who hired technicians to perform the physical tasks of an experiment.[43] When initially appointed by Ferdinand to spy on the Duchess, Bosola refers to himself as an "intelligencer"– a term that has both political and natural philosophical connotations (1.2.182). In *The Advancement of Learning*, Bacon associates the court spy with experimental effects: just as the political "secretaries and spials of princes" bring in secret information so must the experimenter allow the "spials and intelligencers of nature to bring in their bills."[44] The barriers between theoretical knowledge and mechanical knowledge were breaking down in the seventeenth century (following Bacon's promotion that they should). And yet, the relative distance that Ferdinand establishes between himself and his sister through his employment of a proxy also connotes the demonological action-at-a-distance achieved by witchcraft, as indicated by the other title Bosola gives himself – "a familiar," or a "very quaint invisible devil in flesh" (180–81).

Simultaneously invoking the theatrical tricks he ascribed to cheating mountebanks and the witches' charms that aimed to force the will, Ferdinand attempts to provoke the Duchess with what the stage directions in 4.1 identify as a "dead man's hand" and the "artificial figures of Antonio and his children, appearing as if they were dead." After observing her distressed reactions, he pronounces the effects "Excellent; as I would wish: she's plagued in art" (4.1.110–11). Ferdinand's language echoes Bacon's assertion in *The Advancement of Learning* (1605) that we discern a man's true self under duress in the same way that "the passages and variations cannot appear so fully in the liberty of nature, as in the trials and vexations of art."[45] Bacon restates this theme in *Novum Organum* (1620), reiterating the point that the secrets of nature and the secret affections reveal themselves when vexed:

> For even as in the business of life a man's disposition and the secret workings of his mind and affections are better discovered when he is in trouble than at other times; so likewise the secrets of nature reveal themselves more readily under the vexations of art than when they go their own way.[46]

As historians of science have noted, Bacon's conception of experiment transformed how natural philosophers sought knowledge: "Under Bacon's urgings the student of Nature was to participate actively, to *force* things into previously non-existent configurations in order to see how they behaved."[47] Although Ferdinand had dismissed the witches' foolish practices as ineffective (since they failed to move their victims to love), he adopts now what he had learned from the experimental trial that followed.

He initiates his trials by having Bosola observe the Duchess's behavior and report his findings to him. Bosola describes her conduct as impassive and somewhat inscrutable:

> She's sad, as one long us'd to't, and she seems
> Rather to welcome the end of misery
> Than shun it: a behaviour so noble,
> As gives a majesty to adversity:
> You may discern the shape of loveliness
> More perfect in her tears, than in her smiles:
> She will muse four hours together: and her silence,
> Methinks, expresseth more than if she spake. (4.1.3–10)

It is with frustration that Ferdinand concludes that her "melancholy seems to be fortifi'd / With a strange disdain" (11–12). With the pronouncement that he "will no longer study in the book / Of another's heart" (16–17), Ferdinand resorts to plaguing the Duchess with an "art" that will reveal her secrets, hidden, he seems to believe, in "that body of hers" (119). But when Bosola asks Ferdinand why he subjects his sister to these presentations, he confesses his goal is "To bring her to despair" (115). His aims do not differ much from the witch who intends to "force the will." And he relies on what look to be tricks, or "gulleries," to produce a particular affective response from the Duchess.[48]

Part of what drives Ferdinand's experimentation is his foolish conviction that he can maintain divisions between witchcraft, theatrical trickery, and mere experiment. Other characters in *The Duchess of Malfi* prove more cautious in their attempts to navigate superstition. The early modern identification of superstitions executes a kind of boundary work, pinpointing instances of misattributed efficacy, where a person's belief mistakenly ascribes power to an occult agent, or to God, which could only be the work of the devil. When Antonio wonders whether his own fears portend danger, Delio observes that our passions may lead us to dangerous assumptions:

> How superstitiously we mind our evils!
> The throwing down salt, or crossing of a hare;
> Bleeding at nose, the stumbling of a horse:
> Or singing of a cricket, are of power
> To daunt whole man in us. (2.2.68–72)

When Antonio's nose does begin to bleed, Delio's words echo in his mind, prompting him to discount the signs that he and the Duchess are in jeopardy:

> My nose bleeds.
> One that were superstitious, would count
> This ominous: when it merely comes by chance.
> Two letters, that are wrought here for my name
> Are drown'd in blood!
> Mere accident. –   (2.3.41–46)

While Antonio's reluctance to assign significance to his bleeding nose may look to be skepticism, the content of the paper he holds undercuts this perception. Despite the contemporary controversies over astrology, he and the Duchess show no disquiet about setting a figure for the child's nativity. When by chance Antonio drops the horoscope in Bosola's path, he has sealed his family's fate. Although Bosola's discovery may indicate that Antonio stubbornly ignored his own premonitions, it could also imply that his trust in casting figures constitutes a more perilous engagement in demonic arts than the folk beliefs Delio recites.[49]

Ferdinand may feel assured that his employment of representational wax figures and an artificial "dead man's hand" locates his art safely in the realm of counterfeit, but most of his contemporaries would have been apprehensive that his actions necessarily involved demonic forces. The Duchess immediately recognizes that her brother has strayed into ambiguous territory when she exclaims, "What witchcraft doth he practise, that he hath left / A dead man's hand here?" (4.1.54–55). As Katherine Rowe explains, the Duchess's assumption that a dead man's hand signifies witchcraft would have resonated with audiences. Witches, it was understood, cut off the hand of an "exhumed body . . . anointed it with devilish oils," and then either burned the "fingers or used them as a candle-holder." Identified as "the Hand of Glory," its burning allowed the witch to act invisibly.[50] Just as the moss from the skull of an unburied dead man possessed secret properties, giving the weapon-salve (for example) the power to cure at a distance, the dead man's hand signified an uncanny agency, highlighting a gap between will and act. Indeed, the "mandrake," which Ferdinand may have dug up, also alludes to the "Hand of Glory" or in "Old French, *main de gloire*," derived from mandragore, or mandrake.[51] Herbalists recommended that people employ dogs to dig up the mandrake to provide some distance between the gatherer and the plant's deleterious effects, which included a piercing scream when it was yanked from the ground. The associations between the mandrake, canines, and the hand of glory suggest that Ferdinand's digging in the graveyard may have begun well before his diagnosis, underlining the possibility that the dead man's hand he wields, when plaguing his sister, is as genuine as the leg he carries when discovered howling behind the churchyard graves.

Bosola asserts, however, that the hand is artificial – a piece taken from the wax scene of figures. If Ferdinand merely employs a wax representation of a dead man's hand, his intention may be to provoke fear or grief in the Duchess through theatrical trickery rather than witchcraft. And yet even the use of wax figures would raise doubts about the nature of Ferdinand's art. In the Duchess's mind (whether she recognizes the figures as artifice or not), the scene affects her more than if she were cursed with her own "picture, fashioned out of wax" and "stuck with a magical needle." Her apprehension implies that the wax figures themselves may be hanged, or stuck with needles, or manipulated in some way to produce demonic effects at a distance.[52] Stories reciting the use of wax pictures among courtiers were popular at this time. As James Howell observes in 1620, it was believed that Marie de Medici had been enchanted by her lady in waiting, who was arrested for witchcraft on the evidence that the young French king's "picture was found in her closet in virgin-wax, with one leg melted away."[53] Webster stages the Duchess's torture in such a way that audiences are unable to determine the nature of Ferdinand's "art." Is he an experimenting proto-scientist? A gulling mountebank? An equivocating witch? Or an unknowing demonic agent? Implicit in Webster's portrait of Ferdinand's fearful obsession with his sister's body is an association of women's secrets with nature's secrets. But the effects of Ferdinand's experimentation cannot be discerned in the Duchess's response, for despite her understandable misery, she still maintains her sanity and sense of self: "I am Duchess of Malfi still" (4.2.139). A central irony of Ferdinand's failure to plague his sister with art is that he ends up suffering, with *contrapasso* tidiness, from the very passions he attempted to elicit in her. Ferdinand's belief that reliable knowledge can be gained from trials in "witchcraft" identifies him not only with natural philosophers seeking to unlock nature's secrets but also with William Perkins' ignorant cunning folk, who unwittingly engage the devil when they use charms and enchantment.

After he orders his sister's death and Bosola's banishment, Ferdinand reappears in Act 5, scene 2 under a doctor's care, afflicted with "A very pestilent disease . . . lycanthropia." The doctor describes the disease's physical effects and symptoms:

> In those that are possess'd with't there o'erflows
> Such melancholy humour, they imagine
> Themselves to be transformed into wolves,
> Steal forth to churchyards in the dead of night
> And dig dead bodies up: as two nights since
> One met the Duke, 'bout midnight in a lane

> Behind St. Mark's Church, with the leg of a man
> Upon his shoulder; and he howled so fearfully:
> Said he was a wolf: only the difference
> Was, a wolf's skin was hairy on the outside,
> His on the inside; bade them take their swords,
> Rip up his flesh, and try.   (5.2.8–19)

We are compelled to wonder, as Brett Hirsch has asked, why Webster afflicts Ferdinand with this particular disease. Tricomi, who reminds us that early modern audiences accepted the real presence of devilish influence, argues that Ferdinand suffers from a form of demonic possession. Ferdinand tormented the Duchess, Tricomi maintains, as one already possessed by the devil.[54] Hirsch, on the other hand, appeals to the secularization narrative, asserting that an

> Examination of the demonological tracts published in England during this period uncovers a trend from a representation of lycanthropy as a manifestation of the demonic exacerbation of illness, madness, or melancholy, to one set out in wholly medical terms.[55]

For Hirsch, Ferdinand's illness is simply a form of physical melancholy that Webster deploys to symbolize bestial degeneration and "deterioration of . . . society from the civil."[56] It is true that melancholy precipitated lycanthropy, but no writer explicitly ruled out the devil's influence. Indeed, most medical writers in the period recognized the devil's capacity to produce a "natural disease."[57] When lycanthropy provoked controversy, it was in arguments that delineated the exact powers, methods, and limitations of the devil.

With the exception of Reginald Scot, who insisted that the devil only existed as a spiritual force, most writers of the period emphasized the devil's expertise in nature's secrets and the demonological capacity to engender illness, produce illusions, and exacerbate the symptoms of melancholy. Even Edward Jorden, whom scholars have long cited as an early example of the secularization of medicine for his argument that hysteria was a natural disease and not an instance of demonic possession, conceded that the devil was a potential cause of "natural" diseases.[58] Further complicating the devil's role in medical discourse was the argument that a natural disease, even when caused by the devil, often required a natural cure. Consequently, the debate over lycanthropy did not concern whether it had demonological or "natural" origins, for demons were considered a part of nature. Lycanthropy raised the more problematic issue of whether the devil could actually transform a man into an animal. On one extreme, we find Jean Bodin, who contends such metamorphosis is possible. However, most writers insist that since the devil cannot operate outside the bounds of nature, he cannot change man into a beast. Once demonological and medical writers excluded the possibility that lycanthropes had become actual beasts, they puzzled over how to explain werewolf stories. Some argued that the demons, by applying witch-like salves, put the human to sleep, and then the demons masqueraded as werewolves, performing the horrific acts of violence. Others argued that the devil simply fooled the lycanthrope into believing he was a werewolf. Melancholic and vulnerable, lycanthropes were the ultimate victims of demonic illusions.

In his argument that early modern English writers proved increasingly skeptical of lycanthropy as a demonic affliction, Brett Hirsch cites Reginald Scot, Henry Holland, George Gifford, and John Deacon and John Walker. However, as Hirsch himself acknowledges, both Holland and Gifford contend that lycanthropy is generated when the devil produces delusions in those people already oppressed with "melancholy."[59] Both Reginald Scot and Deacon and Walker focus their discussion on the impossibility of bestial metamorphosis; however, on the question of causation, they defer to Johanus Weyer. Scot writes, "For Lycanthropia is of the ancient physicians called *Lupina melancholic*, or *Lupina insania*. J. Wierus declareth verie learnedlie, the cause, the circumstance, and the cure of this disease."[60] In similar terms, Deacon and Walker write, "That which any further concerneth the *nature*, the *causes*, the *circumstances*, and *cure* of *Lycanthropie*: you may see more at large in *Wierus* his workes."[61] For many writers in the period, Johanus Weyer's *De praestigiis daemonum* proves to be the definitive word on the nature and cause of lycanthropy.

As we have observed, Weyer's agenda throughout *De praestigiis daemonum* is to establish the expansive power of the devil and to demonstrate that female witches are nothing more than deluded, melancholic women. While he concedes the possibility that elite male sorcerers may exercise magical powers, he identifies lycanthropes as the devil's male victims. Lycanthropy, he argues, "is not difficult for the Devil when he sets in motion the humors and spirits suitable for these illusions, especially in the case of persons whose brains are oft impaired by mists of black bile." Deluded men "who believe themselves transformed into wolves are found lying somewhere immersed in deep sleep by the efforts of the Devil."[62] In the same way that "toothless old women" can be fooled into thinking they possess magical power, male lycanthropes fail to realize that their supposed metamorphosis is nothing more than demonical illusion.[63] Weyer's thesis, I believe, provides a helpful perspective on the significance of Ferdinand's lycanthropy. Certainly Ferdinand's earlier dismissal of witches failed to acknowledge the devil's power. But his efforts to plague his sister with an art that borders on witchcraft identifies him with Weyer's deluded witches, who mistakenly believe they have the power to intervene in nature without the devil's interference.

As critics have noted, the most distinctive aspect of Ferdinand's lycanthropy is his reported claim that the only difference between himself and a wolf "Was, a wolf's skin was hairy on the outside, / His on the inside." Hirsch and Tricomi both ascribe this detail to an anecdote recited in Simon Goulart's *Admirable and Memorable Histories*, a hodge-podge of many stories, all attributed to other specified authors and texts. The collection includes tales of the devil's material influence, of strange diseases (both humoral and demonic), and of scandalous historical events (including an account of the Duchess of Malfi's life). Here is Goulart's description of the lycanthrope who feels hairy "betwixt the skinne and flesh":

> in the yeare 1541 [he] thought himself to bee a Wolfe, setting upon divers men in the fields, and slew some. In the end being with great difficultie taken, hee did constantlye affirme that hee was a Wolfe, and that there was no other difference, but that Wolves were commonlie hayrie without, and hee was betwixt the skinne and flesh. Some (too barbarous and cruell Wolves in effect) desiring to trie the truth thereof, gave him manie wounds upon the armes and legges; but knowing their owne error, and the innocencie of the poor melancholic man, they committed him to the Surgions to cure, in whose hands hee dyed within fewe dayes after ... I. WIER, *lib. 4. Chap. 13. Of Diuelish deuises.*[64]

While it seems persuasive that Webster read this version of the story, both Hirsch and Tricomi neglect to note that Goulart cites Weyer as his source for this tale. A modern English translation of Weyer reads,

> [a]t Padua in 1541, a farmer thought that he was a wolf, and he attacked and killed many persons in the fields. Finally he was captured (with great difficulty) and he confidently maintained that he was a true wolf and that the only distinction was that his pelt was inside out – with the fur on the inside. Therefore, certain persons stripped themselves of all humanity, and (as truly savage and ravening wolves) hacked at his arms and legs with a sword and cut them off, to find the truth of the matter. And when they realized that the man was innocent, they handed him over to the surgeon to cure him, but he expired after a few days.[65]

Tracing the story to Weyer helps establish that an early modern audience may associate the devil's influence with Ferdinand's conviction that he is "hairy on the inside." Critics of Webster's play have been inclined to assume that the inwardness of Ferdinand's affliction aligns it with the emergence of a modern psychological interiority, or with the secularization of mental illness, but for Weyer and many of his contemporaries, this strange misconception points just as easily to demonic influence. And yet Ferdinand's extraordinary belief that he possesses fur within has distracted scholars from the peculiar way Webster incorporates this anecdote into his tragedy.

Both Goulart and Weyer report that the lycanthrope's insistence that he is hairy on the inside provokes certain people, whom they characterize as the truly savage and cruel wolves, to wound the deluded man with swords in an effort to "find the truth of the matter." It is this violent impulse to gain ocular proof of a hidden affliction that the writers condemn as barbarically wolfish. From Weyer's perspective, a desire to slice open the lycanthrope and find physical evidence of his supposed transformation fails to consider that the devil's expertise in nature's secrets far exceeds human knowledge. What constitutes a crude and brutal anatomy ends up causing the man's death. Webster, however, alters the source on a specific point, for the doctor claims that it is Ferdinand himself, and not his pursuers, who "bade them take their swords, / Rip up his flesh, and try" or test the empirical truth of his statement (5.2.18–19). Ferdinand's lycanthropy functions as the appropriate disease for a man whose arrogant experiments may have unwittingly engaged demonological forces. At the height of his frenzy Ferdinand perversely fulfills his role as destructive empiricist, willingly offering up his own diseased body to a trial that would demonstrate, he believes, the material truth of his occult symptoms.[66]

The physician who attempts to cure the lycanthropy employs treatments that resemble Ferdinand's experiments on his sister: both appear inspired by the Pope's physician who believes that madness is cured by subjecting the patient to more madness:

> A great physician when the Pope was sick
> Of a deep melancholy, presented him
> With several sorts of madmen, which wild object,
> Being full of change and sport, forc'd him to laugh,
> As so th'imposthume broke.   (4.2.39–43)

Ferdinand's physician proposes to "buffet his madness out of him" (5.2.26), arguing that he will inspire awe and fear in his patient by pelting him with "forty urinals filled with rosewater" (68–69). As William Kerwin has argued, the physician's therapy functions as a parody of professional medicine.[67] Not only does the doctor's supposed medical expertise prove ineffective, but it has no apparent superiority to the cures and concoctions identified in the play with female knowledge. Indeed, some audience members may wonder whether the occult items in the Old Lady's closet might prove more effective in remedying a disease of preternatural origins. Certainly, the physician's promise to cure Ferdinand's "cruel sore eyes" with the "white of a cocatrice's egg" (61–62) reminds us of the Old Lady's strange ingredients. As I have suggested, Ferdinand's lycanthropy effeminizes him, for it associates his delusion with the old women who are led by the devil to believe that they are powerful witches. Punished for attempting to pry into nature's secrets, Ferdinand then suffers at the hands of a male physician who has no greater knowledge of occult diseases or cures than his sister or her female attendants.

In the sources to Webster's play, the Duchess marries Antonio out of lust, and he marries her for lust and ambition. In *The Palace of Pleasure*, William Painter writes:

> Now consider hir personage being such, hir easy life and delicate bringing vp, and daily séeing the youthely trade and maner of Courtiers life, whether she felt hir self prickt with any desire, which burned hir heart y^t more incessantly, as the flames were hidden & couert: from the outward shew whereof she stayd hir self so well as she could.[68]

In other words, their secretive behavior, as Ferdinand assumes, is driven by corrupt and sinful motives. Webster, however, takes pains to characterize the marriage as a love-match, and he does so by representing their attraction to each other as a secret sympathy that not only transcends social rank and gender roles but also defies rational inquiry. When making their matrimonial vows, Antonio states that they "may imitate the loving palms, / Best emblem of a peaceful marriage, / That nev'r bore fruit divided" (1.2.398–400). Palm trees emblematized the perfect marriage because they were plants understood to exhibit an occult attraction to one another: drawn to couple, each palm tree preternaturally bends its boughs to its mate.[69] In Thomas Stanley's poem "The Magnet," these amorous trees twine together for the same mysterious reason that the magnet moves iron.[70] For many early modern readers, sympathy – both as an occult attraction and in its more modern sense as commiseration – would also be associated with Echo and her disembodied voice.[71] Webster recognizes the impossibility of knowing whether Antonio hears the Duchess's voice from her grave or merely an empty echo. Those who believe he hears the Duchess may also interpret their sympathetic bond as one of nature's secrets, resisting rational explanation and surviving even death. But it is Delio's advice to Antonio that points us towards a more modern understanding of sympathy, urging him to see in his son "so sweet a figure," that he will feel compassion instead of hopelessness (5.3.52–53). Indeed, this may be the message Webster intends at the moment of the Duchess's death, when Bosola experiences such a pitiful, "manly sorrow" (4.2.355) for her loss that he is determined to execute her "last will: that's deliver / [Her] body to the reverend dispose / Of some good women" (364–66). Not only does the action speak to Bosola's sympathetic response, but his adherence to her request circumscribes, rather than penetrates, a domestic realm of female knowledge and female secrets.[72]

Coda

In his poem "An Anatomy of the World," John Donne famously
declares that the "new Philosophy" had shaken everyone's understanding
of nature:

> And new Philosophy calls all in doubt,
> The Element of fire is quite put out;
> The Sun is lost, and th'earth, and no mans wit
> Can well direct him where to looke for it.
> And freely men confesse that this world's spent,
> When in the Planets, and the Firmament
> They seeke so many new; they see that this
> Is crumbled out againe to his Atomies.
> 'Tis all in peeces, all cohaerence gone.   (205–13)[4]

Donne refers here to Copernican ideas as well as atomism, and his assertion
that the "world's spent" anticipates the barrenness of nature in emergent
notions of mechanical philosophy.[5] It is not coincidental that Donne
analogizes the loss of an animate nature to the death of a young girl.
When alive, her notably magnetic presence unified the now-disparate pieces
of the world:

> She that should all parts to reunion bow,
> She that had all Magnetique force alone,
> To draw, and fasten sundred parts in one.   (220–22)

Ben Jonson notoriously critiqued Donne's poem as "profane and full of Blasphemies" for attaching so much significance and potency to an individual woman.[6] But the strange elegiac center of Donne's poem – a dead girl's once "Magnetique" body – captures the complex associations between women's secrets and the secrets of nature that I have traced throughout this book. Her loss, and the loss of all occult qualities, leaves the natural philosopher, or natural magician, unable to "constellate any thing," for the astral influences now lie "Imprison'd in an Hearbe, or Charme, or Tree" (392–94). An animate cosmos not only acts upon its human subjects but also yields its secret powers to those who know, by experience or learning, how to direct its energies. As we have seen, women were regularly represented as occult objects, as well as possessors of occult knowledge, in a world alive with sympathies, antipathies, and hidden virtues.

Searching for salvific signs, Donne reminds his readers that even dead matter possesses effective properties:

> Since herbes, and roots, by dying lose not all,
> But they, yea Ashes too, are medicinall,
> Death could not quench her vertue so, but that
> It would be (if not follow'd) wondred at.   (403–06)

Stubbornly residual, the occult qualities of the natural world cannot be fully eradicated by the new philosophy's claim of barren matter.[7] As we shall see, even with the advent of mechanical theory, and its articulated hostility towards the concept of self-moving forces in nature, writers and thinkers throughout the seventeenth century found themselves repeatedly occupied with the possibility that the material world possessed secret properties and virtues irreconcilable with the new philosophy. Moreover, the status of women's experiential or embodied knowledge continued to affect, sometimes obliquely and sometimes overtly, the boundary work of scientific discourse.

By way of conclusion, I turn now to an odd triangle of public figures prominent in the Restoration period, some forty to fifty years after the staging of *The Duchess of Malfi* and the publication of Donne's "An Anatomy of the World": Margaret Cavendish, Duchess of Newcastle, Joseph Glanvill, and Robert Boyle. Although she authored eight books of natural philosophy, Margaret Cavendish's primary importance to the history of science rests on her controversial visit to the Royal Society of London in 1667. For the occasion, Robert Boyle presented his "experiments of . . . weighing air in an exhausted receiver; [and] . . . dissolving flesh with a certain liquor."[8] While Cavendish's idiosyncratic perspectives on natural philosophy were met with either "indifference or ridicule," had she been a man (as science historians John Henry and Peter Dear both acknowledge), her books would have found a place in the history of science.[9] At the very least, a male Cavendish would have qualified for membership in the new Society. Certainly her views were no more fantastic or outlandish than those held by some of the leading Society members.

One of those leading Society men, Joseph Glanvill, took Cavendish's views seriously enough to engage in an extended correspondence with her on natural philosophic issues.[10] We only have Glanvill's letters to Cavendish; however, as Jacqueline Broad has demonstrated, we can discern Cavendish's familiarity with and response to his arguments in her other writings. In both *Philosophical letters* (1664) and *Observations upon experimental philosophy* (1666),

> Cavendish is casually dismissive of Glanvill's Platonist-inspired views on the immaterial or supernatural world. Though she does not mention Glanvill by name, she comments directly on passages in his *Lux orientalis* (1662) and *Scepsis scientifica* (1665), a later edition of the *Vanity of dogmatizing*. The comments are unfavourable.[11]

Their differences centered, in particular, on witchcraft. What may surprise modern readers is that Glanvill, a self-identified skeptic, argued for the existence of demonic witchcraft, whereas Cavendish believed that the phenomenon of bewitchment could be ascribed to natural causes.[12] A champion of experimentalism, Joseph Glanvill was the key figure in the Royal Society's investment in scientific demonology. It was, in fact, Robert Boyle who encouraged Glanvill to frame witchcraft and demonic activity as a "proper subject for science."[13]

As exponents of mechanical philosophy, Boyle and Glanvill were insistent upon the complete passivity of matter; however, as Keith Hutchison has established, their views also stipulated a "radically supernaturalist ontology" to account for the non-corporeal causes of physical phenomena.[14] For many mechanical philosophers, an inert nature demanded the existence of demons. Conversely (and surprisingly), occult philosophers could appeal to an animated nature to deny demonic activity.[15] But for our purposes, the exchange between Glanvill and Cavendish also suggests that Glanvill's defense of demonic witchcraft stemmed from his fears and doubts that women could possess secret knowledge or embodied powers. He writes to Cavendish:

> But yet, *Madam*, your Grace may please to consider, That there are things done by mean and despicable persons, transcending all the Arts of the most knowing and improv'd *Virtuosi*, and above all the Essays of known and ordinary Nature. So that we either must suppose that a sottish silly old Woman hath more knowledge of the intrigues of Art, and Nature, than the most exercised Artists, and Philosophers, or confess that those strange things they performe, are done by confaederacy with evil Spirits, who, no doubt, act those things by the ways and applications of Nature, though such as are to us unknown.[16]

When faced with alleged instances of bewitchment or fascination, only two possibilities exist for Glanvill. Either an ignorant woman knows more about nature than the philosophers, or, the ignorant woman is in league with demons. In his *A blow at modern Sadducism in some philosophical considerations about witchcraft* (1668), Glanvill does not deny that the power of fascination may reside in a witch's eyes or imagination, for he affirms the familiar notion that "*pestilential spirits*" may dart from the eye and enter other bodies.[17] However, he contends that the most probable explanation for such power is that a "*Familiar* doth not only *suck* the *Witch*, but the action infuseth some *poisonous ferment* into her, which gives her *imagination* and *spirits* a *magical tincture*."[18] Moreover, he emphasizes, only the "*weak* and *passive*," such as children and "*timorous* persons," prove vulnerable to such invasions. Men, he insists, "of *bold* minds, who have plenty of *strong* and *vigorous spirits* are secure from the *contagion*."[19]

Matter, for Cavendish, is animate and self-moving. And her understanding of the natural world inclines her to view Glanvill's arguments as strained and improbable. Much like the occult philosophers, she attributes "witchcraft" to the secret operations of nature, citing the same motions that produce strange and inexplicable passions:

> My Sense and Reason doth inform me, that there is Natural Witchcraft, as I may call it, which is Sympathy, Antipathy, Magnetisme, and the like, which are made by the sensitive and rational motions between several Creatures, as by Imagination, Fancy, Love, Aversion, and many the like; but these Motions, being sometimes unusual and strange to us, we not knowing their causes . . . by reason we cannot assign any Natural cause for them, are apt to ascribe their effects to the Devil; but that there should be any such devillish Witchcraft . . . I cannot readily believe. Certainly, I dare say, that many a good, old honest woman hath been condemned innocently, and suffered death wrongfully, by the sentence of some foolish and cruel Judges.[20]

Not only does Cavendish lament the tragic ends of wrongly accused witches, but she also objects to the widely held assumption that women are more vulnerable to enchantment than men. Men in love, she argues, may have as "well bewitching *Ideas* as Women, and that they are as hurtful to Men, as to Women."[21] If Glanvill's scientific demonology represents an important component of the Royal Society's new science, then we may be compelled to cast Cavendish's appeals to sympathy and antipathy as intellectually retrograde. But her understanding of witchcraft has affinities with John Webster's *Displaying of Supposed Witchcraft* (1677), a treatise that not only synthesized many of the earlier natural magic suppositions but also aimed to defend the occult tradition against the arguments of Glanvill and his associates. Investment in nature's secret properties induced Webster to diminish the influence and authority of demonic agents.[22]

Experimental philosophy, in particular, struck Cavendish as a foolish enterprise. Indeed, she argues that the Royal Society's experiments distort nature, producing artificial, and even monstrous, results. In delineating the limits of experimental knowledge, she jokes that if the "Art of Micrography" could find out the nature of the female sex, it would prove an "Art of great fame." Cavendish's mockery of experimental philosophy inspires her to suggest that women, owing to their familiarity with household tasks, may be more properly suited to its procedures:

> [O]ur female sex would be the fittest for it, for they most commonly take pleasure in making of Sweet-meats, Possets, several sorts of Pyes, Puddings, and the like ... and it may be, they would prove good Experimental Philosophers, and inform the world how to make artificial Snow by their Creams or Possets beaten into froth, and Ice by their clear, candied or crusted quiddinies or conserves of fruits; and Frost by their candied herbs and flowers ... But the men should study the causes of those Experiments, and by this society the Commonwealth would find a great benefit; for the Woman was given to Man not onely to delight, but to help and assist him; and I am confident, Women would labour as much with Fire and Furnace as Men, for they'll make good Cordials and Spirits ... and then would Men have reason to imploy their time in more profitable studies, then in useless Experiments.[23]

Elaborate recipes for artificial snow, or candied flowers, or good cordials and spirits, could be found in many seventeenth-century books of secrets and receipts. While Cavendish's intentions are satirical, her parody reminds us of the contributions to natural knowledge made by a variety of hands-on practices. She highlights the confectionary art of elite ladies, but we might also cite "empirics, alchemists, old women, compilers of recipe books, manual laborers, artists, and craftsmen."[24] In recent years, historians of science have turned their attention to these everyday practices, tracing their influence on the development of experimental procedures.

On her visit to the Royal Society, Cavendish witnessed Robert Boyle's most famous experiment, a demonstration of his air-pump. If spectators could accept that a product of human art could stand in for nature, the pump was intended to "make accessible and manifest the invisible and normally insensible, effects of the air."[25] In his articulation of the mechanical, or corpuscular, philosophy, Boyle delineated its primary tenets: universal matter had motion (imparted by God) and the attributes of magnitude and shape. On the basis of his experiments, Boyle felt comfortable in stating that his pump demonstrated "spring" as a manifest quality of air, yet the cause of this "spring" remained hidden.[26] Given their understanding of matter, mechanical philosophers would not, as a rule, cite occult *qualities* as an explanation for natural phenomena, even if occult causation remained a reference point when discussing experimental outcomes. But as John Henry and others have demonstrated, mechanical philosophers paid close attention to instances of hidden or occult phenomena and labored to accommodate them within their new philosophy.[27]

When we examine some of Boyle's more speculative pieces, we can find moments in which he entertains the possibility of latent, active principles in matter. In his tract *Suspicions about some hidden qualities of the air* (1674), for example, Boyle confesses in his preface to almost using the title "the Occult Qualities of air."[28] In some passages, we can track Boyle's effort to accommodate an occult event to mechanical theory. Here we see the "peculiar Textures" of bodies do the work of "Sympathies and Antipathies":

> what we call Sympathies and Antipathies, depending indeed on the peculiar Textures and other Modifications of the bodies, between whom these friendships and hostilities are said to be exercised, I see not why it should be impossible, that there be a Cognation betwixt a body of a congruous or convenient Texture, (especially as to the shape and size of its Pores,) and the Effluviums of any other body, whether Subterraneal or Sydereal.[29]

In another passage, it is the very springiness of air that leads Boyle to hint at the presence of an occult quality. He admits his suspicion that there may exist "some *vital substance*, if I may so call it, diffus'd through the Air, whether it be a *volatile Nitre*, or (rather) some *yet anonymous* substance, Sydereal or Subterraneal, but not improbably of kin to that."[30]

But it is in Boyle's discussion of medicinal remedies that we find subtle signs that the preternatural assumptions about women, as well as certain wondrous cures, endure even in the face of the new philosophy's explanatory power.[31] In *Of the reconcileableness of specifick medicines to the corpuscular philosophy* (1685), Boyle acknowledges from the outset that he will focus on providing mechanical accounts of the "occult qualities" presumed to inhere in some medicines:

> Among the several kinds of occult qualities that, which is afforded by Specifick Vertues of Medicines, is not here to be pretermitted. For these Qualities do not only, like other hidden ones, invite our curiosity, but concern our health and may hereafter (if I mistake not) appear to be of much greater importance, than as yet they are commonly thought.[32]

Primarily Boyle reconciles the strange effects of particular medicines to corpuscular theories by noting that "the effects of an agent upon [the human body] are not to be measured so much by the power of that agent considered in it self, as by the effects that are consequently produc'd by the action of the parts of the Living Engine it self upon one another."[33] However, his anecdotes recite marvelous cures that offer no explanation of how they might be accommodated to mechanical philosophy. Wearing or handling the tooth of a hippopotamus or a ring made of an elk's hoof may relieve cramps. By holding the moss of a dead man's skull (a common ingredient in the weapon-salve) in his hand, Boyle cured his own nose bleeds.[34] He repeatedly recommends scent therapy as a cure for hysterical women:

> *as* Perfumes do often enough produce various, and sometimes frightful, Symptoms in many Histerical Women; *so* the fumes of the burnt Feathers of Patridges, Woodcocks, *&c.* do frequently cure the Fit in as little time as the sweet smell procur'd it. And I have often found the smell of strong Spirit of Harts-horn, or Sal-Armoniac, recover such Women in far less time, than the fragrant odours imploy'd to make them [sick].[35]

Recalling the antipathies of *The Changeling*, Boyle claims to have "known several persons, not all of them of the same Sex, very much offended by the smell of Roses."[36] And among his medicinal receipts, Boyle includes a remedy for yellow jaundice that he describes as "An Experienced Magnetical cure":

> TAke the Gall-Bladder of a Sheep, and near the top, without emptying the Liquor, make a small hole, at which put in two or three drops of the Patient's warm Urine; then tye up the upper part of the Bladder, and hang it in the free Air till it dry up, *&c.*[37]

Although Boyle may have a mechanical justification for this remedy, readers will recognize it as a cure that invokes a sympathetic relation between the sheep's bladder and the jaundiced patient.

While the story of occult qualities in the seventeenth century could include many more reports of strange science, demonology, women's maladies, and wondrous cures, I will end with an anecdote that Boyle recounts on the mysterious strength of poisons found in Africa. During a visit to an English colonist who traded "with the Negro's of the Inland Countrey," Boyle inquired whether the poisons found there were as "extraordinarily powerful" as he had heard. The gentleman replied,

> the Blacks had a Poyson, that was, though somewhat slow, yet very mortal; in so small a dose, that it was usual for them to hide enough of it to kill a man, under one of their Nails, which they wear somewhat long: Whence they would drop it so dextrously into the Drink, or Milk, or Broth or other Liquid Aliment of those they owe a spite to, that 'tis scarce possible for a stranger to be watchful enough to prevent it . . . a famous Knight, who commanded the *English* there, and lately died a ship-board in his way home, was so poysoned at a parting Treat, by a young *Negro* Woman of Quality, whom he had enjoy'd and declin'd to take with him, according to his promise, into *Europe*. And though my Relator early gave him notice of what he suspected to be the cause of this Indisposition, and engag'd him thereupon to take Antidotes, and Cordials, as Treacle, *&c.* yet his languishing distemper still increased, till it kill'd him.[38]

Outside the borders of Boyle's philosophical system, and in exotic, "torrid" zones of mysteriously strong poisons, lurk young "Negro" women who possess secret knowledge and secret methods that they can apply in vengeance against European men. Most likely Boyle offers this narrative for its sensational impact, rather than its medical value. But in the context of *Occult Knowledge*, Boyle's story alerts us to the persistent ways women – as objects and agents – help produce the boundaries of "science." And finally, Boyle's anecdote of a "Negro Woman of Quality" moves us beyond the pages of this book to the larger expanse of the early modern Atlantic world. While we have been confined to England, there is no question that new discoveries, environments, diseases, and cures mingled with English natural philosophy and mixed with shifting constructions of gender and race to inform and reform what constituted European science. To put it simply, as the cunning woman faded from view, Indians and African conjurers emerged to take her place.[39]

Notes

INTRODUCTION

1. I am using the word "occult" in its dominant sense at the time, as in "imperceptible" or "secret." For standard accounts of occultism, see Frances A. Yates, *Giordano Bruno and the Hermetic Tradition* (Chicago and London: University of Chicago Press, 1964); D. P. Walker, *Spiritual and Demonic Magic: From Ficino to Campanella* (London: Warburg Institute, University of London, 1958); Wayne Shumaker, *The Occult Sciences in the Renaissance: A Study in Intellectual Patterns* (Berkeley: University of California Press, 1972); Brian P. Copenhaver, "Natural Magic, Hermetism, and Occultism in Early Modern Science" in David C. Lindberg, and Robert S. Westman (eds.), *Reappraisals of the Scientific Revolution* (Cambridge: Cambridge University Press, 1990), 261–302; Copenhaver, "Magic" in Katharine Park and Lorraine Daston (eds.), *The Cambridge History of Science*, vol. 3 (Cambridge: Cambridge University Press, 2003), 518–40; Pierre Hadot, *The Veil of Isis: An Essay on the History of the Idea of Nature*, trans. Michael Chase (Cambridge, MA: The Belknap Press of Harvard University Press, 2006).

2. For ecological approaches to the body, see Mary Floyd-Wilson and Garrett A. Sullivan, Jr. (eds.), *Environment and Embodiment in Early Modern England* (Basingstoke: Palgrave Macmillan, 2007); Mary Floyd-Wilson and Garrett A. Sullivan, Jr. (eds.), *Embodiment and Environment in Early Modern Drama and Performance*, special issue of *Renaissance Drama*, n.s. 35 (2006); Gail Kern Paster, Katherine Rowe, and Mary Floyd-Wilson (eds.), *Reading the Early Modern Passions: Essays in the Cultural History of Emotion* (Philadelphia: University of Pennsylvania Press, 2004); Gail Kern Paster, *Humoring the Body: Emotions and the Shakespearean Stage* (Chicago: University of Chicago Press, 2004); Mary Floyd-Wilson, *English Ethnicity and Race in Early Modern Drama* (Cambridge: Cambridge University Press, 2003). Kristen Poole is a recent exception. Her book *Supernatural Environments* takes up the question of how literary scholars can overcome the problem of disbelief in their approach to the supernatural. See *Supernatural Environments in Shakespeare's England: Spaces of Demonism, Divinity, and Drama* (Cambridge: Cambridge University Press, 2011), 24–35, esp. 24. See also Mary Floyd-Wilson, "English Epicures and Scottish Witches," *Shakespeare Quarterly* 57 (2006): 131–61 and "The

Preternatural Ecology of 'A Lover's Complaint,'" *Shakespeare Studies* 39 (2011): 43–53.

3. Scholarship that attends to the "lived practices of early modern cosmology" includes Paster, *Humoring the Body* (20); Paster, *The Body Embarrassed: Drama and the Disciplines of Shame in Early Modern England* (Ithaca, NY: Cornell University Press, 1993); Michael C. Schoenfeldt, *Bodies and Selves in Early Modern England: Physiology, and Inwardness in Spenser, Shakespeare, Herbert, and Milton* (Cambridge: Cambridge University Press, 1999); Mary Thomas Crane, *Shakespeare's Brain: Reading with Cognitive Theory* (Princeton: Princeton University Press, 2001).

4. Stuart Clark, "Witchcraft and Magic in Early Modern Culture" in Bengt Ankarloo and Stuart Clark (eds.), *Witchcraft and Magic in Europe: The Period of the Witch Trials* (Philadelphia: University of Pennsylvania Press, 2002), 149.

5. Important literary studies of the occult tradition include John S. Mebane, *Renaissance Magic and the Return of the Golden Age: The Occult Tradition and Marlowe, Jonson, and Shakespeare* (Lincoln: University of Nebraska Press, 1989); Lyndy Abraham, *Marvell and Alchemy* (Aldershot: Scolar Press, 1990); Stanton J. Linden, *Darke Hierogliphicks: Alchemy in English Literature from Chaucer to the Restoration* (Lexington: University of Kentucky Press, 1996); Margaret Healy, *Shakespeare, Alchemy and the Creative Imagination: The Sonnets and A Lover's Complaint* (Cambridge: Cambridge University Press, 2011); Genevieve Guenther, *Magical Imaginations: Instrumental Aesthetics in the English Renaissance* (Toronto: University of Toronto Press, 2012).

6. Michel Foucault, *The Order of Things: An Archaeology of the Human Sciences* (New York: Vintage Books, 1973), 30.

7. Most Shakespeare criticism implicitly subscribes to Stephen Greenblatt's argument that early modern theater staged an evacuation of sacred meaning. The falsification of exorcism, however, should not be mistaken for skepticism about demonism or demonic possession. See "Shakespeare and the Exorcists" in Patricia Parker and Geoffrey Hartman (eds.), *Shakespeare and the Question of Theory* (New York: Methuen, 1985), 163–87.

8. See Stuart Clark, *Thinking with Demons: The Idea of Witchcraft in Early Modern Europe* (Oxford: Oxford University Press, 1999); Alexandra Walsham, *Providence in Early Modern England* (Oxford: Oxford University Press, 2001); Peter Lake with Michael C. Questier, *The Anti-Christ's Lewd Hat: Protestants, Papists, and Players in Post-Reformation England* (New Haven: Yale University Press, 2002).

9. See Mary Ellen Lamb, *The Popular Culture of Shakespeare, Spenser, and Jonson* (New York: Routledge, 2006) and Wendy Wall, *Staging Domesticity: Household Work and English Identity in Early Modern Drama* (Cambridge: Cambridge University Press, 2002).

10. On the complexities of superstition in the period, see Clark, *Thinking with Demons*, 472–88, and a special supplement issue of *Past and Present*, "The Religion of Fools? Superstition Past and Present," 199, supplement 3 (2008),

especially the essays by Michael D. Bailey, Alison Rowlands, and Alexandra Walsham.

11. Quoted in Lamb, 53. See *Popular Culture, Desiderius Erasmus: Concerning the Aim and Method of Education*, ed. W. H. Woodward (Cambridge: Cambridge University Press, 1904), 214.

12. Desiderius Erasmus, *A playne and godly exposition or declaration of the commune crede*, trans. William Marshall (London, 1534 [?]), sig. ⊤iiir. Quoted in Clark, *Thinking with Demons*, 500n.

13. Robert W. Scribner, "The Reformation, Popular Magic, and the 'Disenchantment of the World,'" *Journal of Interdisciplinary History* 23 (1993): 475–94, esp. 484. See too Clark, *Thinking with Demons*, 472. On disenchantment and the Reformation, see Keith Thomas, *Religion and the Decline of Magic: Studies in Popular Beliefs in Sixteenth- and Seventeenth-Century England* (London: Penguin Books, 1971). In an important review, Hildred Geertz points out that Thomas dismisses the possibility that magic in this period derived from a "coherent, comprehensive, and general view of the world"; see "An Anthropology of Religion and Magic, 1," *Journal of Interdisciplinary History* 6 (1975): 71–89, esp. 87. For a thorough historiographical assessment of the current status of the disenchantment or secularization thesis among historians, see Alexandra Walsham, "The Reformation and 'The Disenchantment of the World' Reassessed," *Historical Journal* 51 (2008): 497–528. Tracing the thesis from Max Weber through Keith Thomas and others, Walsham surveys the current scholarship on these questions. She shows that historians now agree that the more complex view of the period reveals not just an enduring belief in magic, invisible spirits, and a sacramental universe but, in some cases, an intensification of such convictions. She writes, "The rhetoric of 'disenchantment' that was so central to the reformers' assault upon the Church of Rome paradoxically acquired much of its urgency from a heightened sense that supernatural or preternatural forces were at work in the world" (508).

14. Foucault, *The Order of Things*, 50. See too William B. Ashworth, Jr., "Natural History and the Emblematic World View" in Lindberg and Westman, *Reappraisals of the Scientific Revolution*, 303–31.

15. Foucault, *The Order of Things*, 26.

16. See, for example, James J. Bono's discussion of Paracelsus and experience in *The Word of God and the Languages of Man: Interpreting Nature in Early Modern Science and Medicine* (Madison: University of Wisconsin Press, 1995), 134–40. As Harris L. Coulter observes, even for Paracelsus, "the true value of the remedy is only revealed by its use, whatever its signature may indicate"; see *Divided Legacy: The Patterns Emerge, Hippocrates to Paracelsus*, vol. 1 (Washington, DC: Wehawken Book Co., 1975), 491.

17. Foucault, *The Order of Things*, 30. On occult qualities and seventeenth-century natural philosophy, see John Henry, "Occult Qualities and the Experimental Philosophy: Active Principles in Pre-Newtonian Matter Theory," *History of Science* 24 (1986): 335–81; Ron Millen, "The Manifestation of Occult Qualities in the Scientific Revolution" in Margaret J. Osler and Paul Lawrence Farber

(eds.), *Religion, Science, and Worldview: Essays in Honor of Richard S. Westfall* (Cambridge: Cambridge University Press, 1985), 185–216; Simon Schaffer, "Occultism and Reason" in A. J. Holland (ed.), *Philosophy, Its History and Historiography* (Dordrecht: Reidel, 1985), 117–43; Keith Hutchison, "What Happened to Occult Qualities in the Scientific Revolution?" *Isis* 73 (1982): 233–53. On a "strictly construed" distinction between occult qualities and the theory of sympathies, see James Dougal Fleming, "The Undiscoverable Country: Occult Qualities, Scholasticism, and the End of Nescience" in James Dougal Fleming (ed.), *The Invention of Discovery, 1500–1700* (Aldershot: Ashgate, 2011), 61–78, esp. 61. For a history of the meaning of experience and experiment in the period, see Peter Dear, *Discipline and Experience: The Mathematical Way in the Scientific Revolution* (Chicago: University of Chicago Press, 1995) and "The Meanings of Experience" in Park and Daston, *The Cambridge History of Science*, vol. 3, 106–31. See too Catherine Wilson, *The Invisible World: Early Modern Philosophy and the Invention of the Microscope* (Princeton: Princeton University Press, 1995). Wilson argues that the "conviction that there are subvisible material causes of the most obscure phenomena drove out explanations that involved spiritual entities or correspondences," but that "it would be wrong . . . to think that one is dealing here with exclusive mentalities, rather than with a displacement over the long run" (61).

18. The field is vast, but some significant contributors are Lynn Thorndike, *A History of Magic and Experimental Science*, 8 vols. (New York: Macmillan, 1923–58); Charles B. Schmitt, "Reappraisals in Renaissance Science," *History of Science* 16 (1978): 200–14; Charles Webster, *From Paracelsus to Newton: Magic and the Making of Modern Science* (Cambridge: Cambridge University Press, 1982); Brian Vickers (ed.), *Occult and Scientific Mentalities in the Renaissance* (Cambridge: Cambridge University Press, 1984).

19. Henry, "Occult Qualities," 338.

20. Clark, *Thinking with Demons*, 162.

21. Lorraine Daston, "Preternatural Philosophy" in Lorraine Daston (ed.), *Biographies of Scientific Objects* (Chicago: University of Chicago Press, 2000), 18.

22. Thorndike, *A History of Magic and Experimental Science*, vol. 5, 493. See too Jon Arrizabalaga, John Henderson, and Roger French, *The Great Pox: The French Disease in Renaissance Europe* (New Haven and London: Yale University Press, 1997), 246–51. Fracastoro insists that contagion should be explained not by occult properties but by spiritual qualities, which function as imperceptible substances. Like the mechanical philosophers, he does not simply reject occult qualities but reinterprets them as unseen atoms or corpuscles.

23. Daston, "Preternatural Philosophy," 24–25.

24. As Clark observes, "Insensibility was, after all, at the heart of the corpuscularian conception of matter. Many exponents of the new science were thus able to reconcile the idea of occult properties with mechanical explanations of phenomena – including Robert Boyle, Henry More, Robert Hooke, Walter

Charleton and William Petty"; see *Witchcraft and Magic in Europe*, 159. See too John Henry, "Boyle and Cosmical Qualities" in Michael Hunter (ed.), *Robert Boyle Reconsidered* (Cambridge: Cambridge University Press, 1994), 119–38.

In *Sylva Sylvarum*, Francis Bacon writes: "Certainly, it is agreeable to *Reason*, that there are, at the least, some *Light Effluxions* from *Spirit* to *Spirit*, when *Men* are in *Presence* one with another, as well as from *Body* to *Body*"; see *Sylva Sylvarum: or A naturall historie in ten centuries* (London, 1627), 251.

25. Walter Charleton, *Physiologia Epicuro-Gassendo-Charltoniana, or, A fabrick of science natural, upon the hypothesis of atoms founded by Epicurus repaired [by] Petrus Gassendus* (London, 1654): "But, that [the old lady] may, in some measure, contribute to the indisposition of an Infant, at whom she shoots her maligne Eye-beams, neer at hand; may receive much of credit from the Pollution of a Lookinglass by the adspect of a Menstruous woman" (375). For more on the vexed relationship between occult qualities and mechanical philosophy, see Henry, "Occult Qualities"; Millen, "The Manifestation"; Schaffer, "Occultism and Reason"; Hutchison, "What Happened." Also see my discussion in the Coda.

26. On boundary work in early modern science studies, see John Henry, "The Fragmentation of Renaissance Occultism and the Decline of Magic," *History of Science* 46 (2008): 1–48. Henry cites T. F. Gieryn, "Boundary-Work and the Demarcation of Science from Non-Science: Strains and Interests in Professional Ideologies of Scientists," *American Sociological Review* 48 (1983): 781–95.

27. *Sylva Sylvarum*, 255.

28. Koen Vermeir, "The 'Physical Prophet' and the Powers of the Imagination. Part I: A Case-Study on Prophecy, Vapours, and the Imagination (1685–1710)," *Studies in History and Philosophy of Biological and Biomedical Sciences* 35 (2004): 561–91, esp. 582.

29. Francis Bacon, *The Works of Francis Bacon*, ed. James Spedding, Robert Leslie Ellis, and Douglas Demon Heath, 14 vols. (1861–79), vol. 4 (London: Longman, 1875), 84.

30. Brian P. Copenhaver observes that Bacon did not "deny the existence of occult virtues and sympathies, but he traced them to imperceptible physical structures in bodies called 'latent configurations'"; see "Astrology and Magic" in Charles B. Schmitt and Quentin Skinner (eds.), *The Cambridge History of Renaissance Philosophy* (Cambridge: Cambridge University Press, 1988), 299.

31. Bacon, "The History of the Sympathy and Antipathy of Things" in *The Works of Francis Bacon*, vol. 5 (1877), 203. Thomas Hobbes will follow the same pattern in his pronouncements on occult qualities. In *Leviathan*, he observes that men ignorantly invoke sympathy and antipathy when "they know no cause"; see *Leviathan*, ed. J. C. A. Gaskin (Oxford: Oxford University Press, 1996), 451. But in his "Short Tract of the First Principles," Hobbes acknowledges that, "There is betweene Species conveniency, and discoveniency, by which the Agents whence they issue, attrude and repell one the other. This is manifest by Experience in things that attract or repeal one the other by

Sympathy and Antipathy"; Thomas Hobbes, *The Elements of Law: Natural and Political*, ed. Ferdinand Tonnies (Cambridge: Cambridge University Press, 1928), 160.

32. Katharine Park, "Bacon's 'Enchanted Glass,'" *Isis* 75 (1984): 296.

33. Lorraine J. Daston and Katharine Park, *Wonders and the Order of Nature, 1150–1750* (New York: Zone Books, 1998).

34. Guido Giglioni, "Mastering the Appetites of Matter: Francis Bacon's *Sylva Sylvarum*" in Charles T. Wolfe and Ofer Gal (eds.), *The Body as Object and Instrument of Knowledge: Embodied Empiricism in Early Modern Science* (Dordrecht and New York: Springer, 2010), 166.

35. Bacon, *The Works of Francis Bacon*, vol. 4 (1875), 29.

36. See Paster, *Humoring the Body*; Schoenfeldt, *Bodies and Selves*; Paster, Rowe, and Floyd-Wilson, *Reading the Early Modern Passions*; Floyd-Wilson, *English Ethnicity*; Floyd-Wilson and Sullivan, *Environment and Embodiment*.

37. Paster briefly mentions sympathies and antipathies in *Humoring the Body*, but she does not draw a distinction between the occult unpredictability of these forces and the presumed manifest nature of humors. See her discussion of the "desiring universe" and how the passions are distributed through "a natural world traversed by a host of sympathies and antipathies," 33 and 145.

38. Hutchison, "What Happened," 240.

39. Will Greenwood, *[Apographe storges], or, A description of the passion of love* (London, 1657), 9.

40. William Fenner, *A treatise of the affections, or, The souls pulse whereby a Christian may know whether he be living or dying : together with a lively description of their nature, signs, and symptomes : as also directing men to the right use and ordering of them* (London, 1650), 62.

41. Desiderius Erasmus, "Amicitia, or Friendship" in *The Colloquies of Erasmus*, trans. N. Bailey, vol. 2 (London: Reeves and Turner, 1878), 300–15.

42. Erasmus, "Amicitia, or Friendship," 300.

43. Levinus Lemnius, *The secret miracles of nature* (London, 1658), 198–99.

44. Marsilio Ficino, *Commentary on Plato's Symposium on Love*, trans. Sears Jayne (Dallas, TX: Spring Publications 1985), 127. See too Yates, *Giordano Bruno*, 126–27.

45. Healy, *Shakespeare*, 29–31.

46. Giovanni Pico Della Mirandola, *On the Dignity of Man*, trans. Charles Glenn Wallis (Indianapolis: Bobbs-Merrill, 1965), 28.

47. Hadot, *The Veil of Isis*, 109.

48. See Paster, *Humoring the Body*, 1–24 and Paster, Rowe, and Floyd-Wilson, *Reading the Early Modern Passions*, esp. 16–18; Paster, "The Body and Its Passions," *Shakespeare Studies* 29 (2001): 44–50; Paster, "Nervous Tension: Networks of Blood and Spirit in the Early Modern Body" in David Hillman and Carla Mazzio (eds.), *The Body in Parts: Fantasies of Corporeality in Early Modern Europe* (New York and London: Routledge, 1997), 110–11.

Sympathy has become a key term in American and British literary studies. My survey of the critical literature is not meant to be exhaustive, but I do wish to convey the expansiveness of the field. See Walter J. Slatoff, *The Look of Distance: Reflections on Suffering and Sympathy in Modern Literature – Auden to Agee, Whitman to Woolf* (Columbus: Ohio State University Press, 1985); David Marshall, *The Surprising Effects of Sympathy: Marivaux, Diderot, Rousseau, and Mary Shelley* (Chicago: University of Chicago Press, 1988); Gordon Hutner, *Secrets and Sympathy: Forms of Disclosure in Hawthorne's Novels* (Athens: University of Georgia Press, 1988); Julia A. Stern, *The Plight of Feeling: Sympathy and Dissent in the Early American Novel* (Chicago and London: University of Chicago Press, 1997); Nancy Roberts, *Schools of Sympathy: Gender and Identification through the Novel* (Montreal: McGill-Queen's University Press, 1997); Elizabeth Barnes, *States of Sympathy: Seduction and Democracy in the American Novel* (New York: Columbia University Press, 1997); Thomas J. McCarthy, *Relationships of Sympathy: The Writer and Reader in British Romanticism* (Aldershot: Scolar Press, 1997); Laura Hinton, *The Perverse Gaze of Sympathy: Sadomasochistic Sentiments from Clarissa to Rescue 911* (Albany: State University of New York Press, 1999); Julie Ellison, *Cato's Tears and the Making of Anglo-American Emotion* (Chicago: University of Chicago Press, 1999); Audrey Jaffe, *Scenes of Sympathy: Identity and Representation in Victorian Fiction* (Ithaca, NY: Cornell University Press, 2000); Caleb Crain, *American Sympathy: Men, Friendship, and Literature in the New Nation* (New Haven: Yale University Press, 2001); Kristin Boudreau, *Sympathy in American Literature: American Sentiments from Jefferson to the Jameses* (Gainesville: University Press of Florida, 2002); Benjamin Eric Daffron, *Romantic Doubles: Sex and Sympathy in British Gothic Literature, 1790–1830* (New York: AMS Press, 2002); Amit S. Rai, *Rule of Sympathy: Sentiment, Race, and Power, 1750–1850* (New York: Palgrave Macmillan, 2002); Janis McLarren Caldwell, *Literature and Medicine in Nineteeth-Century Britain: From Mary Shelley to George Eliot* (Cambridge: Cambridge University Press, 2004); Cindy Weinstein, *Family, Kinship, and Sympathy in Nineteenth-Century American Literature* (Cambridge: Cambridge University Press, 2004); David Greven, *Men beyond Desire: Manhood, Sex, and Violation in American Literature* (New York: Palgrave Macmillan, 2005); Lynn Festa, *Sentimental Figures of Empire in Eighteenth-Century Britain and France* (Baltimore: Johns Hopkins University Press, 2006); Brigid Lowe, *Victorian Fiction and the Insights of Sympathy: An Alternative to the Hermeneutics of Suspicion* (London: Anthem Press, 2007); Rachel Ablow, *The Marriage of Minds: Reading Sympathy in the Victorian Marriage Plot* (Stanford: Stanford University Press, 2007); Evan Gottlieb, *Feeling British: Sympathy and National Identity in Scottish and English Writing, 1707–1832* (Lewisberg, PA: Bucknell University Press, 2007); Suzanne Keen, *Empathy and the Novel* (Oxford: Oxford University Press, 2007); Sophie Ratcliffe, *On Sympathy* (Oxford: Oxford University Press, 2008); Laura L. Mielke, *Moving Encounters: Sympathy and the Indian Question in Antebellum Literature* (Amherst: University of Massachusetts Press, 2008). On eighteenth-century adaptations of Shakespeare and the discourse of sympathy, see Jean Marsden,

"Shakespeare and Sympathy" in Peter Sabor and Paul Yachnin (eds.), *Shakespeare and the Eighteenth Century* (Aldershot: Ashgate, 2008), 29–42.

49. Kevis Goodman has argued that we can find the emergence of sympathy as a consciously developed moral position in the poetry of John Milton. See "'Wasted Labor'? Milton's Eve, the Poet's Work, and the Challenge of Sympathy," *ELH* 64 (1997): 415–46. Milton, however, also cites an older sense of sympathies and antipathies in nature as evidence that spousal separation may, upon occasion, be necessary and unavoidable in his defense of divorce. See *John Milton: Selected Prose*, ed. C. A. Patrides (Columbia: University of Missouri Press, 1985), 146–47.

50. On early modern pity and compassion, see John Staines, "Compassion in the Public Sphere of Milton and King Charles" in Paster, Rowe, and Floyd-Wilson, *Reading the Early Modern Passions*, 89–110 and Heather James, "Dido's Ear: Tragedy and the Politics of Response," *Shakespeare Quarterly* 52 (2001): 360–82. For a study that charts the early emergence of a culture of sympathy in the seventeenth century, see Seth Lobis, "The Virtue of Sympathy in Seventeenth-Century England," unpublished Ph.D. thesis, Yale University (2005). In "Sir Kenelm Digby and the Power of Sympathy," Lobis discusses Digby's treatise on the weapon-salve, identifying this work as transitional for the concept of sympathy, where Digby espouses a cure at-a-distance but "discredits the sympathetic interaction between human beings." *Huntington Library Quarterly* 74 (2011): 243–60, esp. 243.

   As Evan Gottlieb observes, David Hume viewed sympathy as an involuntary "mechanism of emotional connection whereby people assume each other's psychological states through an occult process of the transmission of feelings" (*Feeling British*, 31). In *A Treatise of Human Nature*, Hume writes, "As in strings equally wound up, the motion of one communicates itself to the rest; so all the affections readily pass from one person to another, and beget corresponding movements in every human creature"; see David Hume, *A Treatise of Human Nature*, book 3 (Oxford: Clarendon Press, 1896), 576.

51. Anthony Ashley Cooper, Earl of Shaftesbury, "A Letter Concerning Enthusiasm to My Lord" in Lawrence E. Klein (ed.), *Characteristics of Men, Manners, Opinions, Times* (Cambridge: Cambridge University Press, 2000), 10.

52. Edward Reynolds, *A treatise of the passions and faculties of the soule of man* (London, 1640), 74–75.

53. Reynolds, *A treatise*, 119–20.

54. William Shakespeare, *The Merchant of Venice*, in *The Norton Shakespeare*, ed. Stephen Greenblatt (New York: W. W. Norton, 1997), 4.1.46–61. For helpful discussions of this passage, see Paster, *Humoring the Body*, 204–08 and Lara Bovilsky, *Barbarous Play: Race on the English Renaissance Stage* (Minneapolis: University of Minnesota Press, 2008), 146–47.

55. John Baptista Porta [Giambattista della Porta], *Natural Magick (1658)*, ed. Derek J. Price (New York: Basic Books, 1957), 19. In his discussion of the "hidden qualities of natural bodies," Joannes Jonstonus observes "Many will sweat if a Cat be present. *Quercetan in diaetetica*, and make water at the sound

of the harp"; see *An history of the wonderful things of nature* (London, 1657), 6. See too Daniel Sennert, *The sixth book of Practical physick: Of occult or hidden diseases* (London, 1662). In his discussion of occult qualities, Sennert writes: "For who is so foolish or impudent, that will impute the action of the Loadstone drawing iron to qualities fetcht from the Elements? Some hate Cats, that if they be present (though they see them not) they fall into cold sweats, and faint, and cannot endure any Cupboard that contains them" (2).

56. Paster, *Humoring the Body*, 205.
57. Shakespeare, *A Midsummer Night's Dream*, 2.1.195–98.
58. On the presumed value of "old women's knowledge" and the "superiority of 'kitchen physic' to the care of university-trained practitioners," see Joanna Picciotto, *Labors of Innocence in Early Modern England* (Cambridge, MA: Harvard University Press, 2010), 144.
59. *The Book of Secrets of Albertus Magnus of the Virtues of Herbs, Stones and Certain Beasts*, ed. Michael R. Best and Frank H. Brightman (Oxford: Clarendon Press, 1973), 76. On the popularity and audience of Albertus Magnus' *The Book of Secrets* in early modern England, see Allison Kavey, *Books of Secrets: Natural Philosophy in England, 1550–1600* (Urbana and Chicago: University of Illinois Press, 2007), 10–17 and 92–93.
60. Kavey, *Books of Secrets*, 85.
61. William L. Eamon, "Science and Popular Culture in Sixteenth Century Italy: The 'Professors of Secrets' and Their Books," *Sixteenth Century Journal* 16 (1985): 479. See too Eamon, *Science and the Secrets of Nature: Books of Secrets in Medieval and Early Modern Culture* (Princeton: Princeton University Press, 1994). For further discussion on the role of secrets in the development of science and medicine, see Elaine Leong and Alisha Rankin eds., *Secrets and Knowledge in Medicine and Science, 1500–1800* (Aldershot: Ashgate, 2011). For a significant discussion of secrecy in early modern artisanal culture, see Pamela O. Long, *Openness, Secrecy, Authorship: Technical Arts and the Culture of Knowledge from Antiquity to the Renaissance* (Baltimore: Johns Hopkins University Press, 2001). For more on books of secrets, see Chapters 1 and 4.
62. Mary E. Fissell, *Patients, Power, and the Poor in Eighteenth-Century Bristol* (Cambridge: Cambridge University Press, 1991), 19.
63. John Henry, "Doctors and Healers: Popular Culture and the Medical Profession" in Stephen Pumfrey, Paolo L. Rossi, and Maurice Slawinski (eds.), *Science Culture and Popular Belief in Renaissance Europe* (Manchester: Manchester University Press, 1991), 203.
64. *Paracelsus: Selected Writings*, ed. Jolande Jacobi (Princeton: Princeton University Press, 1951), 57.
65. Henry, "Doctors and Healers," 203.
66. Andrew Wear, *Knowledge and Practice in English Renaissance Medicine, 1550–1680* (Cambridge: Cambridge University Press, 2000), 56–57.
67. Wear, *Knowledge and Practice*, 50. See too Sara Pennell, "Perfecting Practice? Women, Manuscript Recipes and Knowledge in Early Modern England" in Victoria E. Burke and Jonathan Gibson (eds.), *Early Modern Women's*

Manuscript Writing: Selected Papers from Trinity/Trent Colloquium (Aldershot: Ashgate, 2004), 237–58. On representations of household practices and domesticity on the English stage, see Wall, *Staging Domesticity*.

68. Doreen G. [Evenden] Nagy, *Popular Medicine in Seventeenth-Century England* (Bowling Green, OH: Bowling Green State University Popular Press, 1988); Linda A. Pollock, *With Faith and Physic: The Life of a Tudor Gentlewoman, Lady Grace Mildmay, 1552–1620* (London: Collins and Brown, 1993); Margaret Pelling, "Thoroughly Resented? Older Women and the Medical Role in Early Modern London" in Lynette Hunter and Sarah Hutton (eds.), *Women, Science, and Medicine 1500–1700: Mothers and Sisters of the Royal Society* (Stroud: Sutton, 1997), 63–88; Pelling, *Medical Conflicts in Early Modern London: Patronage, Physicians, and Irregular Practitioners, 1550–1640* (Oxford: Clarendon Press, 2003), 189–204. Lynette Hunter, "Women and Domestic Medicine: Lady Experimenters, 1570–1620," in Hunter and Hutton, *Women, Science, and Medicine*, 89–107. As Elaine Leong and Sara Pennell observe, receipt books were not "gender-specific"; see "Recipe Collections and the Currency of Medical Knowledge in the Early Modern 'Medical Marketplace'" in Mark. S. R. Jenner and Patrick Wallis (eds.), *Medicine and the Market in England and Its Colonies, c. 1450–c. 1850* (Basingstoke: Palgrave Macmillan, 2007), 133–52, esp. 138. Also on receipt books, Jennifer Stine, "Opening Closets: The Discovery of Household Medicine in Early Modern England," unpublished Ph.D. thesis, Stanford University (1996); Sara Pennell, "The Material Culture of Food in Early Modern England, circa 1650–1750," unpublished Ph.D. thesis, University of Oxford (1997); Lisa K. Meloncon, "Rhetoric, Remedies, Regimens: Popular Science in Early Modern England," unpublished Ph.D. thesis, University of South Carolina (2005); Catherine Field, "'Many Hands': Early Modern Women's Receipt Books and the Politics of Writing Food for the Nation," unpublished Ph.D. thesis, University of Maryland (2006); Field, "'Many Hands': Writing the Self in Early Modern Women's Recipe Books" in Michelle M. Dowd and Julie A. Eckerle (eds.), *Genre and Women's Life Writing in Early Modern England* (Aldershot: Ashgate, 2007); Elaine Leong, "Medical Recipe Collections in Seventeenth-Century England: Knowledge, Text and Gender," unpublished Ph.D. thesis, University of Oxford (2006); Leong, "Making Medicines in the Early Modern Household," *Bulletin of the History of Medicine* 82 (2008): 145–68; Alisha Rankin, "Medicine for the Uncommon Woman: Experience, Experiment, and Exchange in Early Modern Germany," unpublished Ph.D. thesis, Harvard University (2005); Rankin, "Duchess, Heal Thyself: Elisabeth of Rochlitz and the Patient's Perspective in Early Modern Germany," *Bulletin of the History of Medicine* 82 (2008): 109–44; Elizabeth Spiller, "Recipes for Knowledge: Maker's Knowledge Traditions, Paracelsian Recipes, and the Invention of the Cookbook, 1600–1660" in Joan Fitzpatrick (ed.), *Renaissance Food from Rabelais to Shakespeare: Culinary Readings and Culinary Histories* (Aldershot: Ashgate, 2010), 55–72. For more on receipt books, see Chapter 1.

69. Deborah E. Harkness, *The Jewel House: Elizabethan London and the Scientific Revolution* (New Haven: Yale University Press, 2007), and Pamela H. Smith, *The Body of the Artisan: Art and Experience in the Scientific Revolution* (Chicago: University of Chicago Press, 2004). On the rapidly changing conceptions of knowledge production, see Pamela H. Smith and Benjamin Schmidt (eds.), *Making Knowledge in Early Modern Europe: Practices, Objects, and Texts, 1400–1800* (Chicago: University of Chicago Press, 2007). See too Harold J. Cook on the role of medicine in the development of scientific thought, "The New Philosophy and Medicine in Seventeenth-Century England" in Lindberg and Westman, *Reappraisals of the Scientific Revolution*, 397–436.

70. See Bruce T. Moran on how the early modern home was one milieu for "empirical inquiry, experiment, and the production of effects through human agency to extract that which was hidden in nature" in *Distilling Knowledge: Alchemy, Chemistry, and the Scientific Revolution* (Cambridge, MA: Harvard University Press, 2005), 66. Moran cites Sir Hugh Plat's argument in *The Jewell House of Art and Nature* (1594 edition) that through cooking and distillation "women imitated in the home the practical parts of mystical philosophies discussed in the circles of savants" (62).

71. Some critics have suggested that the more bizarre recipes were read less for use than amusement; however, their presence in manuscript receipt books suggests otherwise. See Best and Brightman's introduction to *The Book of Secrets of Albertus Magnus*, xxii.

72. Elizabeth Sleigh and Felicia Whitfeld, "Collection of medical receipts, 1647–1722," MS 751, fo. 20r, Wellcome Library.

73. *English Medical Notebook, 17th Century* (1575–1663), MS 6812, 139, Wellcome Library. Thanks to Emma Smith. On word cures, see Tanya Pollard, "Spelling the Body" in Floyd-Wilson and Sullivan, *Environment and Embodiment*, 171–86.

74. Jane Jackson, "A very shorte and compendious Methode of Phisicke and Chirurgery (1642)," MS 373, fo. 75r–75v, Wellcome Library.

75. Fabián Alejandro Campagne, "Witchcraft and the Sense-of-the-Impossible in Early Modern Spain: Some Reflections Based on the Literature of Superstition (ca. 1500–1800)," *Harvard Theological Review* 96 (2003): 51.

76. From the preface to *De secretis mulierum*, quoted by Katharine Park, *Secrets of Women: Gender, Generation, and the Origins of Human Dissection* (New York: Zone Books, 2006), 82.

77. Park, *Secrets of Women*, 83–84.

78. Mary E. Fissell defines "bodywork" as a wide range of labors attending to the body, including the work of searchers, wet-nurses, watchers, and healers in "Introduction: Women, Health, and Healing in Early Modern Europe," *Bulletin of the History of Medicine* 82 (2008): 1–17.

79. Elizabeth Spiller, "Introductory Note," *Seventeenth-Century English Recipe Books*, vols. 3 and 4 (Aldershot: Ashgate, 2008), xxvii.

80. Deborah E. Harkness, "A View from the Streets: Women and Medical Work in Elizabethan London," *Bulletin of the History of Medicine* 82 (2008): 52–85, esp. 84.

81. Park, *Secrets of Women*, 82.
82. Monica H. Green, "From 'Diseases of Women' to 'Secrets of Women': The Transformation of Gynecological Literature in the Later Middle Ages," *Journal of Medieval and Early Modern Studies* 30 (2000): 15. Also see Green, *Making Women's Medicine Masculine: The Rise of Male Authority in Pre-Modern Gynaecology* (Oxford: Oxford University Press, 2008), 204–45.
83. Green, "From 'Diseases of Women,'" 18.
84. I take this phrase from the collection of essays about empiricism in the period, edited by Wolfe and Gal, *The Body as Object and Instrument of Knowledge: Embodied Empiricism in Early Modern Science*. In this collection, Harold J. Cook argues for the centrality of medicine to the development of scientific thought in the period but also notes the social prejudices raised by experiential knowledge: "If bodily empiricism was the grounding for science, then who was to say whether the empiric, apothecary, or surgeon, or even a peasant woman from South-East Asia, was not better informed about the clinical facts, and therefore a better practitioner, than a well-educated physician?"; see "Victories for Empiricism, Failures for Theory: Medicine and Science in the Seventeenth Century," 27. On the relevance of women and gender difference to the "epistemological experimentation that culminated in the 'new science'" in the seventeenth century, see Rebecca M. Wilkin, *Women, Imagination, and the Search for Truth in Early Modern France* (Aldershot: Ashgate, 2008), 1. On the role of women as both agents and objects in the history of science, see Londa L. Schiebinger, *The Mind Has No Sex? Women in the Origins of Modern Science* (Cambridge, MA: Harvard University Press, 1989) and Sylvia Lorraine Bowerbank, *Speaking for Nature: Women and Ecologies of Early Modern England* (Baltimore: Johns Hopkins University Press, 2004). For pioneering work on this subject, see Carolyn Merchant, *The Death of Nature: Women, Ecology, and the Scientific Revolution* (San Francisco: Harper & Row, 1980) and Evelyn Fox Keller, *Secrets of Life, Secrets of Death: Essays on Language, Gender, and Science* (New York: Routledge, 1992).
85. Pliny, the Elder, *The historie of the vvorld Commonly called, the naturall historie of C. Plinius Secundus*, trans. Philemon Holland, 2 vols. (London, 1601), 2.307–10. Pliny was "expected reading in the universities." Students at Wittenberg, for example, "were taught their 'physics' of the natural world" from Pliny. Moreover, the "sheer volume of editions and the accessibility and interest of Pliny's subject matter . . . suggest that many in fact gathered their notions about the real world from him"; Arrizabalaga *et al.*, *The Great Pox*, 247.
86. Pliny, *The historie*, 2.309.
87. Pliny, *The historie*, 2.309.
88. Joannes Jonstonus, *The idea of practical physic*, 12 books (London, 1657), 6.6 and 6.10. On the "salvific healing power of the ingestible virgin corpse," see Louise Noble, *Medicinal Cannibalism in Early Modern English Literature and Culture* (New York: Palgrave Macmillan, 2011), 131. For a survey of blood and corpse medicine, see Richard Sugg, *Mummies, Cannibals, and Vampires: The History of Corpse Medicine from the Renaissance to the Victorians* (London and

New York: Routledge, 2011). On the use of blood and milk in women's healing practices, see Katharine Park, "Medicine and Magic: The Healing Arts" in Judith C. Brown and Robert C. Davis (eds.), *Gender and Society in Renaissance Italy* (London and New York: Longman, 1998), 141; Luisa Accati, "The Spirit of Fornication: Virtue of the Soul and Virtue of the Body in Friuli, 1600–1800" in Edward Muir and Guido Ruggiero (eds.), *Sex and Gender in Historical Perspective*, trans. Margaret A. Galluci (Baltimore: Johns Hopkins University Press, 1990), 110–40; Guido Ruggiero, *Binding Passions: Tales of Magic, Marriage, and Power at the End of the Renaissance* (Oxford: Oxford University Press, 1993).

89. See Patricia Crawford, "Attitudes to Menstruation in Seventeenth-Century England," *Past and Present* 91 (1981): 59–61. For example, see Girolamo Ruscelli, *The seconde part of the Secretes of Master Alexis of Piemont* (London, 1560), which offers a cure for poison when "some manne hath [been] given menstruall blood to drink, as wicked wemen some time doe" (57). See too Steven Wilson, *The Magical Universe: Everyday Ritual and Magic in Pre-Modern Europe* (London and New York: Hambledon and London, 2000), 399–402; Cathy McClive, "Menstrual Knowledge and Medical Practice in Early Modern France, c. 1555–1761" in Andrew Shail and Gillian Howie (eds.), *Menstruation: A Cultural History* (Basingstoke: Palgrave Macmillan, 2005), 76–89. Carole Levin speculates that Queen Elizabeth I, who regularly healed her subjects with touching, may have refrained from doing so when menstruating; Carole Levin, "'Would I Could Give You Help and Succour': Elizabeth I and the Politics of Touch," *Albion* 21 (1989): 200.

90. On the evil eye and fascination, see Wilson, *The Magical Universe*, 402–08 and Fernando Salmón and Montserrat Cabré, "Fascinating Women: The Evil Eye in Medical Scholasticism" in Roger French, Jon Arrizabalaga, Andrew Cunningham, and Luis García-Ballester (eds.), *Medicine from the Black Death to the French Disease* (Aldershot: Ashgate, 1998), 53–84. Associations between poisonous menstrual blood, fascination, and women's contagious natures can be found in the medieval *De Secretis Mulierum*; see *Women's Secrets: A Translation of Pseudo-Albertus Magnus's* De Secretis Mulierum *with Commentaries*, ed. Helen Rodnite Lemay (Albany: State University of New York Press, 1992). Among its claims, this text avers that men become hoarse in the presence of menstruating women "because the venomous humors from the woman's body infect the air by her breath" (130).

91. Jackson, "A very shorte and compendious Methode of Phisicke and Chirurgery," fo. 104v–105r.

92. *Malleus Maleficarum*, ed. and trans. Montague Summers (London: John Rodker, 1928), 47.

93. Johann Jacob Wecker, *Eighteen books of the secrets of art & nature being the summe and substance of naturall philosophy* (London, 1660), 34.

94. Thomas Johnson, *Cornucopiae, or diuers secrets* (London, 1595), sig. A4v.

95. See Merchant, *The Death of Nature*, 169. The question of how to interpret the metaphorical identification of woman as nature is a subject of dispute,

especially in relation to Bacon's language. See "Focus: Getting Back to *The Death of Nature*: Rereading Carolyn Merchant," *Isis* 97 (2006), as well as selected essays in *Journal of the History of Ideas* 69 (2008): Carolyn Merchant, "Secrets of Nature: The Bacon Debates Revisited," 147–62; Brian Vickers, "Francis Bacon, Feminist Historiography, and the Dominion of Nature," 117–41; Katharine Park, "Response to Brian Vickers, 'Francis Bacon, Feminist Historiography, and the Dominion of Nature,'" 143–46. See too Peter Pesic, "Wrestling with Proteus: Francis Bacon and the 'Torture' of Nature," *Isis* 90 (1999): 81–94.

96. Katharine Park, "Nature in Person: Medieval and Renaissance Allegories and Emblems" in Lorraine Daston and Fernando Vidal (eds.), *The Moral Authority of Nature* (Chicago: University of Chicago Press, 2004), 50–73.

97. Park, *Secrets of Women*, 26–27. See too Jonathan Sawday, *The Body Emblazoned: Dissection and the Human Body in Renaissance Culture* (London: Routledge, 1995) for some discussion of the perceived uncanny nature of women's bodies in relation to the development of science (10).

98. Katharine Park, "Dissecting the Female Body: From Women's Secrets to the Secrets of Nature" in Jane Donawerth and Adele Seeff (eds.), *Crossing Boundaries: Attending to Early Modern Women* (Newark: University of Delaware Press, 2000), 39.

99. Mary E. Fissell, *Vernacular Bodies: The Politics of Reproduction in Early Modern England* (Oxford: Oxford University Press, 2004), 52.

100. Laurinda S. Dixon, *Perilous Chastity: Women and Illness in Pre-Enlightenment Art and Medicine* (Ithaca, NY: Cornell University Press, 1995) and Kaara L. Peterson, *Popular Medicine, Hysterical Disease, and Social Controversy in Shakespeare's England* (Burlington, VT: Ashgate, 2010).

101. On the one-sex model, see Thomas Laqueur, *Making Sex: Body and Gender from the Greeks to Freud* (Cambridge, MA: Harvard University Press, 1990). For challenges to Laqueur, see Katharine Park and Robert A. Nye, "Destiny Is Anatomy," *New Republic* (February 19, 1991): 53–57; Gail Kern Paster, "The Unbearable Coldness of Female Being: Women's Imperfection and the Humoral Economy," *English Literary Renaissance* 28 (1998): 416–40; Michael Stolberg, "A Woman Down to Her Bones: The Anatomy of Sexual Differences in the Sixteenth and Early Seventeenth Centuries," *Isis* 94 (2003): 274–99. Most applicable to my point is W. D. Churchill's argument that early modern writers believed that, during the treatment of disease in men and women, the female body responded to illness and therapy in ways that differed completely from the male body; see "The Medical Practice of the Sexed Body: Women, Men, and Disease in Britain, circa 1600–1740," *Social History of Medicine* 18 (2005): 3–22.

102. Fissell, *Vernacular Bodies*, 88.

103. Jonstonus, *The idea of practical physic*, 10.74.

104. Alexandro Massaria, *De Morbis foemineis, the woman's counsellour*, trans. R. Turner (London, 1657), 3. Massaria published the Latin text *Praelectiones de morbis mulierum* in 1591.

105. On the womb's sympathy, see Peterson, *Popular Medicine*, 24–26 and *passim*.
106. On the importance of Jorden for the history of medicine and mental illness, see Ilza Veith, *Hysteria: The History of a Disease* (Chicago: University of Chicago Press, 1965); Michael MacDonald (ed.), *Witchcraft and Hysteria in Elizabethan London: Edward Jorden and the Mary Glover Case* (London: Routledge, 1991); G. S. Rousseau, "'A Strange Pathology.' Hysteria in the Early Modern World" in Sander L. Gilman, Helen King, Roy Porter, G. S. Rousseau, and Elaine Showalter (eds.), *Hysteria beyond Freud* (Berkeley: University of California Press, 1993), 91–221; Carol Thomas Neely, *Distracted Subjects: Madness and Gender in Shakespeare and Early Modern Culture* (Ithaca, NY: Cornell University Press, 2004); Mark S. Micale, *Approaching Hysteria: Disease and Its Interpretations* (Princeton: Princeton University Press, 1995); Fissell, *Vernacular Bodies*; Peterson, *Popular Medicine*.
107. D. P. Walker, *Unclean Spirits: Possession and Exorcism in France and England in the Late Sixteenth and Early Seventeenth Centuries* (Philadelphia: University of Pennsylvania Press, 1981), 73.
108. Edward Jorden, *A briefe discourse of a disease called the suffocation of the mother* (London, 1603), fo. 5r. Subsequent quotations cited parenthetically in text.
109. Stuart Clark, "Demons and Disease: The Disenchantment of the Sick (1500–1700)" in Marijke Gijswijt-Hofstra, Hilary Marland, and Hans De Waardt (eds.), *Illness and Healing Alternatives in Western Europe* (London: Routledge, 1997), 38–58.
110. Interestingly, Thomas Willis writes at the end of the seventeenth century, "[W]hen at any time a sickness happens in a Woman's Body, of an unusual manner, or more occult original, so that its causes lie hid, and a Curatory indication is altogether uncertain, presently we accuse the evil influence of the Womb ... and in every unusual symptom, we declare it to be something hysterical ... which oftentimes is only the subterfuge of ignorance." Thomas Willis, *An Essay of the Pathology of the Brain and Nervous Stock* (London, 1684), quoted by Veith, *Hysteria*, 134.
111. Jorden's discussion of sympathetic disorders appears to be standard. Early modern medical discourse established several etiological categories of these disorders: they occurred through communication, similarity of substance, similarity of origin, similarity of function, transmission of a substance, and contiguity. See Arrizabalaga *et al.*, *The Great Pox*, 335n.
112. For many classical writers, the womb's perceived independence led to its identification as "an animal within an animal," not only capable of migrating but also driven by an appetite. The ancient therapeutic method of moving the womb up and down by the application of attractive or repellent smells, practiced beyond the seventeenth century, may have derived from this conception of the womb-as-animal. On the ancient use of scent therapy, see Helen King, *Hippocrates' Woman: Reading the Female Body in Ancient Greece* (London: Routledge, 1998), 37–38 and 223–46. See too Audrey Eccles, *Obstetrics and Gynaecology in Tudor and Stuart England* (Kent, OH: Kent State University Press, 1982), 79–80.

113. Misnumbered in the folio as 16r.
114. On the classical history of false deaths and uterine afflictions, see also King, chapter 11 of *Hippocrates' Woman.*
115. The debate over the weapon-salve began in England when a parson, William Foster, published *Hoplocrisma-spongus: or, A sponge to vvipe avvay the weapon-salve A treatise, wherein is proved, that the cure late-taken up amongst us, by applying the salve to the weapon, is magicall and unlawfull* (London, 1631). Foster expresses worry at how commonplace the therapy had become and wishes to dissuade people from using it. While he believes that natural cures can be "wrought by Sympathies" (20), he identifies the weapon-salve as an implicit contract with the devil. Foster named the mystical writer Robert Fludd in his treatise, who replied the same year with a defense of the weapon-salve in *Doctor Fludds answer vnto M· Foster or, The squeesing of Parson Fosters sponge, ordained by him for the wiping away of the weapon-salue VVherein the sponge-bearers immodest carriage and behauiour towards his bretheren is detected* (London, 1631). Also weighing in on the topic were Daniel Sennert (*The weapon-salve's maladie* [London, 1637]) and James Hart (*Klinike, or The diet of the diseased* [London, 1633]), who both grant the power of sympathetic actions on the basis of invisible yet corporeal emanations but worry that the weapon-salve tacitly serves the devil. In Sir Kenelm Digby's treatise on the weapon-salve, he explicitly reconciles sympathetic action with atomistic theories: "if it happens that within that air there be found some dispersed atoms of the same nature, with the body which draws them, the attraction of such atoms is made more powerfully, then if they were bodies of a different nature, and these atoms do stay, stick, and mingle with more willingnesse with the body which draws them. The reason hereof is the resemblance, and Sympathy they have one with the other." See Sir Kenelm Digby, *A late discourse made in a solemne assembly of nobles and learned men at Montpellier in France touching the cure of wounds by the powder of sympathy : with instructions how to make the said powder : whereby many other secrets of nature are unfolded* (London, 1658), 68. For a summary of the controversy, see Allen G. Debus, *The Chemical Philosophy: Paracelsian Science and Medicine in the Sixteenth and Seventeenth Centuries*, 2 vols. (New York: Science History Publications, 1977), vol. 1, 279–90.
116. Elizabeth Jacob and others, "Physicall and chyrurgicall receipts (1654–c. 1685)," MS 3009, 99, Wellcome Library. Fludd states that the wounded should not lie with a "menstruous woman," or it will disrupt the power of the ointment; *Dr Fludds answer*, 1.106. James Hart, who dismisses the ointment, states that the wounded man should not lie with any woman; *Klinike*, 373.
117. *Henslowe's Diary*, ed. R. A. Foakes and R. T. Rickert (Cambridge: Cambridge University Press, 1961), 38–42. S. P. Cerasano has suggested that Henslowe received these receipts from Simon Forman, but the widespread popularity of such knowledge raises the possibility that Henslowe could have derived them from a less professional source than London's notorious astrologer-physician-magician; see "Philip Henslowe, Simon Forman, and the Theatrical Community of the 1590s," *Shakespeare Quarterly* 44 (1993): 145–58.

118. Marshall, *The Surprising Effects*, 1 and 5.
119. William Rankins, "A Mirror of Monsters (1587)"; Stephen Gosson, "Plays Confuted in Five Actions (1582)"; Anthony Munday, "A Second and Third Blast of Retreat from Plays and Theater (1580)", all in Tanya Pollard (ed.), *Shakespeare's Theater: A Sourcebook* (Oxford: Blackwell, 2004), 125, 108, and 79.
120. Stephen Gosson, "The School of Abuse (1579)" in Pollard, *Shakespeare's Theater*, 27.
121. Tanya Pollard, *Drugs and Theater in Early Modern England* (Oxford: Oxford University Press, 2005), 16. Pollard frames the therapeutic potential of early modern theater in Galenic and Paracelsian terms; see 12–19 and *passim*.
122. On theater's potentially humoral effects, see the Induction to Shakespeare's *The Taming of the Shrew* when the servant claims that the physician has prescribed a comedy to purge Christopher Sly's melancholy. For a survey of Italian writing on the allopathic and homeopathic effects of theater, see Federico Schneider, *Pastoral Drama and Healing in Early Modern Italy* (Aldershot: Ashgate, 2010). Schneider quotes sixteenth-century author Lorenzo Giacomini on how humors are moved by a sympathetic process: "Therefore it is clear that, just as humors are moved and purged by means of purging medicaments, due to the natural sympathy and convenience that exists between them, thus in the soul pregnant with melancholy concepts of fear and compassion by means of [the affects of] pity and fear, *alike* concepts are moved and purged" (37). On the contagious power of emotions in an early modern theater of sympathy, see Matthew Steggle, *Laughing and Weeping in Early Modern Theatres* (Aldershot: Ashgate, 2007), esp. 4–8.
123. Sir Philip Sidney, *An Apology for Poetry (or The Defence of Poesy)*, ed. R. W. Maslen, 3rd edition (Manchester: Manchester University Press, 2002), 96.
124. Michel de Montaigne, "On Cato the Younger" in M. A. Screech (trans.), *The Complete Essays* (London: Penguin Books, 2003), 260. See too Plato's *Ion* in *Early Socratic Dialogues*, ed. Trevor J. Saunders (London and New York: Penguin, 2005), 49–68.
125. "The Schoole of Abuse (1579)" in Pollard, *Shakespeare's Theater*, 31.
126. Munday, "A Second and Third Blast of Retreat (1580)," 77. He goes on to relate an anecdote: "I can tell you a story of like practice used of late by a jealous wife to her husband, whose heart being, as she thought, estranged otherwise than of custom, did practice with a sorceress to have some powder, which might have force to renew her husband's wonted goodwill towards her: but it had such a virtue in the operation, as it well nigh brought him his bane: for his memory thereby was gone, so that if God had not dealt miraculously with him, by revealing it, it had cost him his life." "[I]t is a miracle," he exclaims, "if there be found any, either woman or maid [in the audience], which with these spectacles of strange lust is not oftentimes enflamed, even unto fury" (77).
127. Thomas Heywood, *An apologie for actors* (London, 1612), sig. G1v–G2v.
128. On this concept, see Malcolm Gaskill, *Crimes and Mentalities in Early Modern England* (Cambridge: Cambridge University Press, 2000), 211.

129. On the emanating pure spirits of young men, see Wecker, *Eighteen books*, 32 and della Porta, *Natural Magick*, 230. For various manuscript receipts that use a young man's blood to restore the "strength and youth of the body," see Stanhope, 1st Earl of Chesterfield, "A booke of severall receipts (c. 1635)," MS 761, fo. 200r, Wellcome Library.

130. Thomas Heywood, *A Woman Killed With Kindness* in Kathleen E. McLuskie and David Bevington (eds.), *Plays on Women* (Manchester: Manchester University Press, 1999), 13.124–27.

131. Anon., *The English Midwife Enlarged* (London, 1682). See the chapter "Of Leanness and Bewitching," 319.

132. Wecker, *Eighteen books*, 34.

133. Valerie Traub has observed that "Confinement, monumentalization, and death are the typical … means the drama employs to transmute illicit female desire into acceptable form"; see *The Renaissance of Lesbianism in Early Modern England* (Cambridge: Cambridge University Press, 2002), 24.

134. William W. E. Slights has observed of early modern drama that the female characters "not only have secrets, they are often conceived of as actually *being* secrets"; "Secret Places in Renaissance Drama," *University of Toronto Quarterly* 59 (1990): 365.

135. Willem de Blécourt writes, "Because of its haphazard and contingent nature, an actual (but not necessarily formal) witchcraft accusation was an ever lurking threat that could strike a woman at any time … it sufficed [merely for a woman] to cross a boundary at the wrong moment"; see "The Making of the Female Witch: Reflections on Witchcraft and Gender in the Early Modern Period," *Gender and History* 12 (2000): 304.

136. Lorraine Daston and Katharine Park, *Wonders and the Order of Nature*, 330.

137. Daston and Park, *Wonders and the Order of Nature*, 339.

1 WOMEN'S SECRETS AND THE STATUS OF EVIDENCE IN *ALL'S WELL THAT ENDS WELL*

1. For discussions of embodied knowledge in the period, see Pamela H. Smith, *The Body of the Artisan: Art and Experience in the Scientific Revolution* (Chicago: University of Chicago Press, 2004) and Charles T. Wolfe and Ofer Gal (eds.), *The Body as Object and Instrument of Knowledge: Embodied Empiricism in Early Modern Science* (Dordrecht and New York: Springer, 2010).

2. Lisa Jardine notes that the plot of *All's Well That Ends Well* "hinges on Helena's specialist knowledge and on the power that knowledge gives her"; see *Reading Shakespeare Historically* (London: Routledge, 1996), 53. Regina Buccola identifies Helena as a kind of cunning woman whose healing arts have associations with fairy magic. Richard Stensgaard interprets Helena's learning as Paracelsian. Catherine Field maintains that Helena represents the many laywomen who kept household receipt books and practiced domestic medicine in their homes and communities. And David Bergeron views Helena's expertise as a direct

inheritance from her father, the famous physician Gerard de Narbon, who left her his medicinal receipts. See Regina Bucola, *Fairies, Fractious Women, and the Old Faith: Fairy Lore in Early Modern British Drama and Culture* (Selinsgrove, PA: Susquehanna University Press, 2006), 170; Richard K. Stensgaard, *"All's Well That Ends Well* and the Galenico-Paracelsian Controversy," *Renaissance Quarterly* 25 (1972): 173–88; Catherine Field, "'Sweet Practicer, thy Physic I will try': Helena and Her 'Good Receipt' in *All's Well, That Ends Well*" in Gary Waller (ed.), *All's Well, That Ends Well: New Critical Essays* (New York: Routledge, 2007), 194–208; David M. Bergeron, "'The credit of your father': Absent Fathers in *All's Well, That Ends Well*" in Waller, *New Critical Essays*, 169–82. Garrett A. Sullivan, Jr., *Memory and Forgetting in English Renaissance Drama* (Cambridge: Cambridge University Press, 2005), argues that the receipt, as a distillation of Helena's father's memory and knowledge, "figure[s] as 'off-spring'" (53). Mary Polito suggests that Shakespeare ironically presents Helena as an "ideal, active professional citizen" in an effort to boost his own profession as play-maker; see "Professions and 'the Labouring Arts' in *All's Well That Ends Well,*" *Renaissance & Reformation / Renaissance et Reforme* 28 (2004): 90.

3. William Eamon asserts that the experimental knowledge distributed in printed books of secrets provided the "prehistory ... of the Baconian sciences"; see *Science and the Secrets of Nature: Books of Secrets in Medieval and Early Modern Culture* (Princeton: Princeton University Press, 1994), 9. On the intersections between receipt books and books of secrets, see Field, "'Sweet Practicer,'" 204–05 and Elizabeth Spiller, "Introductory Note," *Seventeenth-Century English Recipe Books*, vols. 3 and 4 (Aldershot: Ashgate, 2008), xii–xvi. On the categories of "experience" and "experiment" in the period, see Peter Dear, *Discipline and Experience: The Mathematical Way in the Scientific Revolution* (Chicago: University of Chicago Press, 1995) and "The Meanings of Experience" in Katharine Park and Lorraine Daston (eds.), *The Cambridge History of Science*, vol. 3 (Cambridge: Cambridge University Press, 2003), 106–31.

4. Field, "'Sweet Practicer,'" 204–05.

5. Nancy G. Siraisi, "'Remarkable' Diseases and 'Remarkable' Cures, and Personal Experience in Renaissance Medical Texts" in *Medicine and the Italian Universities, 1250–1600* (Leiden: Brill, 2001), 230.

6. On magic and medicine, see Lauren Kassell, *Medicine and Magic in Elizabethan London. Simon Forman: Astrologer, Alchemist, Physician* (Oxford: Oxford University Press, 2005). On the mingling of Paracelsus, astrology, magic, and Galenic medicine in practice, see Michael MacDonald's study of Richard Napier in *Mystical Bedlam: Madness, Anxiety, and Healing in Seventeenth-Century England* (Cambridge: Cambridge University Press, 1981).

7. Ian Maclean, *Logic, Signs and Nature in the Renaissance: The Case of Learned Medicine* (Cambridge: Cambridge University Press, 2002), 245.

8. William Brockbank, "Sovereign Remedies: A Critical Depreciation of the 17th Century London *Pharmacopoeia*," *Medical History* 8 (1964): 2.

9. Richard Kieckhefer, *Magic in the Middle Ages* (Cambridge: Cambridge University Press, 2000), 66–67.

10. Maclean, *Logic, Signs and Nature*, 245.
11. Nancy G. Siraisi, *The Clock and the Mirror: Girolamo Cardano and Renaissance Medicine* (Princeton: Princeton University Press, 1997), 151.
12. See the "Introduction" in John Henry and J. M. Forrester (eds.), *Jean Fernel's "On the Hidden Causes of Things": Forms, Souls, and Occult Diseases in Renaissance Medicine* (Leiden: Brill, 2005), 63. See too Ron Millen, "The Manifestation of Occult Qualities in the Scientific Revolution" in Margaret J. Osler and Paul Lawrence Farber (eds.), *Religion, Science, and Worldview: Essays in Honor of Richard S. Westfall* (Cambridge: Cambridge University Press, 1985), 185–216; Keith Hutchison, "What Happened to Occult Qualities in the Scientific Revolution?" *Isis* 73 (1982): 233–53; L. Deer Richardson, "The Generation of Disease: Occult Causes and Diseases of the Total Substance" in A. Wear, R. K. French, and I. M. Lonie (eds.), *The Medical Renaissance of the Sixteenth Century* (Cambridge: Cambridge University Press, 1985), 175–94.
13. Fernel, in Henry and Forrester, *Jean Fernel*, 691.
14. John Henry, "Doctors and Healers: Popular Culture and the Medical Profession" in Stephen Pumfrey, Paolo L. Rossi, and Maurice Slawinski (eds.), *Science Culture and Popular Belief in Renaissance Europe* (Manchester: Manchester University Press, 1991), 203. Andrew Wear, *Knowledge and Practice in English Renaissance Medicine, 1550–1680* (Cambridge: Cambridge University Press, 2000), 56.
15. Wear, *Knowledge and Practice*, 49–65.
16. Paul Slack notes that "a strong magical element remained in many sixteenth-century medical recipes"; see "Mirrors of Health and Treasures of Poor Men: The Uses of the Vernacular Medical Literature of Tudor England" in Charles Webster (ed.), *Health, Medicine and Mortality in the Sixteenth Century* (Cambridge: Cambridge University Press, 1979), 265–66. Keith Thomas states that "seventeenth-century prescriptions which seem magical to us were in fact based on obsolescent assumptions about the physical properties of natural substances"; see *Religion and the Decline of Magic: Studies in Popular Beliefs in Sixteenth- and Seventeenth-Century England* (London: Penguin Books, 1971), 224. Throughout his study *Magic in the Middle Ages*, Kieckhefer also acknowledges how sympathetic magic and systematic astrology provided the foundation for many medieval recipes that depended on occult properties. See too Mary E. Fissell, *Patients, Power, and the Poor in Eighteenth-Century Bristol* (Cambridge: Cambridge University Press, 1991), 19–22 and Jennifer Stine, "Opening Closets: The Discovery of Household Medicine in Early Modern England," unpublished Ph.D. thesis, Stanford University (1996), 53–61.
17. "Collection of receipts, household, medical & veterinary (c. 1600)," v.a.140, fo. 35, The Folger Shakespeare Library. Thanks to Alan Stewart who helped me decipher this receipt.
18. For contemporary references to spitting in a dog's mouth, see William Rowley, Thomas Dekker, and John Ford, *The Witch of Edmonton* (1621), ed. Peter Corbin and Douglas Sedge (Manchester: Manchester University Press),

4.1.285–86; Thomas Middleton and Thomas Dekker, *The Roaring Girl (1611)*, ed. Paul A. Mulholland (Manchester: Manchester University Press, 1999), 2.1.408. According to Mulholland's notes, spitting in a dog's mouth is "a not uncommon expression of affection and means of befriending a dog" in the period (120–21). The use of whelps in cures seems to have been customary. See Steven Batman, *Batman uppon Bartholome his book de proprietatibus rerum* (London, 1582): "And yet to this day Authors commaund to take such whelpes wholsomely against venimous bitings: for such whelpes opened & layd hot to the biting of Serpents, draw out venim, & abate the age, and maketh ye sore members whole with remedies laid therto" (356).

19. "Receipt Book (c. 1675)," v.a.365, The Folger Shakespeare Library. Although this cure requires that the chicken's plucked tail be placed "close upon" the plague sore, its effectiveness depends on the same theory underlining action-at-a-distance.

20. Charles Estienne, *Maison rustique, or The countrey farme* (London, 1616), 74. See also Ambroise Paré on poison:

> we may put Hens, or Turkies that lay eggs (which therefore haue their fundaments more wide and open, and for the same purpose put a little salt into their fundaments) vpon the sharpe toppe of the *Bubo*, that by shutting their bills at seuerall times they may draw & sucke the venom into their bodies, farre more strongly and better then cupping glasses, because they are *endewed with a naturall property against poyson*, for they eate and concoct Toades, Efts, and such like virulent beasts: when one hen is killed with the poyson that she hath drawne into her body you must apply another, and then the third, fourth, fift and sixt within the space of halfe an hower. There be some that will rather cut them, or else whelps in the middest, and apply them warme vnto the place, that by the heate of the creature that is yet scarce dead, portion of the venom may be dissipated and exhaled.

A treatise of the plague contayning the causes, signes, symptomes, prognosticks, and cure thereof (London, 1630), 81. My emphasis.

21. "Collection of medical and cookery receipts (c. 1675–c. 1800)," MS 7721, fo. 205, Wellcome Library Collection.

22. In James Hart's discussion of the weapon-salve, which he vehemently refutes, he allows that sympathetic cures may work but demand contact or a narrow distance:

> And as little, or farre lesse for this purpose make the rest of his examples of sympathie: as of the maw or gussord of fowles, alleaged for this same sympathie, good to corroborate the stomacke, braines to braines, lungs to lungs, heart to heart, guts to guts, &c. If I should yet grant all this to be true (whereof I have yet just cause to doubt, if not to deny, whatsoever some others have held to the contrary; and fox lungs working by their abstersive and opening quality) yet would all this make just nothing for the purpose, these working, *per contactum physicum*, by mutuall contact,

and their operation exuscitated and actuated by the internall naturall heat; but none of them producing any such effect at a miles or more remote distance.

Klinike, or The diet of the diseased (London, 1633), 367. For survey of the weapon-salve controversy, see Allen G. Debus, *The Chemical Philosophy: Paracelsian Science and Medicine in the Sixteenth and Seventeenth Centuries*, 2 vols. (New York: Science History Publications, 1977), vol. 1, 279–90.

23. Katherine Packer, "Book of medicines for several diseases wounds & sores (1639)," v.a.387, The Folger Shakespeare Library: "To make children's teeth grow with little paine, Hang about the neck a woules tooth." For the foxes' stones cure, see Katherine Knight, "A Precious Medicine: Tradition and Magic in Some Seventeenth-Century Household Remedies," *Folklore* 113 (2002): 243.

24. On word charms, see Tanya Pollard, "Spelling the Body" in Mary Floyd-Wilson and Garrett A. Sullivan, Jr. (eds.), *Environment and Embodiment in Early Modern England* (Basingstoke: Palgrave Macmillan, 2007), 171–86.

25. "Boyle Family Receipt Book (c. 1675–c. 1710)," MS 1340, fo. 135r, Wellcome Library. See also Katherine and Edward Kidder, "Collection of cookery receipts, with a few medical receipts (1699)," MS 3107, fo. 192, Wellcome Library.

26. *Hocus Pocus Junior The anatomie of legerdemain* (London, 1634).

27. Girolamo Ruscelli, *The seconde part of the Secretes of Master Alexis of Piemont by hym collected out of diuers excellent authours* (London, 1560). See also Thomas Hill, *A briefe and pleasaunt treatise, entituled, Naturall and Artificiall conclusions* (London, 1581) which provides, for example, directions on "How to make thy Chamber appeare full of Snakes and Adders," a receipt that involves boiling a dead snake in a pan of wax and then making a candle. Once lit, the light will appear as if a thousand snakes are "creepying in thy Chamber" (sig. B iv).

28. Ruscelli, *Secretes of Master Alexis*, 17.

29. Philip Butterworth, *Magic on the Early English Stage* (Cambridge: Cambridge University Press, 2005). On the period's tendency to yoke together the effects of natural magic, the illusions of machinery, and mysteries of courtly politics, see Jessica Wolfe, *Humanism, Machinery, and Renaissance Literature* (Cambridge: Cambridge University Press, 2004).

30. *Henslowe's Diary*, ed. R. A. Foakes and R. T. Rickert (Cambridge: Cambridge University Press, 1961), 38–42.

31. Parenthetical citations to *All's Well That Ends Well* are taken from *The Norton Shakespeare*, ed. Stephen Greenblatt, 1st edition (New York and London: W. W. Norton, 1997). The speech is notoriously difficult to interpret; it is unclear whether Helena's "there" refers to her virginity, the court, or both.

32. On the compromise between Paracelsus and Galen in medical circles, see Paul H. Kocher, *Science and Religion in Elizabethan England* (San Marino, CA: Huntington Library, 1953) and Allen G. Debus, *The English Paracelsians* (Chicago: University of Chicago Press, 1968). On the range and importance of Paracelsian ideas, see Charles Webster, "Alchemical and Paracelsian

Medicine" in *Health, Medicine, and Mortality*, 301–34, and Deborah E. Harkness, *The Jewel House: Elizabethan London and the Scientific Revolution* (New Haven: Yale University Press, 2007), 57–96. On the possibility that the play privileges honest empirics, whom he identifies as Paracelsian, over the learned Galenic fellows of the college, see Stensgaard, "*All's Well That Ends Well*," 180–81. Stephanie Moss also maintains that Helena's reliance on "experience" suggests her cure has Paracelsian origins; "Transformation and Degeneration: The Paracelsian / Galenic Body in *Othello*," in Stephanie Moss and Kaara L. Peterson (eds.), *Disease, Diagnosis, and Cure on the Early Modern Stage* (Aldershot: Ashgate, 2004), 155–56.

33. The *OED* defines "empiric" as "A member of the sect among ancient physicians called *Empirici* . . . who (in opposition to the *Dogmatici* and *Methodici*) drew their rules of practice entirely from experience, to the exclusion of philosophical theory." Todd H. J. Pettigrew addresses Shakespeare's use of the word "empiric" and Helena's implicit acceptance of the title in *Shakespeare and the Practice of Physic: Medical Narratives on the Early Modern English Stage* (Newark: University of Delaware Press, 2007), 34–60.

34. Giovanni Boccaccio, *The decameron containing an hundred pleasant nouels*, trans. John Florio, 2 vols. (London, 1620), identifies a "swelling on his stomach," vol. 1, fo. 108r. William Painter, *The Palace of Pleasure* (London, 1566), locates the swelling in the king's breast (fo. 95v).

35. F. David Hoeniger, *Medicine and Shakespeare in the English Renaissance* (Newark: University of Delaware Press, 1992), 297; Nicholas Ray, ""Twas mine, 'twas Helen's': Rings of Desire in *All's Well, That Ends Well*" in Waller, *New Critical Essays*, 183–93; Bard C. Cosman, "*All's Well That Ends Well*: Shakespeare's Treatment of Anal Fistula," *The Upstart Crow* 19 (1999): 78–97; Field, "'Sweet Practicer,'" 195–99.

36. The *OED* gives its first definition of a fistula as "A long, narrow, suppurating canal of morbid origin in some part of the body; a long, sinuous pipe-like ulcer with a narrow orifice."

37. See Siraisi, "'Remarkable' Diseases and 'Remarkable' Cures."

38. Galen "alluded to the powers of specific remedies operating not by contrary qualities but by the similitude of their 'total substance'"; see Millen, "The Manifestation of Occult Qualities in the Scientific Revolution," 188. In his articulation of the doctrine of signatures and homeopathy, Paracelsus believed that the physician-as-magus had the capacity to discern all the secret virtues of Nature through a "process of concentration"; see Nicholas Goodrick-Clarke, "The Philosophy, Medicine, and Theology of Paracelsus" in Keith Whitlock (ed.), *Renaissance in Europe: A Reader* (New Haven: Yale University Press, 2000), 316.

39. Andrew Wear notes that chemical remedies were included in the London College of Physicians' first *Pharmacopeia* (1618), 354. See too Pettigrew, *Shakespeare and the Practice of Physic*, 56.

40. See Field, "'Sweet Practicer,'" 205.

41. Sujata Iyengar maintains that the "something" is surgical intervention and the sanctification of Helena's virginity: "'Handling Soft the Hurts': Sexual Healing and Manual Contact in *Orlando Furioso, The Faerie Queene*, and *All's Well That Ends Well*" in Elizabeth D. Harvey (ed.), *Sensible Flesh: On Touch in Early Modern Culture* (Philadelphia: University of Pennsylvania Press, 2003), 54.

42. Jean Fernel, Paracelsus, and others regularly explained the operations of diseases and medicaments as the consequences of celestial influences.

43. See Kent R. Lehnhof's discussion of the cure's off-stage status in "Performing Women: Female Theatricality in *All's Well, That Ends Well*" in Waller, *New Critical Essays*, 119.

44. From the preface to *De secretis mulierum*, quoted in Katharine Park, *Secrets of Women: Gender, Generation, and the Origins of Human Dissection* (New York: Zone Books, 2006), 82. On the earlier association between women's secrets and occult secrets, see Monica H. Green, "From 'Diseases of Women' to 'Secrets of Women': The Transformation of Gynecological Literature in the Later Middle Ages," *Journal of Medieval and Early Modern Studies* 30 (2000): 5–39, esp. 18. Also Green, *Making Women's Medicine Masculine: The Rise of Male Authority in Pre-Modern Gynaecology* (Oxford: Oxford University Press, 2008), 204–45.

45. On the womb's sympathy, see Kaara L. Peterson, *Popular Medicine, Hysterical Disease, and Social Controversy in Shakespeare's England* (Burlington, VT: Ashgate, 2010), 24–26 and *passim*.

46. Iyengar, "'Handling Soft the Hurts,'" 39–61. In less literal terms, Janet Adelman and Barbara Traister note that Helena's cure draws salacious comments but also observe that there is no evidence that she applies a sexual cure: Janet Adelman, *Suffocating Mothers: Fantasies of Maternal Origin in Shakespeare's Plays, Hamlet to The Tempest* (New York: Routledge, 1992), 82–83; Barbara Howard Traister, "'Doctor She': Healing and Sex in *All's Well That Ends Well*" in Richard Dutton and Jean E. Howard (eds.), *A Companion to Shakespeare's Works: Poems, Problem Comedies, Late Plays*, vol. 4 (Malden, MA: Blackwell, 2003), 343.

47. On the difficulty of interpreting miracles and wonders after the Reformation, see Alexandra Walsham, *Providence in Early Modern England* (Oxford: Oxford University Press, 1999), 230. See too Julie Crawford, *Marvelous Protestantism: Monstrous Births in Post-Reformation England* (Baltimore: Johns Hopkins University Press, 2005).

48. Lisa Jardine suggests that Helena's knowledge may cast her as a wise-woman or even a witch; *Reading Shakespeare*, 56.

49. Walsham, *Providence*, 230.

50. Stuart Clark, *Thinking with Demons: The Idea of Witchcraft in Early Modern Europe* (Oxford: Oxford University Press, 1999), 264.

51. See David M. Bergeron, who argues that the first half of the play is devoted to curing the king and the second half concerns the curing of Bertram; "The Structure of Healing in 'All's Well That Ends Well,'" *South Atlantic Bulletin* 37 (1972): 25.

52. On the play's fairy-tale components, see W. W. Lawrence, *Shakespeare's Problem Comedies* (New York: Macmillan, 1931); David Foley McCandless, *Gender and Performance in Shakespeare's Problem Comedies* (Bloomington: Indiana University Press, 1997), 37–78.
53. The *OED* defines "passport" in 6a as "An authorization to do something" and indicates that this meaning had currency from 1571 to 1605.
54. Traister argues that Helena is greensick and pursues Bertram for healing purposes; see "'Doctor She,'" 334. On the expected curative effects of bed-tricks, see Anthony Cassell, "Pilgrim Wombs, Physicke and Bed-Tricks: Intellectual Brilliance, Attenuation and Elision in *Decameron III:9*," *MLN* 121 (2006): 53–101; Marliss C. Desens, *The Bed-Trick in English Renaissance Drama: Explorations in Gender, Sexuality, and Power* (Newark: University of Delaware Press, 1994), 86; Kaara L. Peterson, "Fluid Economies: Portraying Shakespeare's Hysterics," *Mosaic: A Journal for the Interdisciplinary Study of Literature* 34 (2001): 35–59.
55. See Adelman, *Suffocating Mothers*, on how Helena controls Bertram and the ending of the play by introducing her own ring into the action (82).
56. In Boccaccio, Bertrand's ring has an "especial vertue and property" (*The decameron*, vol. 1, fo. 109v), and in Painter, he keeps it close "for a certaine vertue that he knewe it had" (*The Palace of Pleasure*, fo. 97v), but in Shakespeare's version Bertram's ring signifies his family lineage. See Garrett A. Sullivan, Jr., *Memory and Forgetting in English Drama: Shakespeare, Marlowe, Webster* (Cambridge: Cambridge University Press, 2005), 58. For a discussion of the ring differences in play and source, see Ray, "'Twas mine, 'twas Helen's.'"
57. William Jones, *Finger-Ring Lore: Historical, Legendary, Anecdotal* (London: Chatto & Windus, 1877).
58. On the significance of this legend, see Kieckhefer, *Magic*, 103.
59. Some editions gloss the line by citing Edmund Malone, who conjectures that the expression may allude to "the old tale of *The King and the Beggar*, which was the subject of a ballad"; see *All's Well That Ends Well* in Russell A. Fraser (ed.), *The New Cambridge Shakespeare* (Cambridge: Cambridge University Press, 2003), 154n. Since this tale concerns a king cured by a beggar, the allusion seems plausible, but it makes less sense for the king to allude to his own restoration fast upon the strange revelations of the preceding scene.
60. In *Edward the Confessor* (Berkeley: University of California Press, 1970), Frank Barlow notes that the story was "influential" (274n).
61. Lynn Jones, "From *Anglorum basileus* to Norman Saint: The Transformation of Edward the Confessor," *Haskins Society Journal* 12 (2003): 117. See H. G. Richardson, "The Coronation in Medieval England: The Evolution of the Office and the Oath," *Traditio* 16 (1960): 111–202.
62. Jones, *Finger-Ring Lore*, 161–64. As Shakespeare makes clear in *Macbeth*, King Edward was well known for his capacity to cure his subjects with the royal touch.

63. On other implications of Helena's pilgrimage to the shrine of St. James of Compostela, see Grace Tiffany, *Love's Pilgrimage: The Holy Journey in English Renaissance Literature* (Newark: University of Delaware Press, 2006), 93–97 and Richard Wilson, "To Great St Jaques Bound: *All's Well That Ends Well* in Shakespeare's Europe," *Shakespeare et l'Europe de la Renaissance*, Actes du Congrès de la Société Française Shakespeare (2004): 273–90.

64. Thomas, *Religion*, 224.

65. For a successful Helena, see Susan Synder, "'The King's not here': Displacement and Deferral in *All's Well That Ends Well*," *Shakespeare Quarterly* 43 (1992): 32 and Jay Halio, "*All's Well That Ends Well*," *Shakespeare Quarterly* 15 (1964): 41.

66. David Scott Kastan represents this view when he states, "Love must be freely given, not compelled"; see "*All's Well That Ends Well* and the Limits of ·Comedy," *ELH* 52 (1985): 583–84.

67. Claire Jones discusses the commonplace receipt tag, *probatum est*, in "'Efficacy Phrases' in Medieval English Medical Manuscripts," *Neuphilologische Mitteilungen* 99 (1998): 199–209.

68. Lehnhof, "Performing Women," 119. Lehnhof draws on the work of Bella Mirabella, "'Quacking Delilahs': Female Mountebanks in Early Modern England and Italy" in Pamela Allen Brown and Peter Parolin (eds.), *Women Players in England, 1500–1660: Beyond the All-Male Stage* (Aldershot: Ashgate, 2005), 89–105.

69. See Traister, "'Doctor She,'" 342–43. Carolyn Asp, "Subjectivity, Desire, and Female Friendship in *All's Well That Ends Well*," *Literature and Psychology* 32 (1986): 55.

70. Cathy McClive, "The Hidden Truths of the Belly: The Uncertainties of Pregnancy in Early Modern Europe," *Social History of Medicine* 15 (2002): 215. See also Caroline Bicks, "Planned Parenthood: Minding the Quick Woman in *All's Well*," *Modern Philology* 103 (2006): 299–331; Kathryn M. Moncrief, "'Show me a child begotten of thy body that I am father to': Pregnancy, Paternity and the Problem of Evidence in *All's Well That Ends Well*" in Kathryn M. Moncrief and Kathryn R. McPherson (eds.), *Performing Maternity in Early Modern England* (Aldershot: Ashgate, 2007), 29–43: "the play is uncertain about the nature of the evidence [Helena] presents to prove her success and, in its final moments, rehearses the same anxieties about how to read the pregnant body that are prevalent in the popular guides" (37).

71. Jonathan Gil Harris, "All Swell That End Swell: Dropsy, Phantom Pregnancy, and the Sound of Deconception in *All's Well That Ends Well*," *Renaissance Drama* (2006): 169–89.

72. Painter, *The Palace of Pleasure*, fo. 100v.

73. Catherine Field argues, for example, that Helena's proto-scientific practices leave behind the "older, magical and superstitiously driven" approach to medicine and inquiry; see "'Sweet Practicer,'" 204–05.

74. In the 1959 Arden edition of the play, G. K. Hunter associates Helena's "magic" with an "elder age" in contrast to a youthful and new "scientific

naturalism"; *All's Well That Ends Well* (London: Methuen, 1959), xxxvi–xxxvii. Field, by contrast, identifies Helena with "forces of the Scientific Revolution"; "'Sweet Practicer,'" 205.

75. Siraisi, *The Clock and the Mirror*, 151.

76. John Henry, *The Scientific Revolution and the Origins of Modern Science*, 3rd edition (Basingstoke: Palgrave Macmillan, 2008), 66.

77. On the privileging of probability, see Barbara J. Shapiro, *Probability and Certainty in Seventeenth-Century England: A Study of the Relationships between Natural Science, Religion, History, Law, and Literature* (Princeton: Princeton University Press, 1983).

2 SYMPATHETIC CONTAGION IN *ARDEN OF FAVERSHAM* AND *A WARNING FOR FAIR WOMEN*

1. On contagious sympathy, see Eric Langley, "'Plagued by kindness': Contagious Sympathy in Shakespearean Drama," *Medical Humanities* 37 (2011): 103–09.

2. Cited in Langley, "'Plagued by kindness,'" 104. Thomas Lodge, *A Treatise of the Plague* (London, 1603), sig. L2r. See too Girolamo Fracastoro, *Hieronymi Fracastorii De Contagione and Contagiosis Morbis et Eorum Curatione, Libri III*, trans. Wilmer Cave Wright (New York: G. P. Putnam's Sons, 1930): "the infection is precisely similar in both the carrier and the receiver of contagion; we say that contagion has occurred when a certain similar taint has affected them both" (3).

3. Sergius Kodera, *Disreputable Bodies: Magic, Medicine, and Gender in Renaissance Natural Philosophy* (Toronto: Centre for Reformation and Renaissance Studies, 2010), 47.

4. Although he does not address the sympathetic component of contagion, Darryl Chalk has explored the extensive associations between spectatorship and contagion in the early modern theatre; see "'To creep in at mine eyes': Theatre and Secret Contagion in *Twelfth Night*" in Darryl Chalk and Laurie Johnson (eds.), *"Rapt in Secret Studies": Emerging Shakespeares* (Newcastle upon Tyne: Cambridge Scholars Publishing, 2010), 171–93. See too Chalk, "Contagious Emulation: Antitheatricality and Theatre as Plague in *Troilus and Cressida*" in Brett D. Hirsch and Christopher Wortham (eds.), *"This Earthly Stage": World and Stage in Late Medieval and Early Modern England* (Turnhout: Brepols, 2010), 75–101. For a compatible thesis, see Tanya Pollard, *Drugs and Theater in Early Modern England* (Oxford: Oxford University Press, 2005). For a helpful discussion of contagion tracts in the period, see Margaret Healy, "Anxious and Fatal Contacts: Taming the Contagious Touch" in Elizabeth D. Harvey (ed.), *Sensible Flesh: On Touch in Early Modern Culture* (Philadelphia: University of Pennsylvania Press, 2003), 22–38.

5. Henry Hitch Adams, *English Domestic or Homiletic Tragedy, 1575 to 1642* (New York: B. Blom, 1943); Catherine Belsey, "Alice Arden's Crime," *Renaissance Drama* 13 (1982): 90; Lena Cowen Orlin, *Private Matters and Public Culture in Post-Reformation England* (Ithaca, NY: Cornell University Press, 1994), 91;

Frances E. Dolan, *Dangerous Familiars: Representations of Domestic Crime in England 1550–1700* (Ithaca, NY: Cornell University Press, 1994), 51; Stuart A. Kane, "Wives with Knives: Early Modern Murder Ballads and the Transgressive Commodity," *Criticism* 38 (1996): 219–37; Peter Lake with Michael Questier, *The Antichrist's Lewd Hat: Protestants, Papists and Players in Post-Reformation England* (New Haven: Yale University Press, 2002), 3–53; Peter Berek, "'Follow the Money': Sex, Murder, Print, and Domestic Tragedy," *Medieval and Renaissance Drama in England* 21 (2008): 170–88.

6. Orlin, *Private Matters*, 16. See too Richard Helgerson, *Adulterous Alliances: Home, State, and History in Early Modern European Drama and Painting* (Chicago: University of Chicago Press, 2000), 15.

7. Belsey, "Alice Arden's Crime," 84. For other readings invested in the play's representation of public and private interests, see Dolan, *Dangerous Familiars*; Garrett A. Sullivan, Jr., "'Arden Lay Murdered in That Plot of Ground': Surveying, Land, and *Arden of Faversham*," *ELH* 61 (1994): 231–52; Frank Whigham, *Seizures of the Will in Early Modern Drama* (Cambridge: Cambridge University Press, 1996), 63–120; Michael Neill, "'This Gentle Gentleman': Social Change and the Language of Status in *Arden of Faversham*" in *Putting History to the Question: Power, Politics, and Society in English Renaissance Drama* (New York: Columbia University Press, 2000), 49–72.

8. My emphasis. Raphael Holinshed, *The Third volume of Chronicles, beginning at duke William the Norman, commonlie called the Conqueror* (London, 1586), 1066.

9. Holinshed, *Third volume of Chronicles*, 1066.

10. "Stowe's Historical and Other Collections, Volume vɪ[293], British Library Harl MS 542. Plut xlvɪɪɪ в" in Patricia Hyde (ed.), *Thomas Arden in Faversham: The Man behind the Myth* (Faversham, Kent: Faversham Society, 1996), 124.

11. Holinshed, *Third volume of Chronicles*, third table, sig. g5r.

12. Richard Baker, *A chronicle of the Kings of England* (London, 1643), "The Reigne of King Edward the sixth," 2.86. On the classification of Arden's murder as a wonder, see Helgerson, *Adulterous Alliances*, 21–22.

13. While it is hardly a revelation that Elizabethan tragedies involve supernatural phenomena, domestic tragedies receive more attention for their social relations than their engagement with the occult. *The Witch of Edmonton* is the obvious exception. For attention to the uncanny in domestic tragedies, see Dolan, *Dangerous Familiars*; Margaret Healy, "Bodily Regimen and Fear of the Beast: 'Plausibility' in Renaissance Domestic Tragedy" in Erica Fudge, Ruth Gilbert, and Susan Wiseman (eds.), *At the Borders of the Human: Beasts, Bodies and Natural Philosophy in the Early Modern Period* (Basingstoke: Palgrave Macmillan, 1999), 74–90; Wendy Wall, *Staging Domesticity: Household Work and English Identity in Early Modern Drama* (Cambridge: Cambridge University Press, 2002).

14. Lake, *The Antichrist's Lewd Hat*, 31. Lake's work, in a sense, returns us to the older tradition of reading these plays as "homiletic." Also addressing the play's

"supernatural" elements is Michael T. Marsden, "The Otherworld of *Arden of Faversham*," *Southern Folklore Quarterly* 36 (1972): 36–42.

15. Lake, *The Antichrist's Lewd Hat*, 29.

16. The phrase is from Paul Yachnin, "Eye to eye opposed" in Anthony B. Dawson and Paul Yachnin (eds.), *The Culture of Playgoing in Shakespeare's England: A Collaborative Debate* (Cambridge: Cambridge University Press, 2001), 78. While Yachnin outlines the cultural fear of fascination and the evil eye, he contends that the gaze of characters on the stage was unlikely to "infect or enchant the spectators, because their looks, framed by dramatic and verbal irony, function as signifiers of inward intention" (83).

17. Anonymous, *The Tragedy of Arden of Faversham*, ed. Martin White (London: A&C Black, 1990). Quotations from this edition are cited parenthetically in the text.

18. Frank Whigham interprets these lines as a way for each speaker to absolve themselves "of any personal responsibility or agency for their engagement with" the other, in the same way that witchcraft cases released the accuser from accountability for his or her actions, and in "these specifically erotic cases, the charge also strips from the accused person any personal, non-magical entitlement to past affections" (82).

19. Thomas Lupton, *A thousand notable things* (London, 1579), 102. On the physiology of sight and contagion in lovesickness, see Donald Beecher, "Windows on Contagion" in Claire L. Carlin (ed.), *Imagining Contagion in Early Modern Europe* (Basingstoke: Palgrave Macmillan, 2005), 32–46.

20. Ioan P. Couliano, *Eros and Magic in the Renaissance*, trans. Margaret Cook (Chicago: University of Chicago Press, 1987), 29–30.

21. *The problemes of Aristotle* (London, 1595) sig. L7v.

22. George Hakewill, *The vanitie of the eye* (London, 1615), 33.

23. On the evil eye, see Alan Dundes (ed.), *The Evil Eye: A Folklore Casebook* (New York and London: Garland, 1981); Linda Woodbridge, *The Scythe of Saturn: Shakespeare and Magical Thinking* (Urbana: University of Illinois Press, 1994), esp. 217–27; Sergei Lobanov-Rostovsky, "Taming the Basilisk" in David Hillman and Carla Mazzio (eds.), *The Body in Parts: Fantasies of Corporeality in Early Modern Europe* (New York and London: Routledge, 1997), 195–217; Ferando Salmón and Monteserrat Cabré, "Fascinating Women: The Evil Eye in Medical Scholasticism" in Roger French, Jon Arrizabalaga, Andrew Cunningham, and Luis García-Ballester (eds.), *Medicine from the Black Death to the French Disease* (Aldershot: Ashgate, 1998), 53–84.

24. Lupton, *A thousand notable things*, 140.

25. Kodera, *Disreputable Bodies*, 109.

26. Roger Bacon, *The mirror of alchimy* (London, 1597), 60.

27. Reginald Scot, *The discoverie of witchcraft* (London, 1584), 486.

28. Henry Cornelius Agrippa of Nettesheim, *Three Books of Occult Philosophy*, ed. Donald Tyson, trans. J. Freake (St. Paul, MN: Llewellyn Publications, 2004), 204.

29. Giambattista della Porta explains that, like the cockatrice and the basilisk, some natural creatures "are apt . . . to communicate" their properties to others, especially persons consumed with strong passions; John Baptista Porta [Giambattista della Porta], *Natural Magick (1658)*, ed. Derek J. Price (New York: Basic Books, 1957), 19. As Johann Jacob Wecker asserts, the "Secrets of the Internall parts of Man" encompass the sympathetic influence of virtues, love charms, and enchantment with the eyes. In the same way that the basilisk kills its victims with poisonous eye darts, it seems all men and women have the power to enchant one another through looking and the fixedness of their passions; see Johann Jacob Wecker, *Eighteen books of the secrets of art & nature* (London, 1660), 33.

30. Kodera, *Disreputable Bodies*, 47.

31. See Hakewill, *The vanitie of the eye*, 34, and Andre Du Laurens, *A discourse of the preseruation of the sight* (London, 1599), 44. In his inquiry into whether a basilisk might possess such a power, Sir Thomas Browne rejects the extramissive theory of eyesight but concedes that

> if plagues or pestilentiall Atomes have beene conveyed in the ayre from different Regions, if men at a distance have infected each other; if the shaddowes of some trees be noxious, if Torpedoes deliver their opium at a distance, and stupifie beyond themselves; we cannot reasonably deny, that, beside our grosse and restrained poysons requiring contiguity unto their actions, there may proceed from subtiler seeds, more agile emanations, which will contemne those Laws, and invade at distance unexpected.

See *Pseudodoxia epidemica, or, Enquiries into very many received tenents and commonly presumed truths*, book 3 (London, 1646), 119. On the passive versus extramissive eye, see Eric F. Langley, "Anatomizing the Early-Modern Eye: A Literary Case-Study," *Renaissance Studies* 20 (2006): 340–55 and Stuart Clark, *Vanities of the Eye: Vision in Early Modern European Culture* (Oxford: Oxford University Press, 2007), 17–25.

32. Thomas Johnson, *Cornucopiae, or diuers secrets wherein is contained the rare secrets in man, beasts, foules, fishes, trees, plantes, stones and such like* (London, 1595), sig. A4v.

33. *Natural Magick*, 19. Agrippa contends that in the case of the "harlot," "boldness, and impudence doth infect all that are neer her, by this property, whereby they are made like herself" (50).

34. *The Book of Secrets of Albertus Magnus*, ed. Michael R. Best and Frank H. Brightman (Oxford: Clarendon Press, 1973), 75 and 80.

35. *Ouid's Metamorphosis Englished by G. S.*, book 10 (London, 1628), 238.

36. Martin White notes that Clarke's scheme depends on the extramissive theory of vision; *The Tragedy of Master Arden of Faversham* (London: A&C Black, 1990), 13n. For a discussion of the portrait, Julie R. Schutzman, "Alice Arden's Freedom and the Suspended Moment of *Arden of Faversham*," *Studies in English Literature 1500–1900* 36 (1996): 289–314.

37. Eugene D. Hill, "Parody and History in 'Arden of Feversham' (1592)," *Huntington Library Quarterly* 56 (1993): 363.
38. Hill, "Parody and History," 363.
39. Joseph R. Roach, *The Player's Passion: Studies in the Science of Acting* (Ann Arbor: University of Michigan Press, 1993), 45.
40. For more on the physical and "materially effective" force of early modern theater, see William Egginton, *How the World Became a Stage: Presence, Theatricality, and the Question of Modernity* (Albany: State University of New York Press, 2003), 40.
41. See discussions of this phenomenon in the Introduction. Patricia Crawford acknowledges the prevalence of this belief in "Attitudes to Menstruation in Seventeenth-Century England," *Past and Present* 91 (1981): 59.
42. Stephen Bradwell, *Physick for the Sicknesse* (London, 1636), 9. He and many other plague writers argue that this "analogy" is even stronger among family members: "*nearenesse of Bloud or kinred*, by *Sympathy* of nature, is another aptnesse" (11). On this point, see Richard Kephale, *Medela pestilentiae* (London, 1665), 58 and Ambroise Paré, *A treatise of the plague* (London, 1630), which notes that a "sympathie & familiaritie of Nature" aids in contracting the plague (7).
43. On Paracelsian "predestined sympathy," see Walter Pagel, *Paracelsus: An Introduction to Philosophical Medicine in the Era of the Renaissance*, 2nd revised edition (Basel: S. Karger, 1984), 140. As Jonathan Gil Harris observes in *Foreign Bodies and the Body Politic: Discourses of Social Pathology in Early Modern England* (Cambridge: Cambridge University Press, 1998), Renaissance discussions of the plague tend to fuse a range of conflicting sources and theories, including Hippocrates, Galen, Lucretius, Paracelsus, and Fracastoro (23–25).
44. Pierre Drouet, *A new counsell against the pestilence* (London, 1578), sig. C2r. See too *A general collection of discourses of the virtuosi of France* (London, 1664): "There must be some proportion between the body which communicates this vapour and that which receives it" (568).
45. Thomas Thayre, *A treatise of the pestilence* (London, 1603), 6.
46. See William Simpson, *Zenexton ante-pestilentiale. Or, A short discourse of the plague its antidotes and cure* (London, 1665), which draws a correlation between these secret antipathies and the innate weaknesses that invite infection (29–30).
47. A significant exception is Marguerite A. Tassi, *The Scandal of Images: Iconoclasm, Eroticism, and Painting in Early Modern Drama* (Selinsgrove, PA: Susquehanna University Press, 2005), 130–51.
48. Emma Wilby, *Cunning Folk and Familiar Spirits: Shamanistic Visionary Traditions in Early Modern British Witchcraft and Magic* (Brighton: Sussex Academic Press, 2005), 26–27. See too Owen Davies, *Cunning-Folk: Popular Magic in English History* (London: Hambledon and London, 2003).
49. Wilby, *Cunning Folk*, 28. See Alan Macfarlane, *Witchcraft in Tudor and Stuart England: A Regional and Comparative Study*, 2nd edition (London: Routledge, 1999), 116–19.

50. Stuart Clark, *Thinking with Demons: The Idea of Witchcraft in Early Modern Europe* (Oxford: Oxford University Press, 1997), 463.
51. Davies, *Cunning-Folk*, 9. As Clark observes, "Ordinary people could be persuaded only with difficulty that the devil (and, so, God) lay behind the damage inflicted by the local witch – a causal supplement unfamiliar to them but not inherently implausible ... they were likely to reject out of hand this further idea of demonic responsibility for the *benefits* brought by the local magician"; *Thinking with Demons*, 465.
52. On these porous boundaries, see Alexandra Walsham, *Providence in Early Modern England* (Oxford: Oxford University Press, 1999), 178 and Clark, *Thinking with Demons, passim.*
53. Thomas, *Religion*, 252–300. On cunning folk as specialists, see Willem de Blecourt, "Witch Doctors, Soothsayers and Priests. On Cunning Folk in European Historiography and Tradition," *Social History* 19 (1994): 285–303.
54. On books of secrets, see William Eamon, "Science and Popular Culture in Sixteenth Century Italy: The 'Professors of Secrets' and Their Books," *Sixteenth Century Journal* 16 (1985): 471–85; Eamon, *Science and the Secrets of Nature: Books of Secrets in Medieval and Early Modern Culture* (Princeton: Princeton University Press, 1994); Allison Kavey, *Books of Secrets: Natural Philosophy in England, 1550–1600* (Urbana and Chicago: University of Illinois Press, 2007). See too Eamon, "How to Read a Book of Secrets" and Pamela H. Smith, "What Is a Secret? Secrets and Craft Knowledge in Early Modern Europe" in Elaine Leong and Alisha Rankin (eds.), *Secrets and Knowledge in Medicine and Science, 1500–1800* (Aldershot: Ashgate, 2011), 23–46 and 47–66. Also see discussion in Chapter 1.
55. John Bate, *The mysteries of nature and art* (London, 1634).
56. Bate, *Mysteries*, 177.
57. Bate, *Mysteries*, 190.
58. Holinshed, *Third volume of Chronicles*, 1063.
59. See, for example, Simon Kellwaye, *A Defensative against the Plague* (London, 1593), sigs. 4r–4v.
60. On the belief that "murder will out," see Malcolm Gaskill, *Crimes and Mentalities in Early Modern England* (Cambridge: Cambridge University Press, 2000), 211
61. Thomas Beard (trans.), *The Theatre of God's Judgments* (London, 1597), 270–71.
62. Samuel Clarke, *A mirrour or looking-glasse both for saints and sinners* (London, 1654), 293.
63. *[The] complaint and lamentation of Mistresse Arden of [Fev]ersham* (London, 1633).
64. Robert P. Brittain, "Cruentation: In Legal Medicine and in Literature," *Medical History* 9 (1965): 82–88. See too Henry Charles Lea, *Superstition and Force* (Philadelphia: Collins, 1866), 245–48; Charles Greene Cumston, "A Note on the History of Forensic Medicine of the Middle Ages," *Journal of the American Institute of Criminal Law and Criminology* 3 (1913): 855–65;

Lynn Thorndike, "Mediaeval Magic and Science in the Seventeenth Century," *Speculum* 28 (1953): 692–704.

65. James I, King of England, *Daemonologie in forme of a dialogue, divided into three bookes* (London, 1597), 80.

66. Gaskill, *Crimes and Mentalities*, 227.

67. Hilary M. Nunn, *Staging Anatomies: Dissection and Spectacle in Early Stuart Tragedy* (Aldershot: Ashgate, 2005), 68.

68. Hakewill notes that marvelous emanations of the eye were associated with cruentation, or the bleeding corpse: "[I]t is as commonly receaved not onely among the vulgar, but the learned; that the Basilike by his eie killeth a man . . . by some pestilent vapor, which proceeds from it . . . I here passe over the fresh bleeding of a dead corps, at the looking on of the murtherer"; *The vanitie of the eye*, 33–34.

69. Levinus Lemnius, *The secret miracles of nature* (London, 1658), 104. See also Ludgwig Lavater, *Of ghostes and spirites walking by nyght* (London, 1572), 80.

70. Walter Charleton, *Physiologia Epicuro-Gassendo-Charltoniana, or, A fabrick of science natural* (London, 1654), 365.

71. *The problemes of Aristotle* (London, 1595), sigs. c5v–c6r.

72. Baker, *A chronicle*, 86.

73. "Stowe's Historical and Other Collections," 124.

74. Holinshed, *Third volume of Chronicles*, 1066.

75. Thomas, *Religion*, 600.

76. Thomas, *Religion*, 611.

77. Walsham, *Providence*, 82–85.

78. Holinshed, *Third volume of Chronicles*, 1066.

79. Baker, *A chronicle*, 86.

80. John Webster, *The displaying of supposed witchcraft* (London, 1677), 294.

81. Webster, *Displaying*, 295.

82. Orlin, *Private Matters*, 97.

83. On the question of Arden's culpability, see White, *The Tragedy*, xii; Whigham, *Seizures of the Will*, 71; Belsey, "Alice Arden's Crime," 85; Dolan, *Dangerous Familiars*, 74–75. For another perspective, see Sullivan, "'Arden Lay Murdered,'" 244–47.

84. As Thomas observes, both Protestants and Catholics propagated the "widely disseminated tradition that the monastic estates confiscated by Henry VIII carried with them a divine curse upon their new owners for appropriating to secular uses property once dedicated to God"; *Religion*, 113.

85. Holinshed, *The first and second volumes of Chronicles* (London, 1587), 1062.

86. See Frances E. Dolan, "Gender, Moral Agency, and Dramatic Form in *A Warning for Fair Women*," *SEL: Studies in English Literature, 1500–1900* 29 (1989): 201–18; Berek, "'Follow the Money,'" 173–77; Lake, *The Antichrist's Lewd Hat*, 88–91.

87. Anonymous, *A Warning for Fair Women: A Critical Edition*, ed. Charles Dale Cannon (The Hague: Mouton, 1975). Citations to this edition are provided parenthetically in the text.

88. Lake, *The Antichrist's Lewd Hat*, 91.
89. Arthur Golding, *A briefe discourse of the late murther of master George Saunders* (London, 1573), sig. Ciir.
90. On the rare but significant presence of female surgeons, see Doreen A. Evenden [Nagy], "Gender Differences in the Licensing and Practice of Female and Male Surgeons in Early Modern England," *Medical History* 42 (1998): 194–216.
91. On the exchange of recipes, see Sara Pennell, "Perfecting Practice? Women, Manuscript Recipes and Knowledge in Early Modern England" in Victoria E. Burke and Jonathan Gibson (eds.), *Early Modern Women's Manuscript Writing: Selected Papers from Trinity/Trent Colloquium* (Aldershot: Ashgate, 2004), 237–58. I discuss receipt books in Chapter 3.
92. Sources to the play ascribe Bean's brief survival and testimony to providence; see Holinshed, *First and Second volume*, 1258 and Golding, *A briefe discourse*, Aiiiir.
93. Thomas Heywood, *An apologie for actors* (London, 1612), sig. G1v. In considering the "performance scripts based on actual crimes to which Heywood refers," Dolan suggests that the drama "might elicit responses more unpredictable and disruptive than confession" (*Domestic Familiars*, 50–51).
94. Heywood, *An apologie*, sig. G2v.
95. *The Journal of Richard Norwood*, ed. Wesley Frank Craven and Walter B. Hayward (New York: Scholars' Facsimiles and Reprints, 1945), 42. Norwood is also reading Agrippa's *De Occulta Philosophia* at the time he writes this entry (43). See Henk Gras, *Studies in Elizabethan Audience Response to Theatre Part I: How Easy is a Bush Suppos'd a Bear? Actor and Character in the Elizabethan Viewer's Mind* (Frankfurt am Main: Peter Lang, 1993), 126.
96. Heywood, *An apologie*, sig. B4r.
97. Golding, *A briefe discourse*, sig. D1r.

3 "AS SECRET AS MAIDENHEAD": MAGNETIC WOMBS
AND THE NATURE OF ATTRACTION IN SHAKESPEARE'S
TWELFTH NIGHT

1. William Shakespeare, *Twelfth Night* in *The Norton Shakespeare*, ed. Stephen Greenblatt (New York: W. W. Norton, 1997). References to the play are cited parenthetically in the text.
2. Stephen Greenblatt, *Shakespearean Negotiations: The Circulation of Social Energy in Renaissance England* (Berkeley: University of California Press, 1988), 93.
3. See Patricia Parker, "Gender Ideology, Gender Change: The Case of Marie Germain," *Critical Inquiry* 19 (1993): 337–64; Gail Kern Paster, "The Unbearable Coldness of Female Being: Women's Imperfection and the Humoral Economy," *English Literary Renaissance* 28 (1998): 416–40; Janet Adelman, "Making Defect Perfection: Shakespeare and the One-Sex Model" in Viviana Comensoli and Anne Russell (eds.), *Enacting Gender on*

the English Renaissance Stage (Urbana: University of Illinois Press, 1999), 23–52. See the introduction as well.

4. Greenblatt, *Shakespearean Negotiations*, 77.

5. For critics who have attended to these issues, see Laurinda S. Dixon, *Perilous Chastity: Women and Illness in Pre-Enlightenment Art and Medicine* (Ithaca, NY: Cornell University Press, 1995); Mary E. Fissell, *Vernacular Bodies: The Politics of Reproduction in Early Modern England* (Oxford: Oxford University Press, 2004); Katharine Park, *Secrets of Women: Gender, Generation, and the Origins of Human Dissection* (New York: Zone Books, 2006); Kaara L. Peterson, *Popular Medicine, Hysterical Disease, and Social Controversy in Shakespeare's England* (Burlington, VT: Ashgate, 2010).

6. Although Janet Adelman does not offer a reading of *Twelfth Night*, her monumental study, *Suffocating Mothers*, demonstrates how the matrix and its meanings haunts Shakespeare's entire canon; see *Suffocating Mothers: Fantasies of Maternal Origin in Shakespeare's Plays*, Hamlet *to* The Tempest (New York and London: Routledge, 1992).

   Ben Jonson's play *The Magnetick Lady* (1632) explicitly stages the early modern cultural correlation between the womb and the lodestone. See Julie Sanders, "Midwifery and the New Science in the Seventeenth Century: Language, Print, and the Theatre" in Erica Fudge, Ruth Gilbert, and Susan Wiseman (eds.), *At the Borders of the Human: Beasts, Bodies and Natural Philosophy in the Early Modern Period* (Basingstoke: Palgrave Macmillan, 1999), 74–90.

7. Desiderius Erasmus, "Amicitia, or Friendship" in *The Colloquies of Erasmus*, trans. N. Bailey, vol. 2 (London: Reeves and Turner, 1878), 312. Others suggest more vaguely that the lodestone draws iron by some "hidden virtue or propertie"; see Pedro de Medina, *The arte of nauigation wherein is contained all the rules, declarations, secretes, & aduises, which for good nauigation are necessary* (London, 1581), fo. 68r.

8. Pliny, the Elder, *The historie of the world*, trans. Philemon Holland (London, 1601), 2.586.

9. Henry Cornelius Agrippa of Nettesheim, *Three Books of Occult Philosophy*, ed. Donald Tyson, trans. James Freake (St. Paul, MN: Llewellyn Publications, 2004), 50.

10. Robert Norman, *The new attractive* (London, 1592), sig. B4r.

11. Agrippa writes, the "loadstone, which stone indeed doth not only draw iron rings, but also infuseth a virtue into the rings themselves . . . After this manner it is, as they say, that a common harlot, grounded in boldness . . . doth infect all that are near her" (*Three Books*, 50). On the emotional and spiritual implications of magnetism, see Eileen Reeves, "Of Language and the Lodestone," working papers at The Italian Academy for Advanced Studies in America, Columbia University (see www.italianacademy.columbia.edu/publications/working_papers/2003_2004/paper_fa03_Reeves.pdf) and Angus Fletcher, "Living Magnets, Paracelsian Corpses, and the Psychology of Grace in Donne's Religious Verse," *ELH* 72 (2005): 1–21.

12. Nicholas Coeffeteau, *A table of humane passions* (London, 1621), 120. In *Natural Magick*, Giambattista della Porta similarly maintains that humans in strong affective states are "apt also to communicate [those feelings] unto others" and aligns this with the contagious effect of the magnetism: "The Load-stone doth not only draw to it self that iron which it touches, but also all iron things neer it; the same ring which the Load-stone draws to it self, will draw many rings if they be neer, so it will be like a chain"; see John Baptista Porta [Giambattista della Porta], *Natural Magick (1658)*, ed. Derek J. Price (New York: Basic Books, 1957), 19. Plato compares the contagious effects of magnetism to poetic inspiration; see *The Dialogues of Plato*, vol. 3: *Ion, Hippias Minor, Laches, Protagoras*, trans. R. E. Allen (New Haven: Yale University Press, 1996), 13.

13. [Stephen Batman], *Batman vppon Bartholome his booke de proprietatibus rerum* (London, 1582), fo. 255v.

14. *The Book of Secrets of Albertus Magnus of the Virtues of Herbs, Stones and Certain Beasts*, ed. Michael R. Best and Frank H. Brightman (Oxford: Clarendon Press, 1973), 26.

15. Park, *Secrets of Women*, 169. See too Monica H. Green, "From 'Diseases of Women' to 'Secrets of Women': The Transformation of Gynecological Literature in the Later Middle Ages," *Journal of Medieval and Early Modern Studies* 30 (2000): 5–39. Also Green, *Making Women's Medicine Masculine: The Rise of Male Authority in Pre-Modern Gynaecology* (Oxford: Oxford University Press, 2008).

16. Early modern writers have shifted away from treating the womb as an animal. See note 112 in the Introduction for a brief discussion of classical scent therapy.

17. Alessandro Massaria, *De morbis foemineis, the woman's counsellour*, trans. R. Turner (London, 1657), 12–13.

18. *The problemes of Aristotle* (London, 1595), sig. E3r. Helkiah Crooke in *Mikrokosmographia* (London, 1615) dismisses the bath story (294) but also argues that "the woman conceiueth pleasure more waies, that is in the auoyding of her owne seede and also in the attraction of the mans" (288).

19. Thomas Chamberlayne, *The compleat midwife's practice enlarged* (London, 1659), 74.

20. Jane Sharp, *The midwives book, or, The whole art of midwifry discovered* (1671), 63. Julie Sanders cites Jane Sharp's characterization of the magnetic womb in her discussion of Jonson's play ("Midwifery and the New Science," 86).

21. Galen, *On the Natural Faculties*, trans. Arthur John Brock (London: William Heinemann, 1916), I.IV, 17. On the faculty of attraction, Galen writes, "How else than in the way iron is attracted by the lodestone, the latter having a faculty attractive of this particular quality" (II.VII, 165–67). Robert Burton's analogy in *The anatomy of melancholy* (London, 1621) suggests the comparison is commonplace: "*Attraction* is a ministring facultie, which as a Lodestone doth Iron, drawes meat into the stomacke" (30–31).

22. On the commonplace notion that the womb sympathized with all parts of the body, see the Introduction's discussion of Edward Jorden's *A briefe discourse of*

a disease called the suffocation of the mother (London, 1603). See too Nicholaas Fonteyn, *The womans doctour* (London, 1652), 2.

23. Lazare Rivière, *The practice of physick* (London, 1655), 405–07.

24. On the aetites stone, see *Aristotle's compleat and experience'd midwife* (London, 1700), which recommends placing the stone near the "Privities," for its "magnetick Virtue" will draw the child out as "Iron doth the Load-stone, or as the Load-stone doth the North Star" (55–56). In *The sicke womans private looking-glasse* (London, 1636), John Sadler writes: "Some are of opinion that as long as the loadstone is layd to the navill it keepeth the woman from abortion. The like also is recorded of the stone *Aetites* being hanged about the necke" (163–64). In *The Book of Secrets*, Albertus Magnus argues that the aetites prevents untimely births (45–46). See also Pliny, *The historie*, 2.396, and Thomas Lupton, *A thousand notable things* (London, 1579), 38. Sir Thomas Browne offers a skeptical view on the aetites from *Pseudodoxia epidemica, or, Enquiries into very many received tenents and commonly presumed truths* (London, 1646):

> Many relations are made, and great expectations are raised from the Magnes Carneus, or a Loadstone, that hath a faculty to attract not only iron but flesh; but this upon enquiry, and as Cabeus hath also observed, is nothing else but a weak and inanimate kind of Loadstone, veyned here and there with a few magneticall and ferreous lines, but chiefly consisting of a bolary and clammy substance, whereby it adheres like Hæmatites, or Terra Lemnia, unto the Lipps, and this is that stone which is to be understood, when Physitians joyn it with Ætites, or the Eagle stone, and promise therein a vertue against abortion. (67)

On the common use of the eagle stone, or aetites, see Fissell, *Vernacular Bodies*, 50–52. Also see Keith Thomas, *Religion and the Decline of Magic: Studies in Popular Beliefs in Sixteenth- and Seventeenth-Century England* (London: Penguin Books, 1971), 224.

25. Fonteyn, *The womans doctor*, 18–19. For another perspective, see Gail Kern Paster on Thomas Sydenham's prescription of steel pills in *Humoring the Body: Emotions and the Shakespearean Stage* (Chicago and London: University of Chicago Press, 2004), 94.

26. For an assessment of William Gilbert's contributions to knowledge, see Elizabeth Spiller, *Science, Reading, and Renaissance Literature: The Art of Making Knowledge, 1580–1670* (Cambridge: Cambridge University Press, 2004), 44–58.

27. William Gilbert, *On the Loadstone and Magnetic Bodies* in P. Fleury Mottelay (trans.), *Great Books of the Western World*, vol. 28 (Chicago: Encyclopaedia Britannica, 1952), 1–121.

28. Gilbert, *On the Loadstone*, 104–05.

29. Gilbert, *On the Loadstone*, 77.

30. Gilbert, *On the Loadstone*, 21.

31. Mark Ridley penned *A short treatise of magneticall bodies and motions* (London, 1613), and William Barlow is the author of *The navigators supply* (London, 1597) and *Magneticall Advertisements . . . experiments concerning the nature and properties of the load-stone* (London, 1616).
32. Ridley, *A short treatise*, 22.
33. Ridley, *A short treatise*, 154–55.
34. Ridley, *A short treatise*, 155–56.
35. Aristotle, *Generation of Animals*, trans. A. L. Peck (Cambridge, MA: Harvard University Press, 1953), I.XXII, 119–21.
36. For a thorough survey of early notions of conception, see Joan Cadden, *Meanings of Sex Difference in the Middle Ages: Medicine, Science, Culture* (Cambridge: Cambridge University Press, 1993).
37. Leah DeVun, "The Jesus Hermaphrodite: Science and Sex Difference in Premodern Europe," *Journal of the History of Ideas* 69 (2008): 197.
38. J. M. Thijssen, "Twins as Monsters: Albertus Magnus's Theory of the Generation of Twins and Its Philosophical Contexts," *Bulletin of the History of Medicine* 61 (1987): 240.
39. Thijssen, "Twins as Monsters," 242. See also *Women's Secrets: A Translation of Pseudo-Albertus Magnus's De Secretis Mulierum with Commentaries*, ed. Helen Rodnite Lemay (Albany: State University of New York Press, 1992).
40. *The problemes of Aristotle*, sig. E7r. On the conception of twins, see Sharp, *The midwives book*, 70. On monsters and superfluous seed, see Jakob Rüff, *The expert midwife* (London, 1637), 5.3.153.
41. *Aristoteles Master-piece, or, The secrets of generation displayed* (London, 1684), 123.
42. It was thought that conjoined twins could be generated when natural twins "squashed together"; see Rüff, *The expert midwife*, 5.3.154. See also della Porta, *Natural Magick*, 49. Hence, male and female conjoined twins were considered possible; see Jennifer Spinks, "Wondrous Monsters: Representing Conjoined Twins in Early Sixteenth-Century German Broadsheets," *Parergon* 22 (2005): 110. See also A. W. Bates, *Emblematic Monsters: Unnatural Conceptions and Deformed Births in Early Modern Europe* (Amsterdam and New York: Rodopi, 2005), 178–79.
43. Writers in the period suggest that any strong familial relationship can produce uncanny sympathetic feelings. Francis Bacon attests that he sensed when his father was dying:

> I my Selfe remember, that being in *Paris*, and my *Father* dying in *London*, two or three dayes before my *Fathers* death, I had a *Dreame*, which I told to diuers *English Gentlemen;* That my *Fathers House*, in the *Countrey*, was *Plastered* all ouer with *Blacke Mortar*. There is an Opinion abroad (whether Idle or no I cannot say,) That louing and kinde *Husbands*, haue a *Sense* of their *Wiues Breeding Childe*, by some *Accident* in their owne *Body*.

Bacon also notes that parents sense the presence of their own children, even when they may not recognize them:

> It is mentioned in some *Stories*, that where *Children* haue been *Exposed*,
> or taken away young from their *Parents;* And that afterwards they haue
> approached to their *Parents* presence, the *Parents* (though they haue not
> knowne them,) haue had a *Secret Ioy*, or Other *Alteration* thereupon.

See *Sylva Sylvarum: or A naturall historie in ten centuries* (London, 1627), 262
and 250.

44. For the term "Hippocrates twins," see George Chapman, "*A Good Woman*,"
    Petrarchs seven penitentiall psalms (London, 1612), 60; Chapman, *The
    Gentleman Usher* (London, 1606), sig. GIV; Robert Baron, "Gripus and
    Hegio" in *Erotopaignion, or, The Cyprian academy* (London, 1647), 43–44;
    Richard Head, *The English Rogue, Part I* (London, 1668), 150.

45. St. Augustine, *Of the citie of God*, trans. I.H. (London, 1610), 200.

46. *Women's Secrets*, 118.

47. Della Porta, *Natural Magick*, 18–19.

48. *The Symposium of Plato*, trans. B. Jowett (Boston: Branden Publishing Co.,
    1983), 51–54. See too Penny Gay, "Introduction," *Twelfth Night* (Cambridge:
    Cambridge University Press, 2003), 22.

49. Twinship is the trope Laurie Shannon uses to describe early modern ideal
    conceptions of same-sex friendship, noting that "[w]hile friendship and twin-
    ship discourses alike depend on 'natural' resemblances, what differs most
    between them is that while twinship seems to split or divide a preexisting
    single 'nature,' friendship is understood actively to conjoin preexisting, sepa-
    rate, 'unnaturally' like natures" – what John Donne calls "twins at a later
    conception"; see *Sovereign Amity: Figures of Friendship in Shakespearean
    Contexts* (Chicago: University of Chicago Press, 2002), 43.

50. On the Pantarbe, see Mateo Alemán, *The rogue: or The life of Guzman de
    Alfarache* (London, 1623), which identifies the "Queene of all other stones" as
    the "*Pantaura* . . . And that as the Load-stone draweth the yron vnto it; so this
    Pantaura, attracteth all other stones vnto it selfe" (212). In Ralph Knevet,
    Funerall Elegies (London, 1637), the "Pantarba" is identified as the "brightest of
    all gemmes," which "by her beames / And by a hidden sympathy, attract /
    Adjacent stones" (sig. A4r). On the influence of stones, Francis Bacon writes,
    "There be many *Things* that worke vpon the *Spirits* of *Man*, by *Secret
    Sympathy*, and *Antipathy;* The *Vertues* of *Pretious Stones* worne, haue beene
    anciently and generally Receiued: And curiously assigned to Worke seuerall
    Effects. So much is true; That *Stones* haue in them fine *Spirits;* As appeareth by
    their *Splendour:* And therefore they may worke by *Consort* vpon the *Spirits* of
    Men, to Comfort, and Exhilarate them" (*Sylva Sylvarum*, 257).

51. *Marsilio Ficino: Three Books on Life*, ed. Carol V. Kaske, and John R. Clark
    (Binghamton, NY: Center for Medieval and Early Renaissance Studies, 1989),
    book 3, 309 and 315. The naming of Apollonius of Tyana in this passage further
    associates Ficino's statement with Shakespeare's play: Barnabe Rich's character,
    in one of the sources to *Twelfth Night*, "Apollonius and Silla," may have been
    named for Apollonius of Tyre (whose story was the basis of *Pericles*) or

Apollonius of Tyana. As Elizabeth Archibald notes, it was not uncommon in the period to confuse these figures. See *Apollonius of Tyre: Medieval and Renaissance Themes and Variations* (Cambridge: D. S. Brewer, 1991), 42–43.

52. In her commentary on Antonio's devotion to Sebastian, Nancy Lindheim writes: "'Love' for the period must basically have signified 'attraction': it is a word they can apply to the force driving iron to a magnet"; see "Rethinking Sexuality and Class in *Twelfth Night*," *University of Toronto Quarterly* 76 (2007): 688.

53. Acknowledging that many other critics have made similar observations, Ruth Nevo describes Orsino's language as "truculent, masculine, [and] predatory"; *Comic Transformations in Shakespeare* (London: Methuen, 1980), 203.

54. Levinus Lemnius equates diseases and affections in *The touchstone of complexions*, trans. Thomas Newton (London, 1576): "throwen into sondrye diseases and innumerable affections" (3).

55. On the sexual nature of greensickness, see Lesel Dawson, *Lovesickness and Gender in Early Modern English Literature* (Oxford: Oxford University Press, 2008), 44. In *The practice of physic* (London, 1655), Rivière states, "if Choller or Melancholly be mixed with that flegm, the color will be yellowish, greenish or blew" (401); moreover, "great passions of the mind" such as sorrow can stop menses (403). Rüff also notes that great sadness and lamentation stops menses (*The expert midwife*, 6.11.101).

56. Philip Barrough, *The methode of phisicke* (London, 1583), 145.

57. Paster, *Humoring the Body*, 93.

58. Helen King, *The Disease of Virgins: Green Sickness, Chlorosis and the Problems of Puberty* (London and New York: Routledge, 2004), 74–75 and 79–83. See too Lesel Dawson, "Menstruation, Misogyny and the Cure for Love," *Women's Studies* 34 (2005): 461–84.

59. Robert Record, *The castle of knowledge* (London, 1556), 263.

60. As scholars have noted, Orsino's name may have been suggested by Virginio Orsini, Duke of Bracciano, whose family used the bear as their heraldic device. On the Pole Star, see Thomas Blundeville, *M. Blundevile his exercises containing sixe treatises* (London, 1594): "And that bright starre which is in the very tippe of the little Beares tayle, is commonly called of our English Mariners the Loadstar, of the Latines *Stella polaris*" (fo. 335v). See too Levinus Lemnius, *The Secret Miracles of Nature* (London, 1658), 198–99. Ridley notes that Ficino, Cardano, and Paracelsus all state that the Little Bear constellation is what powers the magnet (*A short treatise*, a2v).

61. See Ridley, "Where a smaller strength *Magneticall* altereth quickely the retention of the whole more vigorous *Magnet*" (*A short treatise*, 100).

62. On the significance of digestion and identity in the period, see Michael C. Schoenfeldt, *Bodies and Selves in Early Modern England: Physiology and Inwardness in Spenser, Shakespeare, Herbert, and Milton* (Cambridge: Cambridge University Press, 1999).

63. See Gail Kern Paster, *The Body Embarrassed: Drama and the Disciplines of Shame in Early Modern England* (Ithaca, NY: Cornell University Press, 1993),

26–63 and Keir Elam, "'In What Chapter of His Bosom?': Reading Shakespeare's Bodies" in Terence Hawkes (ed.), *Alternative Shakespeares 2* (London: Routledge, 1996), 147.

64. On this passage, see Carol Thomas Neely, "Lovesickness, Gender, and Subjectivity: *Twelfth Night* and *As You Like It*" in Dympna Callaghan (ed.), *A Feminist Companion to Shakespeare* (Oxford: Blackwell, 2000), 289. As the *OED* notes, "retentive" can also mean secretive: see Plutarch's *The philosophie, commonlie called, the morals*, trans. Philemon Holland (London, 1603): "If then there be any place in the consideration of the secrets of God, where we ought to be retentive, warie and discret, it is in this" (1352). Intriguingly, *Twelfth Night* also represents a love without retention as admirable when Antonio claims that he has offered his affection to Sebastian without restraint or retention.

65. See Sharp, who insists that after conception the womb shuts up so tight that not even a needle can pass through it (*The midwives book*, 35).

66. Anthony Fletcher, *Gender, Sex, and Subordination in England, 1500–1800* (New Haven: Yale University Press, 1995), 49. As Lesel Dawson points out, critics have often conflated all diseases of the womb, but "lovesickness, hysteria, green sickness, and uterine fury are understood as separate maladies in the early modern period, with their own unique set of symptoms, stereotypical sufferers, and cultural associations"; see *Lovesickness and Gender*, 47.

67. Elam argues that Viola's initial choice to disguise herself as a eunuch is to protect herself from the "potential sexual dangers in the world of Orsino's court"; see "The Fertile Eunuch: *Twelfth Night*, Early Modern Intercourse, and the Fruits of Castration," *Shakespeare Quarterly* 47 (1996): 4.

68. On pictorial representations of Patience on a monument, see William S. Heckscher, "Shakespeare in his Relationship to the Visual Arts: A Study in Paradox," *Research Opportunities in Renaissance Drama* 13–14 (1970–1): 35–56.

69. For example, see Girolamo Cardano, *Cardanus Comforte* (London, 1573), sig. A7v. On consolation in the period, see G. W. Pigman, III, *Grief and English Renaissance Elegy* (Cambridge: Cambridge University Press, 1985).

70. David Schalkwyk, *Shakespeare, Love and Service* (Cambridge: Cambridge University Press, 2008), argues that "Viola is one of the few cross-dressed heroines in Shakespeare who is trapped by her disguise rather than freed by it. The very condition that allows her intimate access to her beloved's 'secret soul' prevents her from revealing her own" (126–27).

71. On the question of whether to equate Viola with Cesario's father's daughter, see Catherine Belsey, "Disrupting Sexual Difference: Meaning and Gender in the Comedies," in John Drakakis (ed.), *Alternative Shakespeares*, 2nd edition (London: Routledge, 2002), 191–92. In her discussion of Rosalind, Paster argues that male costuming and the humoral heat of desire help to dissipate the female's cold and passive sadness, which enables Shakespeare's comic heroines to emerge from a form of virgin melancholia (*Humoring the Body*, 88 and 122). Similarly, Elam states that the only way for Viola to exercise the restraint she attributes to women is to "dress as a man, albeit an imperfect or

'castrated' man; her male disguise itself represents the self-punishing bridling of her sexuality"; see "The Fertile Eunuch," 6.

72. Suzanne Penuel traces the play's nostalgia for mourning rituals and its anxieties over sexual reproduction in "Missing Fathers: *Twelfth Night* and the Reformation of Mourning," *Studies in Philology* 107 (2010): 74–96. For a brief discussion of grief in the play, see Schalkwyk, *Shakespeare*, 130–31. See also Barbara Freedman, *Staging the Gaze: Postmodernism, Psychoanalysis, and Shakespearean* Comedy (Ithaca, NY: Cornell University Press, 1991), 192–235.

73. Nicholas Culpeper, *Culpeper's directory for midwives* (London, 1662), 71, and Sharp, *The midwives book*, 334.

74. On incorporation and mourning, see Valerie Traub, *The Renaissance of Lesbianism in Early Modern England* (Cambridge: Cambridge University Press, 2002), n.76, 468.

75. The sonnet reads, "Then let not winter's ragged hand deface / In thee thy summer, ere thou be distill'd: / Make sweet some vial; treasure thou some place / With beauty's treasure, ere it be self-kill'd." For a reading of vial as both womb and anus, see Jeffrey Masten, "Gee, Your Heir Smells Terrific: Response to 'Shakespeare's Perfume,'" *Early Modern Culture: An Electronic Seminar* 2 (2001) (http://emc.eserver.org/1-2/issue2.html).

76. Stephen Orgel points out that Cesario means "to cut" and suggests the name implies castration; see *Impersonations: The Performance of Gender in Shakespeare's England* (Cambridge: Cambridge University Press, 1996), 53. Yu Jin Ko notes that "cut" can also denote female genitalia; see "The Comic Close of *Twelfth Night* and Viola's *Noli me tangere*," *Shakespeare Quarterly* 48 (1997): 399–400. On the link between Cesario and Caesarian births, see Maurice Hunt, "Viola/Cesario, Caesarian Birth, and Shakespeare's *Twelfth Night*," *The Upstart Crow: A Shakespeare Journal* 21 (2001): 7–14. As Katharine Park has observed, Caesarian births were associated with the anatomist's goal to see inside the mysterious womb (*Secrets of Women*, 239–41).

77. Paul Dean, "'Comfortable Doctrine': *Twelfth Night* and the Trinity," *Review of English Studies* 52 (2001): 511. Dean also references Linda Woodbridge's discussion of Cesario as a "hermaphroditic symbol"; see *Women and the English Renaissance: Literature and the Nature of Womankind* (Urbana: University of Illinois Press, 1984), 141.

78. Greenblatt, *Shakespearean Negotiations*, 72.

79. Park, *Secrets of Women*, 142.

80. See Anthony Dawson on the Eucharistic implications of "participation" and the notion that the "presence of the theatrical person is simultaneously real and unreal"; "Performance and Participation" in Anthony B. Dawson and Paul Yachnin (eds.), *The Culture of Playgoing in Shakespeare's England* (Cambridge: Cambridge University Press, 2001), 11–37, esp. 27. On another treatment of participation in the theater, see Joel B. Altman, "'Vile Participation': The Amplification of Violence in the Theatre of *Henry V*," *Shakespeare Quarterly* 42 (1991): 1–32. The *OED* states that an early and

obsolete definition of "participation" is "sharing or possessing the nature, quality, or substance of a person or thing."

81. Walter Pagel, *Paracelsus: An Introduction to Philosophical Medicine in the Era of the Renaissance*, 2nd revised edition (Basel: S. Karger, 1984), 140. See also Darryl Chalk, "'To creep in at mine eyes': Theatre and Secret Contagion in *Twelfth Night*" in Darryl Chalk and Laurie Johnson (eds.), *"Rapt in Secret Studies": Emerging Shakespeares* (Newcastle upon Tyne: Cambridge Scholars Publishing, 2010), 176. See Chapter 2 for a fuller discussion of contagious sympathy.

82. On the Ovidian influences in *Twelfth Night*, see Jonathan Bate, *Shakespeare and Ovid* (Oxford: Oxford University Press, 1993), 145–50.

83. Dean, "'Comfortable Doctrine,'" 514.

84. James Hart, *Klinike, or The diet of the diseased* (London, 1633), 366–67.

85. Greenblatt, *Shakespearean Negotiations*, 68–71.

86. Laurie Shannon, "Nature's Bias: Renaissance Homonormativity and Elizabethan Comic Likeness," *Modern Philology* 98 (2000): 183–210.

87. Mario DiGangi, *The Homoerotics of Early Modern Drama* (Cambridge: Cambridge University Press, 1997), 39–41. Discussions of the play's representation of sexuality include Belsey, "Disrupting Sexual Difference"; Joseph Pequigney, "The Two Antonios and Same-Sex Love in *Twelfth Night* and *The Merchant of Venice*," *English Literary Renaissance* 22 (1992): 201–21; Valerie Traub, *Desire and Anxiety: Circulations of Sexuality in Shakespearean Drama* (London: Routledge, 1992), 130–44; Michael Shapiro, *Gender in Play on the Shakespearean Stage: Boy Heroines and Female Pages* (Ann Arbor: University of Michigan Press, 1994), 143–72; Elam, "The Fertile Eunuch"; Dympna C. Callaghan, *Shakespeare without Women: Representing Gender and Race on the Renaissance Stage* (London: Routledge, 2000), 26–48; Denise A. Walen, "Constructions of Female Homoerotics in Early Modern Drama," *Theatre Journal* 54 (2002): 411–30; Jami Aki, "Glimpsing a 'Lesbian' Poetics in *Twelfth Night*," *Studies in English Literature 1500–1900* 43 (2003): 375–94. For arguments that consider the eroticism of service in the play, see Lisa Jardine, *Reading Shakespeare Historically* (London: Routledge, 1996), 65–77 and Schalkwyk, *Shakespeare, Love and Service*, 115–63. For a challenge to the criticism's insistent focus on historicizing gender and sexuality through the body, see Lorna Hutson, "On Not Being Deceived: Rhetoric and the Body in *Twelfth Night*," *Texas Studies in Literature and Language* 38 (1996): 140–74.

88. The *OED* offers the following definition of "draw in": *fig*. To induce to come in or take part; to allure, entice, inveigle; to ensnare, "take in." On representations of Nature as veiled, see Pierre Hadot, *The Veil of Isis: An Essay on the History of the Idea of Nature*, trans. Michael Chase (Cambridge, MA.: Harvard University Press, 2006). See too Pamela O. Long, *Openness, Secrecy, Authorship: Technical Arts and the Culture of Knowledge from Antiquity to the Present* (Baltimore: Johns Hopkins University Press, 2001), 171. On the shift from representations of Nature as clothed to unclothed, see Katharine Park, "Nature in Person: Medieval and Renaissance Allegories and Emblems" in

Lorraine Daston and Fernando Vidal (eds.), *The Moral Authority of Nature* (Chicago: University of Chicago Press, 2004), 50–73. See too Catherine Wilson's *The Invisible World: Early Modern Philosophy and the Invention of the Microscope* (Princeton: Princeton University Press, 1995), 39–69. On the play's obsession with the theme of secrecy, see John Kerrigan, "Secrecy and Gossip in *Twelfth Night*," *Shakespeare Survey* 50 (1997): 65–80.

89. Erasmus, "Amicitia, or Friendship," 301.
90. Paula Findlen, "Jokes of Nature and Jokes of Knowledge: The Playfulness of Scientific Discourse in Early Modern Europe," *Renaissance Quarterly* 43 (1990): 292–331.
91. On the implications of Viola's insistence that she and her brother wait to embrace, see Yu Jin Ko, "The Comic Close of *Twelfth Night*."
92. Della Porta writes, "Orpheus in his Verses relates, that iron is drawn by the Loadstone, as a Bride after the Bridegroom, to be embraced" (*Natural Magick*, 201).
93. Greenblatt, *Shakespearean Negotiations*, 88. For a discussion of the transvestite theater, see the Introduction.

4 TRAGIC ANTIPATHIES IN *THE CHANGELING*

1. Thomas Middleton and William Rowley, *The Changeling*, ed. Michael Neill (London: A&C Black, 2006). References to this edition of the play are cited parenthetically in the text. On the play's preoccupation with secrets, see Michael Neill, "'Hidden Malady': Death, Discovery, and Indistinction in *The Changeling*," *Renaissance Drama* 22 (1991): 95–121, and *Issues of Death: Mortality and Identity in English Renaissance Tragedy* (Oxford: Clarendon Press, 1997), 168–97. On the critical condemnations of the virginity test, see Margot Heinemann, who notes that it has been seen as "ludicrous, unrealistic and a blemish on the play"; *Puritanism and Theatre: Thomas Middleton and Opposition Drama under the Early Stuarts* (Cambridge: Cambridge University Press, 1980), 178. For an important defense of the test as giving "serious" and "effective dramatic form ... to the theme of chastity," see Dale B. J. Randall, "Some Observations on the Theme of Chastity in *The Changeling*," *English Literary Renaissance* 14 (1984): 361. For scholars who consider the thematic centrality of this scene to the play, Bruce Boehrer, "Alsemero's Closet: Privacy and Interiority in *The Changeling*," *Journal of English and Germanic Philology* 96 (1997): 349–68; Marjorie Garber, *Symptoms of Culture* (New York: Routledge, 1998), 217–35; Lara Bovilsky, *Barbarous Play: Race on the English Renaissance Stage* (Minneapolis: University of Minnesota Press, 2008), 154–58.
2. For some representative criticism that addresses the play's allusions to the court scandals of Lady Frances Howard, see Heinemann, *Puritanism and Theatre*, 178–79; J. L. Simmons, "Diabolical Realism in Middleton and Rowley's *The Changeling*," *Renaissance Drama* 11 (1980): 135–70; Cristina Malcolmson, "'As Tame as the Ladies': Politics and Gender in *The Changeling*," *English Literary Renaissance* 20 (1990): 320–39; David Lindley, *The Trials of Frances Howard:*

Fact and Fiction at the Court of King James (London: Routledge, 1993); Lisa Hopkins, *The Female Hero in English Renaissance Tragedy* (New York: Palgrave Macmillan, 2002), 18–23; Mara Amster, "Frances Howard and Middleton and Rowley's *The Changeling*: Trials, Tests, and the Legibility of the Virgin Body" in Laurel Amtower and Dorothea Kehler (eds.), *The Single Woman in Medieval and Early Modern England: Her Life and Representation* (Tempe: Arizona Center for Medieval and Renaissance Studies, 2003), 211–32. For a reading of the play as an allegorical coded message of current events, see A. A. Bromham and Zara Bruzzi, The Changeling *and the Years of Crisis, 1619– 1624: A Hieroglyph of Britain* (Cambridge: Cambridge University Press, 1990).

3. As Lara Bovilsky observes, "Alsemero's science . . . presumes its objects – women – will not participate in and distort the results as subjects." (*Barbarous Play*, 156).

4. Allison Kavey, *Books of Secrets: Natural Philosophy in England, 1550–1600* (Urbana and Chicago: University of Illinois Press, 2007), 5. Also see John Ferguson, *Bibliographical Notes on Histories of Inventions and Books of Secrets*, 2 vols. (London: The Holland Press, 1959); William L. Eamon, "Science and Popular Culture in Sixteenth Century Italy: The 'Professors of Secrets' and Their Books," *Sixteenth Century Journal* 16 (1985): 479; Eamon, *Science and the Secrets of Nature: Books of Secrets in Medieval and Early Modern Culture* (Princeton: Princeton University Press, 1994); Paolo Rossi, *The Birth of Modern Science*, trans. Cynthia De Nardi Ipsen (Oxford: Blackwell, 2001); Elaine Leong and Alisha Rankin (eds.), *Secrets and Knowledge in Medicine and Science, 1500–1800* (Aldershot: Ashgate, 2011).

5. Girolamo Ruscelli, *The seconde part of the Secretes of Master Alexis of Piemont*, trans. William Warde (London, 1560), 16–17, 25, 27, 34–35, 54, 57. The receipt for ensuring a good memory reads: "Take a Tooth or the lefte legge of a Badger . . . and binde it about your righte arme nexte vnto the flesh. Take also the gall of a Partridge and rubbe your temples with it that it maie soke into the skin and fleshe, ones in a moneth" (17–18).

6. Ruscelli, *Secretes of Master Alexis*, 17.

7. See Boehrer, "Alsamero's Closet," 353–54.

8. Randall, "Some Observations," 358–59; Boehrer, "Alsamero's Closet," 353.

9. Lupton's text appeared in twelve different editions between 1579 and 1706.

10. Monica H. Green argues that in the twelfth through sixteenth centuries, "men's advantage in literacy" was "key to the regendering of gynaecological knowledge production, and practice." The development of the "women's secrets" genre was crucial to this shift; see *Making Women's Medicine Masculine: The Rise of Male Authority in Pre-Modern Gynaecology* (Oxford: Oxford University Press, 2008), 21 and 204–45.

11. See Randall, "Some Observations," for a survey of medieval and early modern chastity and virginity tests.

12. *The Book of Secrets of Albertus Magnus of the Virtues of Herbs, Stones and Certain Beasts*, ed. Michael R. Best and Frank H. Brightman (Oxford: Clarendon Press, 1973), 26.

13. Anon., *The booke of pretty conceits* (London, 1612), sigs. A3r–A3v. This text includes a second recipe: "A ready and easie way to try whether a Maid be a pure virgin or not. Take roots of red Nettles, and stamp them small, & mire the juice thereof with Ale, and let her drinke therof: and if it doe remaine with her, then she is a maide, otherwise she is not" (sigs. B1r–B1v). Also, Giovanni Benedetto Sinibaldi's *Rare verities: The cabinet of Venus unlocked, and her secrets laid open* (London, 1658) identifies its knowledge, which includes virginity tests, as "occult mysteries" (sig. A4r).

14. Quoted in Randall, "Some Observations," 357. In addition to other tests that involve drinking potions and urinating, Wecker also provides instructions for compelling a woman to confess her secrets. To induce a woman to speak truths against her will, Wecker recommends placing the tongues of creatures that "cry in the night," such as frogs, ducks, or owls, on a woman's breast while she sleeps; Johann Jacob Wecker, *Eighteen books of the secrets of art & nature* (London, 1660), 337. Even the skeptical Laurent Joubert tentatively suggests one put "some perfume of jet; or put a small amount of the oil of this substance into the maiden's privities. If you smell the odour of it in her mouth or in her nose from the air she exhales, there is a great likelihood that her back cloister is open. Yet she could well have such a thick womb that the odor would not rise upward, even if the mouth of her womb were opened"; see *Popular Errors*, trans. Gregory David de Rocher (Tuscaloosa: University of Alabama Press, 1989), 221.

15. [Stephen Batman], *Batman vppon Bartholome his booke de proprietatibus rerum* (London, 1582), fo. 261r. See also Pliny, the Elder, *The historie of the world*, trans. Philemon Holland (London, 1601), 2.589. Thomas Nicols, *Arcula gemmea: or, A cabinet of jewels* (London, 1653), 172.

16. On the gagates stone repelling serpents and proving virginity, see Raphael Holinshed, *The first and second volumes of Chronicles* (London, 1587), 1.239; John Maplet, *A greene forest, or A naturall historie* (London, 1567), fo. 8r.

17. Robert Chester, *The anuals of great Brittaine* (London, 1611), 104–05.

18. On women typified as leaky vessels, see Gail Kern Paster, *The Body Embarrassed: Drama and the Disciplines of Shame in Early Modern England* (Ithaca, NY: Cornell University Press, 1993). Against this trend, Joannes Jonstonus, *An history of the wonderful things of nature* (London, 1657) maintains that drinking jet will cause a virgin to "make water" (100). Marjorie Garber argues that the symptoms produced by Alsemero's receipt are the effects of an orgasm (*Symptoms*, 228–29).

19. Sinibaldi, *Rare verities*, 59–60.

20. John Fletcher, *The faithfull shepheardesse* (London, 1610), sig. B1v. See Randall, "Some Observations," 355.

21. Lindley, *The Trials of Frances Howard*, 110.

22. Kathleen Coyne Kelly, *Performing Virginity and Testing Chastity in the Middle Ages* (London: Routledge, 2000), 32. See too Marie H. Loughlin, *Hymeneutics: Interpreting Virginity on the Early Modern Stage* (Lewisburg, PA: Bucknell University Press, 1997).

23. *A Complete Collection of State-Trials and Proceedings*, 6 vols., 2nd edition, vol. 1 (London, 1730), 329.
24. Alastair Bellany states that James Franklin was "known to have practiced as a cunning-man"; see *The Politics of Court Scandal in Early Modern England: News Culture and the Overbury Affair, 1603–1660* (Cambridge: Cambridge University Press, 2002), 151. Brian Harris mistakenly attributes these words in the trial papers to Anne Turner; *Passion, Poison and Power: The Mysterious Death of Sir Thomas Overbury, A Jacobean Mystery in Fourteen Acts* (London: Wildy, Simmonds & Hill, 2010), 115.
25. Cited in Lindley, *The Trials of Frances Howard*, 48.
26. See Lindley on the commonplace ascription of impotence to *maleficium*: *The Trials of Frances Howard*, 96–101.
27. *A Complete Collection of State-Trials*, 323. See Diane Purkiss's discussion of Anne Turner as a cunning woman among a "whole network of cunning people" involved in the case; see *The Witch in History: Early Modern and Twentieth-Century Representations* (London: Routledge, 1996), 216.
28. See Doreen G. [Evenden] Nagy, *Popular Medicine in Seventeenth-Century England* (Bowling Green, OH: Bowling Green State University Popular Press, 1988), 54–78; Linda Pollock, *With Faith and Physic: The Life of a Tudor Gentlewoman, Lady Grace Mildmay, 1552–1620* (New York: St. Martin's Press, 1993), 92–109; Lynette Hunter, "Women and Domestic Medicine: Lady Experimenters, 1570–1620" in Lynette Hunter and Sarah Hutton (eds.), *Women, Science and Medicine, 1500–1700: Mothers and Sisters of the Royal Society* (Stroud: Sutton, 1997), 89–107; Rebecca J. Tannenbaum, *The Healer's Calling: Women and Medicine in Early New England* (Ithaca, NY: Cornell University Press, 2002).
29. For some discussion of distillation as women's kitchen work, see Wendy Wall, "Distillation: Transformations in and out of the Kitchen" in Joan Fitzpatrick (ed.), *Renaissance Food from Rabelais to Shakespeare: Culinary Readings and Culinary Histories* (Aldershot: Ashgate, 2010), 89–104.
30. Jo Castle, "Amulets and Protection: Pomanders," *Bulletin of the Society for Renaissance Studies* 17 (2000): 12–18; Rudolf Schmitz, "The Pomander," *Pharmacy in History* 31 (1989): 86–90.
31. Nagy, *Popular Medicine*, 43–53.
32. For various methods and receipts for making a "deflowered" woman a "virgin again," see John Baptista Porta [Giambattista della Porta], *Natural Magick (1658)*, ed. Derek J. Price (New York: Basic Books, 1957), 252–53. See also Kelly, *Performing Virginity*, 32.
33. For a reading of this scene in conversation with early modern scientific epistemology, see Bovilsky, *Barbarous Play*, 154–58.
34. Steven Shapin, *A Social History of Truth: Civility and Science in Seventeenth-Century England* (Chicago: University of Chicago Press, 1994).
35. Randall Martin observes that "the domestic expertise and cultural authority ceded to women as medical and food providers generated anxieties about unauthorized combinations of domestic and 'secret' knowledge" (126); see

Women, Murder, and Equity in Early Modern England (New York: Routledge, 2008).

36. On the repetition of "sweet" and "sweetness" in the play, see Michael C. Andrews, "'Sweetness' in *The Changeling*," *Yearbook of English Studies* 1 (1971): 63–67. The *OED* offers a definition of the adjective sweet that denotes health: "3. a. Free from offensive or disagreeable taste or smell; not corrupt, putrid, sour, or stale; free from taint or noxious matter; in a sound and wholesome condition." On the "fille vièrge" as pharmakon, see Louise Noble, *Medicinal Cannibalism in Early Modern English Literature and Culture* (New York: Palgrave Macmillan, 2011), 127–59.

37. See the Introduction on sympathies and antipathies. Drawing on the work of Gail Kern Paster, Bovilsky reads Beatrice's antipathy as derived from the "paradoxical logic with which humoral theory distinguished the different needs, sympathies, and antipathies of different objects and people" (*Barbarous Play*, 145), but as I argue throughout this book, the manifest nature of the humors was often incompatible with the occult properties of antipathy and sympathy. Bovilsky rightly identifies the same language in Shylock's speech in *The Merchant of Venice* 4.1.

38. Della Porta, *Natural Magick*, 9–10.

39. Peter Morrison, "A Cangoun in Zombieland: Middleton's Teratological Changeling" in Kenneth Friedenreich (ed.), *"Accompaninge the Players": Essays Celebrating Thomas Middleton, 1580–1980* (New York: AMS, 1983), 219–41; Joost Daalder, "Introduction," *The Changeling*, 2nd edition (London: A&C Black, 1990), xxvii–xxviii. For a survey of (and challenge to) the Freudian approach among theater critics, see Roberta Barker and David Nicol, "Does Beatrice Joanna Have a Subtext? *The Changeling* on the London Stage," *Early Modern Literary Studies* 10 (2004): 3.1–43 http://purl. oclc.org/emls/10-1/barknico.htm. For a psychoanalytical reading of the play's references to poison, see Maurizio Calbi, *Approximate Bodies: Aspects of the Figuration of Masculinity, Power and the Uncanny in Early Modern Drama and Anatomy* (Salerno: Oedipus, 2001), 121–65.

40. Nicolas Coeffeteau, *A table of humane passions* (London, 1621), 191.

41. Melissa P. Chase has noted that "medieval physicians and natural philosophers believed that poison acts at a distance through occult qualities, which made it a suitable mechanism for contagion"; see "Fevers, Poisons, and Apostemes: Authority and Experience in Montpellier Plague Treatises," *Annals of the New York Academy of Sciences* 441 (1985): 162–63.

42. Robert Fludd, *Mosaicall philosophy grounded upon the essentiall truth, or eternal sapience* (London, 1659), 227.

43. David Gentilcore, *Healers and Healing in Early Modern Italy* (Manchester: Manchester University Press, 1998), 103–04. See too Tanya Pollard, *Drugs and Theater in Early Modern England* (Oxford: Oxford University Press, 2005).

44. For an investigation of the political implications of poisonous pharmacy, see Jonathan Gil Harris, *Foreign Bodies and the Body Politic: Discourses of Pathology in Early Modern England* (Cambridge: Cambridge University Press, 1998).

Harris very rightly traces the application of poison as a cure to the folk notions of homeopathy as well as Paracelsian medicine. He overemphasizes, however, the anti-Galenic tenor of such medicine.

45. See Gilbert Watson, *Theriac and Mithridatium: A Study in Therapeutics* (London: The Wellcome Historical Medical Library, 1966), 74. In the early modern period, many writers interpreted the spread of the plague as an infection of poisonous vapors. As Isabelle Pantin notes, a modified Galenic interpretation of plague held that "its victims inhaled corrupt air that attacked the organism in *tota substantia*, by some occult quality, and putrified it as would an instantaneous poison." Ficino, Ambroise Paré, and Laurent Joubert all subscribe to this theory; see "Fracastoro's *De Contagione* and Medieval Reflection on 'Action at a Distance': Old and New Trends in Renaissance Discourse on Contagion" in Claire L. Carlin (ed.), *Imagining Contagion in Early Modern Europe* (Basingstoke: Palgrave Macmillan, 2005), 3–4 and 10n–11n. Pantin astutely observes that Fracastoro's theory of contagion (adapting Lucretian notions of invisible *semina*) provides a continuation of the medieval theories of action-at-a-distance by proposing that the *species spirituales* of an agent acted on its sympathetic subject (6–10).

46. Many writers agree, however, that if an antidote works by similitude, where a poison drives out a poison, such therapy is less likely to function as a preventive measure. In his argument against arsenic amulets as preservatives against the plague, Herring insists that the ingestion or use of poison cannot prevent poisoning before it has occurred; Francis Herring, *A modest defence of the caveat given to the wearers of impoisoned amulets, as preservatives from the plague* (London, 1604), 4. On the use of amulets as a plague remedy, see Paul Slack, *The Impact of the Plague in Tudor and Stuart England* (Oxford: Oxford University Press, 1991), 32.

47. Ambroise Paré, *The workes of that famous chirurgion Ambrose Parey translated out of Latine and compared with the French*, trans. T. Johnson (London, 1634), 784.

48. Philip Barrough, *The methode of phisicke* (London, 1583), 195.

49. Pliny, *The historie*, 1.211. John Donne writes in *Devotions upon Emergent Occasions*:

> Here we shrink in our proportion, sink in our dignity, in respect of very mean creatures, who are physicians to themselves. The hart that is pursued and wounded, they say, knows an herb, which being eaten throws off the arrow: a strange kind of vomit. The dog that pursues it, though he be subject to sickness, even proverbially, knows his grass that recovers him. And it may be true, that the drugger is as near to man as to other creatures; it may be that obvious and present simples, easy to be had, would cure him; but the apothecary is not so near him, nor the physician so near him, as they two are to other creatures; man hath not that innate instinct, to apply those natural medicines to his present danger, as those inferior creatures have; he is not his own apothecary, his own physician, as they are;

Devotions upon Emergent Occasions and Death's Duel (New York: Random House, 1999), 20. Unlike animals, humans have lost the natural capacity to know the occult qualities that would provide the appropriate antipathetic or sympathetic actions, except by their effects.

50. Hugh Plat, *The jewel house of art and nature* (London, 1653), 219. This appendix, "A rare and excellent discourse of minerals, stones, gums and rosins; with the vertues and use thereof," appears to have been added in 1653 by the editor D.B.

51. Herring, *A modest defence*, 4.

52. Judith Haber notes that the play insists that "Beatrice's loathing is also viewed as the guarantor of her desire – as ultimately contemporaneous with and indistinguishable from that desire"; see "I(t) Could Not Choose but Follow": Erotic Logic in *The Changeling*," *Representations* 81 (2003): 82. On the politics of rape in the play, see Deborah G. Burks, "'I'll want my will else': *The Changeling* and Women's Complicity with Their Rapists," *ELH* 62 (1995): 759–90. For a reading that reconsiders the complexity of Beatrice's position as both agent and victim, see Frances E. Dolan, "Re-reading Rape in *The Changeling*," *Journal for Early Modern Cultural Studies* (2011): 4–29.

53. On the breeding of meteors where "viscous or slimy matter and vapours abound in great quantity," see Robert Basset, *Curiosities: or the cabinet of nature Containing phylosophical, naturall, and morall questions fully answered and resolved*, trans. R.B. (London, 1637), 78–80. On the phenomenon of meteors, see Vladimer Janković, *Reading the Skies: A Cultural History of English Weather, 1650–1820* (Chicago: University of Chicago Press, 2000), 15–43.

54. *The problemes of Aristotle* (London, 1595) sig. L7v. See Chapter 1 on love, poison, and disease transmitted through the eyes.

55. Fludd, *Mosaicall philosophy*, 236.

56. Yet, DeFlores also describes her effect on him in the language of poison, "I shall rest from all love's plagues then; / I live in pain now: that flame-shooting eye / Will burn my heart to cinders" (3.3.150–52).

57. See for example, Levinus Lemnius, *The secret miracles of nature* (London, 1658), 16.

58. Simon Goulart, *Admirable and memorable histories containing the wonders of our time* (London, 1607), 75. On women's purportedly strange appetites, see Helen King, *The Disease of Virgins: Green Sickness, Chlorosis and the Problems of Puberty* (London and New York: Routledge, 2004), 107 and Lesel Dawson, *Lovesickness and Gender in Early Modern English Literature* (Oxford: Oxford University Press, 2008), 49.

59. *Women's Secrets: A Translation of Pseudo-Albertus Magnus's* De Secretis mulierum *with Commentaries*, ed. Helen Rodnite Lemay (Albany: State University of New York Press, 1992), 122, as well as 130–31. Some writers attempted to reconcile pica or odd eating with Galenic medicine; Alexander Ross in *Arcana microcosmi, or, The hid secrets of man's body* (London, 1652) writes that women's stomachs are "coveting after such things as are like to it in malignity, yet contrary to it in some of the prime qualities, heat, cold, humidity and siccity; for Nature looks in the contrary quality to finde remedy" (71).

60. Lemnius, *The secret miracles*, 17.
61. See Chapter 2.
62. On the concept of "bodywork," see Mary E. Fissell, "Introduction: Women, Health, and Healing in Early Modern Europe," *Bulletin of the History of Medicine* 82 (2008): 1–17. On women's presumed knowledge of poisons, see Martin, *Women, Murder and Equity*, 123–54.
63. The first quarto (1653) names Antonio the "changeling." For a discussion of other "changelings" in the play, see Lois E. Bueler, "The Rhetoric of Change in *The Changeling*," *English Literary Renaissance* 14 (1984): 95–113. For readings of the play that highlight its uncanny qualities, see Simmons, "Diabolical Realism," and Madeline Bassnett, "'A Frightful Pleasure, That is All': Wonder, Monstrosity, and *The Changeling*," *Dalhousie Review* 84 (2004): 387–406.
64. Susan Schoon Eberly, "Fairies and the Folklore of Disability: Changelings, Hybrids and the Solitary Fairy," *Folklore* 99 (1988): 58–77 and Joyce Underwood Munro, "The Invisible Made Visible: The Fairy Changeling as a Folk Articulation of Failure to Thrive in Infants and Children" in Peter Narváez (ed.), *The Good People: New Fairylore Essays* (New York: Garland, 1991), 251–83.
65. For a general discussion of changelings, see Katherine Mary Briggs, *The Fairies in Tradition and Literature* (New York: Routledge, 2002). Bovilsky suggests that DeFlores' alienation is an effect of racialization brought on by an aversion to his perceived physical deformities (*Barbarous Play*, 139–54).

5 "TO THINK THERE'S POWER IN POTIONS":
EXPERIMENT, SYMPATHY, AND THE DEVIL IN *THE
DUCHESS OF MALFI*

1. For surveys of the criticism, see David Gunby, "The Critical Backstory" and Dympna Callaghan, "The State of the Art: Critical Approaches 2000–08" in Christina Luckyj (ed.), *The Duchess of Malfi: A Critical Guide* (London: Continuum International Publishing, 2011), 14–41 and 66–86. For some representative discussions of the Duchess's moral status, see D. C. Gunby, "*The Duchess of Malfi*: A Theological Approach" in Brian Morris (ed.), *John Webster* (London: Ernest Benn, 1970), 181–204 and R. S. White, "The Moral Design of *The Duchess of Malfi*" in Dympna Callaghan (ed.), *The Duchess of Malfi* (Basingstoke: Macmillan, 2000), 201–16. On the private/public divide, see Lee Bliss, *The World's Perspective: John Webster and the Jacobean Drama* (New Brunswick, NJ: Rutgers University Press, 1983); Catherine Belsey, *The Subject of Tragedy: Identity and Difference in Renaissance Drama* (London: Methuen, 1985), 197; Frank Whigham, "Sexual and Social Mobility in *The Duchess of Malfi*," *PMLA* 100 (1985): 167–86; Theodore B. Leinwand, "*Coniugium Interruptum* in Shakespeare and Webster," *ELH* 72 (2005): 239–57; Wendy Wall, "Just a Spoonful of Sugar: Syrup and Domesticity in Early Modern England," *Modern Philology* 104 (2006): 149–72. On female subjectivity, see Lisa Jardine,

Still Harping on Daughters: Women and Drama in the Age of Shakespeare (Brighton: Harvester Press, 1983), 68–102; Mary Beth Rose, *The Expense of Spirit: Love and Sexuality in English Renaissance Drama* (Ithaca, NY: Cornell University Press, 1988); Dympna Callaghan, *Women and Gender in Renaissance Tragedy: A Study of* King Lear, Othello, The Duchess of Malfi, *and* The White Devil (Atlantic Highlands, NJ: Humanities Press, 1989); Judith Haber, "'My Body Bestow upon My Women': The Space of the Feminine in *The Duchess of Malfi*," *Renaissance Drama* 28 (1999): 133–59 and *Desire and Dramatic Form in Early Modern England* (Cambridge: Cambridge University Press, 2009), 71–86; Linda Woodbridge, "Queen of Apricots: The Duchess of Malfi, Hero of Desire" in Naomi Conn Liebler (ed.), *The Female Tragic Hero in English Renaissance Drama* (New York: Palgrave, 2002), 161–84. On marriage, see Frank W. Wadsworth, "Webster's *The Duchess of Malfi* in the Light of Some Contemporary Ideas on Marriage and Remarriage," *Philological Quarterly* 35 (1956): 394–407; Christy Desmet, "'Neither Maid, Widow, nor Wife': Rhetoric of the Woman Controversy in *Measure for Measure* and *The Duchess of Malfi*" in Dorothea Kehler and Susan Baker (eds.), *Another Country: Feminist Perspectives on Renaissance Drama* (Metuchen, NJ: Scarecrow, 1991), 71–92; Jennifer Panek, "Why Did Widows Remarry? Remarriage, Male Authority, and Feminist Criticism" in Dympna Callaghan (ed.), *The Impact of Feminism in English Renaissance Studies* (Basingstoke: Palgrave Macmillan, 2007), 281–98; Dympna Callaghan, "*The Duchess of Malfi* and Early Modern Widows" in Garrett A. Sullivan, Jr., Patrick Cheney, and Andrew Hadfield (eds.), *Early Modern English Drama: A Critical Companion* (Oxford: Oxford University Press, 2006), 272–86.

2. David Gunby observes that F. L. Lucas is the first critic to raise the question of incestuous desire with regard to Ferdinand ("The Critical Backstory," 21–22). See F. L. Lucas (ed.), *The Complete Works of John Webster*, 4 vols. (London: Chatto & Windus, 1927), vol. 2, 24. Other early critics who broach the issue are Clifford Leech, *John Webster: A Critical Study* (London: Hogarth Press, 1951), 100–06 and Elizabeth Brennan (ed.), *The Duchess of Malfi* (London: Ernest Benn, 1964), xiv. On lycanthropy, see Albert H. Tricomi, "Historicizing the Imagery of the Demonic in *The Duchess of Malfi*," *Journal of Medieval and Early Modern Studies* 34 (2004): 345–72; Tricomi, "The Severed Hand in Webster's *Duchess of Malfi*," *Studies in English Literature, 1500–1900* 44 (2004): 347–58; Susan Zimmerman, *The Early Modern Corpse and Shakespeare's Theatre* (Edinburgh: Edinburgh University Press, 2005), 155–57; Brett D. Hirsch, "An Italian Werewolf in London: Lycanthropy and *The Duchess of Malfi*," *Early Modern Literary Studies* 11 (2005): 43 paragraphs, http://purl.oclc.org/emls/11-2/hirswere.htm; Hirsch, "Werewolves and Severed Hands: Webster's *The Duchess of Malfi* and Heywood and Brome's *The Witches of Lancashire*," *Notes and Queries* 53 (2006): 92–4; Courtney Lehmann and Bryan Reynolds, "Awakening the Werewolf Within: Self-Help, Vanishing Mediation, and Transversality in *The Duchess of Malfi*" in Bryan Reynolds (ed.), *Transversal*

Enterprises in the Drama of Shakespeare and His Contemporaries: Fugitive Explorations (New York: Palgrave Macmillan, 2006), 227–39.
3. Whigham, "Sexual and Social Mobility," 169.
4. Whigham, "Sexual and Social Mobility," 171.
5. Lynn Enterline, "'Hairy on the In-Side': *The Duchess of Malfi* and the Body of Lycanthropy," *Yale Journal of Criticism* 7 (1994): 85–129. See too Gail Kern Paster's argument that the "cultural role of melancholy adust dries up what might once have been Ferdinand's own normative appetites and desires . . . He becomes a wolf . . . because he cannot identify with his sister *and her desires* as natural"; see *Humoring the Body: Emotions and the Shakespearean Stage* (Chicago: University of Chicago Press, 2004), 162.
6. Tricomi, "Historicizing the Imagery of the Demonic," 353.
7. Since the publication of Barbara Ehrenreich and Deirdre English's *Witches, Midwives, and Nurses: A History of Women Healers* (Old Westbury, NY: The Feminist Press, 1973), which argued that women healers were systematically persecuted as witches, historians have worked to correct, and even dismantle, their thesis. See in particular David Harley, "Historians as Demonologists: The Myth of the Midwife-Witch," *Social History of Medicine* 3 (1990): 1–26. On the stereotypical associations between witches and female healers, Diane Purkiss notes that "Most women used herbal medicines as part of their household skills, some of which were quasi-magical, without arousing any anxiety." She also emphasizes that women were most often the accusers in witchcraft cases, arguing that "witchcraft occurs when women lose control of the processes of housewifery to another woman"; see *The Witch in History: Early Modern and Twentieth-Century Representations* (London: Routledge, 1996), 8 and 102. But as Clive Holmes has demonstrated, not only did men often instigate the involvement of female witnesses, but women "attendant at the sick-bed of the victim" were also "simply better placed than men" to describe the effects of witchcraft; see "Women, Witnesses and Witches," *Past and Present* 140 (1993): 77 and 49. Lyndal Roper suggests that witchcraft themes are generated by "deeply conflicted feelings about motherhood"; see *Oedipus and the Devil: Witchcraft, Sexuality and Religion in Early Modern Europe* (London: Routledge, 1994), 218. See too Deborah Willis, *Malevolent Nurture: Witch-Hunting and Maternal Power in Early Modern England* (Ithaca, NY: Cornell University Press, 1995). But according to Randall Martin, "Popular news accounts mirrored the . . . cultural reflex wherein the traditional knowledge of cookery, physic, herbal remedies, and/or white magic cultivated by daughters, mothers, servants, and cunning-women could quickly turn into accusations of poisoning and witchcraft in suspicious contexts"; see *Women, Murder, and Equity in Early Modern England* (New York: Routledge, 2008), 127. See too the collection of essays in Brian P. Levack (ed.), *New Perspectives on Witchcraft, Magic, and Demonology: Witchcraft, Healing, and Popular Diseases*, vol. 5 (London: Routledge, 2001). Rebecca Laroche has observed that the "intersection between witchcraft pamphlets and the early stages of the English vernacular herbal depicts a world in which the common man may be subjected to the

malevolent/ignorant and female use of herbs and consequently emasculated"; see *Medical Authority and Englishwomen's Herbal Texts, 1550–1650* (Aldershot: Ashgate, 2009), 48.

8. Stuart Clark writes, "It was assumed as a matter of course that those with the special power to heal by magic must know how to harm by the same means"; "Witchcraft and Magic in Early Modern Culture" in Bengt Ankarloo and Stuart Clark (eds.), *Witchcraft and Magic in Europe: The Period of the Witch Trials* (Philadelphia: University of Pennsylvania Press, 2002), 112. On the normative status of female healers, Deborah E. Harkness, "A View from the Streets: Women and Medical Work in Elizabethan London," *Bulletin of the History of Medicine* 82 (2008): 52–85. Katharine Park has argued, moreover, that boundaries between medicine, magic, and religion "in many cases are hardly to be discerned at all"; see "Medicine and Magic: The Healing Arts" in Judith C. Brown and Robert C. Davis (eds.), *Gender and Society in Renaissance Italy* (London and New York: Longman, 1998), 132.

9. Wendy Wall does not discuss witchcraft, but her work highlights the play's attention to women's domestic expertise in the mixing of medicinal syrups.

10. For some of these assumptions about women's bodies, see *Women's Secrets: A Translation of Pseudo-Albertus Magnus's* De Secretis Mulierum *with Commentaries*, ed. Helen Rodnite Lemay (Albany: State University of New York Press, 1992), 130–31. See too Fernando Salmón and Montserrat Cabré I Pairet, "Fascinating Women: The Evil Eye in Medical Scholasticism" in Roger French, Jon Arrizabalaga, Andrew Cunningham, and Luis Garcia-Ballester (eds.), *Medicine from the Black Death to the French Disease* (Aldershot: Ashgate, 1998), 53–84.

11. Peter Dear, *Discipline and Experience: The Mathematical Way in the Scientific Revolution* (Chicago: University of Chicago Press, 1995) and "The Meanings of Experience" in Katharine Park and Lorraine Daston (eds.), *The Cambridge History of Science*, vol. 3 (Cambridge: Cambridge University Press, 2003), 106–31.

12. Deborah E. Harkness, *The Jewel House: Elizabethan London and the Scientific Revolution* (New Haven: Yale University Press, 2007), 197–98.

13. For a discussion of the play in relation to secrecy, gynecology, and anatomy, see Maurizio Calbi, *Approximate Bodies: Aspects of the Figuration of Masculinity, Power and the Uncanny in Early Modern Drama and Anatomy* (Milan: Oedipus, 2001), 43–119. See too Ellen Caldwell, "Invasive Procedures in Webster's *The Duchess of Malfi*" in Linda Woodbridge and Sharon Beehler (eds.), *Women, Violence, and English Renaissance Literature: Essays Honoring Paul Jorgensen* (Tempe: Arizona Center for Medieval and Renaissance Studies, 2003), 149–86. Caldwell identifies Bosola as the surgeon and Ferdinand as the physician in "the dissection theater, managing the interrogation, psychological torture, and 'anatomizing' of the Duchess" ("Invasive Procedures," 150). On the theme of secrecy in the play, see Frances E. Dolan, "'Can this be certain?': The Duchess of Malfi's Secrets" in Luckyj, *A Critical Guide*, 119–35. Kaara Peterson considers the role of the supernatural in the play's representation of

female complaints and argues that Webster expresses a skeptical view; *Popular Medicine, Hysterical Disease, and Social Controversy* (Aldershot: Ashgate, 2010), 176–78.

14. See Stuart Clark on the science of demonology, first outlined in "The Scientific Status of Demonology" in Brian Vickers (ed.), *Occult and Scientific Mentalities in the Renaissance* (Cambridge: Cambridge University Press, 1984), 351–74. As Clark observes, "the history (as well as the anthropology) of science shows that the perceived boundary between nature and supernature, if it is established at all, is local to cultures, and that it shifts according to tastes and interests"; see *Thinking with Demons: The Idea of Witchcraft in Early Modern Europe* (Oxford: Oxford University Press, 1997), 152. G. MacDonald Ross has argued that there "was no clear line of demarcation between occultism, philosophy, religion, and science"; see "Occultism and Philosophy in the Seventeenth Century" in A. J. Holland (ed.), *Philosophy: Its History and Historiography* (Dordrecht: Reidel, 1985), 107. On the epistemological and disciplinary boundary work taking place during this period, see John Henry, "The Fragmentation of Renaissance Occultism and the Decline of Magic," *History of Science* 46 (2008): 1–48.

15. On the vexed relationship between women's secrets and nature's secrets, see Monica H. Green, "From 'Diseases of Women' to 'Secrets of Women': The Transformation of Gynecological Literature in the Later Middle Ages," *Journal of Medieval and Early Modern Studies* 30.1 (2000): 5–39. Also Green, *Making Women's Medicine Masculine: The Rise of Male Authority in Pre-Modern Gynaecology* (Oxford: Oxford University Press, 2008), 204–45 and Katharine Park, *Secrets of Women: Gender, Generation, and the Origins of Human Dissection* (New York: Zone Books, 2006).

16. John Webster, *The Duchess of Malfi*, ed. Elizabeth M. Brennan (London: Ernest Benn, 1964). All quotations from the play are cited parenthetically in the text.

17. Sir Francis Bacon, *The Advancement of Learning* in *The Works of Francis Bacon*, ed. James Spedding, Robert Leslie Ellis, and Douglas Demon Heath, 14 vols. (London: Longman, 1861–79), vol. 3 (1876), 2.331.

18. See *Witches, Devils, and Doctors in the Renaissance: Johann Weyer, De praestigiis daemonum*, trans. John Shea (Binghamton, NY: Medieval and Renaissance Texts and Studies, 1991), 275.

19. On the devil's expertise in nature's secrets, see Clark, *Thinking with Demons*, 245–47.

20. Bacon, *Sylva Sylvarum: or A naturall historie in ten centuries* (London, 1627), 242 and 255. On Bacon's debt to natural magic and alchemy, see Paolo Rossi, *Francis Bacon: From Magic to Science* (Chicago: University of Chicago Press, 1968) and John Henry, *Knowledge Is Power: How Magic, the Government and an Apocalyptic Vision Inspired Francis Bacon to Create Modern Science* (Cambridge : Icon Books, 2002).

21. In discussing Bacon, Clark observes, "the subject of witchcraft had become particularly rich in thought-experiments; experimenting with it in any practical way was not advisable, whereas all manner of insights might be gained by imagining what would have to follow for such a strange phenomenon to be true and what needed to be the case for it to be false"; see *Thinking with Demons*, 257.

22. William Perkins, *A discourse of the damned art of witchcraft* (London, 1608), 170.

23. On how superstition stems from a belief in natural efficacy that leads to a tacit pact with the devil, see Clark, *Thinking with Demons*, 478–88. For more on the complexity of early modern superstition, see Alexandra Walsham, "Recording Superstition in Early Modern Britain: The Origins of Folklore," *Past and Present* 199, Supplement 3 (2008): 178–206; Michael D. Bailey, *Magic and Superstition in Europe: A Concise History from Antiquity to the Present* (Lanham, MD: Rowman and Littlefield), 2007).

24. *Witches, Devils, and Doctors*, 267.

25. On the mandrake causing sleep, see [Stephen Batman], *Batman vppon Bartholome his booke de proprietatibus rerum* (London, 1582), fo. 305v and John Gerard, *The herball or Generall historie of plantes* (London, 1633), 341. Pierre Boaistuau notes that it causes love and puts men to sleep due to its "maruellous virtue"; see *Certaine secrete wonders of nature*, trans. E. Fenton (London, 1569), fo. 73v; Giambattista della Porta contends that the mandrake provokes sleep and makes men mad in larger doses in John Baptista Porta [Giambattista della Porta], *Natural Magick (1658)*, ed. Derek J. Price (New York: Basic Books, 1957), 217–19. On the history of mandrake uses, see Frederick J. Simoons, *Plants of Life, Plants of Death* (Madison: University of Wisconsin Press, 1998). On the significance of sleep in the play, see Garrett A. Sullivan, Jr., *Memory and Forgetting in English Renaissance Drama: Shakespeare, Marlowe, Webster* (Cambridge: Cambridge University Press, 2005), 109–31.

26. William Bullein, *Bulleins bulwarke of defence against all sicknesse* (London, 1579), fo. 42r.

27. Whigham, "Sexual and Social Mobility," 169.

28. See Enterline on the basilisk imagery, "'Hairy on the In-Side,'" 94.

29. Wall, "Just a Spoonful of Sugar," 163.

30. Wall, "Just a Spoonful of Sugar," 172.

31. On the use of human parts in early modern medicine, see Louise Noble, *Medicinal Cannibalism in Early Modern English Literature and Culture* (New York: Palgrave Macmillan, 2011) and Richard Sugg, *Mummies, Cannibals and Vampires: The History of Corpse Medicine from the Renaissance to the Victorians* (New York: Routledge, 2011).

32. See for example the items listed in D. Gordon's *Pharmaco-pinax, or A table and taxe of the pryces of all vsuall medicaments, simple and composed, contayned in D. Gordon's apothecarie and chymicall shop* (London, 1625). Also see

William Brockbank, "Sovereign Remedies: A Critical Depreciation of the 17th Century London *Pharmacopoeia*," *Medical History* 8 (1964): 1–14.

33. Many will recall a similar therapy mentioned in John Donne's *Devotions*, when he mentions the use of a "good pigeon to draw this [venomous] vapor from the head"; see *Devotions upon Emergent Occasions and Death's Duel* (New York: Random House, 1999), 73. Pigeons and other fowl were thought to have a natural antipathy to poison, and their flayed bodies or fundaments were understood to draw out, by an attractive force, diverse poisons in the body, including dog bites and the plague. As discussed in the chapter on *All's Well That Ends Well*, Charles Estienne observes that the birds' natural contrary to poison is seen in its habit of eating "venimous things, as Toades, Vipers, Snakes, Aspes, and other Serpents, without their taking any harme thereby"; see *Maison rustique, or The countrey farme* (London, 1616), 74. See also Ambroise Paré, *The workes of that famous chirurgion Ambrose Parey*, trans. T. Johnson (London, 1644), 784. Among the many writers who recommend flayed pigeons as a counter to poison are John Bates, *The mysteryes of nature, and art* (London, 1634), 175 and Stephen Bradwell, *Helps for sudden accidents endangering life* (London, 1633), 17. On sympathies in early modern medicine, see too Mary E. Fissell, *Patients, Power, and the Poor in Eighteenth-Century Bristol* (Cambridge: Cambridge University Press, 1991), 19–22.

34. Hillary Nunn has done work on the status of the "old lady" and her secrets, including "'Old Women' and 'Old Ladies': Assuming Vocational Identity in Early Modern Theater," presented in the 2010 Shakespeare Association of America seminar "Artisanal Knowledge and the Stage," and "'It seems you are well acquainted with my closet?': Staging Medical Secrets in Early Modern Drama," presented at the Renaissance Society of America Conference in Montreal, 2011. On female practitioners, Doreen G. [Evenden] Nagy, *Popular Medicine in Seventeenth-Century England* (Bowling Green, OH: Bowling Green State University Popular Press, 1988) and *The Midwives of Seventeenth-Century London* (Cambridge: Cambridge University Press, 2000); Margaret Pelling, *Medical Conflicts in Early Modern London: Patronage, Physicians, and Irregular Practitioners, 1550–1640* (Oxford: Oxford University Press, 2003); Lynette Hunter, "Women and Domestic Medicine: Lady Experimenters, 1570–1620" in Lynette Hunter and Sarah Hutton (eds.), *Women, Science and Medicine, 1500–1700: Mothers and Sisters of the Royal Society* (Stroud: Sutton, 1997), 89–107.

35. On the ambiguity of pregnant bodies, see Cathy McClive, "The Hidden Truths of the Belly: The Uncertainties of Pregnancy in Early Modern Europe," *Social History of Medicine* 15 (2002): 209–27. William Kerwin notes that Bosola relies on a "folk medicine similar to that used by women healers" in his essay "'Physicians are like Kings': Medical Politics and *The Duchess of Malfi*," *English Literary Renaissance* 28 (1998): 114. On the sexual implications of the Duchess's appetite, see Katherine Armstrong, "Possets, Pills and Poisons: Physicking the Female Body in Early Seventeenth-Century Drama," *Cahiers Elisabéthains* 61 (2002): 43–56 and Lori Schroeder Haslem, "'Troubled with the

Mother': Longings, Purgings, and the Maternal Body in *Bartholomew Fair* and *The Duchess of Malfi*," *Modern Philology* 92 (1995): 438–59. For a wide-ranging consideration of the significance of apricots in the play and early modern culture, see Dale B. J. Randall, "The Rank and Earthy Background of Certain Physical Symbols in *The Duchess of Malfi*," *Renaissance Drama* 18 (1987): 171–203.

36. In conversation, Edmund Campos suggested these lines pertain to a glass dildo. John Marston refers to a dildo as a "glassie instrument" in *The scourge of villanie* (London, 1598), sig. c8r. On the play's phallic imagery, see Randall, "The Rank and Earthy Background," 173.

37. See Eleanor S. Godfrey, *The Development of English Glassmaking 1560–1640* (Chapel Hill: University of North Carolina Press, 1975); Linda Levy Peck, *Consuming Splendor: Society and Culture in Seventeenth-Century England* (Cambridge: Cambridge University Press, 2005), 74–80. In the late sixteenth century, generating a domestic glass-making industry in England depended on the immigration of Italian glass-makers. In addition to the transfer of Venetian glass-making techniques to native artisans, materials circulated that provided glass-making instructions, despite protests in Italy. In 1612 Antonio Neri published *L'artra vetraria* (*The Art of Glassmaking*), which put glass-house secrets into print for the very first time.

38. Plate from *Opera di Giorgio Agricola de l'arte de metalli* by Georg Agricola (1563). Note the people drinking at a table in the background, seen through an open door. As Roy Booth has observed, other writers in the period indicate that citizens would regularly visit glass-houses to see the burning furnaces and witness the glass-making process; see "John Webster's Heart of Glass," *English* 40 (1991): 99.

39. On the regulation of openness in seventeenth-century experimental spaces, see Betty Jo Teeter Dobbs, "From the Secrecy of Alchemy to the Openness of Chemistry" in Tore Frängsmyr (ed.), *Solomon's House Revisited: The Organization and Institutionalization of Science* (Canton, MA: Science History Publications, 1990), 75–94; William Eamon, "From the Secrets of Nature to Public Knowledge" in David C. Lindberg and Robert S. Westman (eds.), *Reappraisals of the Scientific Revolution* (Cambridge: Cambridge University Press, 1990), 333–65; Pamela O. Long, *Openness, Secrecy, Authorship: Technical Arts and the Culture of Knowledge from Antiquity to the Renaissance* (Baltimore: Johns Hopkins University Press, 2001); William R. Newman, "Alchemical Symbolism and Concealment: The Chemical House of Libavius" in Peter Galison and Emily Thompson (eds.), *The Architecture of Science* (Cambridge, MA: MIT Press, 1999), 59–77. On the development of scientific workspaces, see Steven Shapin, "The House of Experiment in Seventeenth-Century England," *Isis* 79 (1988): 373–404; Maurice Crosland, "Early Laboratories, c. 1600–c. 1800 and the Location of Experimental Science," *Annals of Science* 62 (2005): 233–53; Ursula Klein, "The Laboratory Challenge: Some Revisions of the Standard View of Early Modern Experimentation," *Isis* 99 (2008): 769–82. See too the following entries in

Katharine Park and Lorraine Daston (eds.), *The Cambridge History of Science*, vol. 3 (Cambridge: Cambridge University Press, 2003): Pamela H. Smith, "Laboratories," 290–305; William Eamon, "Markets, Piazzas, and Villages," 206–23; Alix Cooper, "Homes and Households," 224–37; Bruce T. Moran "Courts and Academies," 251–71. As Lady Cressingham observes in Thomas Middleton's *Any thing for a quiet life* (London, 1662), domestic alchemical studies can transform one's very home into a glass-house (sig. B4r–B4v).

40. Park, *Secrets of Women*, 256.

41. Katharine Park, "Dissecting the Female Body: From Women's Secrets to the Secrets of Nature" in Jane Donawerth and Adele Seeff (eds.), *Crossing Boundaries: Attending to Early Modern Women* (Newark: University of Delaware Press, 2000), 39.

42. On Bosola as the surgeon enacting Ferdinand-the-physician's instructions, see Caldwell, "Invasive Procedures," 162.

43. Steven Shapin, "The Invisible Technician," *American Scientist* 77 (1989): 554–63. Also see Shapin, *A Social History of Truth: Civility and Science in Seventeenth-Century England* (Chicago: University of Chicago Press, 1994), 355–407.

44. Bacon, *The Advancement of Learning*, 2.325.

45. Bacon, *The Advancement of Learning*, 2.333.

46. Bacon, *Novum Organum* in *The Works*, vol. 4 (1875), 95.

47. J. E. Tiles, "Experiment as Intervention," *British Journal for the Philosophy of Science* 44 (1993): 466.

48. The parallel I am drawing between Ferdinand's plaguing the Duchess and Bacon's vexations of nature calls to mind the debate taking place among historians of science over whether sexist metaphors play a role in Bacon's scientific enterprise. See "Focus: Getting Back to *The Death of Nature*: Rereading Carolyn Merchant," *Isis* 97 (2006). For more on this topic, see the following essays in *Journal of the History of Ideas* 69 (2008): Carolyn Merchant, "Secrets of Nature: The Bacon Debates Revisited," 147–62; Brian Vickers, "Francis Bacon, Feminist Historiography, and the Dominion of Nature," 117–41; Katharine Park, "Response to Brian Vickers, 'Francis Bacon, Feminist Historiography, and the Dominion of Nature,'" 143–46. See too Peter Pesic, "Wrestling with Proteus: Francis Bacon and the 'Torture' of Nature," *Isis* 90 (1999): 81–94 and Evelyn Fox Keller, *Reflections on Gender and Science* (New Haven: Yale University Press, 1985).

49. On the horoscope, see Johnstone Parr, "The Horoscope in Webster's *The Duchess of Malfi*," *PMLA* 60 (1945): 760–65.

50. Katherine Rowe, *Dead Hands: Fictions of Agency, Renaissance to Modern* (Stanford: Stanford University Press, 1999), 99.

51. Rowe, *Dead Hands*, 103–04.

52. See Lauren Kassell's discussion of Simon Forman's use of sympathetic magic with wax figures in his healing practices; "'The Food of Angels': Simon Forman's Alchemical Medicine" in William R. Newman and Anthony Grafton (eds.), *Secrets of Nature: Astrology and Alchemy in Early*

Modern Europe (Cambridge, MA.: MIT Press, 2001), 369. On the common-place associations between sympathetic magic and wax figures, see Julius von Schlosser, "History of Portraiture in Wax" in Roberta Panzanelli (ed.), *Ephemeral Bodies: Wax Sculpture and the Human Figure* (Los Angeles: Getty Research Institute, 2008), 175–76.

53. See James Howell, *Familiar Letters: or Epistolae Ho-Elianae*, vol. 1 (London: J. M. Dent, 1903), 44.

54. Tricomi, "Historicizing the Imagery of the Demonic," 358.

55. Hirsch, "An Italian Werewolf," para. 8.

56. Hirsch, "An Italian Werewolf," para. 39.

57. Stuart Clark, "Demons and Disease: The Disenchantment of the Sick (1500–1700)" in Marijke Gijswijt-Hofstra, Hilary Marland, and Hans De Waardt (eds.), *Illness and Healing Alternatives in Western Europe* (London: Routledge, 1997), 38–58.

58. See Introduction.

59. Hirsch, "An Italian Werewolf," paras. 8–9.

60. Reginald Scot, *The discoverie of witchcraft* (London, 1584), 102.

61. John Deacon and John Walker, *Dialogicall discourses of spirits and divels* (London, 1601), 161.

62. *Witches, Devils, and Doctors*, 193.

63. *Witches, Devils, and Doctors*, 554.

64. Simon Goulart, *Admirable and memorable histories . . . of our time*, trans. Edward Grimeston (London, 1607), 387–88.

65. *Witches, Devils, and Doctors*, 342–43.

66. Hillary M. Nunn discusses *The Duchess of Malfi* in *Staging Anatomies: Dissection and Spectacle in Early Stuart Tragedy* (Aldershot: Ashgate, 2005), but she does not address these lines or Ferdinand's anatomizing impulse.

67. William Kerwin, *Beyond the Body: The Boundaries of Medicine and English Renaissance Drama* (Amherst and Boston: University of Massachusetts Press, 2005), 163. See too Kerwin, "'Physicians are like Kings,'" 95–117.

68. William Painter, *The second tome of the Palace of pleasure* (London, 1567), fo. 172v. Simon Goulart describes the Duchess as a widow with "lascivious eye" who covered her desire under the "colour of marriage" (*Admirable and memorable histories*, 364). Antonio, he states, was a man "drunke with his owne conceite" who married secretly out of presumption and lust (364–65).

69. Henry Cornelius Agrippa of Nettesheim, *Three Books of Occult Philosophy*, ed. Donald Tyson, trans. J. Freake (St. Paul, MN: Llewellyn Publications, 2004), 138. Paster cites Antonio's lines to discuss how the "self traversed by desire finds its own contradictory longings mimicked everywhere by the sympathies and antipathies that organize and move a desiring universe filled with the strivings of appetite in all things animal, vegetable, and mineral"; see *Humoring the Body*, 31–33.

70. Quoted in Paul J. C. M. Franssen, "Amorous Palms" in Jan Frans van Dijkhuizen, Paul Hoftijzer, Juliette Roding, and Paul Smith (eds.), *Living in*

Posterity: Essays in Honour of Bart Westerweel (Hilversum: Uitgeverij Verloren, 2004), 107.

71. See Ruth HaCohen, "The Music of Sympathy in the Arts of the Baroque; or, the Use of Difference to Overcome Indifference," *Poetics Today* 22 (2001): 619–21.

72. On the play's circumscription of female space in ways that "could be extremely threatening to the dominant order," see Judith Haber, *Desire and Dramatic Form in Early Modern England* (Cambridge: Cambridge University Press, 2009), 73.

CODA

1. Brian Easlea, *Witch-hunting, Magic, and the New Philosophy: An Introduction to the Debates of the Scientific Revolution 1450–1750* (Brighton: Harvester Press, 1980), 246.

2. Steven Shapin, *The Scientific Revolution* (Chicago: University of Chicago Press, 1996), 94.

3. Joseph Glanvill, *The vanity of dogmatizing* (London, 1661), 118.

4. "An Anatomy of the World" in *The Poems of John Donne*, ed. Herbert J. C. Grierson, 2 vols. (Oxford: Clarendon Press, 1912), vol. 1. Line numbers are cited in the text.

5. On Donne and the new philosophy, see Charles M. Coffin, *John Donne and the New Philosophy* (New York: Columbia University Press, 1937); John Haffenden (ed.), *William Empson: Essays on Renaissance Literature*, vol. 1, *John Donne and the New Philosophy* (Cambridge: Cambridge University Press, 1993); Angus [John Stewart] Fletcher, *Time, Space, and Motion in the Age of Shakespeare* (Cambridge, MA: Harvard University Press, 2007).

6. "Ben Jonson's Conversations with Drummond" in *Ben Jonson*, ed. C. H. Herford, Percy Simpson, and Evelyn Simpson, 11 vols. (Oxford: Oxford University Press, 1925–52), vol. 1, 133. On the significance of magnetism in the poem, see Angus Fletcher, "Living Magnets, Paracelsian Corpses, and the Psychology of Grace in Donne's Religious Verse," *ELH* 72 (2005): 1–22.

7. On the poem's representation of life-giving principles retained in bodies after death, see Louise Noble, *Medicinal Cannibalism in Early Modern English Literature and Culture* (New York: Palgrave Macmillan, 2011), 142–59.

8. Samuel Pepys quoted in Londa Schiebinger, "Women of Natural Knowledge" in Katharine Park and Lorraine Daston (eds.), *The Cambridge History of Science*, vol. 3 (Cambridge: Cambridge University Press, 2006), 197.

9. John Henry, *The Scientific Revolution and the Origins of Modern Science*, 3rd edition (Basingstoke: Palgrave Macmillan, 2008), 108. See also Peter Dear, "A Philosophical Duchess: Understanding Margaret Cavendish and the Royal Society" in Juliet Cummins and David Burchell (eds.), *Science, Literature, and Rhetoric in Early Modern England* (Aldershot: Ashgate, 2007), 127. On the development of Cavendish's natural philosophy, see Lisa T. Sarasohn, *The*

Natural Philosophy of Margaret Cavendish: Reason and Fancy during the Scientific Revolution (Baltimore: Johns Hopkins University Press, 2010).

10. He may have been seeking her patronage, too. See Jacqueline Broad, "Margaret Cavendish and Joseph Glanvill: Science, Religion, and Witchcraft," *Studies in History and Philosophy of Science* 38 (2007): 494.

11. Broad, "Margaret Cavendish," 494.

12. On how Glanvill's beliefs prove difficult for modern readers to comprehend, see Thomas Harmon Jobe, "The Devil in Restoration Science: The Glanvill–Webster Witchcraft Debate," *Isis* 72 (1981): 342–56.

13. Stuart Clark, *Thinking with Demons: The Idea of Witchcraft in Early Modern Europe* (Oxford: Oxford University Press, 1997), 297.

14. Keith Hutchison, "Supernaturalism and the Mechanical Philosophy," *History of Science* 21 (1983): 297.

15. Jobe, "The Devil in Restoration Science," 352.

16. Joseph Glanvill in Margaret Cavendish, Duchess of Newcastle, *A Collection of letters and poems* (London, 1678), 139–40. Broad writes that "Glanvill's views were largely the result of uncritical prejudice"; see "Margaret Cavendish," 503.

17. Joseph Glanvill, *A blow at modern Sadducism in some philosophical considerations about witchcraft* (London, 1668), 28.

18. Glanvill, *A blow at modern Sadducism*, 20.

19. Glanvill, *A blow at modern Sadducism*, 29.

20. Cavendish, *Philosophical letters, or, Modest reflections upon some opinions in natural philosophy maintained by several famous and learned authors of this age* (London, 1664), 298.

21. Cavendish, *Philosophical letters*, 244.

22. See Jobe, "The Devil in Restoration Science," 350–52 and Clark, *Thinking with Demons*, 239.

23. Cavendish, *Observations upon experimental philosophy* (London, 1666), 2.12 and 1.102–03. Thomas Vaughn seems quite sincere when he suggests for similar reasons that "*women* are fitter for [chemical experimentation] than men, for in such things they are more neat and patient, being used to a small *Chimistrie* of *Sack-possets*, and other finicall *sugar-sops*"; see *Magia adamica or the antiquitie of magic* (London, 1650), 118.

24. Deborah E. Harkness, *The Jewel House: Elizabethan London and the Scientific Revolution* (New Haven: Yale University Press, 2007), 247.

25. Shapin, *The Scientific Revolution*, 98.

26. Shapin, *The Scientific Revolution*, 103–04.

27. John Henry, "Occult Qualities and the Experimental Philosophy: Active Principles in Pre-Newtonian Matter Theory," *History of Science* 24 (1986): 335–81. See too Keith Hutchison, "What Happened to Occult Qualities in the Scientific Revolution?" *Isis* 73 (1982): 233–53.

28. Robert Boyle, *Suspicions about some hidden qualities of the air* (London, 1674), sig. A2v. See Henry, "Occult Qualities," 345.

29. Boyle, *Suspicions*, sig. D8r.

30. Boyle, *Suspicions*, sig. C6r and Henry, "Occult Qualities," 344.

31. For Boyle's interest in secrets, alchemy, and spirits, see Michael Hunter, "Robert Boyle and Secrecy" in Elaine Leong and Alisha Rankin (eds.), *Secrets and Knowledge in Medicine and Science, 1500–1800* (Burlington, VT: Ashgate, 2011), 87–104; Hunter, *Robert Boyle (1627–91): Scrupulosity and Science* (Woodbridge: The Boydell Press, 2000); and Hunter, *Boyle: Between God and Science* (New Haven: Yale University Press, 2009). See too Lawrence M. Principe, *The Aspiring Adept: Robert Boyle and his Alchemical Quest* (Princeton: Princeton University Press, 1998).

32. Boyle, *Of the reconcileableness of specifick medicines to the corpuscular philosophy* (London, 1685), 3.

33. Boyle, *Of the reconcileableness of specifick medicines*, 34.

34. Boyle, *Of the reconcileableness of specifick medicines*, 119–20 and 125–26.

35. Boyle, *Of the reconcileableness of specifick medicines*, 14.

36. Boyle, *Of the reconcileableness of specifick medicines*, 145.

37. Robert Boyle, *Medicinal experiments, or, A collection of choice and safe remedies for the most part simple and easily prepared, useful in families, and very serviceable to country people* (London, 1693), 112.

38. Boyle, *Of the reconcileableness of specifick medicines*, 25–26.

39. I am paraphrasing Susan Scott Parrish: *American Curiosity: Cultures of Natural History in the Colonial Atlantic World* (Chapel Hill: University of North Carolina Press, 2006), 216. For more on science and indigenous knowledge in the Atlantic world, a good place to start is with the scholarship in James Delbourgo and Nicholas Dew (eds.), *Science and Empire in the Atlantic World* (New York: Routledge, 2008), especially the essays by Parrish and Ralph Bauer.

Bibliography

PRIMARY TEXTS

A Complete Collection of State-Trials and Proceedings. 6 vols. 2nd edition. Vol. 1. London, 1730.

A general collection of discourses of the virtuosi of France. London, 1664.

Agrippa of Nettesheim, Henry Cornelius. *Three Books of Occult Philosophy.* Ed. Donald Tyson. Trans. J. Freake. St. Paul, MN: Llewellyn Publications, 2004.

Alemán, Mateo. *The rogue: or The life of Guzman de Alfarache.* London, 1623.

Anon. *A Warning for Fair Women: A Critical Edition.* Ed. Charles Dale Cannon. The Hague: Mouton, 1975.

Anon. *The booke of pretty conceits.* London, 1612.

Anon. *The English Midwife Enlarged.* London, 1682.

Anon. *The problemes of Aristotle.* London, 1595.

Anon. *The Tragedy of Arden of Faversham.* Ed. Martin White. London: A&C Black, 1990.

Aristoteles Master-piece, or, The secrets of generation displayed. London, 1684.

Aristotle. *Generation of Animals.* Trans. A. L. Peck. Cambridge, MA: Harvard University Press, 1953.

Aristotle's compleat and experience'd midwife. London, 1700.

Augustine, St. *Of the citie of God.* Trans. I. H. London, 1610.

Bacon, Francis. *Sylva Sylvarum: or A naturall historie in ten centuries.* London, 1627.

    The Works of Francis Bacon. Ed. James Spedding, Robert Leslie Ellis, and Douglas Demon Heath. 14 vols. London: Longman, 1861–79.

Bacon, Roger. *The mirror of alchemy.* London, 1597.

Baker, Richard. *A chronicle of the Kings of England.* London, 1643.

Barlow, William. *Magneticall Advertisements . . . experiments concerning the nature and properties of the load-stone.* London, 1616.

    The navigators supply. London, 1597.

Baron, Robert. *Erotopaignion, or, The Cyprian academy.* London, 1647.

Barrough, Philip. *The methode of phisicke.* London, 1583.

Basset, Robert. *Curiosities: or the cabinet of nature Containing phylosophical, naturall, and morall questions fully answered and resolved.* Trans. R.B. London, 1637.

Bate, John. *The mysteries of nature and art.* London, 1634.

Batman, Stephen. *Batman vppon Bartholome his booke de proprietatibus rerum.* London, 1582.

Beard, Thomas, trans. *The Theatre of God's Judgments.* London, 1597.

Blundeville, Thomas. *M. Blundevile his exercises containing sixe treatises.* London, 1594.

Boaistuau, Pierre. *Certaine secrete wonders of nature.* Trans. E. Fenton. London, 1569.

Boccaccio, Giovanni. *The decameron containing an hundred pleasant nouels.* Trans. John Florio. 2 vols. London, 1620.

Boyle Family Receipt Book (c. 1675–c. 1710). MS 1340. Wellcome Library.

Boyle, Robert. *Medicinal experiments, or, A collection of choice and safe remedies for the most part simple and easily prepared, useful in families, and very serviceable to country people.* London, 1693.

Suspicions about some hidden qualities of the air. London, 1674.

Of the reconcileableness of specifick medicines to the corpuscular philosophy. London, 1685.

Bradwell, Stephen. *Helps for sudden accidents endangering life.* London, 1633.

Physick for the Sicknesse. London, 1636.

Browne, Sir Thomas. *Pseudodoxia epidemica, or, Enquiries into very many received tenents and commonly presumed truths.* London, 1646.

Bullein, William. *Bulleins bulwarke of defence against all sicknesse.* London, 1579.

Burton, Robert. *The anatomy of melancholy.* London, 1621.

Cardano, Girolamo. *Cardanus Comforte.* London, 1573.

Cavendish, Margaret, Duchess of Newcastle. *A Collection of letters and poems.* London, 1678.

Philosophical letters, or, Modest reflections upon some opinions in natural philosophy maintained by several famous and learned authors of this age. London, 1664.

Chamberlayne, Thomas. *The compleat midwife's practice enlarged.* London, 1659.

Chapman, George. *Petrarchs seven penitentiall psalms.* London, 1612.

The Gentleman Usher. London, 1606.

Charleton, Walter. *Physiologia Epicuro-Gassendo-Charltoniana, or, A fabrick of science natural, upon the hypothesis of atoms founded by Epicurus repaired [by] Petrus Gassendus.* London, 1654.

Chester, Robert. *The anuals of great Brittaine.* London, 1611.

Clarke, Samuel. *A mirrour or looking-glasse both for saints and sinners.* London, 1654.

Coeffeteau, Nicholas. *A table of humane passions.* London, 1621.

Collection of medical and cookery receipts (c. 1675–c. 1800). MS 7721. Wellcome Library Collection.

Collection of receipts, household, medical & veterinary (c. 1600). v.a.140. The Folger Shakespeare Library.

Complaint and lamentation of Mistresse Arden of [Fev]ersham. London, 1633.

Cooper, Anthony Ashley, Earl of Shaftesbury. "A Letter Concerning Enthusiasm to My Lord." In Lawrence E. Klein (ed.), *Characteristics of Men, Manners, Opinions, Times.* Cambridge: Cambridge University Press, 2000.

Crooke, Helkiah. *Mikrokosmographia.* London, 1615.

Culpeper, Nicholas. *Culpeper's directory for midwives.* London, 1662.

Deacon, John and John Walker. *Dialogicall discourses of spirits and divels.* London, 1601.

Digby, Sir Kenelm. *A late discourse made in a solemne assembly of nobles and learned men at Montpellier in France touching the cure of wounds by the powder of sympathy : with instructions how to make the said powder: whereby many other secrets of nature are unfolded.* London, 1658.

Donne, John. *Devotions upon Emergent Occasions and Death's Duel.* New York: Random House, 1999.

Drouet, Pierre. *A new counsell against the pestilence.* London, 1578.

Du Laurens, Andre. *A discourse of the preseruation of the sight.* London, 1599.

English Medical Notebook, 17th Century (1575–1663). MS 6812. Wellcome Library.

Erasmus, Desiderius. *A playne and godly exposition or declaration of the commune crede.* Trans. William Marshall. London, 1534.

The Colloquies of Erasmus. Trans. N. Bailey. Vol. 2. London: Reeves and Turner, 1878.

Desiderius Erasmus: Concerning the Aim and Method of Education. Ed. W. H. Woodward. Cambridge: Cambridge University Press, 1904.

Estienne, Charles. *Maison rustique, or The countrey farme.* London, 1616.

Fenner, William. *A treatise of the affections, or, The souls pulse whereby a Christian may know whether he be living or dying : together with a lively description of their nature, signs, and symptomes: as also directing men to the right use and ordering of them.* London, 1650.

Ficino, Marsilio. *Commentary on Plato's Symposium on Love.* Trans. Sears Jayne. Dallas, TX: Spring Publications, 1985.

Three Books on Life. Ed. Carol V. Kaske and John R. Clark. Binghamton, NY: Center for Medieval and Early Renaissance Studies, 1989.

Fletcher, John. *The faithfull shepheardesse.* London, 1610.

Fludd, Robert. *Doctor Fludds answer vnto M· Foster or, The squeesing of Parson Fosters sponge, ordained by him for the wiping away of the weapon-salue Vherein the sponge-bearers immodest carriage and behauiour towards his bretheren is detected.* London, 1631.

Mosaicall philosophy grounded upon the essentiall truth, or eternal sapience. London, 1659.

Fonteyn, Nicolaas. *The womans doctour.* London, 1652.

Foster, William. *Hoplocrisma-spongus: or, A sponge to vvipe avvay the weapon-salve A treatise, wherein is proved, that the cure late-taken up amongst us, by applying the salve to the weapon, is magicall and unlawfull.* London, 1631.

Fracastoro, Girolamo. *Hieronymi Fracastorii De Contagione and Contagiosis Morbis et Eorum Curatione, Libri III.* Trans. Wilmer Cave Wright. New York: G. P. Putnam's Sons, 1930.

Galen. *On the Natural Faculties.* Trans. Arthur John Brock. London: William Heinemann, 1916.

Gerard, John. *The herball or Generall historie of plantes.* London, 1633.

Gilbert, William. *On the Loadstone and Magnetic Bodies* in P. Fleury Mottelay, trans., *Great Books of the Western World.* Vol. 28. Chicago: Encyclopaedia Britannica, Inc., 1952. 1–121.

Glanvill, Joseph. *A blow at modern Sadducism in some philosophical considerations about witchcraft.* London, 1668.

 The vanity of dogmatizing. London, 1661.

Golding, Arthur. *A briefe discourse of the late murther of master George Saunders.* London, 1573.

Gordon, D. *Pharmaco-pinax, or A table and taxe of the pryces of all vsuall medicaments, simple and composed, contayned in D. Gordon's apothecarie and chymicall shop.* London, 1625.

Goulart, Simon. *Admirable and memorable histories containing the wonders of our time.* London, 1607.

Greenwood, Will. *[Apographe storges], or, A description of the passion of love.* London, 1657.

Hakewill, George. *The vanitie of the eye.* London, 1615.

Hart, James. *Klinike, or The diet of the diseased.* London, 1633.

Head, Richard. *The English Rogue, Part I.* London, 1668.

Henslowe's Diary. Ed. R. A. Foakes and R. T. Rickert. Cambridge: Cambridge University Press, 1961.

Herring, Francis. *A modest defence of the caveat given to the wearers of impoisoned amulets, as preservatives from the plague.* London, 1604.

Heywood, Thomas. *A Woman Killed With Kindness* in Kathleen E. McLuskie and David Bevington (eds.), *Plays on Women.* Manchester: Manchester University Press, 1999.

 An apologie for actors. London, 1612.

Hill, Thomas. *A briefe and pleasaunt treatise, entituled, Naturall and Artificiall conclusions.* London, 1581.

Hobbes, Thomas. *Leviathan.* Ed. J. C. A. Gaskin. Oxford: Oxford University Press, 1996.

 The Elements of Law: Natural and Political. Ed. Ferdinand Tonnies. Cambridge: Cambridge University Press, 1928.

Hocus Pocus Junior The anatomie of legerdemain. London, 1634.

Holinshed, Raphael. *The first and second volumes of Chronicles.* London, 1587.

 The Third volume of Chronicles, beginning at duke William the Norman, commonlie called the Conqueror. London, 1586.

Howell, James. *Familiar Letters: or Epistolae Ho-Elianae.* Vol. 1. London: J. M. Dent, 1903.

Hume, David. *A Treatise of Human Nature.* Oxford: Clarendon Press, 1896.

Jackson, Jane. "A very shorte and compendious Methode of Phisicke and Chirurgery (1642)." MS 373. Wellcome Library.

Jacob, Elizabeth and others. "Physicall and chyrurgicall receipts (1654–c. 1685)." MS 3009. Wellcome Library.

James I, King of England. *Daemonologie in forme of a dialogue, divided into three books.* London, 1597.

Johnson, Thomas. *Cornucopiae, or diuers secrets.* London, 1595.

Jonson, Ben. *The Magnetick Lady.* London, 1632.

Ben Jonson. Ed. C. H. Herford, Percy Simpson, and Evelyn Simpson. 11 vols. Oxford: Oxford University Press, 1925–52.

Jonstonus, Joannes. *An history of the wonderful things of nature.* London, 1657.

The idea of practical physic. London, 1657.

Jorden, Edward. *A briefe discourse of a disease called the suffocation of the mother.* London, 1603.

Joubert, Laurent. *Popular Errors.* Trans. Gregory David de Rocher. Tuscaloosa: University of Alabama Press, 1989.

Kellwaye, Simon. *A Defensative against the Plague.* London, 1593.

Kephale, Richard. *Medela pestilentiae.* London, 1665.

Kidder, Katherine and Edward, "Collection of cookery receipts, with a few medical receipts (1699)." MS 3107. Wellcome Library.

Knevet, Ralph. *Funerall Elegies.* London, 1637.

Lavater, Ludwig. *Of ghostes and spirites walking by nyght.* London, 1572.

Lemnius, Levinus. *The secret miracles of nature.* London, 1658.

The touchstone of complexions. Trans. Thomas Newton. London, 1576.

Lodge, Thomas. *A Treatise of the Plague.* London, 1603.

Lupton, Thomas. *A thousand notable things.* London, 1579.

Magnus, Pseudo-Albertus. *Women's Secrets: A Translation of Pseudo-Albertus Magnus's* De Secretis Mulierum *with Commentaries.* Ed. Helen Rodnite Lemay. Albany: State University of New York Press, 1992.

Malleus Maleficarum. Ed. and trans. Montague Summers. London: John Rodker, 1928.

Maplet, John. *A greene forest, or A naturall historie.* London, 1567.

Marston, John. *The scourge of villanie.* London, 1598.

Massaria, Alessandro. *De morbis foemineis, the woman's counsellour.* Trans. R. Turner. London, 1657.

Medina, Pedro de. *The arte of nauigation wherein is contained all the rules, declarations, secretes, & aduises, which for good nauigation are necessary.* London, 1581.

Middleton, Thomas and Thomas Dekker. *The Roaring Girl (1611).* Ed. Paul A. Mulholland. Manchester: Manchester University Press, 1999.

Middleton, Thomas and William Rowley. *The Changeling.* Ed. Michael Neill. London: A&C Black, 2006.

Middleton, Thomas and John Webster. *Any thing for a quiet life.* London, 1662.

Milton, John. *John Milton: Selected Prose.* Ed. C. A. Patrides. Columbia: University of Missouri Press, 1985.

Montaigne, Michel de. Trans. M. A. Screech. *The Complete Essays.* London: Penguin Books, 2003.

Nicols, Thomas. *Arcula gemmea: or, A cabinet of jewels.* London, 1653.

Norman, Robert. *The new attractive.* London, 1592.

Norwood, Richard. *The Journal of Richard Norwood.* Ed. Wesley Frank Craven and Walter B. Hayward. New York: Scholars' Facsimiles and Reprints, 1945.

Ouid's Metamorphosis Englished by G.S. London, 1628.

Packer, Katherine. "Book of medicines for several diseases wounds & sores (1639)." v.a.387. The Folger Shakespeare Library.

Painter, William. *The Palace of Pleasure.* London, 1566.

The second tome of the Palace of pleasure. London, 1567.

Paracelsus: Selected Writings. Ed. Jolande Jacobi. Princeton: Princeton University Press, 1951.

Paré, Ambroise. *A treatise of the plague.* London, 1630.

The workes of that famous chirurgion Ambrose Parey translated out of Latine and compared with the French. Trans. T. Johnson. London, 1634.

The workes of that famous chirurgion Ambrose Parey. Trans. T. Johnson. London, 1644.

Perkins, William. *A discourse of the damned art of witchcraft.* London, 1608.

Pico Della Mirandola, Giovanni. *On the Dignity of Man.* Trans. Charles Glenn Wallis. Indianapolis: Bobbs-Merrill, 1965.

Plat, Hugh. *The jewel house of art and nature.* London, 1653.

Plato. *The Dialogues of Plato,* vol. 3: *Ion, Hippias Minor, Laches, Protagoras.* Trans. R. E. Allen. New Haven: Yale University Press, 1996.

Ion in *Early Socratic Dialogues.* Ed. Trevor J. Saunders. London and New York: Penguin, 2005.

The Symposium of Plato. Trans. B. Jowett. Boston: Branden Publishing Co., 1983.

Pliny, the Elder. *The historie of the vvorld Commonly called, the naturall historie of C. Plinius Secundus.* Trans. Philemon Holland. 2 vols. London, 1601.

Plutarch. *The philosophie, commonlie called, the morals.* Trans. Philemon Holland. London, 1603.

Porta, John Baptista [Giambattista della Porta]. *Natural Magick (1658).* Ed. Derek J. Price. New York: Basic Books, 1957.

Receipt Book (c. 1675). v.a.365. The Folger Shakespeare Library.

Record, Robert. *The castle of knowledge.* London, 1556.

Reynolds, Edward. *A treatise of the passions and faculties of the soule of man.* London, 1640.

Ridley, Mark. *A short treatise of magneticall bodies and motions.* London, 1613.

Rivière, Lazare. *The practice of physic.* London, 1655.

Ross, Alexander. *Arcana microcosmi, or, The hid secrets of man's body.* London, 1652.

Rowley, William, Thomas Dekker, and John Ford. *The Witch of Edmonton* (1621). Ed. Peter Corbin and Douglas Sedge. Manchester: Manchester University Press.

Rüff, Jakob. *The expert midwife.* London, 1637.

Ruscelli, Girolamo. *The seconde part of the Secretes of Master Alexis of Piemont.* London, 1560.

Sadler, John. *The sicke womans private looking-glasse.* London, 1636.

Scot, Reginald. *The discoverie of witchcraft.* London, 1584.

Sennert, Daniel. *The sixth book of Practical physick: Of occult or hidden diseases.* London, 1662.

The weapon-salve's maladie. London, 1637.

Shakespeare, William. *The Norton Shakespeare.* Ed. Stephen Greenblatt. New York: W. W. Norton, 1997.

Sharp, Jane. *The midwives book, or, The whole art of midwifry discovered.* London, 1671.

Sidney, Sir Philip. *An Apology for Poetry (or The Defence of Poesy)*. Ed. R. W. Maslen. Third edn. Manchester: Manchester University Press, 2002.

Simpson, William. *Zenexton ante-pestilentiale. Or, A short discourse of the plague its antidotes and cure*. London, 1665.

Sinibaldi, Giovanni Benedetto. *Rare verities: The cabinet of Venus unlocked, and her secrets laid open*. London, 1658.

Sleigh, Elizabeth and Felicia Whitfeld. "Collection of medical receipts, 1647–1722." MS 751. Wellcome Library.

Stanhope, 1st Earl of Chesterfield. "A booke of severall receipts (c. 1635)." MS 761. Wellcome Library.

"Stowe's Historical and Other Collections, Volume VI[293]. British Library Harl MS 542. Plut XLVIII B" in Patricia Hyde (ed.), *Thomas Arden in Faversham: the Man behind the Myth*. Faversham, Kent: Faversham Society, 1996.

Thayre, Thomas. *A treatise of the pestilence*. London, 1603.

The Book of Secrets of Albertus Magnus of the Virtues of Herbs, Stones and Certain Beasts. Ed. Michael R. Best and Frank H. Brightman. Oxford: Clarendon Press, 1973.

Vaughan, Thomas. *Magia adamica or the antiquitie of magic*. London, 1650.

Webster, John. *The displaying of supposed witchcraft*. London, 1677.

Webster, John. *The Duchess of Malfi*. Ed. Elizabeth M. Brennan. London: Ernest Benn, 1964.

Wecker, Johann Jacob. *Eighteen books of the secrets of art and nature being the summe and substance of naturall philosophy*. London, 1660.

Weyer, Johann. *Witches, Devils, and Doctors in the Renaissance: Johann Weyer, De praestigiis daemonum*. Trans. John Shea. Binghamton, NY: Medieval and Renaissance Texts and Studies, 1991.

Willis, Thomas. *An Essay of the Pathology of the Brain and Nervous Stock*. London, 1684.

SECONDARY TEXTS

Ablow, Rachel. *The Marriage of Minds: Reading Sympathy in the Victorian Marriage Plot*. Stanford: Stanford University Press, 2007.

Abraham, Lyndy. *Marvell and Alchemy*. Aldershot: Scolar Press, 1990.

Accati, Luisa. "The Spirit of Fornication: Virtue of the Soul and Virtue of the Body in Friuli, 1600–1800." In Edward Muir and Guido Ruggiero (eds.), *Sex and Gender in Historical Perspective*. Trans. Margaret A. Galluci. Baltimore: Johns Hopkins University Press, 1990. 110–40.

Adams, Henry Hitch. *English Domestic or Homiletic Tragedy, 1575 to 1642*. New York: B. Blom, 1943.

Adelman, Janet. "Making Defect Perfection: Shakespeare and the One-Sex Model." In Viviana Comensoli and Anne Russell (eds.), *Enacting Gender on the English Renaissance Stage*. Urbana: University of Illinois Press, 1999. 23–52.

Suffocating Mothers: Fantasies of Maternal Origin in Shakespeare's Plays, Hamlet to The Tempest. New York: Routledge, 1992.

Aki, Jami. "Glimpsing a 'Lesbian' Poetics in *Twelfth Night*." *Studies in English Literature 1500–1900* 43 (2003): 375–94.

Altman, Joel B. "'Vile Participation': The Amplification of Violence in the Theatre of *Henry V*." *Shakespeare Quarterly* 42 (1991): 1–32.

Amster, Mara. "Frances Howard and Middleton and Rowley's *The Changeling*: Trials, Tests, and the Legibility of the Virgin Body." In Laurel Amtower and Dorothea Kehler (eds.), *The Single Woman in Medieval and Early Modern England: Her Life and Representation*. Tempe: Arizona Center for Medieval and Renaissance Studies, 2003. 211–32.

Andrews, Michael C. "'Sweetness' in *The Changeling*." *Yearbook of English Studies* 1 (1971): 63–67.

Archibald, Elizabeth. *Apollonius of Tyre: Medieval and Renaissance Themes and Variations*. Cambridge: D. S. Brewer, 1991.

Armstrong, Katherine. "Possets, Pills and Poisons: Physicking the Female Body in Early Seventeenth-Century Drama." *Cahiers Elisabéthains* 61 (2002): 43–56.

Arrizabalaga, Jon, John Henderson, and Roger French (eds.), *The Great Pox: The French Disease in Renaissance Europe*. New Haven and London: Yale University Press, 1997.

Asp, Carolyn. "Subjectivity, Desire, and Female Friendship in *All's Well That Ends Well*." *Literature and Psychology* 32 (1986): 48–63.

Bailey, Michael D. *Magic and Superstition in Europe: A Concise History from Antiquity to the Present*. Lanham, MD: Rowman and Littlefield, 2007.

Barker, Roberta and David Nicol. "Does Beatrice Joanna Have a Subtext? *The Changeling* on the London Stage." *Early Modern Literary Studies* 10 (2004): 31–43. http://purl.oclc.org/emls/10-1/barknico.htm.

Barlow, Frank. *Edward the Confessor*. Berkeley: University of California Press, 1970.

Barnes, Elizabeth. *States of Sympathy: Seduction and Democracy in the American Novel*. New York: Columbia University Press, 1997.

Bassnett, Madeline. "'A Frightful Pleasure, That is All': Wonder, Monstrosity, and *The Changeling*." *The Dalhousie Review* 84 (2004): 387–406.

Bate, Jonathan. *Shakespeare and Ovid*. Oxford: Oxford University Press, 1993.

Bates, A. W. *Emblematic Monsters: Unnatural Conceptions and Deformed Births in Early Modern Europe*. Amsterdam and New York: Rodopi, 2005.

Beecher, Donald. "Windows on Contagion." In Claire L. Carlin (ed.), *Imagining Contagion in Early Modern Europe*. Basingstoke: Palgrave Macmillan, 2005. 32–46.

Bellany, Alastair. *The Politics of Court Scandal in Early Modern England: News Culture and the Overbury Affair, 1603–1660*. Cambridge: Cambridge University Press, 2002.

Belsey, Catherine. "Alice Arden's Crime." *Renaissance Drama* 13 (1982): 83–102.
  "Disrupting Sexual Difference: Meaning and Gender in the Comedies." In John Drakakis (ed.), *Alternative Shakespeares*. 2nd edn. London: Routledge, 2002. 191–92.
  The Subject of Tragedy: Identity and Difference in Renaissance Drama. London: Methuen, 1985.

Berek, Peter. "'Follow the Money': Sex, Murder, Print, and Domestic Tragedy." *Medieval and Renaissance Drama in England* 21 (2008): 170–88.

Bergeron, David M. "'The credit of your father': Absent Fathers in *All's Well, That Ends Well.*" In Gary Waller (ed.), *All's Well, That End's Well: New Critical Essays.* New York: Routledge, 2007. 169–82.

"The Structure of Healing in 'All's Well That Ends Well.'" *South Atlantic Bulletin* 37 (1972): 25–34.

Bicks, Caroline. "Planned Parenthood: Minding the Quick Woman in *All's Well.*" *Modern Philology* 103 (2006): 299–331.

Bliss, Lee. *The World's Perspective: John Webster and the Jacobean Drama.* New Brunswick, NJ: Rutgers University Press, 1983.

Boehrer, Bruce. "Alsemero's Closet: Privacy and Interiority in *The Changeling.*" *Journal of English and Germanic Philology* 96 (1997): 349–68.

Bono, James J. *The Word of God and the Languages of Man: Interpreting Nature in Early Modern Science and Medicine.* Madison: University of Wisconsin Press, 1995.

Booth, Roy. "John Webster's Heart of Glass." *English* 40 (1991): 97–113.

Boudreau, Kristin. *Sympathy in American Literature: American Sentiments from Jefferson to the Jameses.* Gainesville: University Press of Florida, 2002.

Bovilsky, Lara. *Barbarous Play: Race on the English Renaissance Stage.* Minneapolis: University of Minnesota Press, 2008.

Bowerbank, Sylvia Lorraine. *Speaking for Nature: Women and Ecologies of Early Modern England.* Baltimore: Johns Hopkins University Press, 2004.

Brennan, Elizabeth (ed.). *The Duchess of Malfi.* London: Ernest Benn, 1964.

Briggs, Katherine Mary. *The Fairies in Tradition and Literature.* New York: Routledge, 2002.

Brittain, Robert P. "Cruentation: In Legal Medicine and in Literature." *Medical History* 9 (1965): 82–88.

Broad, Jacqueline. "Margaret Cavendish and Joseph Glanvill: Science, Religion, and Witchcraft." *Studies in History and Philosophy of Science* 38 (2007): 493–505.

Brockbank, William. "Sovereign Remedies: A Critical Depreciation of the 17th Century London *Pharmacopoeia.*" *Medical History* 8 (1964): 1–14.

Bromham, A. A., and Zara Bruzzi. *The Changeling and the Years of Crisis, 1619–1624: A Hieroglyph of Britain.* Cambridge: Cambridge University Press, 1990.

Bucola, Regina. *Fairies, Fractious Women, and the Old Faith: Fairy Lore in Early Modern British Drama and Culture.* Selinsgrove, PA: Susquehanna University Press, 2006.

Bueler, Lois E. "The Rhetoric of Change in *The Changeling.*" *English Literary Renaissance* 14 (1984): 95–113.

Burks, Deborah G. "'I'll want my will else': *The Changeling* and Women's Complicity with Their Rapists." *ELH* 62 (1995): 759–90.

Butterworth, Philip. *Magic on the Early English Stage.* Cambridge: Cambridge University Press, 2005.

Cadden, Joan. *Meanings of Sex Difference in the Middle Ages: Medicine, Science, Culture.* Cambridge: Cambridge University Press, 1993.

Calbi, Maurizio. *Approximate Bodies: Aspects of the Figuration of Maculinity, Power and the Uncanny in Early Modern Drama and Anatomy.* Salerno: Oedipus, 2001.

Caldwell, Ellen. "Invasive Procedures in Webster's *The Duchess of Malfi.*" In Linda Woodbridge and Sharon Beehler (eds.), *Women, Violence, and English Renaissance Literature: Essays Honoring Paul Jorgensen.* Tempe: Arizona Center for Medieval and Renaissance Studies, 2003. 149–186.

Caldwell, Janis McLarren. *Literature and Medicine in Nineteeth-Century Britain: From Mary Shelley to George Eliot.* Cambridge: Cambridge University Press, 2004.

Callaghan, Dympna C. *Shakespeare without Women: Representing Gender and Race on the Renaissance Stage.* London: Routledge, 2000.

"The State of the Art: Critical Approaches 2000–08." In Christina Luckyj (ed.), *The Duchess of Malfi: A Critical Guide.* London: Continuum International Publishing, 2011. 66–86.

"*The Duchess of Malfi* and Early Modern Widows." In Garrett A. Sullivan, Jr., Patrick Cheney, and Andrew Hadfield (eds.), *Early Modern English Drama: A Critical Companion.* New York: Oxford University Press, 2006. 272–86.

Women and Gender in Renaissance Tragedy: A Study of King Lear, Othello, The Duchess of Malfi, *and* The White Devil. Atlantic Highlands, NJ: Humanities Press, 1989.

Campagne, Fabián Alejandro. "Witchcraft and the Sense-of-the-Impossible in Early Modern Spain: Some Reflections Based on the Literature of Superstition (ca. 1500–1800)." *Harvard Theological Review* 96 (2003): 25–62.

Cassell, Anthony. "Pilgrim Wombs, Physicke and Bed-Tricks: Intellectual Brilliance, Attenuation and Elision in *Decameron III:9.*" *MLN* 121 (2006): 53–101.

Castle, Jo. "Amulets and Protection: Pomanders." *Bulletin of the Society for Renaissance Studies* 17 (2000): 12–18.

Cerasano, S. P. "Philip Henslowe, Simon Forman, and the Theatrical Community of the 1590s." *Shakespeare Quarterly* 44 (1993): 145–58.

Chalk, Darryl. "Contagious Emulation: Antitheatricality and Theatre as Plague in *Troilus and Cressida.*" In Brett D. Hirsch and Christopher Wortham (eds.), *"This Earthly Stage": World and Stage in Late Medieval and Early Modern England.* Turnhout: Brepols, 2010. 75–101.

"'To creep in at mine eyes': Theatre and Secret Contagion in *Twelfth Night.*" In Darryl Chalk and Laurie Johnson (eds.), *"Rapt in Secret Studies": Emerging Shakespeares.* Newcastle upon Tyne: Cambridge Scholars Publishing, 2010. 171–93.

Chase, Melissa P. "Fevers, Poisons, and Apostemes: Authority and Experience in Montpellier Plague Treatises." *Annals of the New York Academy of Sciences* 441 (1985): 162–63.

Churchill, W. D. "The Medical Practice of the Sexed Body: Women, Men, and Disease in Britain, circa 1600–1740." *Social History of Medicine* 18 (2005): 3–22.

Clark, Stuart. "Demons and Disease: The Disenchantment of the Sick (1500–1700)." In Marijke Gijswijt-Hofstra, Hilary Marland, and Hans De Waardt (eds.), *Illness and Healing Alternatives in Western Europe.* London: Routledge, 1997. 38–58.

Thinking with Demons: The Idea of Witchcraft in Early Modern Europe. Oxford: Oxford University Press, 1999.

Vanities of the Eye: Vision in Early Modern European Culture. Oxford: Oxford University Press, 2007.

"Witchcraft and Magic in Early Modern Culture." In Bengt Ankarloo and Stuart Clark (eds.), *Witchcraft and Magic in Europe: The Period of the Witch Trials.* Philadelphia: University of Pennsylvania Press, 2002. 97–169.

Coffin, Charles M. *John Donne and the New Philosophy.* New York: Columbia University Press, 1937.

Copenhaver, Brian P. "Astrology and Magic." In Charles B. Schmitt and Quentin Skinner (eds.), *The Cambridge History of Renaissance Philosophy.* Cambridge: Cambridge University Press, 1988. 264–300.

Cosman, Bard C. *"All's Well That Ends Well:* Shakespeare's Treatment of Anal Fistula." *The Upstart Crow* 19 (1999): 78–97.

Couliano, Ioan P. *Eros and Magic in the Renaissance.* Trans. Margaret Cook. Chicago: University of Chicago Press, 1987.

Coulter, Harris L. *Divided Legacy: The Patterns Emerge, Hippocrates to Paracelsus.* Vol. 1. Washington, DC: Wehawken Book Co., 1975.

Crain, Caleb. *American Sympathy: Men, Friendship, and Literature in the New Nation.* New Haven: Yale University Press, 2001.

Crane, Mary Thomas. *Shakespeare's Brain: Reading with Cognitive Theory.* Princeton: Princeton University Press, 2001.

Crawford, Julie. *Marvelous Protestantism: Monstrous Births in Post-Reformation England.* Baltimore: Johns Hopkins University Press, 2005.

Crawford, Patricia. "Attitudes to Menstruation in Seventeenth-Century England." *Past and Present* 91 (1981): 59–61.

Crosland, Maurice. "Early Laboratories, c. 1600–c. 1800 and the Location of Experimental Science." *Annals of Science* 62 (2005): 233–53.

Cumston, Charles Greene. "A Note on the History of Forensic Medicine of the Middle Ages." *Journal of the American Institute of Criminal Law and Criminology* 3 (1913): 855–65.

Daffron, Benjamin Eric. *Romantic Doubles: Sex and Sympathy in British Gothic Literature, 1790–1830.* New York: AMS Press, 2002.

Daston, Lorraine. "Preternatural Philosophy." In Lorraine Daston (ed.), *Biographies of Scientific Objects.* Chicago: University of Chicago Press, 2000. 15–41.

Daston, Lorraine and Katharine Park. *Wonders and the Order of Nature, 1150–1750.* New York: Zone Books, 1998.

Davies, Owen. *Cunning-Folk: Popular Magic in English History.* London: Hambledon and London, 2003.

Dawson, Anthony B. and Paul Yachnin (eds.). *The Culture of Playgoing in Shakespeare's England: A Collaborative Debate.* Cambridge: Cambridge University Press, 2001.

Dawson, Lesel. "Menstruation, Misogyny and the Cure for Love." *Women's Studies* 34 (2005): 461–84.

Lovesickness and Gender in Early Modern English Literature. Oxford: Oxford University Press, 2008.

de Blécourt, Willem. "The Making of the Female Witch: Reflections on Witchcraft and Gender in the Early Modern Period." *Gender and History* 12 (2000): 287–309.

"Witch Doctors, Soothsayers and Priests. On Cunning Folk in European Historiography and Tradition." *Social History* 19 (1994): 285–303.

Dean, Paul. "'Comfortable Doctrine': *Twelfth Night* and the Trinity." *Review of English Studies* 52 (2001): 500–15.

Dear, Peter. "A Philosophical Duchess: Understanding Margaret Cavendish and the Royal Society." In Juliet Cummins and David Burchell (eds.), *Science, Literature, and Rhetoric in Early Modern England.* Aldershot: Ashgate, 2007. 125–42.

Discipline and Experience: The Mathematical Way in the Scientific Revolution. Chicago: University of Chicago Press, 1995.

Debus, Allen G. *The Chemical Philosophy: Paracelsian Science and Medicine in the Sixteenth and Seventeenth Centuries.* 2 vols. New York: Science History Publications, 1977.

The English Paracelsians. Chicago: University of Chicago Press, 1968.

Delbourgo, James and Nicholas Dew (eds.). *Science and Empire in the Atlantic World.* New York: Routledge, 2008.

Desens, Marliss C. *The Bed-Trick in English Renaissance Drama: Explorations in Gender, Sexuality, and Power.* Newark: University of Delaware Press, 1994.

Desmet, Christy. "'Neither Maid, Widow, nor Wife': Rhetoric of the Woman Controversy in *Measure for Measure* and *The Duchess of Malfi*." In Dorothea Kehler and Susan Baker (eds.), *Another Country: Feminist Perspectives on Renaissance Drama.* Metuchen, NJ: Scarecrow, 1991. 71–92.

DeVun, Leah. "The Jesus Hermaphrodite: Science and Sex Difference in Premodern Europe." *Journal of the History of Ideas* 69 (2008): 193–209.

DiGangi, Mario. *The Homoerotics of Early Modern Drama.* Cambridge: Cambridge University Press, 1997.

Dixon, Laurinda S. *Perilous Chastity: Women and Illness in Pre-Enlightenment Art and Medicine.* Ithaca, NY: Cornell University Press, 1995.

Dobbs, Betty Jo Teeter. "From the Secrecy of Alchemy to the Openness of Chemistry." In Tore Frängsmyr (ed.), *Solomon's House Revisited: The Organization and Institutionalization of Science.* Canton, MA: Science History Publications, 1990. 75–94.

Dolan, Frances E. "'Can this be certain?': The Duchess of Malfi's Secrets." In Christina Luckyj (ed.), *The Duchess of Malfi: A Critical Guide.* London: Continuum International Publishing, 2011. 119–35.

Dangerous Familiars: Representations of Domestic Crime in England 1550–1700. Ithaca, NY: Cornell University Press, 1994.

"Gender, Moral Agency, and Dramatic Form in *A Warning for Fair Women*." *SEL: Studies in English Literature, 1500–1900* 29 (1989): 201–18.

"Re-reading Rape in *The Changeling*." *Journal for Early Modern Cultural Studies* 11 (2011): 4–29.

Dundes, Alan (ed.). *The Evil Eye: A Folklore Casebook*. New York and London: Garland, 1981.

Eamon, William L. "Science and Popular Culture in Sixteenth Century Italy: The 'Professors of Secrets' and Their Books." *Sixteenth Century Journal* 16 (1985): 471–85.

Science and the Secrets of Nature: Books of Secrets in Medieval and Early Modern Culture. Princeton: Princeton University Press, 1994.

Easlea, Brian. *Witch-hunting, Magic, and the New Philosophy: An Introduction to the Debates of the Scientific Revolution 1450–1750*. Brighton: The Harvester Press, 1980.

Eberly, Susan Schoon. "Fairies and the Folklore of Disability: Changelings, Hybrids and the Solitary Fairy." *Folklore* 99 (1988): 58–77.

Eccles, Audrey. *Obstetrics and Gynaecology in Tudor and Stuart England*. Kent, OH: Kent State University Press, 1982.

Egginton, William. *How the World Became a Stage: Presence, Theatricality, and the Question of Modernity*. Albany: State University of New York Press, 2003.

Ehrenreich, Barbara, and Deirdre English. *Witches, Midwives, and Nurses: A History of Women Healers*. Old Westbury, NY: The Feminist Press, 1973.

Elam, Keir. "'In What Chapter of His Bosom?': Reading Shakespeare's Bodies." Terence Hawkes (ed.), *Alternative Shakespeares 2*. London: Routledge, 1996. 140–63.

"The Fertile Eunuch: *Twelfth Night*, Early Modern Intercourse, and the Fruits of Castration." *Shakespeare Quarterly* 47 (1996): 1–36.

Ellison, Julie. *Cato's Tears and the Making of Anglo-American Emotion*. Chicago: University of Chicago Press, 1999.

Enterline, Lynn. "'Hairy on the In-Side': *The Duchess of Malfi* and the Body of Lycanthropy." *Yale Journal of Criticism* 7 (1994): 85–129.

Evenden [Nagy], Doreen A. "Gender Differences in the Licensing and Practice of Female and Male Surgeons in Early Modern England." *Medical History* 42 (1998): 194–216.

Ferguson, John. *Bibliographical Notes on Histories of Inventions and Books of Secrets*. 2 vols. London: The Holland Press, 1959.

Festa, Lynn. *Sentimental Figures of Empire in Eighteenth-Century Britain and France*. Baltimore: Johns Hopkins University Press, 2006.

Field, Catherine. "'Many Hands': Writing the Self in Early Modern Women's Recipe Books." In Michelle M. Dowd and Julie A. Eckerle (eds.), *Genre and Women's Life Writing in Early Modern England*. Aldershot: Ashgate, 2007. 49–64.

"'Sweet Practicer, thy Physic I will try': Helena and Her 'Good Receipt' in *All's Well, That Ends Well*." In Gary Waller (ed.), *All's Well, That Ends Well: New Critical Essays*. New York: Routledge, 2007. 194–208.

"'Many Hands': Early Modern Women's Receipt Books and the Politics of Writing Food for the Nation." Unpublished Ph.D. thesis. University of Maryland, 2006.

Findlen, Paula. "Jokes of Nature and Jokes of Knowledge: The Playfulness of Scientific Discourse in Early Modern Europe." *Renaissance Quarterly* 43 (1990): 292–331.

Fissell, Mary E. "Introduction: Women, Health, and Healing in Early Modern Europe." *Bulletin of the History of Medicine* 82 (2008): 1–17.

Patients, Power, and the Poor in Eighteenth-Century Bristol. Cambridge: Cambridge University Press, 1991.

Vernacular Bodies: The Politics of Reproduction in Early Modern England. Oxford: Oxford University Press, 2004.

Fleming, James Dougal. "The Undiscoverable Country: Occult Qualities, Scholasticism, and the End of Nescience." In James Dougal Fleming (ed.), *The Invention of Discovery, 1500–1700.* Aldershot: Ashgate, 2011. 61–78.

Fletcher, Angus [John Stewart]. *Time, Space, and Motion in the Age of Shakespeare.* Cambridge, MA: Harvard University Press, 2007.

Fletcher, Angus. "Living Magnets, Paracelsian Corpses, and the Psychology of Grace in Donne's Religious Verse." *ELH* 72 (2005): 1–21.

Fletcher, Anthony. *Gender, Sex, and Subordination in England, 1500–1800.* New Haven: Yale University Press, 1995.

Floyd-Wilson, Mary. "English Epicures and Scottish Witches." *Shakespeare Quarterly* 57 (2006): 131–61.

English Ethnicity and Race in Early Modern Drama. Cambridge: Cambridge University Press, 2003.

"The Preternatural Ecology of 'A Lover's Complaint.'" *Shakespeare Studies* 39 (2011): 43–53.

Floyd-Wilson, Mary and Garrett A. Sullivan, Jr. (eds.). *Embodiment and Environment in Early Modern Drama and Performance.* Special issue of *Renaissance Drama,* n.s. 35 (2006).

Environment and Embodiment in Early Modern England. Basingstoke: Palgrave Macmillan, 2007.

Foucault, Michel. *The Order of Things: An Archaeology of the Human Sciences.* New York: Vintage Books, 1973.

Franssen, Paul J. C. M. "Amorous Palms." In Jan Frans van Dijkhuizen, Paul Hoftijzer, Juliette Roding, and Paul Smith (eds.), *Living in Posterity: Essays in Honour of Bart Westerweel.* Hilversum: Uitgeverij Verloren, 2004. 107–16.

Freedman, Barbara. *Staging the Gaze: Postmodernism, Psychoanalysis, and Shakespearean Comedy.* Ithaca, NY: Cornell University Press, 1991.

Garber, Marjorie. *Symptoms of Culture.* New York: Routledge, 1998.

Gaskill, Malcolm. *Crimes and Mentalities in Early Modern England.* Cambridge: Cambridge University Press, 2000.

Gay, Penny. "Introduction." *Twelfth Night.* Cambridge: Cambridge University Press, 2003.

Geertz, Hildred. "An Anthropology of Religion and Magic, 1." *Journal of Interdisciplinary History* 6 (1975): 71–89.

Gentilcore, David. *Healers and Healing in Early Modern Italy.* Manchester: Manchester University Press, 1998.

Gieryn, T. F. "Boundary-Work and the Demarcation of Science from Non-Science: Strains and Interests in Professional Ideologies of Scientists." *American Sociological Review* 48 (1983): 781–95.

Godfrey, Eleanor S. *The Development of English Glassmaking 1560–1640.* Chapel Hill: University of North Carolina Press, 1975.

Goodman, Kevis. "'Wasted Labor'? Milton's Eve, the Poet's Work, and the Challenge of Sympathy." *ELH* 64 (1997): 415–46.

Goodrick-Clarke, Nicholas. "The Philosophy, Medicine, and Theology of Paracelsus." In Keith Whitlock (ed.), *Renaissance in Europe: A Reader*. New Haven: Yale University Press, 2000. 314–21.

Gottlieb, Evan. *Feeling British: Sympathy and National Identity in Scottish and English Writing, 1707–1832*. Lewisberg, PA: Bucknell University Press, 2007.

Gras, Henk. *Studies in Elizabethan Audience Response to Theatre Part I: How Easy is a Bush Suppos'd a Bear? Actor and Character in the Elizabethan Viewer's Mind*. Frankfurt am Main: Peter Lang, 1993.

Green, Monica H. "From 'Diseases of Women' to 'Secrets of Women': The Transformation of Gynecological Literature in the Later Middle Ages." *Journal of Medieval and Early Modern Studies* 30 (2000): 5–39.

Making Women's Medicine Masculine: The Rise of Male Authority in Pre-Modern Gynaecology. Oxford: Oxford University Press, 2008.

Greenblatt, Stephen. "Shakespeare and the Exorcists." In Patricia Parker and Geoffrey Hartman (eds.), *Shakespeare and the Question of Theory*. New York: Methuen, 1985. 163–87.

Shakespearean Negotiations: The Circulation of Social Energy in Renaissance England. Berkeley: University of California Press, 1988.

Greven, David. *Men beyond Desire: Manhood, Sex, and Violation in American Literature*. New York: Palgrave Macmillan, 2005.

Grierson, Herbert J. C. (ed.). *The Poems of John Donne*. Vol. 1. Oxford: Clarendon Press, 1912.

Guenther, Genevieve. *Magical Imaginations: Instrumental Aesthetics in the English Renaissance*. Toronto: University of Toronto Press, 2012.

Gunby, D. C. "*The Duchess of Malfi*: A Theological Approach." In Brian Morris (ed.), *John Webster*. London: Ernest Benn, 1970. 181–204.

Haber, Judith. *Desire and Dramatic Form in Early Modern England*. Cambridge: Cambridge University Press, 2009.

"'I(t) Could Not Choose but Follow': Erotic Logic in *The Changeling*." *Representations* 81 (2003): 79–98.

"'My Body Bestow upon My Women': The Space of the Feminine in *The Duchess of Malfi*." *Renaissance Drama* 28 (1999): 133–59.

HaCohen, Ruth. "The Music of Sympathy in the Arts of the Baroque; or, the Use of Difference to Overcome Indifference." *Poetics Today* 22 (2001): 619–21.

Hadot, Pierre. *The Veil of Isis: An Essay on the History of the Idea of Nature*. Trans. Michael Chase. Cambridge, MA: The Belknap Press of Harvard University Press, 2006.

Haffenden, John (ed.). *William Empson: Essays on Renaissance Literature*, vol. 1, *John Donne and the New Philosophy*. Cambridge: Cambridge University Press, 1993.

Halio, Jay. "All's Well That Ends Well." *Shakespeare Quarterly* 15 (1964): 33–43.

Harkness, Deborah E. "A View from the Streets: Women and Medical Work in Elizabethan London." *Bulletin of the History of Medicine* 82 (2008): 52–85.

The Jewel House: Elizabethan London and the Scientific Revolution. New Haven: Yale University Press, 2007.

Harley, David. "Historians as Demonologists: The Myth of the Midwife-Witch." *Social History of Medicine* 3 (1990): 1–26.

Harris, Brian. *Passion, Poison and Power: The Mysterious Death of Sir Thomas Overbury, A Jacobean Mystery in Fourteen Acts.* London: Wildy, Simmonds & Hill, 2010.

Harris, Jonathan Gil. "All Swell That End Swell: Dropsy, Phantom Pregnancy, and the Sound of Deconception in *All's Well That Ends Well.*" *Renaissance Drama* (2006): 169–89.

Foreign Bodies and the Body Politic: Discourses of Pathology in Early Modern England. Cambridge: Cambridge University Press, 1998.

Haslem, Lori Schroeder. "'Troubled with the Mother': Longings, Purgings, and the Maternal Body in *Bartholomew Fair* and *The Duchess of Malfi.*" *Modern Philology* 92 (1995): 438–59.

Healy, Margaret. "Anxious and Fatal Contacts: Taming the Contagious Touch." In Elizabeth D. Harvey (ed.), *Sensible Flesh: On Touch in Early Modern Culture.* Philadelphia: University of Pennsylvania Press, 2003. 22–38.

"Bodily Regimen and Fear of the Beast: 'Plausibility' in Renaissance Domestic Tragedy." In Erica Fudge, Ruth Gilbert, and Susan Wiseman (eds.), *At the Borders of the Human: Beasts, Bodies and Natural Philosophy in the Early Modern Period.* Basingstoke: Palgrave Macmillan, 1999. 74–90.

Shakespeare, Alchemy and the Creative Imagination: The Sonnets and A Lover's Complaint. Cambridge: Cambridge University Press, 2011.

Heckscher, William S. "Shakespeare in his Relationship to the Visual Arts: A Study in Paradox." *Research Opportunities in Renaissance Drama* 13–14 (1970–1): 35–56.

Heinemann, Margot. *Puritanism and Theatre: Thomas Middleton and Opposition Drama under the Early Stuarts.* Cambridge: Cambridge University Press, 1980.

Helgerson, Richard. *Adulterous Alliances: Home, State, and History in Early Modern European Drama and Painting.* Chicago: University of Chicago Press, 2000.

Henry, John. "Boyle and Cosmical Qualities." In Michael Hunter (ed.), *Robert Boyle Reconsidered.* Cambridge: Cambridge University Press, 1994. 119–38.

"Doctors and Healers: Popular Culture and the Medical Profession." In Stephen Pumfrey, Paolo L. Rossi, and Maurice Slawinski (eds.), *Science Culture and Popular Belief in Renaissance Europe.* Manchester: Manchester University Press, 1991. 191–221.

Knowledge Is Power: How Magic, the Government and an Apocalyptic Vision Inspired Francis Bacon to Create Modern Science. Cambridge: Icon Books, 2002.

"Occult Qualities and the Experimental Philosophy: Active Principles in Pre-Newtonian Matter Theory." *History of Science* 24 (1986): 335–81.

"The Fragmentation of Renaissance Occultism and the Decline of Magic." *History of Science* 46 (2008): 1–48.

The Scientific Revolution and the Origins of Modern Science. 3rd. edn. Basingstoke: Palgrave Macmillan, 2008.

Henry, John and J. M. Forrester (eds.). *Jean Fernel's "On the Hidden Causes of Things": Forms, Souls, and Occult Diseases in Renaissance Medicine.* Leiden: Brill, 2005.

Hill, Eugene D. "Parody and History in 'Arden of Feversham' (1592)." *Huntington Library Quarterly* 56 (1993): 350–82.

Hinton, Laura. *The Perverse Gaze of Sympathy: Sadomasochistic Sentiments from Clarissa to Rescue 911.* Albany: State University of New York Press, 1999.

Hirsch, Brett D. "An Italian Werewolf in London: Lycanthropy and *The Duchess of Malfi.*" *Early Modern Literary Studies* 11 (2005), 43 paragraphs, http://purl. oclc.org/emls/11-2/hirswere.htm.

"Werewolves and Severed Hands: Webster's *The Duchess of Malfi* and Heywood and Brome's *The Witches of Lancashire.*" *Notes and Queries* 53 (2006): 92–94.

Hoeniger, F. David. *Medicine and Shakespeare in the English Renaissance.* Newark: University of Delaware Press, 1992.

Holmes, Clive. "Women, Witnesses and Witches." *Past and Present* 140 (1993): 45–78.

Hopkins, Lisa. *The Female Hero in English Renaissance Tragedy.* New York: Palgrave Macmillan, 2002.

Hunt, Maurice. "Viola/Cesario, Caesarian Birth, and Shakespeare's *Twelfth Night.*" *The Upstart Crow* 21 (2001): 7–14.

Hunter, G. K. *All's Well That Ends Well.* London: Methuen, 1959.

Hunter, Lynette. "Women and Domestic Medicine: Lady Experimenters, 1570–1620." In Lynette Hunter and Sarah Hutton (eds.), *Women, Science and Medicine, 1500–1700: Mothers and Sisters of the Royal Society.* Stroud: Sutton, 1997. 89–107.

Hunter, Michael. *Boyle: Between God and Science.* New Haven: Yale University Press, 2009.

Robert Boyle (1627–91): Scrupulosity and Science. Woodbridge: The Boydell Press, 2000.

Hutchison, Keith. "Supernaturalism and the Mechanical Philosophy." *History of Science* 21 (1983): 297–333.

"What Happened to Occult Qualities in the Scientific Revolution?" *Isis* 73 (1982): 233–53.

Hutner, Gordon. *Secrets and Sympathy: Forms of Disclosure in Hawthorne's Novels.* Athens: University of Georgia Press, 1988.

Hutson, Lorna. "On Not Being Deceived: Rhetoric and the Body in *Twelfth Night.*" *Texas Studies in Literature and Language* 38 (1996): 140–74.

Iyengar, Sujata "'Handling Soft the Hurts': Sexual Healing and Manual Contact in *Orlando Furioso*, *The Faerie Queene*, and *All's Well That Ends Well.*" In Elizabeth D. Harvey (ed.), *Sensible Flesh: On Touch in Early Modern Culture.* Philadelphia: University of Pennsylvania Press, 2003. 39–61.

Jaffe, Audrey. *Scenes of Sympathy: Identity and Representation in Victorian Fiction.* Ithaca, NY: Cornell University Press, 2000.

James, Heather. "Dido's Ear: Tragedy and the Politics of Response." *Shakespeare Quarterly* 52 (2001): 360–82.

Janković, Vladimer. *Reading the Skies: A Cultural History of English Weather, 1650–1820*. Chicago: University of Chicago Press, 2000.

Jardine, Lisa. *Reading Shakespeare Historically*. London: Routledge, 1996.

    Still Harping on Daughters: Women and Drama in the Age of Shakespeare. Brighton: Harvester Press, 1983.

Jobe, Thomas Harmon. "The Devil in Restoration Science: The Glanvill–Webster Witchcraft Debate." *Isis* 72 (1981): 342–56.

Jones, Claire. "'Efficacy Phrases' in Medieval English Medical Manuscripts." *Neuphilologische Mitteilungen* 99 (1998): 199–209.

Jones, Lynn. "From *Anglorum basileus* to Norman Saint: The Transformation of Edward the Confessor." *Haskins Society Journal* 12 (2003): 99–120.

Jones, William. *Finger-Ring Lore: Historical, Legendary, Anecdotal*. London: Chatto & Windus, 1877.

Kane, Stuart A. "Wives with Knives: Early Modern Murder Ballads and the Transgressive Commodity." *Criticism* 38 (1996): 219–37.

Kassell, Lauren. "'The Food of Angels': Simon Forman's Alchemical Medicine." In William R. Newman and Anthony Grafton (eds.), *Secrets of Nature: Astrology and Alchemy in Early Modern Europe*. Cambridge, MA: MIT Press, 2001. 345–84.

    Medicine and Magic in Elizabethan London. Simon Forman: Astrologer, Alchemist, Physician. Oxford: Oxford University Press, 2005.

Kastan, David Scott. "*All's Well That Ends Well* and the Limits of Comedy." *ELH* 52 (1985): 575–89.

Kavey, Allison. *Books of Secrets: Natural Philosophy in England, 1550–1600*. Urbana and Chicago: University of Illinois Press, 2007.

Keen, Suzanne. *Empathy and the Novel*. Oxford: Oxford University Press, 2007.

Keller, Evelyn Fox. *Reflections on Gender and Science*. New Haven: Yale University Press, 1985.

    Secrets of Life, Secrets of Death: Essays on Language, Gender, and Science. New York: Routledge, 1992.

Kelly, Kathleen Coyne. *Performing Virginity and Testing Chastity in the Middle Ages*. London: Routledge, 2000.

Kerrigan, John. "Secrecy and Gossip in *Twelfth Night*." *Shakespeare Survey* 50 (1997): 65–80.

Kerwin, William. *Beyond the Body: The Boundaries of Medicine and English Renaissance Drama*. Amherst and Boston: University of Massachusetts Press, 2005.

    "'Physicians are like Kings': Medical Politics and *The Duchess of Malfi*." *English Literary Renaissance* 28 (1998): 95–117.

Kieckhefer, Richard. *Magic in the Middle Ages*. Cambridge: Cambridge University Press, 2000.

King, Helen. *Hippocrates' Woman: Reading the Female Body in Ancient Greece*. London: Routledge, 1998.

    The Disease of Virgins: Green Sickness, Chlorosis and the Problems of Puberty. London and New York: Routledge, 2004.

Klein, Ursula. "The Laboratory Challenge: Some Revisions of the Standard View of Early Modern Experimentation." *Isis* 99 (2008): 769–82.

Knight, Katherine. "A Precious Medicine: Tradition and Magic in Some Seventeenth-Century Household Remedies." *Folklore* 113 (2002): 237–47.

Ko, Yu Jin. "The Comic Close of *Twelfth Night* and Viola's *Noli me tangere.*" *Shakespeare Quarterly* 48 (1997): 391–405.

Kocher, Paul H. *Science and Religion in Elizabethan England.* San Marino, CA: Huntington Library, 1953.

Kodera, Sergius. *Disreputable Bodies: Magic, Medicine, and Gender in Renaissance Natural Philosophy.* Toronto: Centre for Reformation and Renaissance Studies, 2010.

Lake, Peter with Michael C. Questier. *The Antichrist's Lewd Hat: Protestants, Papists and Players in Post-Reformation England.* New Haven: Yale University Press, 2002.

Lamb, Mary Ellen. *The Popular Culture of Shakespeare, Spenser, and Jonson.* New York: Routledge, 2006.

Langley, Eric. "Anatomizing the Early-Modern Eye: A Literary Case-Study." *Renaissance Studies* 20 (2006): 340–55.

"'Plagued by kindness': Contagious Sympathy in Shakespearean Drama." *Medical Humanities* 37 (2011): 103–09.

Laqueur, Thomas. *Making Sex: Body and Gender from the Greeks to Freud.* Cambridge, MA: Harvard University Press, 1990.

Laroche, Rebecca. *Medical Authority and Englishwomen's Herbal Texts, 1550–1650.* Aldershot: Ashgate, 2009.

Lawrence, W. W. *Shakespeare's Problem Comedies.* New York: Macmillan, 1931.

Lea, Henry Charles. *Superstition and Force.* Philadelphia: Collins, 1866.

Leech, Clifford. *John Webster: A Critical Study.* London: Hogarth Press, 1951.

Lehmann, Courtney, and Bryan Reynolds. "Awakening the Werewolf Within: Self-Help, Vanishing Mediation, and Transversality in *The Duchess of Malfi.*" In Bryan Reynolds (ed.), *Transversal Enterprises in the Drama of Shakespeare and His Contemporaries: Fugitive Explorations.* New York: Palgrave Macmillan, 2006. 227–39.

Lehnhof, Kent R. "Performing Women: Female Theatricality in *All's Well, That Ends Well.*" Gary Waller (ed.), *All's Well, That End's Well: New Critical Essays.* New York: Routledge, 2007. 111–24.

Leinwand, Theodore B. "*Coniugium Interruptum* in Shakespeare and Webster." *ELH* 72 (2005): 239–57.

Leong, Elaine. "Making Medicines in the Early Modern Household." *Bulletin of the History of Medicine* 82 (2008): 145–68.

"Medical Recipe Collections in Seventeenth-Century England: Knowledge, Text and Gender." Unpublished Ph.D. thesis. University of Oxford, 2006.

Leong, Elaine and Sara Pennell. "Recipe Collections and the Currency of Medical Knowledge in the Early Modern 'Medical Marketplace.'" In Mark S. R. Jenner and Patrick Wallis (eds.), *Medicine and the Market in England*

and Its Colonies, c. 1450–c. 1850. Basingstoke: Palgrave Macmillan, 2007. 133–52.

Leong, Elaine and Alisha Rankin (eds.). *Secrets and Knowledge in Medicine and Science, 1500–1800*. Aldershot: Ashgate, 2011.

Levack, Brian P. (ed.). *New Perspectives on Witchcraft, Magic, and Demonology: Witchcraft, Healing, and Popular Diseases*. Vol. 5. London: Routledge, 2001.

Levin, Carole. "'Would I Could Give You Help and Succour': Elizabeth I and the Politics of Touch." *Albion* 21 (1989): 191–205.

Lindberg, David C. and Robert S. Westman (eds.). *Reappraisals of the Scientific Revolution*. Cambridge: Cambridge University Press, 1990.

Linden, Stanton J. *Darke Hierogliphicks: Alchemy in English Literature from Chaucer to the Restoration*. Lexington: University of Kentucky Press, 1996.

Lindheim, Nancy. "Rethinking Sexuality and Class in *Twelfth Night*." *University of Toronto Quarterly* 76 (2007): 679–713.

Lindley, David. *The Trials of Frances Howard: Fact and Fiction at the Court of King James*. London: Routledge, 1993.

Lobanov-Rostovsky, Sergei. "Taming the Basilisk." In David Hillman and Carla Mazzio (eds.), *The Body in Parts: Fantasies of Corporeality in Early Modern Europe*. New York and London: Routledge, 1997. 195–217.

Lobis, Seth. "Sir Kenelm Digby and the Power of Sympathy." *Huntington Library Quarterly* 74 (2011): 243–60.

"The Virtue of Sympathy in Seventeenth-Century England." Unpublished Ph.D. thesis. Yale University, 2005.

Long, Pamela O. *Openness, Secrecy, Authorship: Technical Arts and the Culture of Knowledge from Antiquity to the Renaissance*. Baltimore: Johns Hopkins University Press, 2001.

Loughlin, Marie H. *Hymeneutics: Interpreting Virginity on the Early Modern Stage*. Lewisburg, PA: Bucknell University Press, 1997.

Lowe, Brigid. *Victorian Fiction and the Insights of Sympathy: An Alternative to the Hermeneutics of Suspicion*. London: Anthem Press, 2007.

Lucas, F. L. (ed.). *The Complete Works of John Webster*. 4 vols. London: Chatto & Windus, 1927.

MacDonald, Michael. *Mystical Bedlam: Madness, Anxiety, and Healing in Seventeenth-Century England*. Cambridge: Cambridge University Press, 1981.

(ed.). *Witchcraft and Hysteria in Elizabethan London: Edward Jorden and the Mary Glover Case*. London: Routledge, 1991.

Macfarlane, Alan. *Witchcraft in Tudor and Stuart England: A Regional and Comparative Study*. 2nd edition. London: Routledge, 1999.

Maclean, Ian. *Logic, Signs and Nature in the Renaissance: The Case of Learned Medicine*. Cambridge: Cambridge University Press, 2002.

Malcolmson, Cristina. "'As Tame as the Ladies': Politics and Gender in *The Changeling*." *English Literary Renaissance* 20 (1990): 320–39.

Marsden, Jean. "Shakespeare and Sympathy." In Peter Sabor and Paul Yachnin (eds.), *Shakespeare and the Eighteenth Century*. Aldershot: Ashgate, 2008. 29–42.

Marsden, Michael T. "The Otherworld of *Arden of Faversham.*" *Southern Folklore Quarterly* 36 (1972): 36–42.

Marshall, David. *The Surprising Effects of Sympathy: Marivaux, Diderot, Rousseau, and Mary Shelley.* Chicago: University of Chicago Press, 1988.

Martin, Randall. *Women, Murder, and Equity in Early Modern England.* New York: Routledge, 2008.

Masten, Jeffrey. "Gee, Your Heir Smells Terrific: Response to 'Shakespeare's Perfume.'" *Early Modern Culture: An Electronic Seminar* 2 (2001), http:// emc.eserver.org/1-2/issue2.html.

McCandless, David Foley. *Gender and Performance in Shakespeare's Problem Comedies.* Bloomington: Indiana University Press, 1997.

McCarthy, Thomas J. *Relationships of Sympathy: The Writer and Reader in British Romanticism.* Aldershot: Scolar Press, 1997.

McClive, Cathy. "Menstrual Knowledge and Medical Practice in Early Modern France, c. 1555–1761." In Andrew Shail and Gillian Howie (eds.), *Menstruation: A Cultural History.* Basingstoke: Palgrave Macmillan, 2005. 76–89.

"The Hidden Truths of the Belly: The Uncertainties of Pregnancy in Early Modern Europe." *Social History of Medicine* 15 (2002): 209–27.

Mebane, John S. *Renaissance Magic and the Return of the Golden Age: The Occult Tradition and Marlowe, Jonson, and Shakespeare.* Lincoln: University of Nebraska Press, 1989.

Meloncon, Lisa K. "Rhetoric, Remedies, Regimens: Popular Science in Early Modern England." Unpublished Ph.D. thesis. University of South Carolina, 2005.

Merchant, Carolyn. "Secrets of Nature: The Bacon Debates Revisited." *Journal of the History of Ideas* 69 (2008): 147–62.

The Death of Nature: Women, Ecology, and the Scientific Revolution. San Francisco: Harper & Row, 1980.

Micale, Mark S. *Approaching Hysteria: Disease and Its Interpretations.* Princeton: Princeton University Press, 1995.

Mielke, Laura L. *Moving Encounters: Sympathy and the Indian Question in Antebellum Literature.* Amherst: University of Massachusetts Press, 2008.

Millen, Ron. "The Manifestation of Occult Qualities in the Scientific Revolution." In Margaret J. Osler and Paul Lawrence Farber (eds.), *Religion, Science, and Worldview: Essays in Honor of Richard S. Westfall.* Cambridge: Cambridge University Press, 1985. 185–216.

Mirabella, Bella. "'Quacking Delilahs': Female Mountebanks in Early Modern England and Italy." In Pamela Allen Brown and Peter Parolin (eds.), *Women Players in England, 1500–1660: Beyond the All-Male Stage.* Aldershot: Ashgate, 2005. 89–105.

Moncrief, Kathryn M. "'Show me a child begotten of thy body that I am father to': Pregnancy, Paternity and the Problem of Evidence in *All's Well That Ends Well.*" In Kathryn M. Moncrief and Kathryn R. McPherson (eds.), *Performing Maternity in Early Modern England.* Aldershot: Ashgate, 2007. 29–43.

Moran, Bruce T. *Distilling Knowledge: Alchemy, Chemistry, and the Scientific Revolution*. Cambridge, MA: Harvard University Press, 2005.

Morrison, Peter. "A Cangoun in Zombieland: Middleton's Teratological Changeling." In Kenneth Friedenreich (ed.), *"Accompaninge the Players": Essays Celebrating Thomas Middleton, 1580–1980*. New York: AMS, 1983. 219–41.

Moss, Stephanie. "Transformation and Degeneration: The Paracelsian/Galenic Body in *Othello*." In Stephanie Moss and Kaara L. Peterson (eds.), *Disease, Diagnosis, and Cure on the Early Modern Stage*. Aldershot: Ashgate, 2004. 151–70.

Munro, Joyce Underwood. "The Invisible Made Visible: The Fairy Changeling as a Folk Articulation of Failure to Thrive in Infants and Children." In Peter Narváez (ed.), *The Good People: New Fairylore Essays*. New York: Garland, 1991. 251–83.

Nagy, Doreen G. [Evenden]. *Popular Medicine in Seventeenth-Century England*. Bowling Green, OH: Bowling Green State University Popular Press, 1988.

The Midwives of Seventeenth-Century London. Cambridge: Cambridge University Press, 2000.

Neely, Carol Thomas. *Distracted Subjects: Madness and Gender in Shakespeare and Early Modern Culture*. Ithaca, NY: Cornell University Press, 2004.

"Lovesickness, Gender, and Subjectivity: *Twelfth Night* and *As You Like It*." Dympna Callaghan (ed.), *A Feminist Companion to Shakespeare*. Oxford: Blackwell, 2000. 276–98.

Neill, Michael. "'Hidden Malady': Death, Discovery, and Indistinction in *The Changeling*." *Renaissance Drama* 22 (1991): 95–121.

Issues of Death: Mortality and Identity in English Renaissance Tragedy. Oxford: Clarendon Press, 1997.

Putting History to the Question: Power, Politics, and Society in English Renaissance Drama. New York: Columbia University Press, 2000.

Nevo, Ruth. *Comic Transformations in Shakespeare*. London: Methuen, 1980.

Newman, William R. "Alchemical Symbolism and Concealment: The Chemical House of Libavius." In Peter Galison and Emily Thompson (eds.), *The Architecture of Science*. Cambridge, MA: MIT Press, 1999. 59–77.

Noble, Louise. *Medicinal Cannibalism in Early Modern English Literature and Culture*. New York: Palgrave Macmillan, 2011.

Nunn, Hilary M. *Staging Anatomies: Dissection and Spectacle in Early Stuart Tragedy*. Aldershot: Ashgate, 2005.

Orgel, Stephen. *Impersonations: The Performance of Gender in Shakespeare's England*. Cambridge: Cambridge University Press, 1996.

Orlin, Lena Cowen. *Private Matters and Public Culture in Post-Reformation England*. Ithaca, NY: Cornell University Press, 1994.

Pagel, Walter. *Paracelsus: An Introduction to Philosophical Medicine in the Era of the Renaissance*. 2nd revised edition. Basel: S. Karger, 1984.

Panek, Jennifer. "Why Did Widows Remarry? Remarriage, Male Authority, and Feminist Criticism." In Dympna Callaghan (ed.), *The Impact of Feminism in English Renaissance Studies*. Basingstoke: Palgrave Macmillan, 2007. 281–98.

Pantin, Isabelle. "Fracastoro's *De Contagione* and Medieval Reflection on 'Action at a Distance': Old and New Trends in Renaissance Discourse on Contagion." In Claire L. Carlin (ed.), *Imagining Contagion in Early Modern Europe*. Basingstoke: Palgrave Macmillan, 2005. 3–15.

Park, Katharine. "Dissecting the Female Body: From Women's Secrets to the Secrets of Nature." In Jane Donawerth and Adele Seeff (eds.), *Crossing Boundaries: Attending to Early Modern Women*. Newark: University of Delaware Press, 2000. 29–47.

"Medicine and Magic: The Healing Arts." In Judith C. Brown and Robert C. Davis (eds.), *Gender and Society in Renaissance Italy*. London and New York: Longman, 1998. 129–49.

"Nature in Person: Medieval and Renaissance Allegories and Emblems." In Lorraine Daston and Fernando Vidal (eds.), *The Moral Authority of Nature*. Chicago: University of Chicago Press, 2004. 50–73.

"Response to Brian Vickers, 'Francis Bacon, Feminist Historiography, and the Dominion of Nature.'" *Journal of the History of Ideas* 69 (2008): 143–46.

Secrets of Women: Gender, Generation, and the Origins of Human Dissection. New York: Zone Books, 2006.

"Bacon's 'Enchanted Glass.'" *Isis* 75 (1984): 290–302.

Park, Katharine and Lorraine Daston (eds.). *The Cambridge History of Science*. Vol. 3. Cambridge: Cambridge University Press, 2003.

Park, Katharine and Robert A. Nye, "Destiny Is Anatomy." *New Republic* (February 19, 1991): 53–57.

Parker, Patricia. "Gender Ideology, Gender Change: The Case of Marie Germain." *Critical Inquiry* 19 (1993): 337–64.

Parr, Johnstone. "The Horoscope in Webster's *The Duchess of Malfi*." *PMLA* 60 (1945): 760–65.

Parrish, Susan Scott. *American Curiosity: Cultures of Natural History in the Colonial Atlantic World*. Chapel Hill: University of North Carolina Press, 2006.

Paster, Gail Kern. *Humoring the Body: Emotions and the Shakespearean Stage*. Chicago: University of Chicago Press, 2004.

"Nervous Tension: Networks of Blood and Spirit in the Early Modern Body." In David Hillman and Carla Mazzio (eds.), *The Body in Parts: Fantasies of Corporeality in Early Modern Europe*. New York and London: Routledge, 1997. 110–11.

"The Body and Its Passions." *Shakespeare Studies* 29 (2001): 44–50.

The Body Embarrassed: Drama and the Disciplines of Shame in Early Modern England. Ithaca, NY: Cornell University Press, 1993.

"The Unbearable Coldness of Female Being: Women's Imperfection and the Humoral Economy." *English Literary Renaissance* 28 (1998): 416–40.

Paster, Gail Kern, Katherine Rowe, and Mary Floyd-Wilson (eds.). *Reading the Early Modern Passions: Essays in the Cultural History of Emotion*. Philadelphia: University of Pennsylvania Press, 2004.

Peck, Linda Levy. *Consuming Splendor: Society and Culture in Seventeenth-Century England*. Cambridge: Cambridge University Press, 2005.

Pelling, Margaret. *Medical Conflicts in Early Modern London: Patronage, Physicians, and Irregular Practitioners, 1550–1640*. Oxford: Oxford University Press, 2003.

"Thoroughly Resented? Older Women and the Medical Role in Early Modern London." In Lynette Hunter and Sarah Hutton (eds.), *Women, Science, and Medicine 1500–1700: Mothers and Sisters of the Royal Society*. Stroud: Sutton, 1997. 63–88.

Pennell, Sara. "Perfecting Practice? Women, Manuscript Recipes and Knowledge in Early Modern England." In Victoria E. Burke and Jonathan Gibson (eds.), *Early Modern Women's Manuscript Writing: Selected Papers from Trinity/Trent Colloquium*. Aldershot: Ashgate, 2004. 237–58.

"The Material Culture of Food in Early Modern England, circa 1650–1750." Unpublished Ph.D. thesis. University of Oxford, 1997.

Penuel, Suzanne. "Missing Fathers: *Twelfth Night* and the Reformation of Mourning." *Studies in Philology* 107 (2010): 74–96.

Pequigney, Joseph. "The Two Antonios and Same-Sex Love in *Twelfth Night* and *The Merchant of Venice*." *English Literary Renaissance* 22 (1992): 201–21.

Pesic, Peter. "Wrestling with Proteus: Francis Bacon and the 'Torture' of Nature." *Isis* 90 (1999): 81–94.

Peterson, Kaara L. "Fluid Economies: Portraying Shakespeare's Hysterics." *Mosaic: A Journal for the Interdisciplinary Study of Literature* 34 (2001): 35–59.

Popular Medicine, Hysterical Disease, and Social Controversy in Shakespeare's England. Burlington, VT: Ashgate, 2010.

Pettigrew, Todd H. J. *Shakespeare and the Practice of Physic: Medical Narratives on the Early Modern English Stage*. Newark: University of Delaware Press, 2007.

Picciotto, Joanna. *Labors of Innocence in Early Modern England*. Cambridge, MA: Harvard University Press, 2010.

Pigman, III, G. W. *Grief and English Renaissance Elegy*. Cambridge: Cambridge University Press, 1985.

Polito, Mary. "Professions and 'the Labouring Arts' in *All's Well That Ends Well*." *Renaissance & Reformation / Renaissance et Reforme* 28 (2004): 77–94.

Pollard, Tanya. *Drugs and Theater in Early Modern England*. Oxford: Oxford University Press, 2005.

"Spelling the Body." In Mary Floyd-Wilson and Garrett A. Sullivan, Jr. (eds.), *Environment and Embodiment in Early Modern England*. Basingstoke: Macmillan, 2007. 171–86.

Pollard, Tanya (ed.). *Shakespeare's Theater: A Sourcebook*. Oxford: Blackwell, 2004.

Pollock, Linda A. *With Faith and Physic: The Life of a Tudor Gentlewoman, Lady Grace Mildmay, 1552–1620*. London: Collins and Brown, 1993.

Poole, Kristen. *Supernatural Environments in Shakespeare's England: Spaces of Demonism, Divinity, and Drama*. Cambridge: Cambridge University Press, 2011.

Principe, Lawrence M. *The Aspiring Adept: Robert Boyle and his Alchemical Quest*. Princeton: Princeton University Press, 1998.

Purkiss, Diane. *The Witch in History: Early Modern and Twentieth-Century Representations*. London: Routledge, 1996.

Rai, Amit S. *Rule of Sympathy: Sentiment, Race, and Power, 1750–1850.* New York: Palgrave Macmillan, 2002.

Randall, Dale B. J. "Some Observations on the Theme of Chastity in *The Changeling.*" *English Literary Renaissance* 14 (1984): 347–66.

"The Rank and Earthy Background of Certain Physical Symbols in *The Duchess of Malfi.*" *Renaissance Drama* 18 (1987): 171–203.

Rankin, Alisha. "Duchess, Heal Thyself: Elisabeth of Rochlitz and the Patient's Perspective in Early Modern Germany." *Bulletin of the History of Medicine* 82 (2008): 109–44.

"Medicine for the Uncommon Woman: Experience, Experiment, and Exchange in Early Modern Germany." Unpublished Ph.D. thesis. Harvard University, 2005.

Ratcliffe, Sophie. *On Sympathy.* Oxford: Oxford University Press, 2008.

Ray, Nicholas. "''Twas mine, 'twas Helen's': Rings of Desire in *All's Well, That Ends Well.*" Gary Waller (ed.), *All's Well, That Ends Well: New Critical Essays.* New York: Routledge, 2007. 183–93.

Reeves, Eileen. "Of Language and the Lodestone," working papers at The Italian Academy for Advanced Studies in America, Columbia University. www.italianacademy.columbia.edu/publications/working_papers/2003_2004/paper_fa03_Reeves.pdf.

Richardson, H. G. "The Coronation in Medieval England: The Evolution of the Office and the Oath." *Traditio* 16 (1960): 111–202.

Richardson, L. Deer. "The Generation of Disease: Occult Causes and Diseases of the Total Substance." In A. Wear, R. K. French, and I. M. Lonie (eds.), *The Medical Renaissance of the Sixteenth Century.* Cambridge: Cambridge University Press, 1985. 175–94.

Roach, Joseph R. *The Player's Passion: Studies in the Science of Acting.* Ann Arbor: University of Michigan Press, 1993.

Roberts, Nancy. *Schools of Sympathy: Gender and Identification through the Novel.* Montreal: McGill-Queen's University Press, 1997.

Roper, Lyndal. *Oedipus and the Devil: Witchcraft, Sexuality and Religion in Early Modern Europe.* London: Routledge, 1994.

Rose, Mary Beth. *The Expense of Spirit: Love and Sexuality in English Renaissance Drama.* Ithaca, NY: Cornell University Press, 1988.

Ross, G. MacDonald. "Occultism and Philosophy in the Seventeenth Century." In A. J. Holland (ed.), *Philosophy: Its History and Historiography.* Dordrecht: Reidel, 1985. 95–115.

Rossi, Paolo. *Francis Bacon: From Magic to Science.* Chicago: University of Chicago Press, 1968.

The Birth of Modern Science. Trans. Cynthia De Nardi Ipsen. Oxford: Blackwell, 2001.

Rousseau, G. S. "'A Strange Pathology.' Hysteria in the Early Modern World." In Sander L. Gilman, Helen King, Roy Porter, G. S. Rousseau, and Elaine Showalter (eds.), *Hysteria beyond Freud.* Berkeley: University of California Press, 1993. 91–221.

Rowe, Katherine. *Dead Hands: Fictions of Agency, Renaissance to Modern*. Stanford: Stanford University Press, 1999.

Ruggiero, Guido. *Binding Passions: Tales of Magic, Marriage, and Power at the End of the Renaissance*. Oxford: Oxford University Press, 1993.

Salmón, Fernando and Montserrat Cabré I Pairet. "Fascinating Women: The Evil Eye in Medical Scholasticism." In Roger French, Jon Arrizabalaga, Andrew Cunningham, and Luis Garcia-Ballester (eds.), *Medicine from the Black Death to the French Disease*. Aldershot: Ashgate, 1998. 53–84.

Sanders, Julie. "Midwifery and the New Science in the Seventeenth Century: Language, Print, and the Theatre." In Erica Fudge, Ruth Gilbert, and Susan Wiseman (eds.), *At the Borders of the Human: Beasts, Bodies and Natural Philosophy in the Early Modern Period*. Basingstoke: Palgrave Macmillan, 1999. 74–90.

Sarasohn, Lisa T. *The Natural Philosophy of Margaret Cavendish: Reason and Fancy during the Scientific Revolution*. Baltimore: Johns Hopkins University Press, 2010.

Sawday, Jonathan. *The Body Emblazoned: Dissection and the Human Body in Renaissance Culture*. London: Routledge, 1995.

Schaffer, Simon. "Occultism and Reason." In A. J. Holland (ed.), *Philosophy, Its History and Historiography*. Dordrecht: Reidel, 1985. 117–43.

Schalkwyk, David. *Shakespeare, Love and Service*. Cambridge: Cambridge University Press, 2008.

Schiebinger, Londa L. *The Mind Has No Sex? Women in the Origins of Modern Science*. Cambridge, MA: Harvard University Press, 1989.

Schlosser, Julius von. "History of Portraiture in Wax." In Roberta Panzanelli (ed.), *Ephemeral Bodies: Wax Sculpture and the Human Figure*. Los Angeles: Getty Research Institute, 2008. 171–314.

Schmitt, Charles B. "Reappraisals in Renaissance Science." *History of Science* 16 (1978): 200–14.

Schmitz, Rudolf. "The Pomander." *Pharmacy in History* 31 (1989): 86–90.

Schneider, Federico. *Pastoral Drama and Healing in Early Modern Italy*. Aldershot: Ashgate, 2010.

Schoenfeldt, Michael C. *Bodies and Selves in Early Modern England: Physiology and Inwardness in Spenser, Shakespeare, Herbert, and Milton*. Cambridge: Cambridge University Press, 1999.

Schutzman, Julie R. "Alice Arden's Freedom and the Suspended Moment of *Arden of Faversham*." *Studies in English Literature 1500–1900* 36 (1996): 289–314.

Scribner, Robert W. "The Reformation, Popular Magic, and the 'Disenchantment of the World.'" *Journal of Interdisciplinary History* 23 (1993): 475–94.

Shannon, Laurie. "Nature's Bias: Renaissance Homonormativity and Elizabethan Comic Likeness." *Modern Philology* 98 (2000): 183–210.

 Sovereign Amity: Figures of Friendship in Shakespearean Contexts. Chicago: University of Chicago Press, 2002.

Shapin, Steven. *A Social History of Truth: Civility and Science in Seventeenth-Century England*. Chicago: University of Chicago Press, 1994.

"The House of Experiment in Seventeenth-Century England." *Isis* 79 (1988): 373–404.

"The Invisible Technician." *American Scientist* 77 (1989): 554–63.

The Scientific Revolution. Chicago: University of Chicago Press, 1996.

Shapiro, Barbara J. *Probability and Certainty in Seventeenth-Century England: A Study of the Relationships between Natural Science, Religion, History, Law, and Literature.* Princeton: Princeton University Press, 1983.

Shapiro, Michael. *Gender in Play on the Shakespearean Stage: Boy Heroines and Female Pages.* Ann Arbor: University of Michigan Press, 1994.

Shumaker, Wayne. *The Occult Sciences in the Renaissance: A Study in Intellectual Patterns.* Berkeley: University of California Press, 1972.

Simmons, J. L. "Diabolical Realism in Middleton and Rowley's *The Changeling.*" *Renaissance Drama* 11 (1980): 135–70.

Simoons, Frederick J. *Plants of Life, Plants of Death.* Madison: University of Wisconsin Press, 1998.

Siraisi, Nancy G. *Medicine and the Italian Universities, 1250–1600.* Leiden: Brill, 2001.

The Clock and the Mirror: Girolamo Cardano and Renaissance Medicine. Princeton: Princeton University Press, 1997.

Slack, Paul. "Mirrors of Health and Treasures of Poor Men: The Uses of the Vernacular Medical Literature of Tudor England." In Charles Webster (ed.), *Health, Medicine and Mortality in the Sixteenth Century.* Cambridge: Cambridge University Press, 1979. 237–61.

The Impact of the Plague in Tudor and Stuart England. Oxford: Oxford University Press, 1991.

Slatoff, Walter J. *The Look of Distance: Reflections on Suffering and Sympathy in Modern Literature – Auden to Agee, Whitman to Woolf.* Columbus: Ohio State University Press, 1985.

Slights, William W. E. "Secret Places in Renaissance Drama." *University of Toronto Quarterly* 59 (1990): 364–82.

Smith, Pamela H. *The Body of the Artisan: Art and Experience in the Scientific Revolution.* Chicago: University of Chicago Press, 2004.

Smith, Pamela H. and Benjamin Schmidt (eds.). *Making Knowledge in Early Modern Europe: Practices, Objects, and Texts, 1400–1800.* Chicago: University of Chicago Press, 2007.

Spiller, Elizabeth. "Introductory Note." *Seventeenth-Century English Recipe Books.* Vols. 3 and 4. Aldershot: Ashgate, 2008.

"Recipes for Knowledge: Maker's Knowledge Traditions, Paracelsian Recipes, and the Invention of the Cookbook, 1600–1660." In Joan Fitzpatrick (ed.), *Renaissance Food from Rabelais to Shakespeare: Culinary Readings and Culinary Histories.* Aldershot: Ashgate, 2010. 55–72.

Science, Reading, and Renaissance Literature: The Art of Making Knowledge, 1580–1670. Cambridge: Cambridge University Press, 2004.

Spinks, Jennifer. "Wondrous Monsters: Representing Conjoined Twins in Early Sixteenth-Century German Broadsheets." *Parergon* 22 (2005): 77–112.

Staines, John. "Compassion in the Public Sphere of Milton and King Charles." Gail Kern Paster, Katherine Rowe, and Mary Floyd-Wilson (eds.), *Reading the Early Modern Passions: Essays in the Cultural History of Emotion.* Philadelphia: University of Pennsylvania Press, 2004. 89–110.

Steggle, Matthew. *Laughing and Weeping in Early Modern Theatres.* Aldershot: Ashgate, 2007.

Stensgaard, Richard K. "*All's Well That Ends Well* and the Galenico–Paracelsian Controversy." *Renaissance Quarterly* 25 (1972): 173–88.

Stern, Julia A. *The Plight of Feeling: Sympathy and Dissent in the Early American Novel.* Chicago and London: University of Chicago Press, 1997.

Stine, Jennifer. "Opening Closets: The Discovery of Household Medicine in Early Modern England." Unpublished Ph.D. thesis, Stanford University, 1996.

Stolberg, Michael. "A Woman Down to Her Bones: The Anatomy of Sexual Differences in the Sixteenth and Early Seventeenth Centuries." *Isis* 94 (2003): 274–99.

Sugg, Richard. *Mummies, Cannibals and Vampires: The History of Corpse Medicine from the Renaissance to the Victorians.* London and New York: Routledge, 2011.

Sullivan, Jr., Garrett A. "'Arden Lay Murdered in That Plot of Ground': Surveying, Land, and *Arden of Faversham.*" *ELH* 61 (1994): 231–52.
  Memory and Forgetting in English Drama: Shakespeare, Marlowe, Webster. Cambridge: Cambridge University Press, 2005.

Synder, Susan. "'The King's not here': Displacement and Deferral in *All's Well That Ends Well.*" *Shakespeare Quarterly* 43 (1992): 20–32.

Tannenbaum, Rebecca J. *The Healer's Calling: Women and Medicine in Early New England.* Ithaca, NY: Cornell University Press, 2002.

Tassi, Marguerite A. *The Scandal of Images: Iconoclasm, Eroticism, and Painting in Early Modern Drama.* Selinsgrove, PA: Susquehanna University Press, 2005.

Thijssen, J. M. "Twins as Monsters: Albertus Magnus's Theory of the Generation of Twins and Its Philosophical Contexts." *Bulletin of the History of Medicine* 61 (1987): 237–46.

Thomas, Keith. *Religion and the Decline of Magic: Studies in Popular Beliefs in Sixteenth- and Seventeenth-Century England.* London: Penguin Books, 1971.

Thorndike, Lynn. *A History of Magic and Experimental Science.* 8 vols. New York: Macmillan, 1923–58.
  "Mediaeval Magic and Science in the Seventeenth Century." *Speculum* 28 (1953): 692–704.

Tiffany, Grace. *Love's Pilgrimage: The Holy Journey in English Renaissance Literature.* Newark: University of Delaware Press, 2006.

Tiles, J. E. "Experiment as Intervention." *British Journal for the Philosophy of Science* 44 (1993): 463–75.

Traister, Barbara Howard. "'Doctor She': Healing and Sex in *All's Well That Ends Well.*" In Richard Dutton and Jean E. Howard (eds.), *A Companion to Shakespeare's Works: Poems, Problem Comedies, Late Plays.* Vol. 4. Malden, MA: Blackwell, 2003. 333–46.

Traub, Valerie. *Desire and Anxiety: Circulations of Sexuality in Shakespearean Drama.* London: Routledge, 1992. 130–44.

The Renaissance of Lesbianism in Early Modern England. Cambridge: Cambridge University Press, 2002.

Tricomi, Albert H. "Historicizing the Imagery of the Demonic in *The Duchess of Malfi.*" *Journal of Medieval and Early Modern Studies* 34 (2004): 345–72.

"The Severed Hand in Webster's *Duchess of Malfi.*" *Studies in English Literature, 1500–1900* 44 (2004): 347–58.

Veith, Ilza. *Hysteria: The History of a Disease.* Chicago: University of Chicago Press, 1965.

Vermeir, Koen. "The 'Physical Prophet' and the Powers of the Imagination. Part 1: A Case-Study on Prophecy, Vapours, and the Imagination (1685–1710)." *Studies in History and Philosophy of Biological and Biomedical Sciences* 35 (2004): 561–91.

Vickers, Brian. "Francis Bacon, Feminist Historiography, and the Dominion of Nature." *Journal of the History of Ideas* 69 (2008): 117–41.

(ed.). *Occult and Scientific Mentalities in the Renaissance.* Cambridge: Cambridge University Press, 1984.

Wadsworth, Frank W. "Webster's *The Duchess of Malfi* in the Light of Some Contemporary Ideas on Marriage and Remarriage." *Philological Quarterly* 35 (1956): 394–407.

Walen, Denise A. "Constructions of Female Homoerotics in Early Modern Drama." *Theatre Journal* 54 (2002): 411–30.

Walker, D. P. *Spiritual and Demonic Magic: From Ficino to Campanella.* London: Warburg Institute, University of London, 1958.

Unclean Spirits: Possession and Exorcism in France and England in the Late Sixteenth and Early Seventeenth Centuries. Philadelphia: University of Pennsylvania Press, 1981.

Wall, Wendy. "Distillation: Transformations in and out of the Kitchen." In Joan Fitzpatrick (ed.), *Renaissance Food from Rabelais to Shakespeare: Culinary Readings and Culinary Histories.* Aldershot: Ashgate, 2010. 89–104.

"Just a Spoonful of Sugar: Syrup and Domesticity in Early Modern England." *Modern Philology* 104 (2006): 149–72.

Staging Domesticity: Household Work and English Identity in Early Modern Drama. Cambridge: Cambridge University Press, 2002.

Waller, Gary (ed.). *All's Well, That Ends Well: New Critical Essays.* New York: Routledge, 2007.

Walsham, Alexandra. *Providence in Early Modern England.* Oxford: Oxford University Press, 2001.

"Recording Superstition in Early Modern Britain: The Origins of Folklore." *Past and Present* 199, Supplement 3 (2008): 178–206.

"The Reformation and 'The Disenchantment of the World' Reassessed." *Historical Journal* 51 (2008): 497–528.

Watson, Gilbert. *Theriac and Mithridatium: A Study in Therapeutics.* London: The Wellcome Historical Medical Library, 1966.

Wear, Andrew. *Knowledge and Practice in English Renaissance Medicine, 1550–1680.* Cambridge: Cambridge University Press, 2000.

Webster, Charles. *From Paracelsus to Newton: Magic and the Making of Modern Science.* Cambridge: Cambridge University Press, 1982.

Weinstein, Cindy. *Family, Kinship, and Sympathy in Nineteenth-Century American Literature.* Cambridge: Cambridge University Press, 2004.

Whigham, Frank. *Seizures of the Will in Early Modern Drama.* Cambridge: Cambridge University Press, 1996.

"Sexual and Social Mobility in *The Duchess of Malfi.*" *PMLA* 100 (1985): 167–86.

White, Martin. *The Tragedy of Master Arden of Faversham.* London: A&C Black, 1990.

White, R. S. "The Moral Design of *The Duchess of Malfi.*" In Dympna Callaghan (ed.), *The Duchess of Malfi.* Basingstoke: Macmillan, 2000. 201–16.

Wilby, Emma. *Cunning Folk and Familiar Spirits: Shamanistic Visionary Traditions in Early Modern British Witchcraft and Magic.* Brighton: Sussex Academic Press, 2005.

Wilkin, Rebecca M. *Women, Imagination, and the Search for Truth in Early Modern France.* Aldershot: Ashgate, 2008.

Willis, Deborah. *Malevolent Nurture: Witch-Hunting and Maternal Power in Early Modern England.* Ithaca, NY: Cornell University Press, 1995.

Wilson, Catherine. *The Invisible World: Early Modern Philosophy and the Invention of the Microscope.* Princeton: Princeton University Press, 1995.

Wilson, Richard. "To Great St Jaques Bound: *All's Well That Ends Well* in Shakespeare's Europe." *Shakespeare et l'Europe de la Renaissance*, Actes du Congrès de la Société Française Shakespeare (2004): 273–90.

Wilson, Steven. *The Magical Universe: Everyday Ritual and Magic in Pre-Modern Europe.* London and New York: Hambledon and London, 2000.

Wolfe, Charles T. and Ofer Gal (eds.). *The Body as Object and Instrument of Knowledge: Embodied Empiricism in Early Modern Science.* Dordrecht and New York: Springer, 2010.

Wolfe, Jessica. *Humanism, Machinery, and Renaissance Literature.* Cambridge: Cambridge University Press, 2004.

Woodbridge, Linda. "Queen of Apricots: The Duchess of Malfi, Hero of Desire." In Naomi Conn Liebler (ed.), *The Female Tragic Hero in English Renaissance Drama.* New York: Palgrave, 2002. 161–84.

The Scythe of Saturn: Shakespeare and Magical Thinking. Urbana: University of Illinois Press, 1994.

Women and the English Renaissance: Literature and the Nature of Womankind. Urbana: University of Illinois Press, 1984.

Yates, Frances A. *Giordano Bruno and the Hermetic Tradition.* Chicago and London: University of Chicago Press, 1964.

Zimmerman, Susan. *The Early Modern Corpse and Shakespeare's Theatre.* Edinburgh: Edinburgh University Press, 2005.

Index